DATE DUE

Second Edition

PRESCHOOL CHILDREN

DEVELOPMENT AND RELATIONSHIPS

Mollie S. Smart and Russell C. Smart

Macmillan Publishing Co., Inc.
NEW YORK

Collier Macmillan Publishers
LONDON

80737

Earlier edition copyright © 1973 by Macmillan Publishing Co., Inc.

Reprinted with modifications from *Children: Development and Relationships,*
Third Edition, by Mollie S. Smart and Russell C. Smart, copyright © 1967,
1972, and 1977 by Macmillan Publishing Co., Inc., and *Readings in Child
Development and Relationships,* by Russell C. Smart and Mollie S. Smart,
copyright © 1972 and 1977 by Macmillan Publishing Co., Inc.

Macmillan Publishing Co., Inc.
866 Third Avenue, New York, New York 10022

Collier Macmillan Canada, Ltd.

Library of Congress Cataloging in Publication Data

Smart, Mollie Stevens.
  Preschool children.

  "Reprinted with modifications from [the authors']
Children: development and relationships, third
edition . . . and Readings in child development and
relationships."
  Includes bibliographies and indexes.
  1. Child psychology. I. Smart, Russell Cook,
joint author. II. Title.
BF721.S5713   1978   155.4'23   77–5407
ISBN 0–02–412040–5

Printing: 1 2 3 4 5 6 7 8   Year: 8 9 0 1 2 3 4

Contents

Introduction

Children between the ages of two and five or six are called preschool children, even though they are learning very fast and developing their cognitive and other powers enormously. Most school systems require attendance of children at age 6. Earlier schooling is offered widely throughout the world, but not to all young children. In North America, many young children go to nursery schools, pre-schools, prekindergartens, and day-care centers.

This book is designed for all people who teach and care for young children, including teachers, day-care workers, nurses, social workers, and parents. Parents are still the primary teachers and caregivers, although they may share their efforts with teachers and others who nurture children. Children and communities benefit when parents can work in partnership with others who teach, protect, and care for children.

Intuition, sensitivity, and love are indispensable in working with little children, but knowledge of their development is also needed. Preschool children's thinking is quite different from adults'. Even though a young child is free about telling what he is thinking, an adult may not fully understand what he means.

Piaget calls preschool thinking the stage of preoperational thought. The child uses words, imitation, and play as means of thinking. Play is the young child's special resource for dealing with his experiences, making sense out of the world, enjoying, communicating, and learning. Reasoning is highly influenced by wishes and does not conform to the rules of logic as used by adults. Chapter 2 deals with mental development, with play and imagination.

Young children have special physical needs. In order to give adequate care, adults need to know what and how to feed them, how to plan schedules that allow for rhythms of rest and activity, how to arrange an environment that offers protection, and how to encourage children in caring for their own health. An adequate environment also provides opportunities for movement and increasing bodily coordination and competency. In learning to control his body in space, along with using growing mental powers, the young child expands in personality. Erikson describes two personality stages that occur in the preschool years. In developing the sense of autonomy, the child makes choices that tend to turn out well and about which he has a feeling of self-satisfaction. In developing the sense of initiative, the child explores widely, tries out new actions, new modes, and new roles, exercising curiosity and imagination. Chapter 1 is concerned with physical and personality development.

Social and emotional development are discussed in Chapter 3. Learning to play with other children is a reason given by many parents when they send their children to nursery school. Playing with peers is quite different from living with adults and siblings. Through play with equals, children stimulate each other to thought, action, imagination, and feeling.

Because the preschool years are packed with potential for all sorts of growth, provisions made for young children are crucial. Instead of trying to make up later for developmental deficits, it is more humane as well as more economical to give young children what they need for healthy growth of body, mind, and personality. Chapter 4 of this book tells of various programs that provide for growth and development of young children and their parents, and of some that are therapeutic in special ways.

Each of the five chapters of the book consists of a text section followed by readings from other authors. Some of the readings report research; others review and discuss topics concerning preschool children. Chapter 5 is philosophical and theoretical, concerned with life and development of human beings and dealing with topics that apply to all age levels. We urge the teacher to consider assigning the last chapter first. Some teachers like to start the course by focusing first on the preschool child, while others prefer to lay a theoretical background first. The text sections are taken from the third edition of our book *Children: Development and Relationships;* the articles by other authors are from the second edition of our *Readings in Child Development and Relationships.*

Suggestions to the Student

TAKING NOTES ON DIFFERENT KINDS OF READINGS

The first part of each chapter, which is from our textbook *Children,* Third Edition, gives basic subject matter. We show you by means of the headings what we think most important. When you are taking notes, we suggest that you use our headings as a framework. Put under them, in your own words, what the section says to you.

The articles in each chapter elaborate on something mentioned much more briefly in the chapter, or they may lay a background for the chapter. You will need to adapt your note taking to the style of the article. Reviews of research and statements of theoretical positions require about the same kinds of notes. There are usually not a great many main points, although some of them may have subsidiary points made in connection with them. Often these points are reiterated in a summary that may come at the beginning or the end of the selection. If there is no summary, the author may have omitted it because he thought he made his points so clearly that they would not be missed. In any case, assume the author had a message and ask yourself, "What does the author want me to learn? Why does he think it important? What evidence does he present for accepting the truth of his statements?"

The selections that are research reports are more specialized kinds of writing and therefore require a different kind or form of note taking. Here is an outline that we have developed over our years of teaching. Students have found it helpful.

HOW TO MAKE AN ABSTRACT OF RESEARCH ARTICLES

Author, Name of. The complete title of the article, as stated in the journal. Name of journal, year, volume, inclusive pages. (Month). For the selections in this book add the bibliographic reference for this book also, in the same form. Note that so far you have been copying, exercising your writing muscles. You should not do much more copying.

Purpose. State the purpose in the author's words if he has not been too verbose. Do you see why copying may be a good idea here? But make an active decision to copy. Do not just keep on writing.

Subjects. Name, ages, sex, socioeconomic status, hereditary factors, environmental factors, all the important identifying material that the author gives. Put it in tabular form if possible.

Apparatus and Procedure. A brief description of any special apparatus, tests, or techniques. If a standard test is used, be sure to mention any deviations from the usual method of presentation or scoring. If the length of time the test continued or the number of determinations is important, be sure to include these facts.

Results. What the investigator found, in terms of scores, and so on. Put these in tabular form also if you can. Keep in mind that you are writing a summary, but do not leave out any important items. Also remember that you usually make abstracts for use over a long period of time, and that later you may want to know the results of this study for a purpose different from your present one.

Conclusions. How the author interprets his findings. Does he think his hypothesis is substantiated? What does he think is the "next step?" Does he tie his results into the main body of knowledge in his field?

Remarks. This is the place, and the *only* place, for you to say what you think. Is it a good study? Are there any points on which you disagree? Can you offer any interpretations other than those given by the author? What are the theoretical implications? Are there implications for practice? What further studies does this one suggest to you?

The following questions are some of the points you should investigate under each of the major headings. All of them, of course, are not applicable to any one study, and there may be others in some instances. A beginning student will not have the background for answering all of them.

Purpose. Does the author state the purpose clearly? Allowing for personal enthusiasms, was the purpose worthwhile?

Subjects. Is the number adequate? Is the sample clearly described as to age, sex, SE status, education, race, and so on? Remember that in different studies different things are important. The two criteria here are whether the sampling is good and whether the sample is reproducible. That is, if you wanted to check the experiment, has the author given you enough information so that you could reproduce the group in all important characteristics?

Apparatus and Procedure. As far as you can tell, did the investigator set up his procedure so that his results are not biased by it? Are factors controlled that might invalidate the results? Is there a better way of testing the same hypothesis? If statistics were used, are they adequate? Why did the investigator use the ones he did? If statistics were not used, why did he handle the data as he did? Do you approve of his methods? Why?

Results. Are the results clearly stated? Are sufficient raw data given so that someone else could rework them? Would the results be different if better methods of handling the data had been used? What effect does the sampling have on the results? Do you know of any other studies that bear on this one, either substantiating it or contradicting it?

Conclusions. Do the author's conclusions follow from the results he has stated? Do they bear any relation to his stated purpose? Do the conclusions as stated take into account any limitations in the sampling or method?

This is not the only way of keeping track of research articles. This outline, however, is as exhaustive as most people will need for ordinary purposes. Only occasionally, when you are engaged in writing a minute analysis of the literature on one topic, will you want to keep a more inclusive record of the details in an article. More often you will want to record less material than this outline requires. It is a lot of work to make a complete abstract, but when you have done it, your thinking becomes clearer and your files are that much more well stocked. Complete abstracts should not be neglected.

A VERY SHORT COURSE IN STATISTICS

Many students who read this book will not have had a course in statistics. Usually the authors of research articles interpret the statistics they use and state the conclusions that follow from them. But because you should not get into the lazy habit of skipping over them, we include this section in order to help you to understand some of the important kinds of statistics. When you come across a statistic (correlation, for instance), refer back to this section. Some that are used only occasionally, like the sign test and the Mann-Whitney test, are not described here. A text on statistics will explain these.

Averages or Measures of Central Tendency. What a nonstatistician calls the average, a statistician calls the *mean* or the *arithmetic mean*. The average (mean) cost of your textbooks for this semester is the sum of what you paid for all the books divided by the number of books. A mean is a number that, mathematically, is most representative of a series of similar numbers.

Another kind of average is the *median*. A median is the middle number when a series of numbers is arranged from small to large. There are two conditions under which it is used. The median is used when some of the numbers are much larger or smaller than the others. If you were able to get four used textbooks for $4, $4.75, $5, and $7, but had to spend $15 for a new edition, the mean cost would be $7.15. The median cost of $5 is more representative of the series of numbers. The median is also used when the unit of measurement is not divisible into smaller units. The mean number of children per family is an incorrect use of the mean, although it is sometimes reported, because there can be no such thing as a fractional child, and means rarely come out as integers. Since a median can be an integer, the average number of children per family should always be stated as a median.

The *mode* and the *harmonic mean* are occasionally used as a measure of central tendency. A statistics textbook will explain them.

Tests of Significance. In most research two or more groups are compared with each other. The important question is, "Are the differences due to chance or to a real difference in condition or treatment of the groups?" The researcher sets up the hypothesis (called the null hypothesis) that there is no true difference. He applies an appropriate statistical test, on the basis of which he decides to accept or reject the null hypothesis. He would accept the null hypothesis that there is no significant difference if the test showed that a difference as large as the one discovered could have arisen by chance. If the test showed that the difference could have arisen by chance less than five times out of 100 repetitions of the study, he rejects the null hypothesis and concludes there *is* a true, or significant, difference. The statistical notation for such a statement is $p < .05$, which is read, "the probability is less than five in 100." Occasionally a more stringent test of significance is used, which is written $p < .01$. This means that the result could be obtained by chance less than 1 per cent of the time. Note that a statistician does not say a difference could *never* occur by chance, but the probability of its occurring by chance is so many in 100.

There are many different kinds of tests of significance, depending on the kind of data being used. Some of the more usual are χ^2 (chi-squared), the t test, and the F test of analysis of variance. Always a test of significance gives the basis for deciding whether the difference could have arisen by chance.

The t test and analysis of variance (ANOVA) are statistical tests that are similar: In the t test two conditions or situations can be compared; in a one-way ANOVA more than two (high, moderate, and no nutritional supplement, for instance) can be compared. A two-way ANOVA makes it possible to compare the effects of two variables (nutritional supplement and sex of subject) and also determine the effect of the interaction between the variables. In such a study, there would be boys and girls in the three nutritional supplement groups. All of them would be measured for height at the beginning of the period of nutritional supplement and again at the end. The gains of all the children, both boys and girls, in each of the nutritional supplement groups would be compared; this would be a one-way ANOVA. Similarly, the gains of all the girls, regardless of level of supplement, would be compared with all the boys' gains, another one-way. The analysis of variance is two-way, because it is possible, also, to find out if there is an interaction between nutritional supplement and sex of subject—do high-level boys react differently from high-level girls *and* from moderate-level and no-level boys. Because there are computers to do the immense number of calculations, there are three-variable and even four-variable ANOVAs reported in the literature, although they are rare, for very large numbers of subjects are necessary in order to make the subgroups big enough.

Correlation. A coefficient of correlation measures the degree to which two measures (height and weight, for instance) vary together—positive correlation if one measure gets bigger as the second one does, and negative correlation if one gets smaller as the other one gets bigger. Zero correlation means that there is no relationship between the two. Note carefully that correlation coefficients do not say anything about causation. Heights and weights are positively correlated, but a person's weight does not cause her height, nor does her height cause her weight.

Coefficients of correlation range in size between $+1.00$ and -1.00. If the coefficient is .00, there is no relationship between the two measures. The closer it is to 1.00, either positive or negative, the closer is the relationship. If there was discovered to be a correlation of $+1.00$ between height and weight in a group of children, the tallest child would be the heaviest, the second tallest would be second heaviest, and so on to the shortest, the lightest. If you knew the height of one of these children in relation to the others, you could place him exactly in weight in relation to the others. If a correlation coefficient is -1.00, the relationship is perfectly inverse. Suppose the coefficient between reading and arithmetic scores is .00 or not significantly different from .00. The best prediction of any child's reading test score, knowing what his arithmetic test score is, would be the mean reading score of the group of children. Such a prediction would not be very helpful, unless the score in arithmetic (the independent variable) is itself close to the mean.

Most often the correlation coefficient reported is the Pearson product-moment coefficient (r). Another one often used is the rank-order coefficient (rho, or ρ).

Factor Analysis. As noted above, correlation coefficients are measures of the degree to which pairs of scores vary together. Therefore a set of coefficients can be used to obtain an indication of the *factors* underlying the co-variation of the scores. The method is called *factor analysis*. Although factor analysis was invented before there were computers, the number of calculations involved in the method prevented its wide use. If there are 50 variables to be correlated with each other, 1225 correlation coefficients are necessary, and each coefficient involves several arithmetic calculations. Then many more calculations must be made on those coefficients in order to measure the factors. These kinds of repetitive calculations are what a modern computer does very well. More factor analyses are reported in the research journals now than were reported even five years ago.

A factor analysis yields from two up to nine or ten factors. Each variable (test) in the analysis has a loading on each factor. Loadings range from .00 up to .99. A loading not significantly different from zero means that that factor does not contribute anything to that test. The bigger the loading, the more important is that factor in influencing the variability of the test scores. When several tests or measures all have large loadings on a factor, there is evidence that all of them share something in common. The investigator then sets about naming the factor, by considering what it is that all members of the group have in common, and that the rest of the tests have not at all or in only small amounts. Unlike the calculation of correlation coefficients and factor loadings, the naming of the factors is not precise, since judgments have to be made about what the members of each subset share. Often, perhaps usually, the naming of the factors is obvious when the reader of the research considers what the original measures are. But sometimes an investigator has not considered all the possibilities of the meanings of the factors the computer has extracted from his data.

Chapter 1
Personality and Body

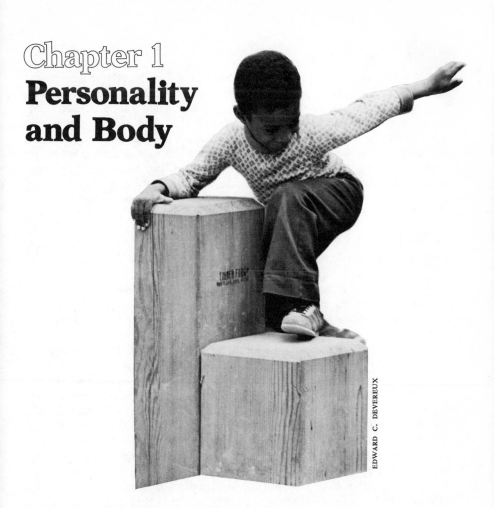

EDWARD C. DEVEREUX

No longer a baby, the preschool child interacts with an expanding world of people and things. Although physical growth is slower than it was during infancy, he is still growing faster than he will in the years that follow this period. Personality development is dramatic, as he moves from infantile concerns to the stage that gives color and focus to the preschool years.

Directions in Personality Growth

Two threads dominate the fabric of personality growth during the preschool years: the sense of autonomy and the sense of initiative. If all has gone well during infancy, a firm sense of trust is established by now. Further satisfactory experiences strengthen it, although shreds of mistrust are also present throughout life. Upon the foundation of a sense of trust, the child builds his sense of autonomy, and upon trust and autonomy, his sense of initiative. The success of his preschool interactions determine the adequacy of the sense of initiative and imagination that he builds.

1

AUTONOMY

The sense of autonomy blossoms as the child of 2 or thereabouts experiences the power of doing and deciding that comes with his wealth of budding abilities. Walking freely, although in a jerky trudging style, running a bit stiffly, climbing, bear-walking, knee-walking, galloping, riding a kiddy car, he has many independent modes of locomotion to exploit and choose from. The house and yard are for exploring. His hands easily do his bidding in reaching, grasping, letting go, throwing, turning, pulling, pushing. Toys to manipulate, tools that extend the powers of his hands, milk bottles with clothespins, Daddy's old hat, Mummy's old purse, crayons and paper, sand and water, mud—all give him choices and successes. "Shall I play with it or not? . . . I'll do what I want with it. . . . What I do is all right."

Talking brings control over both the self and others and a corresponding strengthening of the sense of autonomy. Between 18 months and 2½ years the average child's vocabulary increases from about 20 words to about 20 times that number. These four hundred words represent a great many things, activities, people, and ideas brought into the child's orbit of influence. She has made the discovery that everything has a name and that when she can say the name, she can exert some control over the thing.

Even headier is the power to cooperate with people or not. If you ask a 2-year-old, "Do you want to go outdoors?" the chances are that he'll say *no*. Even though he really would like to go out, he gets tremendous momentary satisfaction out of deciding thus. If you say, "We're going out now," he'll most likely trot along happily, the decision having been kept out of his hands. Similarly, with helping him finish a job that is too hard, like putting his rubbers on, it is better to do it than to ask, "Shall I help you?" There are many opportunities for choosing and deciding, even when adults limit them. The child decides whether to kiss, hug, and give other endearments, whether to finish his dinner and whether to urinate on the toilet or in his pants. The last decision mentioned, the question of toileting, is the one which, to the psychoanalysts, symbolizes the whole stage of developing autonomy. It is indeed an area where the sternest of parents has a hard time forcing the child and where the child can retain his autonomy under severe pressure. In the normal course of events in Western society, the child exercises autonomy as he brings his sphincters under control and takes on the toileting patterns approved by his family.

Autonomy in a group of nursery school children was measured by ratings of their behavior in separating themselves from their parents and becoming involved with peers and play in the nursery school [42]. Questionnaires answered by their parents showed the degree to which each parent expected autonomous behavior from the child. Significant relationships were found between the parents' expectations of autonomous behavior and the children's actual behavior. Autonomous behavior included practical independent performance that was helpful to the parent and also the child's insistence on doing for himself or acting on his own. For example, "Johnny is two years old. He refuses to eat at mealtime unless he can feed himself."

The negative side of a healthy sense of autonomy is a sense of shame and worthlessness. These negative feelings creep in when the youngster cannot choose enough and act independently enough, when the results of his choices and actions are disastrous, and when adults use shaming as a method of control. Because the young child is vulnerable to shaming, adults may use it as a discipline technique, not realizing its dangers for personality development [19]. When a person is shamed, he does not want to be seen or noticed. The use of shaming as a technique of control does not promote good behavior but, rather, defiance and trying to get away with doing what one wants to do. Another unfortunate outcome of poor guidance of autonomy is compulsive repetition of certain acts, a stubborn exerting of power. This type of behavior is probably the source of conforming rigidly to rules as written, in contrast to flexible interpretation of meaning.

> Outer control at this age, therefore, must be firmly reassuring. The infant must come to feel that the basic faith in existence, which is the lasting treasure saved from the rages of the oral stage, will not be jeopardized by this about-face of his, this sudden violent wish to have a choice, to appropriate demandingly, and to eliminate stubbornly. Firmness must protect him against the potential anarchy of his yet untrained sense of discrimination, his inability to hold on and to let go with discretion. As his environment encouraged him to "stand on his own feet," it must protect him against meaningless and arbitrary experiences of shame and of early doubt [19, p. 252].

INITIATIVE

Just as development of a sense of autonomy dominates the early part of the preschool period, the sense of initiative is the central theme of the latter part. Personality growth is never in a straight line. There is always some backing up and reworking of old problems. Even with a firm sense of trust, there are frights over Mother's being away too long or strangers threatening. Even with a strong sense of autonomy, a child occasionally asserts it in a temper tantrum, a refusal to eat, or a toilet "accident." Little threads of problems run through life as imperfections in trust and autonomy, demanding attention and solutions.

Now at 4 years or so, the sense of initiative claims the center of the stage. The preschool child is an explorer, curious and active. He seeks new experiences for their own sake, the sheer pleasure of sensing and knowing. He also seeks experience in order to fit it in with something he already knows and to make it more understandable. He pushes vigorously out into the world, seeking a wide range of information about it, about people and what they do, about what he himself can do. Grasping a piece of reality, like Mother's high heels and handbag, Daddy's briefcase, or a doctor's kit, he creates the experience he wants, trying on the role of a mother or father or doctor, contemplating what these adults do, imagining how it would be if he himself were doing it. Building a store with cartons, he becomes a storekeeper. He paints a picture. He creates a new world in a stream bed. It is at this stage that children put beans in their ears and stir eye shadow into cold cream. If the child's seeking is successful, then he finds a wide variety of things he can do, make, and create, with the approval of his family and other adults. If he succeeds, he continues as an older child and adult to look for new ideas, solutions, answers, reasons, creative experiences. Imagination is discussed in greater detail in Chapter 3, where its development is related to cognitive growth and

where both these functions are seen as integrated in play, which is the business of the preschool child.

Aggression, also, is a function of the sense of initiative, since aggression involves pushing out into the world and attacking. Since aggression is also involved with anger, its discussion is postponed until Chapter 4, which deals with emotional development and control. Assertive behavior is similar to aggression in being a reaching out and pushing into the environment to explore and manipulate it.

Assertion, unlike aggression, does not imply anger. Assertive behavior in five-year-olds was studied by testing, observations, and teachers' ratings, focusing on the exploration-manipulation sort of behavior and upon destructiveness in the service of learning or exploring [17]. The test of instrumental destructiveness involved telling the child that he could get and keep an attractive top if he would first knock over a pile of plastic glasses that stood in front of the toy. Results showed that this test, as well as teachers' and observers' ratings, was correlated with intelligence as measured by the Stanford–Binet. The measures of assertion were reflections of the child's ability to interact with his environment and to master it. Since intelligence tests measure knowledge and mastery, the child who dealt assertively with his world would be more likely to score high on such tests.

Conscience begins to develop at this time, regulating initiative and imagination. The child takes the voice of his parents into himself, saying what he may do and what he may not do. When he does not obey it, he may feel guilty. Sometimes he even feels guilty for his thoughts and wishes which run counter to the commands of his conscience. His vigorous imagination can easily hit or kill people who oppose him or it can, more deviously, create a bear or a wolf to eat the annoying people. The bear may get out of control and threaten the child himself, especially in a dream. Conscience development is considered further in the framework of parent–child relationships. Thus do the forces of creativity and social control struggle in the person of a young child, producing dreams of beauty and fright, glimpses of new worlds of achievement, the constriction of guilt. The establishment of a healthy sense of initiative means that the child can interact vigorously under the control of a conscience that is strong enough but not too punishing.

Activity and Passivity. Although the expression of initiative includes pushing out, exploring, and making beginnings, being active is also an aspect of initiative. Therefore, it is worthwhile to note what has been found about activity and passivity in the early years of life. Individual differences in activity have been observed in infancy, as well as during the preschool and school years [20]. Differences were seen in motor activity and in sensitivity to the environment. Motor differences included those in total amount of activity and those in ways of using the body. For example, some babies were very active with their arms and legs, whereas others turned and rolled more. Some moved quickly, others slowly, some mildly, some forcefully. They varied in the distribution and length of periods of quiet and activity. At each age, degree of activity and degree of perceptual sensitivity determine certain aspects of interactions with the environment, including people, and thus affect the course of personality development [20, pp. 21–29].

Another approach to the understanding of activity was through a longitudinal study that followed children from birth to maturity [32]. Passivity was defined as the tendency to acquiesce to or withdraw from frustrating situations, instead of dealing with them actively. The opposite of passivity, then, sounds very much like the sense of initiative. Passivity was found to be a highly stable personality characteristic during the first ten years of life. Another characteristic studied was dependency, defined as the child's tendency to seek affection, help, and company of female adults, usually his mother. The opposite of dependency also sounds like an aspect of initiative, since initiative includes independent action. Dependency was found to be a moderately stable personality characteristic during the first ten years of life [32, pp. 50–54].

Achievement and Competence. During the preschool years, when the development of the sense of initiative dominates life, it seems more important to get things started than to finish them. Planning, undertaking, exploring, pushing out, and attacking are all of the essence of this period. Achieving (finishing jobs, doing well) becomes much more important during the stage that follows, the period of the development of a sense of industry. Since preparations for each stage of personality development are made during preceding stages, some of the foundations for later achievement can be studied during the preschool years. The young child has experiences that affect his efforts, persistence, and expectations of himself in regard to excellence. As the youngster pushes forward to explore and to try new activities, his parents take certain attitudes toward what he is doing. Some parents hold high standards of excellence for their children; others hold lower standards. Some push children to do well; others let them do more as they will. Some give them a large measure of independence; others control them tightly. There are steps in between each of these pairs of extremes. Research shows that achievement motivation and behavior are affected by experience during the period of development of the sense of initiative and even more in the years that follow [14].

Competence in preschool children is correlated with parental practices that are intellectually stimulating and somewhat tension producing, such as demands for mature behavior and firm discipline. These conclusions came from factor-analytic studies of parent interviews and ratings of children's behavior. Parental techniques that fostered self-reliance, such as demanding self-control and encouraging independent decision making, promoted responsible, independent behavior. In another study, a group of preschool children were chosen for being highly socialized and independent, as shown by their self-reliance, exploring, self-assertion, self-control, and affiliation. The parents of these children, as contrasted with the parents of a control group, were consistent, loving, and demanding, respecting the child's decisions, using reason, and maintaining a firm stand when a stand was taken. These parents displayed high nurturance, high control, clear communication, and clear policies of regulation. Thus, the parents encouraged initiative in children, but limited the area within which the child could operate. The children were therefore protected from disastrous failure while benefiting from appropriate freedom [6].

Sex and Ethnic Differences. Up to about age 3, observational studies of children do not consistently show that boys or girls are more active. Between the ages of 3 and 6, sex differences in activity level are most frequently detected, with boys on the average showing more curiosity and exploratory behavior than girls [39]. Such a summary of research results does not come as a surprise to teachers of preschool children. The greater amount of curiosity and activity in boys has been linked by some authors to the tendency for males across species to be more active than females, but it is probably also true that North American males are given more encouragement than females to fit the stereotype of what a boy is like.

Cultural influences in traditional Chinese and Japanese families encourage children to be dependent, obedient, and cautious, and discourage them from exploring, behaving impulsively, and deciding [35]. We have observed the same phenomena in India. Especially when children live in joint families, adults are ever present to supervise, restrain, and protect, preventing an active reaching out and intrusion by young children. Often we have seen young Indian children taken to parties or visiting by their parents. The little child sits beside the mother or close to her, simply looking and listening, or maybe daydreaming, or if given something to play with, quietly playing. A North American child his age would most likely explore the room and objects in it, approach some of the people and intrude upon his mother's conversations. Such differences in Asian and North American child behavior reflect different cultural values as well as child-rearing methods that support the values.

Physical Characteristics, Experiences, and Their Implications

Although much more independent than infants, preschool children are able to operate independently only within circumscribed areas. The protective and nurturing roles of parents are understood best in the light of the young child's physical characteristics.

GROWTH RATES

Height and Weight. Growth in height is not so fast as it was during infancy. The growth rate decelerates slowly throughout the preschool period. At 2 years, the average child is 175 per cent of birth length, whereas at 4 years she has added only another 25 per cent, so that her height is increased by 100 per cent, or doubled. It takes the average child another nine years to triple her length at birth [37, p. 77]. Another way of showing the overall deceleration of growth is in the formula of doubling a boy's height at age 2 to arrive at an approximation of his adult height; for a girl, one doubles her height at age 2 and subtracts 10 or 12 centimeters [37, p. 88]. Thus, the first doubling of height takes place in 4 years, whereas the doubling that results in final height takes from 14 to 16 years. Birth weight is quadrupled by age 2½, showing the rapid rate for weight gain in infancy. Between 2 and 5, the weight gain is less than the amount gained during the first year of life, showing the slower rate at which weight is gained in the preschool period as contrasted with infancy. The average child's weight at age 2 is doubled by the first half of the eighth year, quadrupled by age 14, and by age 18 is about five times what it was age 2 for boys and four and one half times for girls. These multiples of height and weight at age 2 are true of averages, but may not be very accurate predictors of the growth of individual children.

Slow growth in height and weight has been reported for children in lower socioeconomic groups all over the world, including the United States. Most of the children in underdeveloped countries are retarded in height and weight, the usual average being below the sixteenth percentile for well-nourished children in the United States and Western Europe. In these same countries, the growth of children in the favored socioeconomic groups has been found to be comparable with that of children in the United States and Western Europe [62]. Such studies strongly suggest that nutrition, rather than racial or genetic factors, plays the main role in the growth failure occurring in deprived parts of the world [31, 62].

Tissues and Proportions. Rates of growth change for various tissues, as well as for height and weight. The growth of fat and muscle is especially interesting, because of the consequent change from babylike to childlike appearance. Fat increases rapidly during the first 9 months of life, decreases rapidly in thickness from 9 months to 2½ years, and decreases slowly until 5½. At 5½, it is half as thick as at 9 months. Thus does the chubby baby grow into a slender child. Muscle tissue follows a different pattern, growing at a decelerating rate throughout infancy and childhood, lagging behind other types of tissue growth until the puberal growth spurt.

Sex differences show up in tissue growth, too. Boys have more muscle and bone than girls; girls have more fat than boys. Of course, there are individual differences, too, in all aspects of growth. Individual differences in amount of fat are greater than sex differences [11, pp. 260–262].

Bodily proportions change because of differential growth rates of various parts of the body. The principle of developmental direction is illustrated here by the growth that takes place in a cephalo-caudal (head to tail) direction. Development is at first more rapid in the head end of the body, with the tail end reaching maturity later. At age 2, the head is still large in relation to the trunk and legs. The abdomen and chest measure about the same but after 2, the chest becomes larger in relation to the abdomen [37, p. 74]. The abdomen sticks out, since a relatively short trunk has to accommodate the internal organs, some of which are closer to adult size than is the trunk. Thus the toddler is top-heavy. The head itself grows according to the same principle, with the upper part closer to completion than the lower part. A large cranium and a small lower jaw give the characteristic baby look to a 2-year-old's face. These proportions, plus fat, result in the diminutive nature of immature creatures that adults find emotionally appealing. Americans call baby humans, puppies, kittens, and other animal infants *cute*. Germans add *chen* to babies' names, and the French add *ette*. As the legs, trunk, and jaw grow in relation to the head, the baby loses his "cute" or diminutive look. This is what happens to the human baby between 2 and 5 years of age. By the time he starts to kindergarten or first grade, his proportions more nearly resemble those of the children in the rest of the grades than they resemble his preschool brothers and sisters at home. The photograph seen here illustrates the proportions of a child between 5 and 6.

Bones of preschool children have their own qualitative as well as proportional characteristics. The younger the child the more cartilage there is in his skeletal system and the less the density of minerals in the bones. The joints are more flexible; the ligaments and muscles are attached more tenuously than in an older child. Thus it is easier to damage young bones, joints, and muscles by pressure and pulling and by infections. The skeletal system is very responsive to changes in environment that produce malnutrition, fatigue, and injury [37, p. 260]. Bone maturation, evaluated by the thickness, number, and shape of small bones showing

EDWARD C. DEVEREUX

Sun bathing on a Yugoslavian beach, this child shows the proportions typical at 5 or 6 years of age.

in X rays of the hand and wrist, has been found to be retarded by two or three years in preschool children of poor, underdeveloped countries [48]. Head circumference was found to be smaller in malnourished preschool children as compared with well-nourished children of the same ethnic origin [48].

The brain is more nearly complete, as to total weight, than the rest of the body. By 3 years, the brain is about 75 per cent of its adult weight and by 6 years of age almost 90 per cent. At age 5 the total nervous system is one twentieth the total weight, in contrast to the adult nervous system, which is one fiftieth the total weight [37, p. 201].

The fact that there is relatively little increase in brain weight at this time does not mean that brain development is not proceeding rapidly. There is every reason to believe that during the preschool period, there is a continuous increase in the number, size, and complexity of connections between cells in the cortex and in connections between the different levels of the brain [54]. Evidence strongly suggests that Piaget's successive stages of cognitive growth occur as the cortex matures and becomes progressively organized. The connections between the two hemispheres (corpus callosum) are structurally immature through the preschool period [15].

By two years, most children have a full set of 20 primary (deciduous) teeth. At between six and seven years, these teeth begin to shed, starting with the lower central incisors. The first permanent teeth, the "six-year" or first molars, erupt. Parents often do not realize the importance of taking good care of the "baby" teeth because they know they will be replaced. Physical examinations of lower-income children in Tennessee revealed 42 per cent of the urban children and 71 per cent of the rural children with teeth that had active caries that were so severe that crowns were broken down, pulp involved, or extraction indicated [13]. One of the rural children had 19 such teeth. Dental care includes much more than attention to cavities, although treatment of caries is very important. A dentist also monitors the development of teeth in order to see whether intervention is needed, and if so, to plan for it at the best time. Dental maturity can be measured by matching X rays with standards [16].

Of the special senses, *vision* and *taste* are noteworthy in the preschool years. The macula of the retina is not completely developed until about 6 years, and the eyeball does not reach adult size until 12 or 14 [37]. The young child is farsighted because of the shape of the eyeball. Estimates for visual acuity, taken from several studies [18] are: at two years, 20/100 to 20/40; at three, 20/50 to 20/30; at four, 20/40 to 20/20; at five, 20/35 to 20/25; at six, 20/27. Thus, even at 6 years of age, the estimated acuity is not yet 20/20. Investigations of the ways in which children use their visual mechanism show that they function in immature ways during the preschool years. An analysis of 109 vision-screening projects shows that 6 per cent of the children were referred for professional eye examinations and that 75 per cent of those examined had abnormal eye conditions. One to 3 per cent of preschool children require glasses [56].

Taste buds are more generously distributed in the young child than in the adult, being scattered on the insides of the cheeks and the throat as well as on the tongue. He probably is highly sensitive to taste. The ear, too, is significantly different in the young child because of the Eustachian tube which connects the middle ear with the throat. The tube is shorter, more horizontal, and wider in the infant and preschool child than in the older child and adult. Invading organisms find an easy entrance route from the young child's throat to his middle ear. Hence he is more susceptible to ear infections than is the older child.

The internal organs show various immaturities, with implications for child care. For example, the stomach, at 4 to 6 years, has less than half the capacity of the average adult stomach. Calorie requirements at that age, however, are more than half as great as that of an active adult. The shape of the stomach is straighter than in older children and is more directly upright than an infant's or older child's. Thus, it empties rather readily in either direction. The lining of the digestive tract is easily irritated by seasonings and roughage. The respiratory system matures sufficiently during the preschool years to establish the adult type of breathing, combining abdominal and chest movements. However, air passages are relatively small at this time and the lymphatic system is prominent so that tonsils and adenoids are at their maximum size.

METHODS OF ASSESSING GROWTH

A child can be compared with other children his age or he can be evaluated in terms of his own past growth. As was mentioned in Chapter 3, heredity can be taken into account by using a mid-parent height table when considering his height. Speed of growth can be calculated between two points in time. An individual's speed of growth can be compared with that of other children.

Comparisons with Peers. Height and weight tables represent the most common instrument used for making such assessments of growth. Tables 1-1 and 1-2 give for each age and sex the heights and weights that are at seven points on a percentile scale. For example, 4-year-old David is 107.3 centimeters tall and weighs 75 kilograms. Table 1-2 shows that he weighs less than 75 per cent of children his age, whereas Table 1-1 indicates his height to be above that of 75 per cent of children. These figures suggest that David is slim and tall.

If David is a subject in a carefully controlled experiment or investigation (of nutritional status, for instance), the norms given here should probably not be used but should be replaced by norms established on a group that is similar to David in as many aspects as possible. For clinical use, to decide if David's growth up to this time is satisfactory, these tables, based on studies done on United States children in the 1940s, are quite satisfactory. Studies of black and white children up to two years of age [61], between two and five [44], and between six and 12 years [26], indicate that although black children are smaller at birth than white, they gain relatively to the whites so that during the years from two to five they are consistently, but only slightly, taller and heavier than white children. These three studies, done in the 1960s, give norms very similar to the 1940s figures.

Table 1-1. Percentile Distribution of Heights of Males and Females from Age $2\frac{1}{2}$ Years Through $5\frac{1}{2}$ Years; United States, 1940s.

Age	Percentile in Centimeters for Females						
	3	10	25	50	75	90	97
$2\frac{1}{2}$ years	85	86	90	91	94	97	99
3 years	88	90	93	96	98	101	104
$3\frac{1}{2}$ years	92	94	96	100	102	105	108
4 years	95	98	100	102	105	109	112
$4\frac{1}{2}$ years	98	101	104	107	109	114	116
5 years	102	104	107	109	112	116	119
$5\frac{1}{2}$ years	105	108	110	113	116	119	122

Age	Percentile in Centimeters for Males						
	3	10	25	50	75	90	97
$2\frac{1}{2}$ years	87	88	90	92	94	97	100
3 years	91	92	94	97	98	100	103
$3\frac{1}{2}$ years	94	96	98	100	102	104	107
4 years	98	99	101	104	107	109	110
$4\frac{1}{2}$ years	100	102	104	107	110	112	114
5 years	103	105	107	110	113	116	118
$5\frac{1}{2}$ years	105	108	111	114	117	120	122

SOURCE: Adapted from E. H. Watson and G. H. Lowrey. *Growth and development of children*. Chicago: Year Book Medical Publishers, 1967.

Table 1-2. Percentile Distribution of Weights of Males and Females from Age 2½ Through Age 5½; United States, 1940s.

Age			_Percentile in Kilograms for Females_				
	_3_	_10_	_25_	_50_	_75_	_90_	_97_
2½ years	10.7	11.6	12.5	13.4	14.5	16.1	17.4
3 years	11.6	12.5	13.4	14.4	15.6	17.0	18.9
3½ years	12.5	13.4	14.3	15.4	16.8	18.4	20.5
4 years	13.3	14.2	15.2	16.4	17.9	19.7	21.9
4½ years	13.9	15.0	16.0	17.4	19.0	21.2	23.1
5 years	15.0	16.1	17.2	18.6	20.2	22.1	23.7
5½ years	15.9	17.2	18.5	20.0	21.4	23.2	25.2
Age			_Percentile in Kilograms for Males_				
2½ years	11.5	12.0	12.9	13.6	14.6	15.6	16.8
3 years	12.2	13.0	13.7	14.6	15.6	16.7	17.8
3½ years	12.9	13.8	14.6	15.5	16.7	17.7	18.8
4 years	13.6	14.5	15.4	16.6	17.7	18.8	20.0
4½ years	14.2	15.3	16.2	17.5	18.8	20.0	21.5
5 years	15.4	16.3	17.5	18.8	20.5	21.9	23.5
5½ years	16.4	17.6	19.0	20.6	22.3	24.0	25.6

SOURCE: Adapted from E. H. Watson and G. H. Lowrey. _Growth and development of children_. Chicago: Year Book Medical Publishers, 1967.

Comparisons with Self. For judging how well a child is growing from point to point of time, a child's status at each successive measurement can be entered on a graph or chart. Such a chart shows a curve that represents the average height or weight of representative groups of children at each age, and curves connecting percentile points on either side of the mean, often the 10th and 90th. A line connecting the child's successive measurements will be roughly parallel to the printed lines if the growth progress is satisfactory. A child with small parents, for instance, whose curves for height and weight stay from year to year at about the 25th percentile may be growing satisfactorily; a point at the mean, or above it, is not necessarily desirable for all children. (See Appendix B.)

Cross-Culture Comparisons. Body size varies in different parts of the world. Physical measurements on 160 samples of 4-year-old children represent Africa, Asia, Australia, Europe, the Americas, West Indies, and the Malay archipelago [41]. These samples differed as much as 17 centimeters in average height and 5.9 kilograms in average weight.

The shortest group was from Bihar, an Indian state known for its famines. The sample of over 3,000 children averaged 85.8 centimeters in height. The diet in Bihar is commonly deficient in calories, proteins, calcium, and vitamins. The Bihar children were fifth lightest, at an average weight of 11.8 kilograms. The lightest sample was from East Pakistan, another area prone to famine and found by a survey team to be deficient in total calories, protein, vitamin A, riboflavin, and iron. The Pakistani 4-year-olds were taller than only three other groups: the Indians, Kwango Negroes, and Vietnamese.

The tallest sample was Czech, having an average height of 103.8 centimeters. Next tallest was Dutch, 103.5, and next, United States whites, 102.9. The heaviest children were Lithuanians, at 17.3 kilograms, then Latvian, 17.2, and Czech, 17.1. Norwegian and Dutch were also heavier than United States white children, who averaged 16.7 kilograms.

In the middle of the height ranks were Polynesians, at 96.6 centimeters. Children in the West Indies and Jamaica were midway in weight, averaging 6.6 kilograms.

Growth in weight among preschool children from several underdeveloped countries is shown in Figure 1-1. The children are compared with INCAP standards (Institute of Nutrition of Central America and Panama). The children from Thailand and New Guinea followed an almost normal course of growth for the first 3 months, fell farther and farther below normal for the next year, and then maintained a low level of weight growth. The Guatemalan and Indian children showed a pattern similar to the other two groups in the first 3 months, but after

Figure 1-1.   Average weight-for-age of children in four underdeveloped countries, shown in relation to average weight according to the standards of the Institute for Nutrition in Central America and Panama. The median of Iowa curves is also indicated, showing that averages for normal Central American children are very close to those for a sample of North American children.

SOURCE: Data from M. Béhar. Prevalence of malnutrition among preschool children of developing countries, in N. S. Scrimshaw and J. E. Gordon (eds.). *Malnutrition, learning and behavior.* Cambridge: M.I.T. Press, 1968. Also from R. L. Jackson and H. G. Kelly. Growth charts for use in pediatric practice. *Journal of Pediatrics,* 1945, **27,** 215–229.

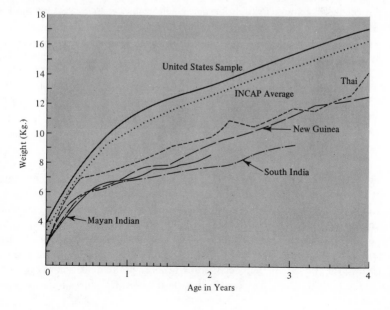

that diverged farther from the INCAP standard. As far as these graphs show, the children do not seem to be dropping farther below the standard line.

SKELETAL AGE

Another way of assessing growth is to measure the maturity of the skeleton, by means of X rays. Early in prenatal life the precursors of most bones appear as cartilage. (The bones of the upper part of the skull develop from membranous tissue.) The cartilage is gradually replaced by bone beginning in the sixth week after fertilization. From this time until the individual is in his twenties, bone is being laid down, starting from centers of ossification that appear in highly uniform places in each cartilage. Ossification takes place in the cells through a process of formation of organic salts of calcium and phosphorus. The centers of ossification appear in a fairly uniform order. Bones grow in width or diameter by the addition of bony material on the outer surface of the bone underneath the *periosteum* (a membrane that surrounds the bone). Long bones grow longer by the addition of ossified materials at their ends. The shape of a bone is developed and maintained by the action of cells that remove calcified material, as well as of those that deposit it.

In long bones another ossification center appears at the end of the cartilage that forms the model of the growing bone. This separate piece of bone is called the *epiphysis*. The cartilage between the epiphysis and the shaft of the bone (the *diaphysis*) appears to become thinner and thinner as growth proceeds. Eventually, in normal human beings the epiphysis and diaphysis fuse into one piece of bone, and lengthwise growth in that bone ceases. Just as the timetable of the appearance of centers of ossification is fairly regular for the individual, so the fusion of epiphyses and diaphyses follows a time pattern [45]. As each piece of bone grows, its size and shape changes in a systematic fashion that varies relatively little from one person to another.

All of these changes in body tissue can be followed in X rays of the bones. The cartilaginous material is transparent to X rays; the ossified material, opaque. Most of the studies of skeletal development have been done using X rays of the left hand and wrist. The developed film is compared with standard illustrations in order to match it as closely as possible to one of them. The skeletal status of a child is expressed in terms of skeletal age, which corresponds to the chronological age at which the children on whom the standards were based usually attained that same degree of skeletal development. Mental age, which is discussed in the next chapter, is a similar derived measure of development and is defined in much the same way as skeletal age.

Bone Growth as a Record of Health. X rays of the hand yield information about the quality of a child's growth. Lightly mineralized bones may be caused by insufficient intake of calcium, or insufficient metabolism of calcium, or both. An X ray film may therefore yield supplemental information concerning the nutritional status of a child. Some kinds of illnesses and other traumatic events in the child's life may result in bands of increased density of the bone at the growing end of the long bones [45a, p. 19]. If they occur, they become permanent records of disturbances in the body's metabolism during that period of the child's life.

The principle of critical periods (Chapter 5) is apparent in the disruption of the orderly sequence of appearance of ossification centers during illness [45a, p. 18]. If there is a disturbance in the calcium metabolism, such as occurs during illnesses, at the time when an ossification center is due to appear, its appearance may be delayed until a later time, even until after the appearance of the next scheduled center. When this happens, an X ray film taken subsequently, even perhaps several years later, will show imbalances in the development of individual bones and centers of ossification. Since the age of the bones that are present can be judged from their appearance, it becomes possible to make a judgment as to the time of the crisis and about how severe was the impact on the skeleton (and presumably the total organism). Later X ray examinations can tell at what point the child has made complete recovery.

MINOR PHYSICAL ANOMALIES

In order to explore relationships between congenital factors and behavior, a longitudinal study has been done on a group of nursery school children who had been judged normal at birth [57, 58]. Each child was scored for anomalies of hair, eyes, ears, mouth, hands, and feet, such as very fine electric hair, eyelid fold, ears set low, curved fifth finger, and third toe longer than second. These anomalies are so slight that they are ordinarily not noticed. Each child's total score was based upon the degree as well as the presence of such anomalies. Behavior measures were obtained at 2½ years by observers who measured time spent in various activities and counted incidences of specific actions, and by teachers' ratings. High scores for anomalies were associated with inability to delay gratification, nomadic play, frenetic play, spilling, throwing, opposing peers, and intractability.

Five years later, a replication of the study [57] showed stable anomaly scores and poor motor control associated with high scores. Such children shifted location more, were less able to delay response, and showed more frenetic behavior than children with low anomaly scores. High-scoring girls were more likely to be fearful and withdrawn, high-scoring boys were more likely to be hyperactive.

The results of this study suggest that the slight physical anomalies and the somewhat disturbed behavior have a common source, rather than that one caused the other. One might reason that very noticeable physical abnormalities cause negative reactions toward children, who then behave poorly. The subjects of this study were normal physically, however, with deviations that could be noticed only through a careful examination. It is very unlikely that they experienced negative reactions because of their appearance. It is possible, however, that hyperactive behavior in infancy elicited hostility from parents, which intensified the condition.

FEEDING THE YOUNG CHILD

The majority of the world's preschool children, hundreds of millions, are malnourished. Although most underfed children live in poor countries, there are substantial numbers of them in prosperous areas of the world, including North America. The first cause of malnutrition, unavailability of food, is everybody's business, a problem of political, economic, agricultural, educational, religious, and social dimensions. A second cause of malnutrition is ignorance of how to feed young children. Mothers' knowledge and practices of nutrition were shown to be

A two-year-old child with marasmus was photographed on admission to the Nutrition Rehabilitation Unit, Kampala, and again after six weeks on a high protein diet based on local foods.

SOURCE: D. B. Jelliffe. *Child nutrition in developing countries.* Washington, D.C. Agency for International Development, 1969.

highly correlated with the degree of adequate growth achieved by preschool children in low-income families in Beirut [4]. In many parts of the world, much better use could be made of available foods if parents only knew what nutrients children need and how to prepare foods appropriately.

Nutrients. Although one child may lack a certain nutrient because his mother does not offer it, another may refuse to eat any or enough of the valuable food given to him. Even when the family diet is adequate for adults, it may be unsuitable for young children. For example, peppers and other strong seasonings, common in Asia and Africa, may damage young gastrointestinal systems. Children may not be able to chew rough foods sufficiently. Preschool malnutrition can result from unsuitable foods, poor preparation, poor timing, and emotional disturbances.

Even when a special diet is provided for young children, it may be high in starch and low in protein. Thus, the 4-year-old, who needs 50 per cent more protein per pound of body weight than his father, receives bananas, arrowroot, maize, and rice gruel, while his father gets meat or beans. The problem of the man's getting the best food may also occur during pregnancy. The inequity continues throughout the childhood period, and is most serious when growth is most rapid. The Food and Nutrition Board of the National Research Council regularly publishes recommended allowances of food elements for people of all ages. The most recent table of recommended nutrients can be found in Appendix A. The following guide [3] for feeding the preschool child translates the nutrients into foods for each day:

3 or more cups of milk and milk products
2 or more servings of meat, poultry, fish, and eggs
4 or more servings of vegetables and fruits, including a citrus fruit or other
      fruit or vegetable high in vitamin C, and a dark-green or deep-yellow vege-
      table for vitamin A at least every other day
4 or more servings of bread and cereal of whole grain, enriched or restored
      variety
Plus other foods as needed to provide additional energy and other food values

Figures are not to be taken completely literally. Individuals vary in the amounts they need and in the amounts they eat from one day to another and from one meal to another. If the foods offered are chosen along the lines of this plan, most preschool children will take what they need from it.

Little is known of the roles played by trace elements in human growth and health, but many such elements are essential. Fluorine is one element that is well known for its contribution to sound teeth. If a family lives where the water supply is not adequate in fluorine, all members, especially young children, should have fluorine supplements. Parents should get guidance from their dentist on this matter, along with regular attention to the teeth of their preschool children.

Timing. Because a small child's capacity is limited while his needs for growth-promoting and protective foods are great, his nutritional program merits careful planning. Menus and timing are both important. Although feeding a new baby when he cries for food contributes to the early building of a sense of trust, the preschool child benefits from a structured program, including regular mealtimes that fit his stage of maturity. If the child comes to meals hungry but not famished, and exercised but not exhausted, he is likely to take in adequate nutrients.

Snacks are an important part of young children's nutrient intake. A longitudinal study of a group of middle-class children showed that during the preschool years, 22 per cent of their calories came from snacks [8]. Since only 12 per cent of their protein came from snacks, it can be seen that better planning could have resulted in more valuable snacks and a better balancing of nutrients throughout the day. If completely unplanned, snacks are all too likely to be long on carbohydrates and fats and short on proteins, minerals, and vitamins. With his limited capacity for intake and high need for growth-promoting foods, a preschool child cannot afford to eat many empty calories (foods devoid of proteins, minerals, and vitamins).

With good planning, eating and sleeping can be tied together in rhythms that assure adequate sleep for the young child. Insufficient sleep leads to fatigue, which depresses the appetite.

Sensory Aspects. Taste sensitivity varies from one individual to another, in preschool children as well as in older children and adults. An investigation [34] of preschool children's thresholds for the basic tastes—salt, sweet, bitter, and sour—showed degrees of sensitivity to all four tastes to be highly correlated. Preschool children tended to be at the extreme ends of the scale for tasting bitter. That is, they either tasted it or they did not, whereas for sweet, salt, and sour, they could be arranged into groups of high, medium, and low sensitivity. The number of subjects who reported that they were always hungry for meals increased as taste sensitivity decreased. Breakfast was the meal most enjoyed, in contrast to teenage girls who liked breakfast least.

A few years ago, baby foods were made with excessive salt and other flavorings in order to please mothers who tasted them. This mistake has been corrected, but many mothers flavor young children's food the way they themselves like it instead of realizing that preschool children are satisfied with bland food, and that it is better for them than highly flavored food. Sugar may be an even worse detriment than salt in the diets of many young children. Fruits and simple desserts provide enough sweets, but candy, sugar-coated cereals, sugar-containing beverages, and gum are all devoid of growth-promoting nutrients. These substances displace useful nutrients from the diet and also promote tooth decay.

Cooked vegetables were disliked by over half the preschool children who took part in a study of food attitudes [8]. Probably the flavor of vegetables is the main offender, although the texture may also be unpleasant. (Since many North Americans overcook vegetables, the results are often strong, mushy, and dull-colored.) Young children often prefer raw vegetables to the cooked vegetables typically served to them. Very few, only 1.7 per cent, of the children disliked milk, and only 3.5 per cent disliked fruit. When favorite foods were discussed, meat was at the top, with 38.8 per cent nominating it as best liked.

Touch and texture are also important in eating. A meal is made attractive by a combination of crisp, chewy, and soft foods. Children often want to feel the

STANLEY SUMMER

slipperiness of gelatin and spaghetti, the crinkliness of lettuce, and the cloudlike softness of a soufflé. Bright colors and color contrasts are thought to be effective in making meals attractive to children as well as to adults. Young children prefer lukewarm food to hot food [11, p. 201]. The sense of smell doubtless plays an important part in the enjoyment of eating.

Emotional Aspects. Emotional surroundings can enhance or depress appetite. Conversely, hunger disposes the child toward anger outbursts. Excitement and upset conditions cause the stomach to stop its movements. To eat with the family may be too stimulating for a young child, or it may add to his happiness and feelings of belonging, depending on what goes on at the family table. Whatever the arrangements, the preschool child has the best chance of eating an adequate diet in an atmosphere that is calm and pleasant.

Avoiding Problems. The year between age 2 and 3 is a time when eating problems often begin. Because the rate of growth has slowed down, appetite is likely to be smaller. Parents, remembering the joyous abandon with which their baby waded into his food, may worry when they see that the same child at 2½ toys with his food and fusses over what he will eat and what he will not eat. Urging and forcing at this point often prolong and complicate the problem. Eager to exercise his autonomy, the 2-year-old wants to choose and decide for himself. It is satisfying to decide to eat a small serving and then to ask for more or to refuse it; it can be very annoying to have too large an amount presented, especially if it is poked at you in spoonfuls. If the child can do it himself, his sense of autonomy is enhanced. He can make progress with a spoon and even more with his fingers if given foods that are easy to pick up. Custard and soup are easier to drink than to spoon up. The young child profits from all arrangements that facilitate self-help and from wide limits within which to do it himself. He does need limits, though, for healthy development of the sense of autonomy. The child suffers, as well as the family, when he is allowed to throw his applesauce on the floor or to grab the food from his neighbor's plate. It is important for him to feel that what he does is all right, and for him to have that feeling, his behavior has to be acceptable to the people around him.

Changing Behavior. Since vegetables supply some frequently lacked nutrients and since young children often dislike vegetables, several programs of nutrition improvement have focused on teaching children to like vegetables. Various methods have proved successful. In one nursery school nutrition program, children received stickers for each portion of vegetables they ate [30]. The stickers were exchangeable for a dessert. The subjects duly tasted and ate more vegetables, dropping their intake somewhat after the reinforcements were discontinued. Another approach consisted of demonstration, discussion, games, dramatic play, and pointing out qualities such as color, texture, shape, growth properties, and food value [28]. Beets, Brussels sprouts, cauliflower, and squash, upon which all these activities were focused, were more accepted after the experiment than before. The children ate larger quantities, and more children ate the vegetables. Good nursery schools include nutrition education as part of the program, by planning and serving nutritious, attractive meals, by letting children help with food preparation, and by stimulating interest through art, games, and stories.

PLANNING FOR SLEEP AND REST

Sleep is a protective function that allows for repair and recovery of tissues after activity. Cognition is more adequate and emotional life more positive under conditions of enough sleep.

As children mature, they sleep less. The average total hours of sleep at age 2 to 3 is almost 12 and at age 3 to 5, about 11 [47]. During the second year a common pattern is two naps a day and an all-night sleep. One nap is more usual between age 2 and 5 and after that, no nap. In some cultures an afternoon nap is normal for everybody, adults as well as children.

Children vary widely, in hours of sleep, consistency of patterns, distribution of sleep between night and day, soundness of sleep, and effects of various influences on sleep. How much sleep is enough? This is a very difficult question to answer with scientific evidence or even to answer in a home situation. A practical way for adults to judge whether children are getting enough sleep is to use as criteria such signs as readiness to get up in the morning, good appetite, emotional relaxation, cheerfulness, warm skin with good color, bright eyes, good posture, activeness in play, curiosity, and enthusiasm.

Pediatricians have commented that mothers often find it more difficult to let children establish their own sleep patterns than to let them regulate their own feeding. Only 7 per cent of parents in an American study [49, p. 269] and 9 per cent in an English study [43, p. 246] said that they had no particular bedtime and let the child go to bed when he liked. The majority of parents had a certain bed hour in mind, but they varied considerably as to how strictly they maintained it. Among the English parents variations in strictness were related to class, those in higher occupations reporting more insistence upon prompt bed-going.

Although unspecified bed hours may be infrequent, many children manage to postpone bed-going and sleep, with the result that they sleep for shorter periods of time than children who go to bed promptly. Whether permissively reared children get enough sleep is a difficult question to answer because of the problem of defining *enough* sleep. In countries such as Italy and India, where babies and preschool children go out in the evening with their parents, falling asleep here and there on a friend's sofa or an extra chair at a concert, we have not noticed hyperactivity or signs of fatigue. Young children seemed to sit around more than Americans, but in a relaxed, not tense, way. Extra sitting around might be the result of more relaxed adults, fewer toys, less stimulating conditions, and possibly lower available energy because of poor nutrition.

Avoiding Problems. Children generally benefit from parental supervision that makes regular sleep and rest a part of their lives. At developmental periods when certain influences disturb sleep, guidance is appropriate. For instance, toward the end of the first year, when strangers are recognized as strange and frightening, it is important for baby-sitters to be well acquainted with the baby, in order to prevent fright when he wakens from sleep. In the latter part of the second year and for some time after that, when motor activities are thrilling and the sense of autonomy is at a crucial stage of growth, a child may find it very hard to accept bed and sleep. Here is where a routine and careful guidance can prevent sleep problems from getting established. It is easiest to go to bed and to sleep after a period when stimulation has been cut down (that is, excitement minimized), and when a regular series of steps toward bed (such as washing, tooth brushing, story, putting teddy bear in bed), and an affectionately firm parent have indicated that sleep is imminent. Dreams are likely to be disturbing, because they are not clearly distinguished from reality. Reassurance after a fright or disturbance is conducive to sleep, as long as it is calm, confident, and given in the child's room. When parents make a big entertainment production out of the incident or take the youngster into their bed, reassurance may come to be a goal in itself.

ILLNESS AND ACCIDENTS

Prevention. Maintaining life and health in young children is no simple matter for parents, even in the favored environment of Western civilization. (In some parts of the world, the odds are against an infant's surviving.) Preventive care means taking a young child regularly to a physician or to a well-baby clinic, where he is immunized against diseases, assessed as to growth and health, and his mother

STANLEY SUMMER

is given advice as to nutrition, physical care, and attention to defects. Dental care is necessary from the preschool period onward. It has been estimated that among American children under 5 years of age, 10 per cent have more than eight cavities [7, p. 5]. In areas without fluoridated water, 70 to 80 per cent of preschool children have decay requiring treatment, whereas in communities with fluoridation, only 30 to 40 per cent suffer such decay [56].

Figure 1-3. Incidence of acute conditions as per cent of total number of acute conditions reported for children under six years: United States, July 1972–June 1973.

SOURCE: C. S. Wilder. Acute conditions: incidence and associated disability. National Center for Health Statistics. Series 10, no. 98. DHEW Publication (HRA) 75-1525. Washington, D.C.: U.S. Government Printing Office, 1975.

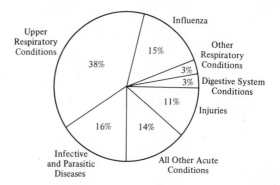

Promotion of health and growth through routines of feeding, sleep, and activity have been discussed. Parents also have the jobs of promoting community health measures, supervising general hygiene in the home, nursing ill children, and keeping children from injury. Although most of the serious childhood diseases are preventable through immunization and many of the lesser illnesses are preventable through home hygiene, many respiratory disturbances and some gastrointestinal illnesses are common even in preschool children living under favorable circumstances. The immaturity of the systems involved makes them prone to infections and disturbances.

Figure 1-3 shows that in a sample of United States children under six, 38 per cent of the acute conditions suffered by these children were upper respiratory conditions, and another 15 per cent were diagnosed as influenza. Sixteen per cent of the acute conditions were the result of infective and parasitic diseases. In 1974, the president of the American Medical Association gave warning that the American people had become too complacent about the communicable diseases of childhood. During the previous year, 5.8 million (of the total 14 million) children between 1 and 4 years of age were not immunized against either polio, measles, rubella, diphtheria, whooping cough, or tetanus. In ten years, polio immunizations had dropped from 84 per cent to 60 per cent [55].

Accidents. During the same year in which the statistics shown in Figure 1-3 were collected, accidents took the lives of more children between the ages of 1 and 4 than did the next seven ranking causes combined. For at least the last ten years, the rate of deaths of children from accidents has stayed about the same while the rate of deaths from causes other than accidents have decreased by about 30 per cent [1]. Figure 1-4 gives the death rates from all types of accidents combined, and the percentage caused by accidents of all deaths, for boys and girls separately.

Accident rates have increased during the past decade largely because of the increase in the number of motor vehicle accidents. The other main types of accidents to young children are the result of traffic, fires, explosions, burns, drowning, poisoning, falls, and inhaling or ingesting food and other objects. Supervision of children outdoors is thus seen to be vital—not only telling them what not to do but watching them and keeping them out of the way of traffic, water, and other hazards. Making and keeping the home safe for young children require constant

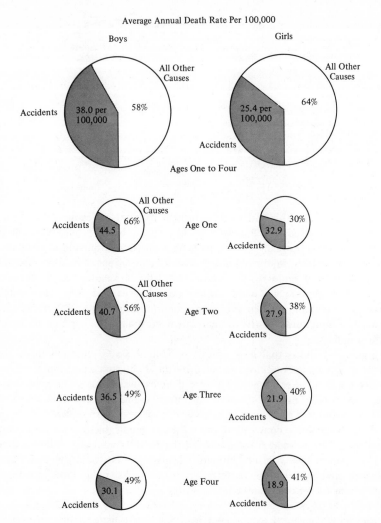

Average Annual Death Rate Per 100,000

Figure 1-4. Death rates from accidents among boys and girls aged one through four, and accidental deaths as a per cent of all deaths. United States, 1972–1973.

SOURCE: Accident mortality at the preschool age. *Statistical Bulletin*, 1975, 56: **5**, 7–9.

planning and vigilance. Over two fifths of accidents to young children occur in the home.

Another study [2] showed that about 25 per cent of the annual deaths from accidental poisoning in the United States were deaths of children between 2 and 4 years of age. The agents of death were chiefly aspirin and other salicylates, petroleum products, lead, and household pesticides. The obvious implications are that safety of preschool children requires keeping them away from many substances of common use in the home. Saying *no* is not enough at this age. Since preschool children tend to be good climbers, the problem of where to keep poisons out of their grasp is an important one to solve.

Parents as Sources of Injuries. A large proportion of accidents that befall children in the United States occur in the home, because of lack of safety precautions. In recent years it has become evident that a large number of children suffer bruises, lacerations, broken bones, and even death at the hands of their parents. A review of several studies of child abuse showed that many of the victims of parental violence were children between the ages of 3 months and 3 years [22]. The same review surmised that the vulnerability of children under three years of age as compared with older children is one of the reasons for so many reported cases at these ages. It is also generally agreed that there are many unreported cases of child abuse.

International Differences in Threats to Children. International differences in mortality and illness rates are greatest at the 1-to-4 age-level. Countries with low death rates include the United States, Great Britain, Denmark, the Netherlands, Norway, Sweden, and Australia. Death rates in some of the nations with high rates are as much as 40 times the rates in the countries with low rates [50, pp. 206–207]. Preschool mortality rates are not only ever so much higher in Colombia, Mexico, and Guatemala, but the leading cause is different. Disturbances of the gastrointestinal tract rank last among the principal causes of death in the United States and first in the other countries. Accidents (or violence), the first cause of death in the United States, does not appear as a principal cause in the other countries. The infectious diseases, whooping cough, and measles are still important in Colombia, Mexico, and Guatemala [59].

A new threat to child health knows no national boundaries. *Air pollution* most likely has adverse effects on health and development, according to a committee of the American Academy of Pediatrics [5]. A review of studies suggests that toxic substances in the air are now contributing to respiratory infections and that they may lead to permanent lung damage. Since pollutants emitted in England may fall on Sweden, to cite only one example, the problem is truly international.

Psychological Care of Ill and Injured Children. It is frightening to be hurt or sick—frightening to anyone, but especially to a preschool child. Pain itself can be frightening as well as unpleasant. Reduced to a lower level of autonomy, the child is disturbed at not being able to control himself and the environment as efficiently as normally. His thinking and his actions are less adequate for coping with the world.

Reassurance from parents makes the pain and fright possible to bear, just as Mother's presence in a disturbingly new situation gives a young child courage to explore. The most reassuring parent is one who combines sympathy with the calm expectation that balance and normalcy will be restored in due time. The ill or injured child is comforted and strengthened by having the limits of his activity redefined appropriately. For instance, "You are going to stay in your bed, but you can move around it all you like. I'll give you this box of toys to play with now

After your nap, you can choose a story for me to read to you." If toys and activities require less effort than his normal top speed, then he can still feel satisfied with what he achieves.

Canadian children living in Calgary have an opportunity to learn about hospitals when they are well [53]. Kindergarten children go in groups of 15 or 20 to one of five participating hospitals for an orientation program that takes one and one-half hours. Using a large panda bear that has a rectum, children observe and practice taking temperatures, giving hypodermics, and other nursing and treatment procedures that a child is likely to experience when she becomes a patient in hospital. They see the playroom, kitchen, and other parts of the hospital. Guides encourage questions and discussion. Such a program probably reduces somewhat the child's dread of going to a hospital when hospitalization is necessary.

Hospital care for young children has been slowly undergoing a revolution, sparked by the research of Bowlby [9] and Spitz [51, 52] and pushed along by writers such as Robertson [46]. Gradually doctors, nurses, and parents are accepting the evidence that it is damaging for children between 6 months and 3 years to be separated from their mothers, and that even after 3 years of age, separation may be harmful. Some hospitals now permit and even encourage parents to stay with their young children so as to give them the emotional support that they need every day but all the more when they are ill. Visiting rules have been liberal-

These African children have the security of their mothers' staying with them when they go to the hospital. In Africa and Asia, a family member usually stays with a patient, no matter how old the patient is.

JOHN E. BALL

ized in many places, too. Continuing research efforts confirm the earlier findings on young children's need for closeness to loved people while undergoing traumatic experiences. For example, when 197 British children under 6 years of age underwent surgery for tonsils and/or adenoids, half were admitted to the hospital with their mothers and half were alone. The young patients accompanied by their mothers suffered significantly fewer complications afterwards, both emotional and infective [10]. Interviews with parents of Swiss preschool children showed that emotional reactions after discharge were less frequent among children whose parents had visited them frequently in the hospital and who had had close contact with their parents. The differences between frequently visited, closely contacted children and infrequently visited children were very significant [12]. There is still a big educational job to be done in adapting hospitals to children's emotional needs. Unfortunately many medical personnel still interpret a young child's stony silence as good adjustment, and the flood of tears released by his parents' arrival as evidence that parents are bad for him.

Motor Development

Watch a group of preschool children playing. The first impression is of constant motion. Closer inspection reveals some children sitting looking at books, others squatting in the sandbox, and one or two in dreamy silence beside the record player. The younger the child, the shorter is the interval during which he is likely to stay put. Carrying out simple motor acts, he tends to finish quickly. In contrast, the older preschooler weaves simple acts together into more complicated units that take longer to perform. To crawl through a piece of culvert, for instance, takes only a minute and to crawl through several times takes only five, whereas to make that culvert into the Holland Tunnel and to use it as such may take half the morning.

Motor control includes inhibiting actions as well as initiating them and controlling their speed of execution. The ability to perform certain motor acts very slowly was found to be associated with high levels of intelligence in preschool children [38]. In a group ranging from average to very high IQs, the higher IQ children were more likely to do well in tests of drawing a line slowly, walking slowly between two lines, and making a truck move slowly by means of a winch. The experiment also showed that children of higher IQ were just as active in free play as those of average intelligence. It is not certain whether superior ability to inhibit motor acts is the result of superior intelligence or if a common cause, superior development of the nervous system, is responsible for the high scores on both types of tests.

THE DEVELOPMENT SEQUENCE

The chart of motor behavior, Table 1-3, drawn from several sources, shows how development between age 2 and 5 results in a child who moves and manipulates more like an adult than he does like the toddler he used to be. Having worked through stages of using a spoon and fork, holding a glass, and pouring from a pitcher, he can feed himself neatly without having to try very hard. He can even

Table 1-3. Some Landmarks in Motor Development During the Years from Two to Five, from Basic Normative Studies. The Item Is Placed at the Age Where 50 Per Cent or More of Children Perform the Act. (Initials in parentheses refer to sources. See footnotes.)*

	Age Two	Age Three	Age Four	Age Five
Eye-Hand	Builds tower of 6 or 7 blocks (KP) Turns book pages singly (KP) Spoon into mouth without turning (KP) Holds glass in one hand (KP) Imitates vertical and circular strokes (KP) Puts on simple garment (KP)	Builds tower of 9 blocks (KP) Makes bridge of 3 blocks (TM) Catches ball, arms straight (MW) Spills little from spoon (KP) Pours from pitcher (KP) Unbuttons, puts shoes on (KP) Copies circle (TM) Draws straight line (TM)	Cuts on line with scissors (GI) Makes designs and crude letters (GI) Catches small ball, elbows in front of body (MW) Dresses self (GI) Throws ball overhand (KP)	Folds paper into double triangle (TM) Copies square (TM) and triangle (KP) Copies designs, letters, numbers (GI) Catches small ball, elbows at sides (MW) Throws well (G) Fastens buttons he can see (GI)
Locomotion	Wide stance, runs well (KP) Walks up and down stairs alone (KP) Kicks large ball (KP) Descends large ladder, marking time (MW) Jumps 12 inches (MW)	Walks tiptoe (KP, B) Jumps from bottom stair (KP, B) Stands on one foot (KP, B) Hops, both feet (MW) Propels wagon, one foot (J) Rides tricycle (KP) Descends long steps, marking time, unsupported (MW) Jumps 18 inches (MW)	Gallops (G) Descends small ladder, alternating feet easily (MW) Stunts on tricycle (G) Descends short steps, alternating feet, unsupported (G) Skips on one foot (KP)	Narrow stance (GI) Skips (G, MW) Hops on one foot, ten or more steps (MW) Descends large ladder, alternating feet easily (MW) Walks straight line (GI)

* SOURCES:

B —N. Bayley. Development of motor abilities during the first three years. *Monographs of the Society for Research in Child Development*, 1935, **1.**
GI —A. Gesell, and F. L. Ilg. *Child development.* New York: Harper & Row, Publishers, Inc., 1949.
G —M V. Gutteridge. A study of motor achievements of young children. *Archives of Psychology*, 1939, **244.**
J —T. D. Jones. *Development of certain motor skills and play activities in young children,* Child Development Monographs. New York: Teachers College, Columbia University, 1939, No. 26.
KP —H. Knobloch and B. Pasamanick. *Developmental diagnosis* 3rd ed. New York: Harper & Row, Publishers, Inc., 1974.
MW —C. L. McCaskill and B. L. Wellman. A study of common motor achievements at the preschool ages. *Child Development*, 1939, **9,** 141–150.
TM —L. M. Terman and M. A. Merrill. *Stanford-Binet intelligence scale.* Boston: Houghton Mifflin Company, 1960.

carry on a conversation at meals. He can cut and fold paper. From imitating a circular stroke at 2, drawing a vertical line at 3, and copying a square with some accuracy at 5, he is poised on the brink of learning to write. The 2-year-old, to whom walking steadily, running, and climbing are thrilling achievements, advances through walking tiptoe, hopping, jumping, tricycling, agile climbing, and stunting to the graceful age of 5. Skipping, hopping skillfully, running fast, he looks into an exciting future of skating, swimming, and riding a two-wheeler. Balls, the toys beloved by babies, children, and adults, are used with increasing maturity.

Individual Differences. One child differs from another in the speed with which he progresses through a sequence of behavior patterns. We have seen 4-year-olds who could swim and ride bicycles and 6-year-olds who spilled their food consistently. Children differ also in speed, power, and accuracy of their muscular coordinations, as witness the "natural athletes" who throw and catch balls efficiently in the preschool years. They differ, too, in balance and grace. When reading a chart that shows average development for various ages, it is important to keep in mind that this is a summary of a group of children and that it does not picture any one child as he is.

Sex Differences. Girls begin early to show superiority in manual dexterity. Between age 2 and 6, boys have been found to excel in going up and down ladders and steps, throwing, catching and bouncing balls, and jumping from boxes and ladders [40]. Girls performed better than boys in hopping, skipping, and galloping [24]. The latter can be confirmed by observing a kindergarten in the fall, where there are almost sure to be several little boys who merely run or gallop while the other children skip.

Boys and girls differed in their use of outdoor space in a nursery school where every effort was made to offer freedom of choice to all [27]. The children's parents showed little interest in sex-differentiated behavior. Even so, boys played outdoors more than girls, spending more time in sand, on a tractor, on climbing equipment, and near an equipment shed. Girls spent more time indoors, using the craft tables and kitchen more than boys did.

HYPERACTIVITY

Highly active, impulsive behavior was observed and rated in a nursery school, as part of an extensive longitudinal study [25]. We have already mentioned the part of this research that showed minor physical anomalies to be associated with hyperactive behavior. When the preschool children were assessed five years later, at age 7½, hyperactivity, or the inability to inhibit motor behavior, was negatively related to intellectual functioning. Hyperactive children were more likely than normally active children to score lower on IQ, especially performance IQ, on field independence, and on inferential concepts.

POSTURE

Posture is the way in which the whole body is balanced, not only in sitting and standing but also in play and rest. Posture is neuromuscular behavior, just as surely as bouncing a ball and drawing a circle are. Parents and teachers rarely make great headway when they try to get children to stand up straight or otherwise consciously improve their posture according to standard ideas of what good posture is. The ways in which a child stands, sits, and moves are the results of a dynamic interplay of forces that cannot be controlled by holding his head up or throwing back his shoulders. This is not to say that good posture is unimportant in its influence on health, growth, and efficiency of movement. It is very important indeed, but it is achieved through good muscle tone and healthy skeletal development, as well as through general physical and mental health. Figure 1-5 illustrates good and poor posture in the preschool child.

The child's own personality is expressed in his posture, both his general attitudes toward himself and the world and his specific ups and downs. Sometimes a sagging, slumping body is the first indication that something is wrong. A handicap,

Figure 1-5.   The child on the left shows good posture, the child on the right poor posture. The first child's body is arranged symmetrically about a line that passes through his center of gravity. The head and chest are high, chin in, abdomen in, shoulder blades in, and curves of back small and knees straight.

SOURCE: Fig. 4.3 on p. 90 of *Good posture and the little child*. Children's Bureau Publication 219. Washington, D.C.: U.S. Government Printing Office, 1935.

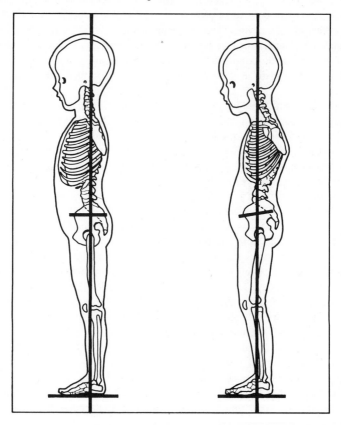

such as blindness or deafness, often leads to a characteristic posture. A beautifully balanced body is one indication of a healthy child.

MOVEMENT EDUCATION

For the harmonious development of the person, movement experiences and education are significant during the preschool years. At this time, the brain is immature, with communication between the two hemispheres limited. It is suggested that the child needs experiences that will stimulate even development of both hemispheres, rather than getting a concentration of speech, reading, and counting that involves mostly the left hemisphere. "Perhaps, then, as much emphasis should be given to music, rhythmic exercises, body awareness, graphics, and solid constructions as to speaking, listening, reading and counting" [60].

Movement has many important meanings to the young child [21]. It means life, since she thinks that things that move are alive. Movement helps her to discover her body and to form a body image and concept of self. Through movement, she explores the environment, builds concepts of space, and orients herself in space. Being able to control her movements means being able to control what happens to her and to keep her safe. Communication can take place through movement, the language of behavior. Controlled movement brings pleasure in itself as well as the satisfaction of mastery.

Unfortunately, many people still think of physical education as exercise drills and, therefore, inappropriate for the young child. The old point of view is that because young children are very active, they get all the exercise they need.

Young children will educate themselves to a large degree if they have a physical environment that makes it possible for them to do so. The planning of such an environment is, in itself, teaching. Much of the educating carried on by preschool teachers and parents consists of arranging the environment, or setting the stage, including dressing the child for easy movement. Children will use space and equipment for developing and perfecting the movements of which they are capable, whether they be the basic movements of walking, running, crawling, climbing, jumping, pushing, pulling, and grasping, or the skilled movements of throwing, catching, tricycle riding, swimming, and so on. The designing and equipping of movement centers can be observed in a good nursery school and can be studied through the writings of specialists in movement education for young children, such as Flinchum's book, *Motor Development in Early Childhood* [21].

Teachers teach young children through encouragement and enthusiasm, rather than showing them just how to execute a movement, by asking questions rather than telling them, by setting up situations that encourage exploration and practice [21, pp. 80–92]. For example, children are encouraged to discover different ways of throwing, catching, and carrying a beanbag, or different ways of moving around, into, and out of a circle. Teachers do not suggest that the child may fail by saying, "Be careful, don't fall." If a young child is very limited in his movements, he may need remedial work in terms of a careful program of extra reinforcement, encouragement, and exposure to appropriate materials and situations.

Dance Movement. Music and rhythm provide links between movement, emotional expression, creativity, and self-awareness. With their limited verbal capacities, children can use music and suggestion to move happily and sadly, to express moods and experiences, and to understand relationships with space. From watching other children, a child gets notions of how they are feeling and thinking, perhaps by imitating the motions and savoring his own experience as an elephant or a butterfly.

LATERALITY

Most preschool children prefer the right hand and a few the left. A few others show little or no preference. During the years from 2 to 5, hand preference becomes more firmly established, as the left and right hemispheres of the brain become more specialized.

Choice of hand was noted when children ate with a spoon, ate with fingers, threw a ball, and drew with crayons [29]. About 11 per cent of the children showed left-hand preference, but mainly in actions where they had been taught, as in the use of implements. In eating with fingers, there was little preference.

Boys show a slightly greater incidence of left-handedness and ambidexterity than girls. There are several possible reasons for the sex difference. Boys are more immature physiologically. Girls tend to respond more to social pressure. Boys are more vulnerable to neurological injury in prenatal and early life.

Stuttering and handedness have long been thought to be associated. Low left-dominance or partially converted dominance has been found to occur in stutterers more often than in the general population. Stuttering may begin at 3 or 4 years of age and then disappear at the time that manual dominance is more fully established [29]. The speech center is normally in the left hemisphere of the brain, as is the center of control of the right hand. There seems to be some overlap between these systems [33].

The left-handed person incurs many disadvantages. In a world designed for right-handed people, he has to adjust to golf clubs, classroom chairs, table settings, and countless other arrangements that are awkward for him. There are certain prejudices against left-handers, although feelings against them vary from time to time and from culture to culture. A small percentage of children develop a strong preference for the left hand, in spite of living among right-handed arrangements. It seems wise for teachers and parents to respect such a preference and to help the child by giving him left-handed equipment when possible and showing him how to adapt in places where he has to use right-handed tools and arrangements.

Perceptual-Motor Learning. Many motor acts, both large and small, are started and guided by a child's perceptions, or interpretations of sensory experience. In catching a ball or coloring a picture, the hands are seen and coordinated in relation to the ball or the crayon and paper. Body awareness is involved in perceptual-motor learning, since a person has to know where the different body parts are in space in order to control what they do. Thus, dance and creative expression contribute to perceptual-motor development through heightening body awareness. Sensory experience is linked to motor in drawing, cutting, painting, clay work, carpentry, playing with balls, blocks, and puzzles, and, in fact, with most nursery school activities.

Finger movement and awareness have been studied for the insight they give into the development of body schemas, body image, and sensory integration [36]. Children from 3 to 5 were given tasks involving their fingers. The easiest task, done by 85 per cent of 3-year-olds and by nearly all 5-year-olds, was to oppose each finger to the thumb, after the examiner had touched the finger while the child was watching. The subject thus had both visual and tactile cues to use in guiding his finger movements. The task of opposing fingers to thumb was much more difficult when only visual cues were given by the examiner demonstrating the action. Three-year-olds apparently did not discriminate fully one finger from the others. The most difficult of all tasks was to point to the fingers of a model after the examiner had touched the corresponding fingers of the child, but with the child's hand shielded so that he could not watch. Only about 10 per cent of 3-year-olds and 50 per cent of 5-year-olds succeeded. This task involved integrating tactile information with visual discrimination, as well as transferring representation from self to model. The tasks thus explored perceptual differentiation, intersensory integration, and symbolic representation, all of which develop rapidly between 3 and 5 years of age. These processes provide a basis for organizing bodily experiences and for building a body image.

Summary

Two stages of personality development occur during the preschool period: the development of the sense of autonomy, during the early years, and the development of the sense of initiative, from about 3 years to 6 or 7 years. The sense of autonomy is promoted by clear, firm guidance that permits successful decision making within the limits it imposes. The opposite of sense of autonomy includes feelings of shame and doubt. Initiative and imagination grow as the child explores the world of people and things, as he imagines himself into a variety of roles and activities, and as he successfully seeks reasons, answers, solutions, and new ideas. Conscience develops, along with guilt, requiring a balancing with initiative for adequate personality development. Beginnings of initiative can be seen in infancy, when children differ in activity and passivity. During the preschool years, differences in achievement behavior represent differences in the sense of initiative. Parental encouragement of achievement behavior at this age is likely to have lasting effects. The sense of initiative results from the interaction of a variety of influences, including genetic, constitutional, cultural, and familial.

Physical growth is slower than it is in infancy. The rate of growth in height decelerates slowly during the preschool years. Although boys are slightly larger than girls, girls are closer to maturity than boys. Retarded growth occurs in children in the lower socioeconomic levels in the United States and in the majority of children in underdeveloped countries. Appearance and proportions change from the chubby, babylike configuration to the more slender, childish pattern, as a result of changes in the amount and distribution of fat, as well as the growth of muscle and skeletal tissues. Evidence of changes in the nervous system is more in terms of function and structure than of size. The structures of vision are immature. Taste buds are more numerous than in the older child. Characteristic shape, position, and structure make for significant differences, as compared with older children, in the preschool child's middle ear, digestive system, and respiratory system. Dental care is important.

Assessment of growth is most often done in terms of a child's height and weight, which are compared with a standard derived from measurements of a large number of children. Or the present status may be evaluated according to a record of past growth. Growth can also be judged from skeletal development. X rays of the bones provide information on the health history of the child, as well as on his present status. Minor physical anomalies are related to mild behavior disturbances.

The majority of the world's children are malnourished. Their food is insufficient in quantity and quality. Since fatigue depresses appetite, health care includes careful guidance of rhythms of eating and sleeping. Eating problems are avoided by such guidance plus attention to the physiological, sensory, and emotional aspects of preschool children's eating and by recognition of his eagerness for autonomy. Sleep problems, also, are avoided by appropriate timing, nonstimulating bed-going routines, reassurance in frightening situations, and gentle firmness.

Many illnesses and accidents are preventable by planning, guidance, careful arrangement of the environment, hygiene, immunizations, and medical supervision. Preschool children are especially vulnerable to illness. International differences in preschool illness and death are enormous. Gastrointestinal disturbances rank first as cause of death in many poor countries; accidents rank first in the United States. Parental child abuse contributes heavily to the high "accident" rate. Easily frightened by illness or injury, the young child is reassured by the presence of a loved person, especially if that person is calmly sympathetic.

Motor development proceeds through a fairly stable sequence of patterns. Individual children differ in speed of sequential development as well as in quality of performance, as shown in speed, power, and accuracy. In many, but not all, large muscle performances, boys excel girls. Posture, or body balance, expresses health and influences it. Dance and movement education are valuable for young children. They vary in muscular strength and flexibility. Hand preference is established in most children during the first five years of life. Right-handedness increases with age. Left-handedness and ambidexterity occur more often in boys than in girls. Disturbances in lateral dominance are associated with poor perceptual-motor performances, implying an underlying neurological deficit.

References

1. Accident mortality at the preschool ages. *Statistical Bulletin*, 1975, **56**:5, 7–9.
2. Accidental deaths high at the preschool ages. *Statistical Bulletin*, 1969, **50**:9, 6–8.
3. Agricultural Research Service. *Food for fitness*. Washington, D.C.: United States Department of Agriculture, 1964.
4. Al-ki, I. J., A. A. Kanawati, and D. S. McLaren. Formal education of mothers and their nutritional behavior. *Journal of Nutrition Education*, 1975, **7**:1, 22–24.
5. Altman, L. K. Pollution danger to children seen. *Wall Street Journal*, 1970, November 15.
6. Baumrind, D. Socialization and instrumental competence in young children. In

W. W. Hartup. *The young child: Reviews of research.* vol. 2. Washington, D.C.: National Association for the Education of Young Children, 1972, pp. 202–224.

7. Berland, T., and A. Seyler. *Your children's teeth.* New York: Meredith Corporation, 1968.

8. Beyer, N. R. and P. M. Morris. Food attitudes and snacking patterns of young children. *Journal of Nutrition Education,* 1974, **6:**4, 131–134.

9. Bowlby, J. *Child care and the growth of love.* London: Pelican, 1953.

10. Brain, D. J., and I. Maclay. Controlled study of mothers and children in hospital. *British Medical Journal,* 1968, **1,** 278–280.

11. Breckenridge, M. E. and M. N. Murphy. *Growth and development of the young child* 8th ed. Philadelphia: W. B. Saunders Company, 1969.

12. Cardinaux-Hilfiker, V. Elternbesuche bei hospitalisierten vorschulpflichtigen Kindern. Heilpädagogische Workblätter, 1969, **38,** 6–15. (Abstract)

13. Carter, J., B. Gilmer, R. Vanderzwaag, and K. Massey. Health and nutrition in disadvantaged children and their relationship with intellectual development. Nashville, Tenn.: George Peabody College for Teachers and Vanderbilt University School of Medicine, undated.

14. Crandall, V. C. Achievement behavior in young children. In W. W. Hartup and N. L. Smothergill (eds.). *The young child: Reviews of research.* vol. 2. Washington, D.C.: National Association for the Education of Young Children, 1967, pp. 165–85.

15. Crinella, F. M., F. W. Beck, and J. W. Robinson. Unilateral dominance is not related to neurological integrity. *Child Development,* 1971, **42,** 2033–2045.

16. Demirjian, A., H. Goldstein, and J. M. Tanner. A new system of dental assessment. *Human Biology,* 1973, **45,** 211–227.

17. Dorman, L. and F. Rebelsky. Assertive behavior and cognitive performance in pre-school children. Paper presented at the meeting of the Society for Research in Child Development, Santa Monica, Calif., March 29, 1969.

18. Eichorn, D. H. Biological correlates of behavior. In H. W. Stevenson, J. Kagan, and C. Spiker. *Child psychology.* The Sixty-second Yearbook of the National Society for the Study of Education, Part I. Chicago: University of Chicago Press, 1963, pp. 4–61.

19. Erikson, E. H. *Childhood and society.* New York: W. W. Norton, & Co., 1963.

20. Escalona, S. K. *The roots of individuality.* Chicago: Aldine Publishing Company, 1968.

21. Flinchum, B. M. *Motor development in early childhood.* St. Louis: The C. V. Mosby Co., 1975.

22. Gelles, R. J. Child abuse as psychopathology: A sociological critique and reformulation. *American Journal of Orthopsychiatry,* 1973, **43,** 611–621.

24. Gutteridge, M. V. A study of motor achievements of young children. *Archives of Psychology,* 1939, **244.**

25. Halverson, C. F., Jr. and M. F. Waldrop. The relations between preschool activity and aspects of intellectual and social behavior at age seven and one-half. *Developmental Psychology,* 1976, **12,** 107–112.

26. Hamill, P. V., F. E. Johnston, and W. Grams. Height and weight of children: United States. Public Health Service Publication No. 1000. Series 11, No. 104. Washington, D.C.: U.S. Government Printing Office, 1970.

27. Harper, L. V., and D. M. Sanders. Preschool children's use of space: Sex differences in outdoor play. In R. C. Smart and M. S. Smart (eds.) *Readings in child development and relationships.* New York: Macmillan, 1977, pp. 99–111.

28. Harrill, I., C. Smith, and J. A. Gangever. Food acceptance and nutritional intake of preschool children. *Journal of Nutrition Education,* 1972, **4,** 103–106.
29. Hildreth, G. Manual dominance in nursery school children. *Journal of Genetic Psychology,* 1948, **72,** 29–45.
30. Ireton, C. L., and H. A. Guthrie. Modification of vegetable-eating behavior in preschool children. *Journal of Nutrition Education,* 1972, **4,** 100–103.
31. Jackson, R. L. Effect of malnutrition on growth of pre-school child. In National Research Council, *Pre-school child malnutrition: Primary deterrent to human progress.* Washington, D.C.: National Academy of Sciences, 1966, pp. 9–21.
32. Kagan, J., and H. A. Moss. *Birth to maturity.* New York: John Wiley & Sons, Inc., 1962.
33. Kimura, D. The asymmetry of the human brain. *Scientific American,* 1973, **228:**3, 70–78.
34. Korslund, M. K. Taste sensitivity and eating behavior of nursery school children. Unpublished Master's thesis. Iowa State University, 1962.
35. Kurokawa, M. Acculturation and childhood accidents among Chinese and Japanese Americans. *Genetic Psychology Monographs,* 1969, **79,** 89–159.
36. Lefford, A., H. G. Birch, and G. Green. The perceptual and cognitive bases for finger location and selective movement in preschool children. *Child Development,* 1974, **45,** 335–343.
37. Lowrey, G. H. *Growth and development of children.* 6th ed. Chicago: Year Book Medical Publishers, Inc., 1973.
38. Maccoby, E. E., E. M. Dowley, and J. W. Hagen. Activity level and intellectual functioning in normal preschool children. *Child Development,* 1965, **36,** 761–770.
39. Maccoby, E. E., and C. N. Jacklin. *The psychology of sex differences.* Stanford, Ca.: Stanford University Press, 1974.
40. McCaskill, C. L., and B. L. Wellman. A study of common motor achievements at the preschool ages. *Child Development,* 1938, **9,** 141–150.
41. Meredith, H. V. Body size of contemporary groups of preschool children studied in different parts of the world. *Child Development,* 1968, **39,** 335–377.
42. Nakamura, C. Y., and M. M. Rogers. Parents' expectations of autonomous behavior and children's autonomy. *Developmental Psychology,* 1969, **1,** 613–617.
43. Newson, J., and E. Newson. *Four years old in an urban community.* Chicago: Aldine Publishing Co., 1968.
44. Owen, G. M., and H. Lubin. Anthropometric differences between black and white preschool children. *American Journal of Diseases of Children,* 1973, **126,** 168–69.
45. Pyle, S. I., H. C. Stuart, J. Cornoni, and R. Reed. Onsets, completions and spans of the osseous stage of development in representative bone growth centers of the extremities. *Monographs of Society for Research in Child Development,* 1961, **26:**1.
45a. Pyle, S. I., A. M. Waterhouse, and W. W. Greulich. *A radiographic standard of reference for the growing hand and wrist.* Cleveland: Press of Case Western Reserve University, 1971.
46. Robertson, J. *Young children in hospitals.* New York: Basic Books, Inc., 1958.
47. Roffwarg, H. P., J. N. Muzio, and W. C. Dement. Ontogenetic development of the human sleep-dream cycle. *Science,* 1966, **152,** 604–617.
48. Scrimshaw, N. S. Malnutrition, learning and behavior. *American Journal of Clinical Nutrition,* 1967, **20,** 493–502.
49. Sears, R. R., E. E. Maccoby, and H. Levin. *Patterns of child rearing.* Evanston, Ill.: Row, Peterson, 1957.
50. Shapiro, S., E. R. Schlesinger, and E. L. Nesbitt. *Infant, perinatal and childhood mortality in the United States.* Cambridge, Mass.: Harvard University Press, 1968.

51. Spitz, R. A. Hospitalism: An inquiry into the genesis of psychiatric conditions in early childhood. *Psychoanalytical Studies of Children,* 1945, **1,** 53–74.
52. Spitz, R. A. Hospitalism: A follow-up report. *Psychoanalytical Studies of Children,* 1946, **2,** 113–117.
53. Stainton, C. Preschoolers' orientation to hospital. *Canadian Nurse,* 1974, **70:**9, 38–41.
54. Tanner, J. M. *Education and physical growth.* London: University of London, 1961.
55. *Toronto Globe and Mail,* October 3, 1974.
56. U.S. Public Health Service News Release. Quoted by A. F. North, Jr., in Research Issues in Child Health I: An Overview. In E. Gotberg (ed.). *Critical issues in research related to disadvantaged children.* Princeton, N.J.: Educational Testing Service, 1969.
57. Waldrop, M. F., and C. F. Halverson, Jr. Minor physical abnormalities and hyperactive behavior in young children. In J. Hellmuth (ed.) *Exceptional infant.* Vol. 2. New York: Brunner/Mazel, 1971.
58. Waldrop, M. F., F. A. Pedersen, and R. Q. Bell. Minor physical anomalies and behavior in preschool children. *Child Development,* 1968, **39,** 391–400.
59. Whipple, Dorothy V. *Dynamics of development: Euthenic pediatrics.* New York: McGraw-Hill, Inc., 1966.
60. Whitehurst, K. E. The young child: What movement means to him. In *The significance of the young child's motor development.* Washington, D.C.: National Association for the Education of Young Children, 1971.
61. Wingerd, J., E. J. Schoen, and I. L. Solomon. Growth standards in the first two years of life based on measurements of white and black children in a prepaid health care program. *Pediatrics,* 1971, **47,** 818–825.
62. Woodruff, C. W. An analysis of the ICNND data on physical growth of the preschool child. In National Research Council, *Preschool child malnutrition: Primary deterrent to human progress.* Washington, D.C.: National Academy of Sciences, 1966, pp. 22–28.

Readings in
Personality and Body

Motor development is intimately related to other areas of development, as the readings in this chapter show. The stage of bodily growth and the condition of the body, of course, set limits upon possible movements and coordinations. The physical and social environments often acting in interaction, offer opportunities for various kinds of learning and expression.

Boys and girls differ in their use of space and in their choice between indoor and outdoor play. Lawrence V. Harper and Karen M. Sanders discuss reasons for their findings, weighing biological sex differences against differential gender socialization. These questions are important ones in the culture of present-day North America, where gender-role equality is an issue. An ethological interpretation is also offered, placing boys' and girls' modes of using space in perspective as inherited behavior patterns that had survival value in man's early environment.

Hyperactivity was studied in 2½-year-old children and again when the children were 7½ years old, by Charles F. Halverson Jr., and Mary F. Waldrop. Relationships were shown between behaviors at the two ages and between hyperactivity and bodily structure, cognitive performance, and social behavior. The unity of the child as body, mind, and social being is indicated by this study.

Perceptual development involves motor action and bodily experience as well as cognitive operations. Arthur Lefford, Herbert G. Birch, and George Green studied finger localization and finger movement of children from ages 3 to 6. Performance is related to sensory and cognitive behavior. The authors see practical implications for understanding learning disabilities.

Severely malnourished children usually come from environments that are low in social and intellectual stimulation, as well as those that are physically inadequate. After nutritional rehabilitation, children often have to return to the poor social and intellectual environment. Myron Winick, Knarig K. Meyer, and Ruth C. Harris report on a group of previously malnourished children who were adopted into excellent environments. The study analyzes the contributions of nutritional and social environments upon previously deprived and non-deprived children.

Preschool Children's Use of Space: Sex Differences in Outdoor Play *

Lawrence V. Harper and Karen M. Sanders
UNIVERSITY OF CALIFORNIA AT DAVIS

Abstract

Over a two-year period time-sampled observations were made of the free-play behavior of 65 children between 3 and 5 years of age in a half-acre nursery school complex. In both years, the boys used more space and consistently spent more time playing outdoors than did the girls. Consideration of the possible determinants of this sex difference led to the conclusion that endogenous factors could account for the data as readily as traditional models of socialization.

According to Wynne-Edwards (1962), in most mammals, males range more widely than females. Studies of the free play of primate (Crook, 1966) and human young (Terman and Tyler, 1956) indicate that males expend more physical energy than females. Garai (1970) states that boys are less concerned than girls with security and are more likely to seek large areas for exploration and play. The sex difference in activity level in human children cannot be explained by the greater incidence of perinatal insult in males because Pedersen and Bell (1970) observed that, in a sample carefully screened to exclude perinatal or congenital abnormality, boys still displayed more gross motor output and more frequent changes in activity than girls. According to Money and Ehrhardt (1972), a preference for outdoor pursuits is one of the elements of "tomboyism" in human females who were masculinized anatomically as the result of synthetic progestins administered to their mothers during early pregnancy.

Several recent studies have provided evidence that boys are more likely than girls to wander afield. In laboratory settings, 13-month-old girls played nearer to the mothers than did boys (Messer and Lewis, 1972). Between preschool and grammar school, boys spent more time away from thir teachers, covering more ground per minute than did girls (Omark and Edelman, 1973). Among the !Kung Bushmen of Africa, male children were more likely than females to stray from the central campsite (Draper, 1973). Early studies using self-reported behavior preferences of American children indicated that boys were more likely than girls to engage in outdoor activities (Terman and Tyler, 1956). However, there exists a paucity of observational data directly comparing the sexes with respect to the spontaneous use of indoor and outdoor space.

Thus, quantitative data on the spontaneous behavior of children in settings allowing them free access to buildings and open areas have considerable

Extended report of a paper by the same title published as a "Brief Report" in *Developmental Psychology*, 1975, **11**, 119.

* This study was supported by a grant from the California Agricultural Experiment Station. The authors wish to express their thanks to Dr. E. E. Werner for her comments and suggestions on this manuscript, and to Ms. Jane Welker, director of the Early Childhood Education Center, for her cooperation and encouragement.

theoretical as well as practical value. The following report is based upon a 2-year observational study of pre-school children's free-play use of space and play equipment in a half-acre nursery school compound.

METHOD

Subjects   Children enrolled in the University of California, Davis laboratory nursery school during the 1971–72 and 1972–73 academic years served as subjects for this study. Admission to the nursery school was limited to children between 3 and 5 years of age. An attempt was made to keep the population mixed with respect to sex, and ethnic and socio-economic background; however, a majority of the children were from middle-class, white families. The total number of children attending at any one time was limited to 30, but with quarter-to-quarter turnover as many as 40 different children were enrolled throughout the course of an academic year. Children with gross physical or behavioral abnormalities were usually excluded from the nursery school program.

We observed the behavior of 65 apparently normal, English-speaking children, 16 girls and 16 boys in 1971–72, and 16 girls and 17 boys in 1972–73. Despite the fact that a child may attend for two consecutive years, only one boy upon whom observations were reported from 1971–72 was represented in the 1972–73 sample. As of January 1972, the mean ages of the 1971–72 sample were 53.2 months for the boys and 53.8 months for the girls. In January 1973, for the 1972–73 group, the boys averaged 46.9 months of age and the girls 44.2. The age differences between the two yearly samples were significant at the .05 level ($t_{31} = 2.30$) for the boys and at the .001 level for the girls ($t_{30} = 4.21$). The sex differences in age within samples were not statistically significant. Sample size varied from one season to the next because a number of children did not attend for the entire year; the data reported here are from children who were present during at least 75% of the season under discussion.

Setting   The nursery school facility included a "main building" (1,340 ft^2 floor space available to the children) in which the children deposited belongings and kept a dry change of clothes. In addition to the locker area there were two bathrooms, a kitchen, two craft areas, a music area, a "nature study" area, a room with a toy kitchen, a "book" room, and an area in which puzzles were stored. A second building, the "block house," (678 ft^2 available for use) had two rooms for block play, a room with craft tables, a "book" room, and a kitchen. A third, smaller, building served as a research house for faculty and graduate students; it was not available for free play.

These structures were surrounded by about 19,000 ft^2 outdoor space landscaped with trees and shrubs. The open region was divided from north to south by a long, low, unlighted storage shed (180 ft^2) and a 3 ft-high wooden fence, running from the shed toward the main building, partially separating the main building from the regions to the southeast. The space directly in front (south) of the main building, (620 ft^2), including the steps and porch, was covered by a corrugated plastic roof extending about 15 ft from the main building to the storage shed. A small, paved, fenced courtyard (1335 ft^2)

separated the main building from the block house. The fully open spaces included a sandy region (3900 ft²) in front of the main building in which there were two jungle gyms, a farm tractor, a 3-swing set, and a sandbox. East of the shed there were two large lawns (4800 and 1500 ft²). The larger contained an open, raised platform with a ladder and a fireman's pole, and, as of early spring 1972, a tire swing suspended from a tree. Various large oil drums, packing crates and modular climbing toys were available in this region. The smaller grassy space faced the larger one; late spring 1972 an enclosed climbing structure was erected in this region and by fall 1973 a pen and shelter were constructed behind the research house for rabbits, chickens, and guinea pigs. Directly in front of the block house, separated from the large lawn by a cement pathway was a smaller lawn (512 ft²) in which there was a tree swing. The remaining outdoor space included shrubbery around the buildings and along the south fence, a paved patio between the research house and the block house, and paved pathways around the large lawn and between the various buildings. During free play, few restrictions were placed upon the children's access to these spaces although the block house was occasionally closed.

Procedure   Each child was observed once each week during free play from the time he or she arrived in the morning (around 9:00 a.m.) until snack time, at about 10:00, or until 35–50 minutes' observation were completed. Each observer followed one child per day recording his or her location and activity every 15 seconds on a prepared checksheet. Recording intervals were signaled by portable, battery-powered, timing devices that delivered an audible click to the observer through an earphone. All play areas were de-signated by a number posted in a conspicuous location. In 1971–72, areas were defined in terms of specific fixed structures (e.g., the sand box), or for large, apparently homogeneous regions, on an *a priori* basis, in terms of roughly equal sized central and peripheral segments. For 1972–73 several of the latter areas were redefined according to the patterns of use observed in 1971–72; the indoor areas remained the same.

The observers' presence had little effect on the subjects; the nursery school served as a demonstration laboratory for students enrolled in child development and related fields, and the children rapidly habituated to the presence of a large number of adults. Throughout both years there were six to seven observers; thus, each of 30 selected subjects was observed at least once each week and each observer was paired with every other observer to conduct at least one reliability check every week throughout the course of the study. Inter-observer agreement on time spent in each area, as indicated by the number of agreements divided by the number of agreements plus disagreements averaged over 90% over both years for all areas to be discussed in this report.

RESULTS

Since the first four to six weeks of the fall quarter were characterized by warm, sunny weather, the year was divided into three seasons: "Fall" weather extended until the end of the last consistently "warm" (at least 60°F; range 60–90°F) week. "Winter" weather lasted until the end of the rainy season and until temperatures consistently remained above 60°F (range 38°–70°F). "Spring" weather was characterized by temperatures consistently above 60°F (range 60–100°F) and predominantly sunny days. The data were analyzed for the year as a whole, and by each season.

As column 1 of Table 1 indicates, the children spent nearly half their time indoors. The boys spent more time outdoors than did the girls. A tally of the number of indoor and outdoor areas in which the boys' total scores exceeded the girls' showed that, for both the 1971–72 and 1972–73 observations, the boys

TABLE 1

Proportions of Free-Play Time Spent Out of Doors According to Sex, Region, Year, and Season

			MEAN TOTAL TIME OUTSIDE ÷ TOTAL TIME OBSERVED	MEAN TIME OUTSIDE IN "NEAR" REGION ÷ TOTAL TIME OUTSIDE	MEAN TOTAL OBSERVATION TIME
Total for Year	71–72	Boys N = 12 p^* < .001	.552	.594	20.26 hrs
		Girls N = 13	.288	.621	20.01
	72–73	Boys N = 10 p < .002	.609	.658	18.08
		Girls N = 8	.400	.678	17.55
Fall	71	Boys N = 15 p < .02	.642	.673	5.33
		Girls N = 13	.411	.671	5.08
	72	Boys N = 12 p < .01	.665	.682	4.82
		Girls N = 11	.467	.645	4.35
Winter	71–72	Boys N = 13 p < .002	.316	.614	6.33
		Girls N = 13	.120	.631	7.57
	72–73	Boys N = 13 p < .001	.491	.683	8.22
		Girls N = 11	.235	.645	7.88
Spring	72	Boys N = 13 p < .0001	.687	.531	8.62
		Girls N = 15	.371	.533	7.59
	73	Boys N = 14 p < .005	.744	.605	5.47
		Girls N = 12	.580	.676	5.43

* Mann-Whitney Test.

used more outdoor areas than did the girls in every season. The yearly totals showed the boys dominating 43 of 54 outdoor areas that were used in 1971–72 ($p < .0001$, binomial approximation) and 39 of 51 used in 1972–73 ($p < .005$, binomial approximation). The girls dominated the indoor areas; in the first year they spent more time in 19 of the 22 indoor areas ($p < .001$, binomial test) but in the second, they dominated only 14 of the 22 (N.S.). Another measure of area use, the ratio of time spent playing outside to total play time, was computed. For all seasons of both years, the boys spent significantly more of their time outdoors than did the girls (See Table 1, column 1). Since the outdoor areas generally were considerably larger, it follows that the boys used more space than the girls. A rough estimate of the amount of space utilized was obtained by multiplying the per cent of total time spent by each sex in each area by the per cent of total space (inside plus outside) covered by each area. As expected, this total "score" for each season, for both years, favored the boys ($p < .05$, binomial test). According to this measure, the boys used between 1.2 (Spring, 1973) and 1.6 (Winter, 1972–73) times as much space as the girls.

Given that the boys spent more time outside and thus used more space than the girls, it seemed important to see whether there existed a qualitative difference; that is, whether the boys used different regions proportionately more than the girls. Since the enclosed patio and sandy region directly south of the main building were most obviously accessible to the "home base," a ratio of total time in these areas to total time spent outdoors was computed. None of the sex differences were significant; both sexes spent slightly less than two thirds of their outdoor play time in the region directly communicating with the front door of the main building. Recalling that nearly half their time was spent in the main building, for both years, the children thus spent three quarters of their time in about one third of the total space available to them.

Over the course of the 1971–72 school year there was a tendency for the children to spend progressively more outdoor time in the spaces beyond the sandy regions (See Table 1, column 2). Compared to fall, in 1971–72, 11 of 12 boys spent proportionately less time in these areas in spring ($p < .006$, binomial test), but in 1972–73 only 6 of 9 boys showed the same decline (N.S.). Similar trends were apparent for the girls: 11 of 12 showed less outdoor time in the sandy area in spring 1972 as compared to fall 1971 ($p < .006$), but for the 1972–73 year, only 4 of the 8 girls showed a comparable shift. This difference most probably reflects the introduction of the tire swing and fort in the grassy areas in early spring 1971–72; no comparable changes in the physical setting were made in 1972–73.

As is evident from Table 1, bad weather kept the children indoors more (although the staff was instructed to be permissive in this regard). For both years and both sexes, the proportion of time spent outdoors in fall and spring was greater than in winter; almost every child spent less time outdoors in winter (all within-sex p's $\leq .05$, binomial tests). Between fall and spring 1972–73 the boys increased their outdoor time significantly (8 of 9, $p < .05$, binomial test) but the difference for boys in 1971–72 was non-significant; the girls showed no comparable changes in either year.

To further evaluate the existence of qualitative differences in the children's use of space, an analysis was conducted area by area. The individual records were scanned to determine the number of areas that accounted for 75–85% of each child's time for each season of the year. Only those areas that were thus determined to be among the most frequently used by at least three children of one sex were subjected to further analysis. On this basis, the sexes were compared for their use of 40 (of 75) designated areas for 1971–72 and 42 (of 74) areas for 1972–73. Sex differences were evaluated by Mann-Whitney or Chi-square tests. See Table 2 for a summary of the results.

For fall 1971, there were eight areas for which there were significant sex differences in usage at the .05 level or better; in winter 1971–72, there were 12, and by spring 1972 there were 15 areas that received significantly different utilization by the sexes. Over the entire year there were 20 areas in which the sex differences were statistically significant. The only "outdoor" area used more by girls was the sheltered porch in front of the main building. The indoor areas receiving more use by the boys were confined to the equipment shed and the block room of the block house. The areas in which significant sex differences occurred were those in which the boys spent 59% and the girls spent 62% of their time over the year.

In 1972–73, despite a younger group, a new head teacher, and new assistants, the same pattern emerged. In fall, the boys dominated the equipment shed and four of five outdoor areas in which significant sex differences were found; the girls dominated the remaining indoor area. While the fall season was short, winter 1972–73 was long and the rainiest on record for a decade. During this period, the boys spent more time than the girls in all of the 10 outside areas for which there were significant differences and the shed; five of the remaining six significant inside differences favored the girls. The boys' tendency to dominate the block room in the block house only approached significance ($p < .10$). In spring 1973 the girls "took over" the swings, but the boys predominated in the other seven outdoor areas for which there were significant differences. Again the boys' only indoor area was the storage shed while the girls spent more time in the remaining two indoor areas for which there were differences. Over the entire year there were 11 significant differences; the boys dominated the outside areas, the storage shed and block room of the block house while girls dominated the remaining inside areas. The areas in which significant sex differences occurred during 1972–73 accounted for 58% of the boys' and 59% of the girls' free play time.

In addition to the time spent in the different areas, a record was kept of the amount of time during which the children were "in transit" from one area to another (defined as entering three or more areas within a single 15-second period). In 1971–72 the boys spent more time in transit than the girls in every season; the yearly total difference was significant ($p < .05$, Mann-Whitney). In 1972–73, the boys spent significantly ($p < .05$) more time in transit than the girls only in winter; they also spent more time in transit than the girls for the year as a whole but the difference was not statistically significant. A simple tally of the number of areas entered at least once showed the boys entering more areas in spring 1972 ($p < .01$) and for the entire 1971–72 observation year ($p < .001$). In 1972–73 the boys entered more areas in winter ($p < .01$) and for the year as a whole ($p < .01$).

Wherever possible, within-sex comparisons were made to determine whether age or prior experience were related to the children's use of space.

Fewer significant differences than would be expected by chance were found, although it must be emphasized that the subsamples were uniformly small.

DISCUSSION

Consistent with Omark and Edelman's (1973) findings that nursery school children spent more of their free-play time indoors than did older children, even our male subjects spent nearly half their time indoors. Perhaps due to the small size of the subsamples or the limited age ranges, we found no evidence for an age-related increase in the amount of outdoor play. Of possible practical significance is the observation that much of the available space received relatively little use by either the boys or the girls. However, this finding should be viewed with caution given the fact that several structural features of the outdoor regions presented physical, and, insofar as they defined an area "belonging to" the main building, perhaps psychological barriers to free movement. We are currently pursuing this question further.

Our findings support the views that males are more attracted to the outdoors (Money and Ehrhardt, 1972) while females spend more time in sheltered areas (Garai, 1970). Although our data do not bear directly upon the question of the mechanisms underlying the development of sex differences in childrens' use of space, several of our incidental observations during the course of the study and two *post hoc* analyses are pertinent. Whereas cultural expectations of female "passivity" and selective reinforcement for conformity to sex-role stereotypes may account for some of the observed differences (Kagan, 1964), our data do not support such an interpretation. During both years of this study, the nursery school staff was composed of women who held liberal, egalitarian views; there was no reason to suspect that the children were under pressure to conform to traditional expectations. Indeed, on the basis of the 1971–72 findings, deliberate attempts were made by the staff to entice the girls outdoors during 1972–73. Thus if girls actually tend to rebel at adult demands for traditional sex-role behavior (Kagan, 1964), sex differences should have been minimized in this permissive atmosphere.

However, it is still possible that pressures exerted by parents at home could have accounted for the observed differences. To evaluate this possibility, an attempt was made to assess the existence of sex-typed socialization pressures on the basis of questionnaire responses submitted by the children's parents. In 1972–73, parents of each child enrolled in the nursery school were required to fill out a questionnaire concerning, among other things, five things they "enjoyed doing" most and least with their child and five things about the child they liked most and least. These questionnaires were collected and the items such as "friendliness," "dirtiness," and so on, were listed. These items were rated as in keeping with either the traditional "male" or "female" stereotypes by 71 students in an advanced class in Child Development. Items receiving over 75% agreement were taken as areas of potential parental pressure. Giving "male" items a score of -1 and "female" items a score of $+1$, and assigning parental enjoyment or liking a positive sign and parental dislike a negative sign, each child was assigned a "socialization pressure" score. These "scores" were then compared with the proportion of time that the children spent outdoors.

TABLE 2
Areas in which Sex Differences in Use Occurred: By Year and Season

	3 WOODEN CLIMBING GYM	4 TRACTOR	5 SWINGS	5a†† SAND ADJACENT TO SWINGS	6 SANDBOX	7 SAND	8 SAND BY SHED	9 SAND BY PORCH	9a†† CENTRAL SANDY AREA	10 TOOL TABLE	12 PORCH	14 EQUIPMENT SHED	16 BUSHES	22 GRASS	23 GRASS/FORT	26§ GRASS/TREE SWING
Fall 1971 Boys: Mean % Time		4.45			1.68	2.79	10.23					2.11				
p		**			**	†	*					**				
Girls: Mean % Time		.57			.17	.14	3.27					.36				
Winter 1971–72 Boys	2.73				1.04	.75	2.04					.45		.42	2.47	
p	*				†	**	**					*		**	*	
Girls	.56				.01	.04	.97					.11		.03	.07	
Spring 1972 Boys	2.67	1.77			.68		5.71					1.33			1.94	7.75
p	*	*			*		†					†			**	*
Girls	.88	.45			.08		.27					.22			.55	3.38
Year 1971–72 Boys	2.27	1.95			1.18	2.27	5.98			3.62	.75	1.29		.53	2.14	3.91
p	**	**			†	†	†			*	*	†		†	†	*
Girls	.66	.42			.06	.39	1.23			1.61	1.34	.22		.17	.47	1.53
Fall 1972 Boys		2.99					8.61	1.78		1.87		1.78			2.95	
p		*					†	*		*		**			**	
Girls		.61					1.26	.62		1.77		.39			1.45	
Winter 1972–73 Boys	1.83	1.74	3.35	.87	.24		4.70		5.05	3.45		2.03				
p	†	**	*	**	*		†		**	**		**				
Girls	.12	.37	.64	.24	.05		.36		1.40	.98		.35				
Spring 1973 Boys			1.43	1.61	3.33	.98	10.40	1.94				1.32	1.43	.35		
p			*	**		*	*	**				†		*		
Girls			8.00	.39	.83	.13	.97	.45				.36	.06	.35		
Year 1972–73 Boys		2.12		1.74			8.02		4.65			1.85	.37		1.94	
p		**		**			†		*			**			*	
Girls		.22		.22			.65		2.53			.35	.05		.76	

		Central Grass Area	Grass	Paved Court	Fort	Lockers	Table Activity	Table Activity	Music	Nature Study	Play House	Book Room	Cabinets	Puzzles	Bathroom	Kitchen	Block Room	Block Room
Fall 1971	Boys: Mean % Time						3.43	4.51			3.50							
	p						**	*			*							
	Girls: Mean % Time						9.05	10.46			8.66							
Winter 1971–72							6.20		1.08	2.64			1.07		.64			
							**		**	*			*		**			
							18.04		4.31	6.80			2.64		1.58			
Spring 1972		1.30	1.10					2.13		2.85	1.02			1.50	.92	1.72		
		*	*					*		*	*			*	*	**		
		.40	.47					6.44		7.34	2.88			5.23	1.61	3.85		
Year 1971–72		2.61					5.82		.61	2.60			.56	4.16	.79	1.40	6.32	
		†					**		†	†			†	*	**	*	*	
		.50					13.12		2.50	6.91			1.98	8.91	1.56	3.27	3.10	
Fall 1972		.25												2.99				
		*												**				
		.49												10.38				
Winter 1972–73				.43		2.23	5.39	6.20				6.39			.25	4.90		
				**		*	**	**				*			†	**		
				.01		4.00	14.71	14.61				2.82			1.51	10.76		
Spring 1973							1.78									4.25		.86
							†									*		*
							9.80									5.73		.21
Year 1972–73					1.83		3.86	4.12										
					*		**	**										
					.74		11.17	8.92										

* $p \leq .05$ ** $p \leq .01$ † $p \leq .001$ †† Designated only in 1972–73 § Structure erected spring 1972

For the seven girls for whom both maternal reports and year-long data were available, the *rho* was −.348; that is, in the opposite direction predicted by socialization theory. There were too many ties to permit the use of *rho* among the nine boys for whom adequate data were available; however, a median split indicated no relationship. Further, a comparison of the socialization pressure scores for these boys and girls (whose outdoor usage differed significantly; $p < .005$, Mann-Whitney) revealed only a non-significantly greater tendency for girls (mean = +4.71) to receive more pressure than boys (mean = +3.33; $t_{14} = 1.457$, $p < .10 > .05$). An additional check of the items revealed that only 4 of the 9 boys' parents mentioned liking to take their children "on walks" while 3 of the 7 girls' parents did so and, in addition 2 girls' parents who did not mention walks and one who did, listed hiking or going on outdoor trips as being activities they enjoyed doing with their daughters. Thus, there was little evidence of overt parental pressure to conform to sex-stereotyped behavior in general, and no indication of differential encouragement of outdoor activity.

If such pressures did exist covertly it was thought that they might be expressed indirectly by discouraging the girls' getting dirty and encouraging them to "look nice," and that they would be reflected in the clothing typically worn by the girls. Thus we compared the proportion of outdoor play of girls who consistently wore dresses with that of those who consistently wore jeans, etc. The distribution of scores according to attire was essentially random; combining extreme groups across years, there was only a non-significant tendency for the *dress-wearers* to spend more time outside.

It is possible that the nature of the activities or apparatus favored the girls' staying indoors and the boys' going outside. However, such reasoning accepts the premise that boys are more attracted than girls to gross motor activity, without attempting to account for it. Furthermore, analyses of the locations in which popular, movable equipment was used suggest that the observed sex differences reflect more than toy location. For example, containers such as pots, bowls, etc. were used by the boys outdoors 81% of the time *vs* 16% of the time outdoors for the girls in 1971–72; for 1972–73 the corresponding percentages were 66 and 38 respectively. Of 15 classes of items that could be used either indoors or outdoors, the boys played more outdoors than the girls with 13 ($p < .02$, Binomial test) in 1971–72, and with 11 ($p < .06$, Binomial test) in 1972–73. Thus it seems that portable items were often moved to favored play-spaces; their location did not necessarily determine the children's choice or use of space.

In summary, we found little evidence that the behavior of the nursery school staff, the expressed concerns or the overt practices of the children's parents, or the nature of the available apparatus could account for the observed sex differences in behavior. Explanations invoking endogenous factors are consistent with our data. Terman and Tyler (1956) suggest that the greater muscle strength and vital capacity of boys might account for their more vigorous activity as compared with girls. Recent studies of the effects of androgens on the behavior of primates and humans indicate that prenatal exposure to male sex hormones predisposes genetic females to engage in male-typical behaviors, including a preference for vigorous, outdoor activity even in the absence of continued androgenic stimulation. (See Money and Ehrhardt, 1972, for review.) Our finding that there was no sex difference in the relative proportion of time spent in the outdoor regions beyond the sandy areas might appear to contradict the idea that endogenous factors such as androgens could account for the data. However, experiments with infrahuman mammals (Beach, 1971) and observations of the effects of hormonal influences on human behavior (Money and Ehrhardt, 1972) indicate that prenatal androgenic stimulation leads to sex differences in the frequency or intensity of behavior rather than to qualitative differences. Thus our data are consistent with the hypothesis of endogenous causation.

The greater outdoorishness of males might be attributed to the fact that they have a higher basic metabolic rate (BMR) than do girls (Tanner, 1970). Assuming that their lower BMR would render girls more sensitive to cold, our finding of an intensification of sex differences in outdoor activity in the long and relatively severe winter of 1972–73 would seem to support such a hypothesis. However, the fact that the same pattern of sex differences was apparent during the spring and early summer months of both years, when temperatures were consistently in the neighborhood of 75–85°F, suggests that females' possibly greater sensitivity to cold is insufficient to account for our data. The greater activity level of the boys, as represented by their greater time in transit, could reflect any of several factors: higher BMR, greater muscle strength and vital capacity, a direct androgenic influence on motor output, or greater biological immaturity (cf. Tanner, 1970) and hence, relatively lower capacity to sustain a particular focus (Kagan, 1971). However, Money and Ehrhardt's (1972) observation of greater vigor in prenatally androgenized females supports the hypothesis of a central, hormonal effect, since these girls also tended to be intellectually precocious, and thus presumably suffering no attentional deficits.

Our data are thus more consistent with hypotheses implicating the role of endogenous factors than with a hypothesis of environmental determination of sex differences in children's use of space. In particular, they support hypotheses involving the effects of androgenic stimulating during the first trimester.

However, from a biological perspective (Blurton-Jones, 1972) the analysis of the proximate mechanisms such as androgenic stimulation or differences in muscle strength represents only part of the picture; a complete account should also consider the possible selective pressures leading to the evolution of such mechanisms. That is, one should be able to indicate how a greater tendency for males to move about—in unsheltered regions—would confer an advantage upon the species.

While the details of man's prehistory are still the subject of debate, a plausible explanation can be offered if one accepts the view that many significant features of human evolution were the result of man's adopting a hunting-gathering way of life (Lee and De Vore, 1968). According to Watanabe (1968), among contemporary hunter-gatherers, the male's (hunter's) geographical range of food-seeking activity is considerably greater than the female's (gatherer's), whose collecting tends to be concentralized in the vicinity of the group's base camp. Assuming that the exigencies of the hunting-gathering strategy, *per se*, forced such a division of labor upon humans, a selective advantage might well have accrued to groups in which there developed endogenous predispositions toward appropriate behavior [particularly if there already existed sexual dimorphism in size and activity as that which now exists among many old-world primates (Crook, 1966; 1972)]. As a result of these predispositions, the males would have become more familiar with the group's home range, hunting grounds, and with the habits of available prey, thereby enhancing the likelihood of successfully obtaining game.

Furthermore, endogenous tendencies for males to undertake the more risky enterprise of hunting large game makes "biological sense" in view of the generally accepted principle that the potential "cost" to a population of accidentally losing a male (child) is less; that a stable population is more dependent upon the number of females, and that, other things being equal, the number of males may vary more radically without severely threatening the ability of a population to maintain itself (Wynne-Edwards, 1962). Given the greater expendability of males, and assuming that camps tended to serve as safe or protected sites in an otherwise dangerous or hostile environment, another benefit would have derived from the males' tendency to range afield and to be more "on the move." The males' activity would have provided a screen of expendable individuals about the periphery of the camp in the same way that young Japanese monkey males provide an outer defense perimeter for the females and infants who congregate at the center of the group (Imanishi, 1963).

Thus, the greater centrifugal movement of males would have maximized their opportunities to become successful hunters and, at the same time, provided an early warning or buffer zone around the periphery of the group while the more centripetal tendencies of the females would have caused them to remain in areas of relatively greater safety. Groups in which these patterns did not exist, or were reversed, presumably would have been more at risk biologically and therefore would have been at a reproductive disadvantage.

In conclusion, our findings indicate the existence of a marked sex difference in preschool children's tendency to play in unsheltered areas. Our data are more compatible with explanations based upon the existence of endogenous determination of gender-dimorphic behavioral traits than with explanations based upon the existence of sex-role expectations. An argument is presented in support of the hypothesis that natural selection may have favored the development of such sex differences in man. The problem for future investigations is to specify the nature of and the ways in which the environmental factors co-act with endogenous sensitivities to produce behavioral differences.

References

BEACH, F. A. Hormonal factors controlling the differentiation, development, and display of copulatory behavior in the ramstergig and related species. In E. Tobach, L. R. Aronson and E. Shaw (Eds.) *The biopsychology of development.* New York: Academic Press, 1971. Pp. 249–296.

BLURTON-JONES, N. G. Characteristics of ethological studies of human behaviour. In N. G. Blurton-Jones (Ed.) *Ethological studies of child behaviour.* Cambridge: Cambridge University Press, 1972. Pp. 3–33.

CROOK, J. H. Gelada baboon herd structure and movement. A comparative report. In P. A. Jewell and C. Loizos (Eds.) *Play, exploration and territory in mammals.* New York: Academic Press, 1966. Pp. 237–258.

CROOK, J. H. Sexual selection, dimorphism and social organization in the primates. In B. Campbell (Ed.) *Sexual selection and the descent of man 1871–1971*. Chicago: Aldine, 1972. Pp. 231–281.

DRAPER, P. Crowding among hunter-gatherers: The !Kung bushmen. *Science*, 1973, **182**, 301–303.

GARAI, J. E. Sex differences in mental health. *Genetic Psychology Monographs*, 1970, **81**, 123–142.

IMANISHI, K. Social behavior in Japanese monkeys, *Macaca fuscata*. In C. H. Southwick (Ed.) *Primate social behavior*. New York: Van Nostrand, 1963. Pp. 68–81.

KAGAN, J. Acquisition and significance of sex typing and sex role identity. In M. L. Hoffman and L. W. Hoffman (Eds.) *Review of child development research*. Vol. 1. New York: Russell Sage, 1964. Pp. 137–167.

KAGAN, J. *Change and continuity in infancy*. New York: Wiley, 1971.

LEE, R. B. & DeVore, I. (Eds.) *Man the hunter*. Chicago: Aldine, 1968.

MESSER, S. B. & LEWIS, M. Social class and sex differences in attachment and play behavior in the year-old infant. Merrill-Palmer Quarterly, 1972, **18**, 295–306.

MONEY, J. & EHRHARDT, A. A. *Man and woman, boy and girl*. Baltimore: Johns Hopkins, 1972.

OMARK, D. R. & EDELMAN, M. Peer group social interactions from an evolutionary perspective. Paper presented at the biennial meeting of the Society for Research in Child Development. Philadelphia, Pa., March, 1973.

PEDERSEN, F. A. & BELL, R. Q. Sex differences in preschool children without histories of complications of pregnancy and delivery. *Developmental Psychology*, 1970, **3**, 10–15.

TANNER, J. M. Physical growth. In P. H. Mussen (Ed.) *Carmichael's manual of child psychology*, Third Ed., Vol. 1. New York: Wiley, 1970. Pp. 77–155.

TERMAN, L. M. & TYLER, L. E. Psychological sex differences. In L. Carmichael (Ed.) *Manual of child psychology*, Second Ed. New York: Wiley, 1956. Pp. 1064–1114.

WATANABE, H. Subsistence and ecology of northern food gatherers with special reference to the Ainu. In R. B. Lee and I. DeVore (Eds.) *Man the Hunter*. Chicago: Aldine, 1968. Pp. 69–77.

WYNNE-EDWARDS, V. C. *Animal dispersion in relation to social behaviour*. New York: Hafner, 1962.

Preschool Hyperactivity: Social and Cognitive Relations in Middle Childhood *

Charles F. Halverson, Jr., and Mary F. Waldrop

NATIONAL INSTITUTE OF MENTAL HEALTH

Abstract

The relations between preschool hyperactivity and school age behavior were explored. Consistent clusters of observed behaviors were associated with teacher ratings of hyperactivity; namely, two independent and replicated factors, Activity

A paper presented at the meetings of The Society for Research in Child Development, Denver, 1975. A different version appears in *Developmental Psychology*, 1976, **12**, 107–112. Printed by permission.

* The authors wish to thank Gale Inoff and Richard Q. Bell for their help on various aspects of this study.

Level and Social Participation. These two factors and the hyperactivity ratings were significantly related to behavior at 7½. For both boys and girls, hyperactivity showed considerable stability over five years. Hyperactivity expressed by high activity levels is negatively related to various measures of cognitive and intellective performance at 7½. Hyperactivity as expressed in social participation is positively related to the same measures of intellectual performance. The activity level component is highly related to an index of minor physical anomalies, while the social participation component is not.

There has been some evidence and considerable speculation that early hyper-kinetic and impulsive behavior is implicated in the development of cognitive style differences and related social behavior in children. For example, Kagan, Moss, and Sigel (1963); Witkin (1963); Sigel, Jarman, and Hanesian (1967); and Pedersen and Wender (1968) have speculated that high magnitude activity level may be an important antecedent of various intellectual and social be-haviors. The general hypothesis has been that high levels of activity and impulsivity tend to interfere with the development of behaviors conducive to cognitive and social development. For example, Kagan (1971) has presented evidence that children with "fast tempos" (short attention span and impulsive) do not maintain an active involvement in hypothesis verification when con-fronted with a new event. They act quickly on the first hypothesis and go on to a new situation. What generally has been lacking are longitudinal data on early high-activity behaviors and their relations to later cognitive functioning.

High levels of impulsive play activity are presumably one index of this impulsive cognitive processing which interferes with a more complete examina-tion of alternate hypotheses about new events. In the present paper, therefore, there are two major emphases; (a) the assessment of impulsive, hyperactive play in unselected, non-clinical samples of preschool children and, (b) the implications of that preschool hyperactivity for later cognitive and social functioning. Because this investigation concerned results obtained on non-clinical, unselected samples of children, the term "hyperactive play" must be interpreted as not referring to a clinical syndrome but as a convenient summary term for a set of behaviors shown to a greater or lesser degree by most children in free, unrestrained situations.

Hyperactivity was initially assessed in this sample by a rating system developed by Bell, Waldrop, and Weller (1972). These ratings have been con-densed by factor analysis to form an internally consistent and highly reliable rating factor describing hyperactive play behavior in nursery school settings. It was felt that further understanding of the structure of hyperactivity could be obtained by identifying and subjecting to analysis the *observed* behaviors that related to the rating factor. Before assessing the implications of early hyper-activity for later cognitive and social functioning, we first examined the stability of both rated and observed hyperactivity between age 2½ and 7½ years.

METHOD

PRESCHOOL STUDY   At the preschool phase, relations between the rating factor of hyperactivity and independently observed samples of play and social behavior were assessed. The children were 60 boys and 60 girls ranging from 30 to 34 months of age with a mean age of 32 months. All children were white and from middle-class intact families living in the suburbs of Washington, D.C. (Hollingshead index classes II, III, and IV). They attended a research nursery school in same sex groups of 5 or 6 for five weeks.

The setting was designed to make the children as comfortable and at ease as quickly as possible. Play and social behavior was coded daily in a free-play setting indoors, a quiet room for rest, and a free play setting outdoors. Except for free play outdoors, observations were made by two independent observers from behind one-way vision glass. The behavioral codes consisted essentially of the cumulative time spent in various categories of activity and frequency counts of specific types of behaviors such as opposes peer, water play, running. A total of 6 days of observation distributed over a 1-month period was obtained for each child. Interobserver reliabilities were all above $r = .90$ for measures used in the present study and odd-even stabilities were consistently above $r = .60$. Details of the procedures can be found in Bell, Weller, and Waldrop (1971).

A male and a female teacher were with the children in all settings, and two days each week, independently, made six ratings concerning hyperactive behavior. The ratings were on 11-point scales and dealt with frenetic play, spilling and throwing, nomadic play, aggression, inability to delay, and induction of intervention. The children were given composite scores based on the six ratings using the procedure described by Bell et al. (1972).

Because the observational codings were not directed toward the description of hyperactivity per se but were, rather, focused on general play and social variables across all settings, an empirical strategy which would guard against chance correlates was devised to assess the observation correlates of rated hyperactivity. The sample was divided into two subsamples of 60 children each (30 boys and 30 girls in each subsample). For each subsample intercorrelations were computed between the hyperactivity rating factor and all reliable observation codes. Six behavioral variables from indoor free play, five from outdoor free play, and two from the rest period replicated as being significant in their relation to the hyperactivity rating and were, thus, retained for further analysis. These 13 measures were then subjected to a principal component factor analysis with two factors being rotated by the varimax procedure. The result was two orthogonal observation factors which related significantly to the hyperactivity rating. Table 1 lists the variables and their loadings on the two orthogonal factors. The first observation factor, Activity Level, had high loadings on running, walking, and a pedometer measure of activity level; negative loadings on inactivity. The second factor, termed Social Participation, had positive loadings on positive peer interaction, squealing, and following games; negative loadings on watching peers and stationary watching. These two factors emerged for both subsamples. Between-sample comparisons (Ryder, 1967b) of the two factors yielded high correlations (Factor 1, r (58) $= +.88, p < .001$; Factor 2, r (58) $= +.78, p < .001$). These two observational factors together, however, only accounted for 43% of the variance associated with the rated hyperactivity factor, indicating considerable non-shared variance. For this reason, the longitudinal analyses were done on all three factors: the observational factors of Activity Level and Social Participation as well as the rating factor of hyperactivity.

TABLE 1

Varimax Rotated Observation Factors of Hyperactivity Replicated Across Two Samples

VARIABLES	FACTOR 1 ACTIVITY LEVEL	FACTOR 2 SOCIAL PARTICIPATION
Activity Recorder (O)	.83	−.11
Runs (O)	.67	−.08
Opposes peer (I)	.59	.15
Up and about (R)	.55	.34
Direct walking (I)	.55	.38
Squeals (O)	.21	.53
Positive interaction (I)	.14	.42
Water play (I)	.01	.36
Withdraws from peer conflict (I)	.00	−.48
Stationary watching (I)	−.18	−.72
Follows game (R)	−.37	.61
Watch peer (O)	−.44	−.70
Sustained play (O)	−.72	−.24

(I) = Indoor free play.
(R) = Rest period.
(O) = Outdoor free play.

FOLLOW-UP STUDY AT AGE $7\frac{1}{2}$ Sixty-two of the children from the preschool sample were studied at a follow-up five years later (35 boys and 27 girls). The setting for the follow-up study was a well-equipped playroom in which mother and child were observed together for 20 minutes. During that time, each child was free to play while the mother was occupied with a questionnaire. A narrative account of the child's behavior was recorded by an observer from behind one-way vision glass and subsequently coded for number of play shifts and rate of shifts. These two variables measured the amount of sustained, directed play. In addition, 9 general behavioral ratings of the child were done by a person who had not known the child in the earlier preschool study, (interrater reliabilities of the 11-point scales ranged from $r = .70$ to $r = .94$, with a mean of $r = .82$). These ratings covered such concepts as Frenetic Play, Inability to Delay, Cooperativeness, and Vigor. Later, while the child was being given tests of intelligence and cognitive style, including the WISC, the Children's Embedded Figures Test (Karp & Konstadt, 1963) and the Sigel Sorting Task (Sigel et al., 1967), the mother was interviewed about her child's social behavior. The mother's detailed diary account of the child's social contacts for the prior week was discussed. From the mother's diary account and from the observations of the child's social interactions, three summary ratings were made regarding the child's social ease, dominance in peer relations, and tendency to play with a group of children vs. play with close friend (Extensity). Further analyses of peer data can be found elsewhere (Waldrop & Halverson, 1975).

From the three cognitive tasks that were administered individually, the following classes of measures were obtained:

Verbal and Nonverbal Intelligence   This was assessed by the Wechsler Intelligence Scale for Children (WISC).

Categorization-Style   The Sigel Sorting Task (Kagan et al., 1963) was used to evaluate conceptual style. The test consists of 12 arrays containing four pictures each, a stimulus picture and three response pictures. After the children identified the stimulus picture, they were asked to pick out one response picture that was most like the stimulus picture. They were then asked to give reasons for making the choice. The three response pictures were designed to elicit one of three "styles" of responding—the *analytic*, involving pairings based on objective attributes, the *relational*, response selections based on functional relations between pictures, and the *inferential*, responses based on a conceptual category. Items were scored using the child's verbal statement. Interrater agreement was adequate ($r = .94$), and the split-half reliabilities ranged from $r = .70$ to $.80$ for the three categories of response.

Field Dependence–Independence   This was measured by the Children's Embedded Figures Test (CEFT), developed by Karp and Konstadt (1963). The test is a downward extension of the Witkin (1950) Embedded Figures Test suitable for children as young as 5 years. It contains 25 items arranged approximately in order of increasing difficulty in a format essentially similar to the adult form. Karp and Konstadt reported adequate internal consistency and, for children 9 years of age and older, high-order correlations with the adult form of the Embedded Figures Test.

In addition to the behavioral measures, each child was assessed for the presence of multiple minor anomalies (Waldrop & Halverson, 1971) and administered the Lincoln-Oseretsky Motor Scale (Sloan, 1955). This latter scale is an objectively scored series of items pertaining to fine and gross motor coordination and development. Earlier research (Waldrop & Halverson, 1971; Halverson & Victor, 1975) has consistently shown minor physical anomalies and motor coordination problems to be related to other indices of hyperactivity in young children.

RESULTS

Data will be presented first with respect to the longitudinal stability of hyperactivity and then with respect to the longitudinal and concurrent implications of hyperactivity for cognitive and social functioning. Analyses of the cross-stage correlations done separately for the sexes revealed no significant differences, therefore, all correlational analyses are presented for the combined sample of 62 children.[1]

Stability of Hyperactivity   To assess as closely as possible the same rating construct of hyperactivity at $7\frac{1}{2}$ as was rated at $2\frac{1}{2}$, three highly intercorrelated

[1] An intercorrelation matrix of the follow-up variables and the preschool hyperactivity variables is available from Dr. Halverson.

ratings at $7\frac{1}{2}$ were summed together to form a hyperactivity rating composite: Frenetic Play, Inability to Delay, and Cooperativeness (negatively weighted). These ratings were defined and rated to match as closely as possible the same ratings done at $2\frac{1}{2}$. The concurrent correlations of this factor at age $7\frac{1}{2}$ and longitudinal correlations are presented in Table 2. The $7\frac{1}{2}$ rating cluster of hyperactivity showed a highly significant correlation with the preschool rating of this dimension (r (62) = .57, p < .001), indicating a fair degree of stability over 5 years. Of the two observation components of preschool hyperactivity, Activity Level showed some predictability over 5 years while Social Participation is only marginally related to later hyperactivity. The two observation codings of fast-paced behavior at $7\frac{1}{2}$ (shifts in play and rate of shifts) related positively to hyperactivity at both age periods.

The correlates of the other general behavior ratings done at $7\frac{1}{2}$ are listed in Table 1 and they reveal considerable consistency in the pattern of relations as well. Children high on rated and observed hyperactivity at $2\frac{1}{2}$ tended to be rated as animated, vigorous, and excitable at follow-up.

TABLE 2

Longitudinal and Concurrent Relations of Hyperactivity at $7\frac{1}{2}$

	MEASURES AT $7\frac{1}{2}$	MEASURES AT $2\frac{1}{2}$		
	Hyper-activity Factor (Rating)	Hyper-activity Factor (Rating)	Activity Level Factor (Behavior)	Social Participation Factor (Behavior)
Hyperactivity Factor	—	.57†	.31*	.14
Inability to delay	—	.56†	.33**	.00
Frenetic play	—	.49†	.47†	−.04
Cooperativeness (negative)	—	−.33**	−.32**	.00
Free Play Observations				
$\overline{X}$ number of shifts	.49†	.34**	.33**	.00
Rate of shifts	.39**	.38**	.35**	.13
General Behavior Ratings				
Animation	.48†	.25*	.11	.20
Dependency	−.18	−.26*	−.28*	−.27*
Vigor in play	.62†	.42†	.29*	.26*
Coping	−.20	−.04	.13	.17
Fearfulness	−.20	.00	.13	−.22
Excitability	.82†	.47†	.32**	.18
Lincoln Oseretsky Motor Scale	−.50†	−.54†	−.44†	.12
Minor Physical Anomalies	.44†	.51†	.37**	−.03

* p < .05.
** p < .01.
† p < .001.

Two other variables gave added importance to the hyperactivity measures at 2½ and 7½. Performance on the Lincoln-Oseretsky Motor Scale showed significant negative correlations to both concurrent rated hyperactivity and to hyperactivity measured at 2½. These correlations indicate that children who score high on hyperactivity in terms of ratings and observed activity level tend to be less coordinated. Further evidence of the importance of the hyperactivity dimension over time comes from the positive relations of 2½ and 7½ hyperactivity to an index of minor physical anomalies assessed at age 7½. The relations between aspects of hyperactivity and anomalies as well as the stability of rated hyperactivity associated with anomalies have also been reported earlier (Waldrop & Halverson, 1971). The relations of hyperactivity to anomalies suggest that there is a possible congenital factor (anomalies being present from birth) contributing to the stability of this dimension in early childhood, particularly as referenced by the Activity Level factor.

Cognitive Correlates of Hyperactivity   Relations of cognitive performance at 7½ years of age with concurrent and antecedent hyperactivity are presented in Table 3. Both 2½ and 7½ hyperactivity ratings are significantly and consistently negatively related to FSIQ, VIQ, and PIQ on the WISC. The observation factor of Activity Level is also negatively related to intellectual performance. These findings are similar to the relation between preschool hyperactivity and performance on the CEFT at 7½. High levels of rated hyperactivity and high levels of the observation factor of Activity Level were related

TABLE 3
Hyperactivity Correlates of Cognitive Variables

	MEASURES AT 7½	MEASURES AT 2½		
	Hyper-activity Factor (Rating)	Hyper-activity Factor (Rating)	Activity Level Factor (Behavior)	Social Participation Factor (Behavior)
WISC				
Full scale IQ	−.31*	−.38**	−.47†	.14
Verbal IQ	−.21	−.29*	−.38**	.24*
Performance IQ	−.33**	−.33**	−.40**	−.05
Children's Embedded Figures Test	−.28*	−.34**	−.34**	.25*
Sigel Sorting Test				
Relational	.20	.22	.11	.00
Analytic	.00	.03	.23	.12
Inferential	−.24	−.31**	−.30*	−.08

* $p < .05$.
** $p < .01$.
† $p < .001$.

to *field dependent* behavior on the CEFT. These findings are consonant with cross-sectional data reported by Witkin (1963) who reported field dependent behavior to be associated with impulse control problems. It should be noted, however, that the observation factor of Social Participation is *positively* related to VIQ and was associated with a tendency toward field *independent* behavior.

Relations between hyperactivity and the cognitive style data differed from our expectations: hyperactivity was unrelated to both relational and analytic functioning, at $2\frac{1}{2}$ and $7\frac{1}{2}$ years of age. There were only modest negative correlations with inferential responding. When IQ was partialed out of these correlations, no relationship remained. In general, then, early hyperactivity was not found to be an important antecedent of the analytic style as Kagan et al. (1963) hypothesized.

Social correlates of Hyperactivity   An examination of the relations of the rated hyperactivity factor and social behavior at $7\frac{1}{2}$ reveals only one significant relation, a correlation of $+.41$ between the preschool hyperactivity rating and dominance in peer relations at $7\frac{1}{2}$. Interestingly, it is not the observed Activity Level component that is important but rather observed Social Participation. The Social Participation component of hyperactivity at $2\frac{1}{2}$ was related to social behavior at $7\frac{1}{2}$, as shown by positive relations to social ease (r (60) $= +.49$, $p < .001$), the tendency to play with groups of children (r (60) $= +.36$, $p < .01$), and dominance with peers (r (60) $= +.40, p < .01$). These relations show, perhaps not surprisingly, some predictability of the Social Participation component of hyperactivity to peer relations at $7\frac{1}{2}$ but only marginal predictability for other facets of hyperactivity as examined in the present study. It should be remembered that the children were seen individually at $7\frac{1}{2}$ and in groups at $2\frac{1}{2}$. Therefore, at $7\frac{1}{2}$ there are no observed social measures.

TABLE 4
Social Correlates of Hyperactivity

	MEASURES AT $7\frac{1}{2}$	MEASURES AT $2\frac{1}{2}$		
	Hyper-activity Factor (Rating)	Hyper-activity Factor (Rating)	Activity Level Factor (Behavior)	Social Participation Factor (Behavior)
Extensity	$-.02$	.03	.07	.36**
Social ease	.15	.08	.00	.49†
Dominance	.18	.41†	.14	.40**

** $p < .01$.
† $p < .001$.

DISCUSSION

The data in the present study provide longitudinal evidence confirming the importance of hyperactive behaviors for the development of differences in intellectual and social behavior in young children. There is, for both boys and girls, stability of rated impulsive and hyperkinetic behavior over five years. Even though all of the variables comprising both observational factors correlated individually with rated hyperactivity, these two factors relate to different criterion behaviors at $7\frac{1}{2}$. The observed preschool factor of Activity Level replicates most of the relations obtained with the rating alone while the concurrent social behaviors associated with rated preschool hyperactivity only showed implications for later social behavior. While both factors correlate with preschool rated hyperactivity (Activity Level r (60) = .62, p < .001; Social Participation r (60) = .39, p < .01) it is the Activity Level factor which carries the negative implications for later intellectual functioning (as does rated hyperactivity). It is, then, motoric hyperkinesis and not high levels of positive social interaction which seem to affect negatively those behaviors important for the development of intellectual functioning. In fact, the social behaviors identified with hyperactivity in preschoolers tend to be positively related to verbal intelligence and field independence in this sample.

The relations between hyperkinesis and intellectual functioning closely paralleled the findings reported by Kagan et al. (1963). In the Fels data, they found rated hyperkinesis for ages 3 to 6 to be negatively correlated with adult intellectual mastery for both males and females. These results and the data from the present study strongly suggest that the inability to inhibit motor behavior during early childhood is inimical to the development of sustained involvement in cognitive skills.

The findings in the present study also corroborate Witkin's (1963) contention that impulsive, hyperactive behaviors are related to field dependent functioning on the Embedded Figures Test. These data did not replicate, however, the findings of Kagan et al. (1963) that hyperkinesis is one class of behavior negatively related to analytic responding. In general, it was only the inferential-categorical style which was related negatively to hyperactivity, and this correlation appears due to the high relation of IQ and inferential-categorical responding, (r (60) = +.61, p < .001).

The longitudinal relations of preschool Social Participation reveal straightforward predictability to social behavior at age $7\frac{1}{2}$. High activity level, however, was not related to the aspects of social functioning measured at $7\frac{1}{2}$. Added significance of the positive relations of preschool Social Participation with Social Ease and Dominance at age $7\frac{1}{2}$ may be found in Ryder's (1967a) canonical reanalysis of the Fels data reported by Kagan and Moss (1962). Ryder found Dominance in peer relations and Social Ease with peers from ages 6–10 to be predictive of adult achievement orientations. It is possible that data in the present study may have identified one potential early preschool antecedent, Social Participation, to this developmental line from early childhood to adulthood.

Finally, the results of the present study are consonant with Kagan's (1971) contention that there is a stable disposition of play tempo in early childhood, and, further, that play tempo, as indexed by variations in play activity levels, has important consequences for social and intellectual functioning in the young child.

References

BELL, R. Q., WALDROP, M. F., & WELLER, G. M. A rating system for the assessment of hyperactive and withdrawn children in preschool samples. *American Journal of Orthopsychiatry*, 1972, **42**, 23–34.

BELL, R. Q., WELLER, G. M., & WALDROP, M. F. Newborn and preschooler: organization of behavior and relations between periods. *Monographs of the Society for Research in Child Development*, 1971, **36**, (Whole No. 142).

HALVERSON, C. F., Jr., & VICTOR, J. B. Minor physical anomalies and problem behavior in elementary school children. *Child Development*, 1976, **47**, 281–285.

KAGAN, J. *Change and continuity in infancy*. New York: Wiley, 1971.

KAGAN, J., & MOSS, H. A. *Birth to maturity: a study in psychological development*. New York: Wiley, 1962.

KAGAN, J., MOSS, H. A., & SIGEL, I. Psychological significance of styles of conceptualization. In J. C. Wright and J. Kagan (Eds.), Basic cognitive processes in children. *Monographs of the Society for Research in Child Development*, 1963, **28**, (2, Serial No. 86): 73–112.

KARP, S. A., & KONSTADT, N. L. *Manual for the children's embedded figures test*. New York: Cognitive Tests, 1963.

PEDERSEN, F. A., & WENDER, P. H. Early social correlates of cognitive functioning in six-year-old boys. *Child Development*, 1968, **39**, 185–193.

RYDER, R. G. Birth to maturity revisited: a canonical reanalysis. *Journal of Personality and Social Psychology*, 1967, **7**, 168–172. (a)

RYDER, R. G. Computational remarks on a measure for comparing factors. *Educational and Psychological Measurement*, 1967, **27**, 301–304. (b)

SIGEL, I. E., JARMAN, P., & HANESIAN, H. Styles of categorization and their intellectual and personality correlates in young children. *Human Development*, 1967, **10**, 1–17.

SLOAN, W. The Lincoln-Oseretsky motor development scale. *Genetic Psychology Monographs*, 1955, **51**, 183–252.

WALDROP, M. F., & HALVERSON, C. F., Jr. Minor physical anomalies and hyperactive behavior in young children. In J. Hellmuth (Ed.), *Exceptional infant: studies in abnormalities. Vol. 2.* New York: Brunner/Mazel, 1971.

WALDROP, M. F., & HALVERSON, C. F., Jr. Intensive and extensive peer behavior: longitudinal and cross-sectional analyses. *Child Development*, 1975, **46**, 19–26.

WITKIN, H. A. Discussion of psychological significance of styles of conceptualization. In J. C. Wright and J. Kagan (Eds.), Basic cognitive processes in children. *Monographs of the Society for Research in Child Development*, 1963, **28** (2, Serial No. 86): 118–122.

WITKIN, H. A. Individual differences in ease of perception of embedded figures. *Journal of Personality*, 1950, **19**, 1–15.

The Perceptual and Cognitive Bases for Finger Localization and Selective Finger Movement in Preschool Children[*]

Arthur Lefford, Herbert G. Birch, and George Green

ALBERT EINSTEIN COLLEGE OF MEDICINE

This study reports the development of the ability of 167 children from 3 to 6 years of age to selectively oppose fingers to the thumb and to localize digits. 12 tasks were administered. The data indicate a clearly defined age-specific developmental course for digital competence over the preschool years. First, different sensory modalities are effective as guides for selective action; then, intersensory transfer develops as an effective guide for action at a later stage; and finally, the ability to use representational information as a guide for behavior is demonstrated. Findings are discussed in relation to the development of body schemata and to neuropathological conditions. The tasks investigated may have diagnostic potential for preschool children at risk for learning disabilities.

This study reports the development of the ability of children from 3 to 6 years of age to selectively oppose their fingers to the thumb and to localize the fingers. It derives from two different traditions in research. The study of development of finger-thumb opposition is related to the tradition of normative studies of psychomotor development in children (Gesell & Amatruda 1947; Kuhlman 1939). The impetus to pursue the course of finger differentiation derived from the observation in clinical examination in neurology by Gerstmann (1924, 1958) that finger agnosia was associated with right-left disorientation, dyslexia, agraphia, and acalculia.

The disturbance of finger awareness was part of a syndrome which involved disturbances in such primary education skills as reading, writing, and arithmetic (Critchley 1953; Nielson 1938; Stengel 1944) in adults who had acquired them but lost them after suffering some form of brain damage. The phenomenon has also been studied in normal and defective children (Benton 1955, 1959; Benton, Hutcheon, & Seymour 1951; Kinsbourne & Warrington 1963a, 1963b; Mathews & Falk 1964; Orton 1937; Strauss & Carrison 1942; Strauss & Werner 1938, 1939). With the exception of the Kinsbourne and Warrington study (1963b), detailed examination of the preschool child's developing awareness of the fingers of his hand has not been forthcoming. The findings suggest that in many subjects disturbances in finger awareness or agnosia are associated with deficiencies in scholastic skill, or what now is called learning disabilities. In view of the numerous and diverse disorders of intellective and

[*] This study was supported by the National Institutes of Health, National Institute of Child Health and Human Development (HD 00719), and by the Association for the Aid of Crippled Children. This report is being published after the untimely and tragic death of Dr. Herbert G. Birch. Reprints may be obtained from Arthur Lefford, Ph.D., Yeshiva University, Ferkauf Graduate School, 55 Fifth Avenue, New York, New York 10003. An extended description of procedures is available on request. George Green is now at Saint Dominic's Home, Blauvelt, New York.

scholastic functions with which finger awareness has been associated, it appeared essential to have more detailed norms of the normal development of these functions with a view to exploring their potential as an index of normal and aberrant development of the central nervous system. Because it would be of value to have the earliest indication of normal or pathological development, an attempt was made to study finger differentiation from the age at which it first starts, 3 years, to the age of school entry, 6 years.

In an earlier study (Birch & Lefford 1967) evidence was found to suggest that the control of voluntary action was dependent at least in part on the child's ability to utilize sensory information and to integrate information from the different sense modalities. The present study therefore also represents an examination of the effects of different conditions of indication or stimulation of the fingers and conditions for performance on the ability of preschool children to selectively oppose fingers and thumb and to localize them by pointing.

METHOD

The ability of the child to differentiate among his fingers was studied by examining three modes of response. Selective finger-thumb opposition required the child to oppose his thumb to a particular digit when both thumb and digit have previously been indicated by the examiner. Finger localization on the child's own hand involved the demand that the child point to his thumb and to a finger of his own hand which the examiner had previously indicated. Finger localization on a drawing required that the child point to the thumb and finger which pictorially represented the pair previously indicated by the examiner on the child's own hand. Conditions of indication of the fingers were varied systematically for each type of response. This resulted in a set of 12 tasks administered in the serial order in which they are described below. All tasks were presented twice. The second presentation of the series was administered immediately after the first presentation in reverse order to the first presentation to control for practice effects. The children were required to respond with their preferred hand. Only three children preferred the left hand.

All children were tested individually either in a separate room, or, if preferred, in an isolated section of the normal nursery school room. Interest was high, and all children readily participated in the "new game." The tasks were given in the order in which they are described below.

1. Visual imitation of finger-thumb opposition (V Imit). In this task, the examiner said to the subject: "We are going to play a game. Let me see if you can bring your fingers together in the way that I bring mine together." The demonstration was then given of the finger-thumb opposition with the palmar surface of the hand up and alongside the corresponding level of the child and held until a response was made.

2. Nonvisual imitation of finger-thumb opposition (nV Imit). This task was administered in exactly the same manner as the previous one except that now an 8 × 10 card was interposed between the subject's hand and eyes.

3. Visual-tactual finger-thumb opposition (VT FTO). In this task the subject was required to make the particular finger-thumb opposition

movements on the basis of the examiner indicating the fingers to be opposed by heavily touching the subject's thumb and fingers while the subject visually observed what was being done.

4. Visual finger-thumb opposition (V FTO). This task was given exactly in the same manner as the previous test except that the examiner pointed to the fingers without touching them.

5. Tactual finger-thumb opposition (T FTO). The finger to be opposed to the thumb was indicated to the subject by the examiner touching the finger to be opposed. The child's view of the hand was obstructed by interposing an 8 × 10 card between the subject's hand and his eyes. (The card was removed before the subject responded.)

6. Tactual-nonvisual finger-thumb opposition (T nVFTO). This task was the same as the T FTO test just described except that the subject was not permitted to see his own hand while attempting to respond.

7. Visual-tactual pointing to self (VT Self). On this examination the thumb and other fingers were indicated as in VT FTO. The subject was then required to point with this contralateral hand to the fingers which had been indicated to him.

8. Visual pointing to self (V Self). The thumb and finger were indicated to the subject as in V FTO, and he was required to point to the fingers which had been indicated to him by pointing to them with his contralateral hand.

9. Tactual pointing to self (T Self). On this test the thumb and finger to be localized by the subject were indicated to him as in T FTO. The subjects were required to respond as in the previous localization tests.

10. Visual-tactual pointing to model (VT Mod). The subject's fingers in this test were stimulated as in the VT Self task. He was required to respond, however, by designating the previously indicated fingers by pointing with his other hand to the fingers represented by a line drawing of the hand. The picture of the hand was placed in line with and just above the hand which was stimulated. The model was in view of the subject during indication and at all other times during the examination by this procedure.

11. Visual pointing to model (V Mod). The subject was stimulated as in the V Self task. He was required to respond as in the above task.

12. Tactual pointing to model (T Mod). The fingers were indicated to the subject as in the T Self task and he was required to respond as above.

Subjects   The subjects for the study consisted of a total of 167 nursery school children from the Bronx, New York. Four nursery schools participated in this study with a pupil population drawn from lower- and middle-class communities of mixed ethnic and religious backgrounds. Boys and girls were approximately equal at each age level. None of the subjects selected for study showed any signs of deviant intellectual or social development, as noted by pediatrician, parents, teachers, or examiners.

Scoring   The first finger-thumb opposition or finger-thumb localization made by the child was taken as his response to the demand. Any changes made by him were not scored. The score was a simple quantitative measure and consisted of the sum of numbers of correct responses made on the two trials. Since the thumb and another finger on the hand were stimulated on each trial and two trials were given for each finger-thumb combination, scores ranging from 0 to 8 were possible. For the needed χ^2 tests it was necessary to develop a criterion measure of pass or fail. A child was judged to have passed the task if each of the four different finger-thumb combinations had been correctly opposed or identified for a given condition on a given trial.

RESULTS

The data were analyzed in two ways. First, the findings were considered with respect to the adequacy with which finger-thumb opposition and finger-thumb localization developed with age as reflected in the average number of correct responses made by the subjects at each half-yearly interval. Second, the effect of the various experimental conditions on response competence was considered. In order to statistically evaluate these differences, age-specific fourfold

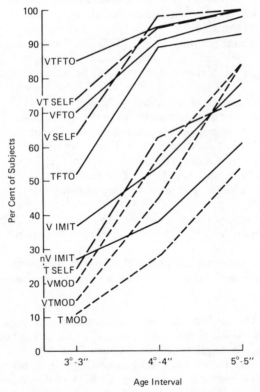

F I G U R E 1.   *Percentage of children at the different age intervals who succeeded to criterion under the various conditions of stimulation and response.*

tables at yearly levels across pairs of conditions were tested by the McNemar χ^2 test for correlated proportions (McNemar 1955). These values are shown in Table 3. Because of the large number of χ^2s calculated, the 1% level was used. This procedure resulted in three age groups: 3-, 4-, and 5-year-old. The number of subjects who correctly opposed or identified all the finger-thumb combination of the hand at least once on the two series was used to construct the fourfold tables. From these data, it was also possible to calculate the percentage of subjects who successfully met the aforementioned criterion measure at each year level. These data are represented in Figure 1 and reflect the development of age-related competence.

The Development of Finger-Thumb Opposition   The performances of children ranging in age from 3 years to 5 years 11 months, on tasks which demand that they selectively oppose the fingers of the hand to the thumb, are summarized in Table 1, which shows the mean number of correct responses made under the different conditions. The least difficult tasks are VT FTO and V FTO. Next, in order of greater difficulty, are the T nVFTO and the T FTO tasks. Visual Imit and nV Imit are the most difficult tasks. The percentage of

TABLE 1

Age Differences in FTO Competence under Different Conditions of Testing

CONDITION	AGE					
	3–0 to 3–5 ($N = 15$)	3–6 to 3–11 ($N = 31$)	4–0 to 4–5 ($N = 30$)	4–6 to 4–11 ($N = 36$)	5–0 to 5–5 ($N = 30$)	5–6 to 5–11 ($N = 25$)
Visual-tactual FTO:						
M	6.00	7.16	7.53	7.81	7.90	7.92
SD	2.17	1.61	1.33	.62	.40	.40
Visual FTO:						
M	5.67	6.35	7.28	7.08	7.70	7.96
SD	2.65	2.32	1.04	1.84	.79	.20
Tactual FTO:						
M	4.71	5.32	7.07	7.22	7.43	7.80
SD	2.83	2.76	1.39	1.07	1.10	.50
Visual imitation:						
M	4.05	5.13	5.43	5.78	6.57	6.88
SD	2.25	1.98	2.06	1.87	1.45	1.42
Tactual-nonvisual FTO:						
M	4.71	5.87	7.03	7.43	7.73	7.76
SD	2.59	2.51	1.33	.97	.78	.66
Nonvisual imitation:						
M	3.14	4.32	4.88	5.36	5.76	6.64
SD	2.31	1.94	2.07	1.73	1.56	1.50

TABLE 2

Finger Localization Scores

CONDITION OF INDICATION	AGE					
	3-0 to 3-5 ($N = 15$)	3-6 to 3-11 ($N = 31$)	4-0 to 4-5 ($N = 30$)	4-6 to 4-11 ($N = 36$)	5-0 to 5-5 ($N = 30$)	5-6 to 5-11 ($N = 25$)
	On Self					
Visual-tactual:						
M	5.00	6.32	7.67	7.54	7.87	7.96
SD	3.26	2.68	.55	1.27	.35	.20
Visual:						
M	4.48	5.90	7.33	7.11	7.67	8.00
SD	3.28	2.95	.84	1.79	.66	.00
Tactual:						
M	2.57	3.81	5.23	5.46	5.53	7.24
SD	1.99	2.48	1.83	2.06	1.98	1.05
	On Model					
Visual-tactual:						
M	1.67	2.87	4.87	5.67	6.37	7.40
SD	1.83	2.75	2.30	2.01	1.27	.76
Visual:						
M	.95	2.90	5.33	5.44	6.10	7.28
SD	1.75	2.95	2.23	1.87	1.60	.84
Tactual:						
M	.52	1.94	3.80	4.19	5.17	5.64
SD	.93	2.21	2.46	1.92	1.84	1.78

children who correctly oppose every finger of the hand to the thumb is shown in Figure 1. Although the trends for each condition are different, statistically significant differences by the McNemar χ^2 test (see Table 3) were found at all ages only between the V Imit and the VT FTO and the V FTO at beyond the 1% level. Only at the 3-year age level was the VT FTO different from the T FTO beyond the 1% level. Though the children performed very slightly better on the T nVFTO task than on the T FTO task, no significant statistical difference was found. As seen in Figure 1, considerably fewer children succeeded on the nV Imit task than on the V Imit; however, the differences were not found to be significantly statistically different.

The Development of Finger Localization   Age difference in the subjects' competence to localize by pointing to the fingers on their hands and on the model in terms of mean number of correct responses is presented in Table 2. The percentage of subjects at the three yearly age levels is presented in Figure 1.

TABLE 3

McNemar χ^2 Values for Correlated Proportions at Three Annual Age Levels for Different Conditions

| | AGE (YEARS) | | |
| | 3 | 4 | 5 |
CONDITION	($N = 46$)	($N = 66$)	($N = 55$)
VT FTO vs. V FTO	4.08*	1.13	.00
VT FTO vs. T FTO	11.53**	1.13	2.25
VT Self vs. T Self	19.05**	17.39**	12.07**
V Self vs. T Self	12.50**	20.05**	12.07**
VT Mod vs. T Mod	.25	4.51	11.13**
V Mod vs. T Mod	2.25	11.12**	11.13**
V FTO vs. V Imit	8.52**	15.61**	7.69**
T FTO vs. T Self	7.56**	13.47**	5.79**
VT FTO vs. T. Self	4.17*	.17	.00
V Self vs. V. Mod	18.05**	24.07**	7.11**
T Self vs. T Mod	4.90*	13.79**	6.27**
VT Self vs. VT Mod	23.31**	30.31**	7.11**

* $p < .05$.
** $p < .01$.

Localization on Self   The subjects' ability to localize their fingers and thumbs by pointing to them on their own hands was well developed when VT and V indication of the fingers to be localized were used. The T Self task proved to be far more difficult than the two previous conditions. The differences between the T condition of indication and the two other conditions were statistically significant beyond the 1% level at all age levels, as indicated in Table 3.

Localization on Model   Requiring the subjects to localize the finger and thumb on a model of the hand proved to be the most difficult set of tasks, as can be seen from mean number of correct responses made, as shown in Table 2, and the percentage of subjects who met the criterion, as shown in Figure 1. There were statistically significant differences between the visual and tactual indication at the 4-year level and between VT, V, and T indication at the 5-year level, as seen from Table 3.

Other Differences in Performance   At all age levels more children could effectively use T information as an indicator for finger-thumb opposition than could use it for correctly pointing to their own fingers. The difference is statistically significant beyond the 1% level, as indicated in Table 3.

Localization of the fingers on the subject's own hand and localization on the model involved a basic difference with respect to whether the terminus of the action was on the subject's own body or on a representation of it. Fewer subjects at all ages were able to localize the fingers on the model than were able to do so on their own hands. This difference was statistically significant, as shown in Table 3, for all three conditions of indication, V, T, and VT.

The localization on the model and the imitation of finger-thumb opposition are similar in that they involve the translation of information from the examiner's hand as a model to the subject's body or from his own body to a model, the drawing of the hand; V Imit and V Mod differences were not statistically significant.

Finger Individuation   Successful finger-thumb opposition and localization do not develop uniformly in all fingers. To evaluate the differential rates of development, the percentage of subjects able to correctly oppose or localize a given finger was ranked at each 6-month interval and for each condition, and the ranks were summed across the age intervals. The differences among the sums of ranks for each of the fingers were then evaluated by Friedman ANOVA for ranks. Statistically significant differences about the 2% level of confidence were found only for those tasks requiring the subject to point to the model and to imitate the finger-thumb opposition demonstrated by the examiner. Under all conditions of indication, pointing to the little finger and thumb was most frequently correctly indicated on the model; the index finger and thumb, the middle finger and thumb, and ring finger and thumb followed in that rank order. For V Imit and nV Imit, the fingers were most successfully opposed to the thumb in the following rank order: index finger, little finger, middle finger, and ring finger. Generally, it appeared that the index and little fingers are differentiated first, followed by the middle and ring fingers.

DISCUSSION

The observations of the study provide evidence delineating certain factors which underlie the emergence of skilled differentiated action and the development of the body schema using the hand as a microcosm. The findings of finger-thumb opposition development indicate that it is not the lack of motor ability which makes the child unable to direct a given finger and thumb to each other. What is lacking is sensory and perceptual discrimination among the fingers. By 6–9 months the child can oppose the forefinger and thumb in picking up a small object. By 3 years 2 months, most children can imitate finger-thumb opposition to each finger in succession (Kuhlman 1939). Motor ability required for the task is present, but perceptual discrimination among the fingers appears to be lacking. When tactual stimulation of the fingers is used only 52% of the 3-year-old children selectively discriminate among all the fingers, and when visual indication is used, only 70% of the 3-year-old children correctly oppose the fingers and thumb.

By $1\frac{1}{2}$ years, children can point to familiar pictures or objects when asked to do so. However, when the children are asked to point to their fingers which are visually indicated, only 63% of the 3-year-old children respond correctly. Since they can make a pointing movement, it would appear that at that age they do not yet fully discriminate differentially among the fingers. It appears, therefore, that one factor which determines a correct movement of one part of the body to another, by finger-thumb opposition or pointing, is the sensory differentiation of the point or locus which is the goal of the movement. The movements as actions are already possible among the 3-year-old children; it is a lack of orientation to the locus or place to which the movement is to be made which is lacking.

A second factor which is critical in making a movement or action possible is that of intersensory integration. When the fingers are stimulated tactually and the subject must point to the fingers of his own hand or to those on the model, the movement is guided visually. This involves an intersensory integration of the two sense-modalities schemata. That there may be intrasensory differentiation but a lack of intersensory integration is suggested by the fact that the T Self task is statistically significantly more difficult than both the T FTO task and V Self task at all age levels. Of the 3-year-old children, 52% showed evidence of tactual differentiation and 70% showed visual differentiation. However, only 26% of the children passed the T Self task, suggesting that 26% lacked intersensory integration. Among the 4-year-olds, 27% lacked intersensory integration, and among the 5-year-olds 17% of the children still lacked the integration. To pass the T Self task the Ss must be able to distinguish which fingers were stimulated tactually and translate the tactual information into a visual equivalent which guides the localization on the subject's own hand. The lack of intersensory equivalence would make a correct response not feasible.

Another factor implicated in the attainment of a successful action in several of the tasks presented the children is the ability to understand representation or symbolization (i.e., the functional equivalence of two different objects). Both in the imitation of the examiner's FTO movements and in the pointing to the fingers on the drawing of the hand, visual equivalence or representations have to have been established for a correct response. In the case of imitation, the children must understand that the fingers on the examiner's hand symbolize or represent the equivalent fingers on their own hand. When the Ss are required to point to fingers on the drawing of the hand, they must also understand that the drawing symbolizes or represents the fingers of their own hand. The V Imit task is significantly more difficult than the V FTO task, and the V Self is significantly easier than the V Mod task. There are no statistically significant differences between the percentage of subjects who succeed to criterion on V Imit and the V Mod at any age level. The ability to understand representation and correspondence of the fingers increases between the third and fifth years. By the fifth year about 80% of the subjects succeeded, and by extrapolation it might be expected that all children would succeed at these tasks by 7 years of age.

The most difficult task in the battery was the T Mod task. This task involves both intersensory equivalence and representation. The fingers are indicated to the Ss tactually, and they must visually identify the fingers on the model as well as guide their pointing fingers visually. To complete this task successfully, the Ss must be able to discriminate among the fingers within a sense modality; intersensory equivalence must have been established between the visual and tactual senses; and the representation of the fingers on the model to those on the children's own hands must have been understood.

With respect to the problem of body image, the development of finger differentiation and control may be taken as a microcosm in which the processes and developmental changes underlying the development of bodily adaptation as a whole are reflected. Thus, the data we have analyzed have relevance for the concepts of body schema and body image which have been considered both in the context of development (Benton et al. 1951; Schilder 1950) and of neuropathology (Critchley 1953).

Despite the fact that the concept of body image was first advanced as an explanatory idea in neurology almost a century ago, little is still understood of its origins. Henry Head (1926) suggested that body image was composed of schemata which represented the organized "storehouse of past impressions" which affect the organization and interpretation of incoming sensory impulses. Benton (1959); Birch, Proctor, and Bortner (1961); and Oldfield and Zangwill (1942) have all viewed such schemata as learned organizations of sensory inputs and sensory integrations. Bartlett (1932) was the first to recognize in an explicit way that "schemata are built up chronologically." Both he and Schilder (1950) as well as Benton (1955) subscribe to the view that developmental factors were instrumental in the emergence of the body scheme. However, these speculations have remained unaccompanied by any serious developmental investigation of underlying processes.

The processes of intrasensory differentiation, intersensory integration, and symbolic representation we have described as underlying the development of finger selection and opposition in young children can be considered as the emerging developmental competences from which the schemata of Bartlett (1932) and Head (1926) derive. Such processes emerge in the preschool years (or earlier) and provide a basis for the organization of experience out of which body image can be acquired. The data suggest that in the early stages of development there are independent schemata for the particular sense systems. This finding supports the speculation advanced by Bartlett (1932) that intrasensory schemata are the first to emerge in the course of development. Our findings also suggest that he was right in anticipating that such sensory system schemata soon interrelate and acquire an intermodal structure. At a later stage the schemata intrinsic to the body itself become linked to the perceptions of other bodies and objects in the external world which are first-order representations. When a child correctly designates his own fingers on the drawing of a hand or is able to oppose selected digits on the basis of another person's movements, he is treating the external environment as the equivalent of stimuli deriving from his own body surface. How he acquires these equivalences and the nature of the learning process which is involved in their acquistion remain unknown but represent fruitful areas for subsequent investigation.

PRACTICAL IMPLICATIONS

The explication of the developmental course of such a typically human behavior as finger-thumb opposition and differential finger awareness provides a simple and useful evaluative technique for neurologic intactness and developmental progress in preschool children. The behavior is particularly intriguing because manual functioning is a ubiquitous human activity whose emergence may be relatively unaffected by particular social and cultural settings. If this is the case it may be a useful method for the comparative evaluation of development across cultures and provide a relatively culture-free basis for the evaluation of developmental course.

The method of examination may be of particular potential value for the early identification of children at later risk of school failure. The early studies of

Orton (1937), Strauss and Carrison (1942), and Strauss and Werner (1938, 1939) suggest that finger agnosia may be associated as a clinical finding with difficulties in such primary educational skills as reading, writing, and arithmetic. The demonstrations by Benton et al. (1951) and Strauss and Carrison (1942) suggest, too, that children of school age have the ability to successfully engage in finger selection which has a consistent relationship with mental age. It is possible therefore that an earlier evaluation of digitual competence may well be one basis for the early identification of subnormality.

References

BARTLETT, F. C. *Remembering: an experimental and social study.* London: Cambridge University Press, 1932.

BENTON, A. L. Development of finger-localization capacity in school children. *Child Development*, 1955, **26**, 225–230.

BENTON, A. L. *Right-left discrimination and finger localization.* New York: Hoeber-Harper, 1959.

BENTON, A. L., HUTCHEON, J. F., & SEYMOUR, E. Arithmetic ability, finger-localization capacity and right-left discrimination in normal and defective children. *American Journal of Orthopsychiatry*, 1951, **21**, 756–766.

BIRCH, H. G., & LEFFORD, A. Visual differentiation, intersensory integration and voluntary motor control. *Monographs of the Society for Research in Child Development*, 1967, **32**(Serial No. 110).

BIRCH, H. G., PROCTOR, F., & BORTNER, M. Perception in hemiplegia, IV: Body surface localization in hemiplegic patients. *Journal of Nervous and Mental Disease*, 1961, **113**, 192–202.

CRITCHLEY, M. *The parietal lobes.* London: Arnold, 1953.

GERSTMANN, J. Fingeragnosie: eine umschriebene Störung der Orientierung am eigenen Körper. *Wiener Klinische Wochenschrift*, 1924, **37**, 1010–1012.

GERSTMANN, J. Psychological and phenomenological aspects of disorders of the body image. *Journal of Nervous and Mental Disease*, 1958, **126**, 499–512.

GESELL, A. E., & AMATRUDA, C. S. *Developmental diagnosis.* (2d ed.) New York: Hoeber-Harper, 1947.

HEAD, H. *Aphasia and kindred disorders of speech.* London: Cambridge University Press, 1926.

KINSBOURNE, M., & WARRINGTON, E. K. Developmental factors in reading and writing backwardness. *British Journal of Psychology*, 1963, **54**, 145–156. (a)

KINSBOURNE, M., & WARRINGTON, E. K. The development of finger differentiation. *Quarterly Journal of Experimental Psychology*, 1963, **15**, 132–137. (b)

KUHLMAN, F. *Tests of mental development.* Minneapolis: Educational Test Bureau, 1939.

McNEMAR, Q. *Psychological statistics.* (2d ed.) New York: Wiley, 1955.

MATHEWS, C. G., & FALK, E. D. Finger localization, intelligence, and arithmetic in mentally retarded subjects. *American Journal of Mental Deficiency*, 1964, **69**(1), 107–113.

NIELSON, J. M. Gerstmann syndrome: finger agnosia, agraphia, confusion of right and left acalculia. *AMA Archives of Neurology and Psychiatry*, 1938, **39**, 536–560.

OLDFIELD, R. C., & ZANGWILL, O. L. Head's concept of the schema and its application in contemporary British psychology. *British Journal of Psychology*, 1942, **33**(Pt. 2), 58–64.

ORTON, S. T. *Reading, writing and special problems in childhood.* London: Chapman & Hall, 1937.

SCHILDER, P. *Image and appearance of the human body*. New York: International Universities Press, 1950.

STENGEL, E. Loss of spatial orientation, constructional apraxia and Gerstmann's syndrome. *Journal of Mental Science*, 1944, **90**, 753–760.

STRAUSS, A., & CARRISON, D. Measurement and development of finger schema in mentally retarded children. *Journal of Educational Psychology*, 1942, **33**, 252–264.

STRAUSS, A., & WERNER, H. Deficiencies in finger schema in relation to arithmetic disability. *American Journal of Orthopsychiatry*, 1938, **8**, 719–724.

STRAUSS, A., & WERNER, H. Finger agnosia in children. With a brief discussion on defect and retardation in mentally handicapped children. *American Journal of Psychiatry*, 1939, **95**, 1215–1225.

Malnutrition and Environmental Enrichment by Early Adoption: Development of Adopted Korean Children Differing Greatly in Early Nutritional Status Is Examined

Myron Winick, Knarig Katchadurian Meyer, and Ruth C. Harris

COLUMBIA UNIVERSITY

Numerous studies conducted in several different countries have demonstrated that malnutrition during the first two years of life, when coupled with all the other socioeconomic deprivations that generally accompany it, is associated with retarded brain growth and mental development which persist into adult life (1–3). What is not clear is the contribution of the malnutrition relative to that of the other social and cultural deprivations. When malnutrition has occurred in human populations not deprived in other ways the effects on mental development have been much less marked (4). Animal experiments have shown that early isolation results in the same type of persistent behavioral abnormalities as does early malnutrition (5). A stimulatory environment has been shown to counteract the untoward behavioral effects of early malnutrition in rats (6). These observations have led to the hypothesis that malnutrition and environmental deprivation act synergistically to isolate the infant from the normal stimulatory inputs necessary for normal development (6). In addition, they suggest that enriching the environment of previously malnourished children might result in improved development. To test this hypothesis, we have examined the current status of a group of Korean orphans who were adopted during early life by U.S. parents and who had thereby undergone a total change in environment.

From *Science*, December 1975, **190**, 1173–1175. Copyright 1975 by the American Association for the Advancement of Science. Reprinted by permission.

EXPERIMENTAL SAMPLE

The sample was drawn from records of children who had been admitted to the Holt Adoption Service in Korea between 1958 and 1967. The following criteria were established for inclusion in the sample:

1. The child must be female. This was decided in order to eliminate sex differences; and because many more female than male infants were brought to the agency they provided a larger adoptive sample to choose from.

2. Date of birth and results of physical examination at the time of admission to Holt care, including height and weight, must be available on the records.

3. The child must have been less than two years old when first admitted to Holt care and less than three years old when adopted.

4. The child must have been reported to be full term at birth.

5. The physician's examination at time of initial contact must have revealed no physical defect or chronic illness.

6. The child must have been followed by the adoption service for at least six years and must be currently in elementary school (grades 1 to 8).

7. The child must have a current mailing address in the United States.

From 908 records chosen at random 229 children were found who met all these criteria. We divided these 229 into three groups, as follows, on the basis of how their height and weight at time of admission to Holt related to a reference standard of normal Korean children of the same age (7): group 1, designated "malnourished"—below the 3rd percentile for both height and weight; group 2, "moderately nourished"—from the 3rd through the 24th percentile for both height and weight; group 3, "well-nourished" or control—at or above the 25th percentile for both height and weight.

There were 24 children, randomly distributed through the three groups, whose height and weight were not in the same percentile grouping. These were eliminated from the sample. The remaining 205 consisted of 59 children in group 1, 76 in group 2, and 70 in group 3.

A letter was sent by the Holt Adoption Service to the parents describing the general objectives of the study and asking their cooperation. It was followed by a letter from us explaining the study in more detail and asking for permission to request information about the child from the school. Where possible, the parents were called by telephone so that any questions they had about the study could be answered. For various reasons, 64 children could not be followed—17 in group 1, 24 in group 2, and 23 in group 3. Most of this loss resulted from inability to reach the parents, from an inadequate response, or from parental refusal. The final sample thus consisted of 141 children—42 in group 1, 52 in group 2, and 47 in group 3.

Information on health, growth and nutrition, and family socioeconomic background was obtained from the families of these 141 children by means of a checklist questionnaire (8). Information about scores on standardized tests of intelligence and school performance for the years 1971 to 1973 was requested from the schools on a mailed form constructed for this purpose.

TABLE 1
Number of Cases in Each Group

		NUMBER MEASURED FOR			
GROUP	TOTAL NUMBER	Current Height	Current Weight	IQ	School Achievement
1	42	41	41	36	40
2	52	50	51	38	38
3	47	47	47	37	37

The outcome data presented here consist of current height, which was obtainable for 138 children; current weight, obtainable for 139; current IQ (9), for 111; and current achievement scores, for 115. Table 1 shows the number of children in each group about whom these data were obtained.

RESULTS

As may be seen in Tables 2 and 3, all three groups have surpassed the expected mean (50th percentile) for Korean children in both height and weight. There is a tendency for the children in groups 1 and 2 to be smaller and lighter than in group 3, but the differences are statistically significant only between the mean heights of children in groups 1 and 3 (Table 2). Although all three groups are heavier and taller than would be expected if they had remained in Korea, their means all fall below the 50th percentile of an American standard.

The mean IQ of group 1 is 102: of group 2, 106; and of group 3, 112 (Figure 1). Only the difference between groups 1 and 3 is statistically significant ($P \leq .005$). All the groups have reached or exceeded mean values of American children. When the data are converted to stanines (Table 4) the results are the same as with the IQ scores.

TABLE 2
Current Height (Percentiles, Korean Reference Standard): Comparison of the Three Nutrition Groups. F Prob. Is the Probability That the Calculated F Ratio Would Occur by Chance

						t-TEST	
GROUP	N	MEAN PERCENTILE	S.D.	F PROB.	CONTRAST GROUPS	t	P
1	41	71.32	24.98	.068	1 vs. 2	1.25	.264
2	50	76.86	21.25		1 vs. 3	2.22	.029*
3	47	82.81	23.36		2 vs. 3	1.31	.194
Total sample	138	77.24	23.41				

* Statistically significant.

TABLE 3

Current Weight (Percentiles, Korean Reference Standard): Comparison of the Three Nutrition Groups. F Prob. Is the Probability That the Calculated F Ratio Would Occur by Chance

Group	N	Mean Percentile	S.D.	F Prob.	Contrast Groups	t-Test t	P
1	41	73.95	24.60	.223	1 vs. 2	1.24	.218
2	51	79.94	20.78		1 vs. 3	1.61	.141
3	47	82.11	22.66		2 vs. 3	.49	.624
Total sample	139	78.91	22.68				

TABLE 4

IQ Stanines: Comparison of the Three Nutrition Groups. F Prob. Is the Probability That the Calculated F Ratio Would Occur by Chance

Group	N	Mean Percentile	S.D.	F Prob.	Contrast Groups	t-Test t	P
1	37	5.25	1.32	.005	1 vs. 2	1.42	.160
2	38	5.74	1.62		1 vs. 3	3.45	.001*
3	37	6.46	1.66		2 vs. 3	1.91	.061
Total sample	112	5.82	1.61				

* Statistically significant.

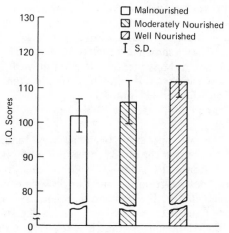

FIGURE 1.   *The IQ's of the three nutrition groups—means and standard deviations (S.D.).*

TABLE 5

Achievement Stanines: Comparison of the Three Nutrition Groups. F Prob. Is the Probability
That the Calculated F Ratio Would Occur by Chance

						t-TEST	
GROUP	N	MEAN PERCENTILE	S.D.	F PROB.	CONTRAST GROUPS	t	P
1	40	5.07	1.51	.002	1 vs. 2	2.12	.038*
2	38	5.79	1.47		1 vs. 3	3.60	.001*
3	37	6.48	1.89		2 vs. 3	1.80	.080
Total sample	115	5.76	1.72				

* Statistically significant.

Results for achievement scores (Table 5) are similar to those for IQ's. All
the groups have achieved at least to stanine 5 (the mean for U.S. school children
of the same age). There is a highly statistically significant difference between
group 1 and group 3 ($P \le .001$). Differences in achievement between groups 1
and 2 just reach the level of statistical significance. All the groups are doing at
least as well as would be expected from an average U.S. population.

DISCUSSION

In the studies referred to earlier which showed persistent retardation in
children malnourished during the first two years of life (1–3), after successful
nutritional rehabilitation the children were sent back to the environment from
which they came. Even by comparison with nonmalnourished siblings or other
children from similar socioeconomic environments their growth and development were retarded (3). Thus severe malnutrition itself during the first two
years of life appears to exacerbate the developmental retardation that occurs
under poor socioeconomic conditions. What happens to the child from a high
socioeconomic background who becomes malnourished early in life? In the few
such cases that have been studied (children with cystic fibrosis or pyloric
stenosis) the children have shown a much smaller degree of retardation in
growth and development and have tended to catch up with time (4). What has
not been determined yet and what is a much more important practical problem
is the fate of a malnourished child from a poor socioeconomic background who
is subsequently reared in the relatively "enriched" environment of a higher
socioeconomic stratum.

In a few instances attempts have been made to modify the subsequent
environment either by keeping the child longer in the hospital in a program of
environmental stimulation or by sending the child home but enrolling him or
her in a special preschool program designed to provide a variety of enriching
experiences. Improvement in development has been noted with both these
approaches but there have been reversals as soon as the special program was
discontinued (10). The data suggest that if a severely malnourished child is
subsequently to develop adequately, any program of environmental enrichment

must be of long duration. In the present study, severely malnourished children were compared with moderately malnourished and well-nourished children after all had undergone a radical and permanent change in their environments by being adopted into primarily middle-class American homes. (The adoptive parents had no knowledge of the previous nutritional status of the child, and the distribution of these children into their adoptive homes was entirely random.) The results are in striking contrast to those obtained from similar groups of children returned to the environments from which they came (1, 2). Even the severely malnouished adopted Korean children have surpassed Korean norms of height and weight. Moreover, the marked initial size differences between the malnourished and the well-nourished infants have almost entirely disappeared, leaving only a small difference in height. None of the groups reach mean values for American children of the same age. This may reflect either genetic size differences between Korean and American children or the effects of chronic undernutrition extending for several generations in developing countries such as South Korea.

Perhaps even more striking and less in accord with previously reported experience is the fact that the mean IQ of the severely malnourished children is 102 and slightly skewed to the right. It is about 40 points higher than that reported in similar populations that were returned to their early home environments (1, 3). In addition, achievement in school for the severely malnourished group is equal to that expected of normal U.S. children. However, the stigmata of malnutrition had not entirely disappeared by the time these children were studied. There are statistically significant differences between the previously malnourished and well-nourished children in IQ and achievement scores. Whether these are permanent differences it may be too soon to judge. It should be noted, however, that the initially well-nourished children attained a mean IQ and achievement score higher than that of middle-class American children. It may be that these attainments (and those of the other two groups as well) reflect the select character of adoptive parents and of the environment they provide to their adopted children.

In this study all the children came to their U.S. homes before the age of three—the mean age was 18 months. Thus they spent a major portion of their early developmental years in their adoptive homes. It would be important both theoretically and practically to determine whether adoption at later ages produces similar results. Such studies are being planned.

References and Notes

1. M. B. STOCH and P. M. SMYTHE, *Arch. Dis. Child.* **38**, 546 (1963): H. G. Birch. *Am. J. Public Health* **62**, 73 (1972).
2. J. CRAVIOTO, E. R. DE LICARDIE, H. G. BIRCH. *Pediatrics* **38**, 319 (1966).
3. M. E. HERTZIG, H. G. BIRCH, S. A. RICHARDSON, J. TIZARD, *ibid.* **49**, 814 (1972).
4. J. D. LLOYD-STILL, paper presented at the annual meeting of the Society for Pediatric Research, San Francisco, May 1974; P. S. Klein, G. B. Forbes, P. R. Nader, *Pediatrics*, in press.
5. S. LEVINE, in *Stimulation in Early Infancy*, A. Ambrose, Ed. (Academic Press, London, 1969), p. 21: V. Denenberg, *ibid.*, p. 62.
6. D. A. LEVITSKY and R. H. BARNES, *Science*, **176**, 68 (1972).

7. Chang Yu Hong, *Pediatric Diagnosis and Treatment* (Yongrin, Korea, 1970).
8. A publication showing the questionnaire is in preparation.
9. Results of only four tests of mental ability, all of them group tests, were used in this study: Lorge-Thorndike Intelligence Test, Otis-Lennon Mental Ability Test, Cognitive Abilities Test, and California Test of Mental Maturity. Each of these tests has a mean of 100 and a standard deviation of 15; they were chosen, on the advice of two consulting educational psychologists, because of their equivalency. Results of the following achievement tests were used: California Achievement Test, California Test of Basic Skills, Metropolitan Achievement Test, Stanford Achievement Test, and SRA Achievement Series. To facilitate comparison of ability and achievement scores both were converted to stanine scores, the former by chronological age, the latter by school grade. In stanine scores 9 is high, 1 is low, and the mean is 5. The conversion to stanine scores was done by two educational psychologists who had no knowledge of the nutrition group assignments.
10. D. S. McLaren et al., *J. Ment. Defic. Res.* **17**, 273 (1973); H. McKay and A. McKay, paper presented at the Western Hemisphere Conference, Mayaguez. Puerto Rico, October 1970.
11. Acknowledgment is made to the Agency for International Development and the Grant Foundation for support of this research. We thank J. Justman and M. Sontag for consultations on how to evaluate the school data, L. Burrill for help with converting the IQ and achievement scores into standard stanines, B. Miller for technical assistance with the sampling and mailing, and G. Raabe and B. Milcarek for computer programming.

Chapter 2
Development in Cognition, Imagination, and Language

Jennifer is sorting the nails out of her father's toolbox into three glass jars, one for each size of nail. She looks serious as she says, "This is a baby nail and it goes in here. The mommies go in this jar. This big nail is a daddy and it goes in here." Is she working or playing? Is she thinking or imagining? She is doing useful work for her father. She chose to do this work and therefore is probably enjoying it. She is classifying objects according to size, a cognitive activity. At the same time, she pretends that nails are people in a family, who can also be sorted according to size. She is simultaneously carrying on processes of thinking, imagining, and language that we often separate in order to discuss and study. Older children and adults can separate work from play, thinking from talking, and reasoning from pretending, but young children are less differentiated. They react more globally, more as wholes. Their mode of operation has a strong imaginative component that operates in concert with language and controlled thought. Children do much of their problem solving through play.

Sensory Experience

The raw material for thinking, imagination, and language comes in through the senses, is selected by perceptual processes, sorted, organized, and stored for further use. Children actively seek sensory experience, enjoying sensorimotor play. Exploration is one facet of the developing sense of initiative. The young child touches objects eagerly, grasps them, runs his fingers and palms over them, even scratches them with his fingernails. Although he has learned, to a large extent, to keep objects out of his mouth, such inhibitions are not complete and he may explore an object with his lips and tongue. Color is important, often featured in his comments, and greatly enjoyed in toys, art, clothing, and nature. He experiments with sounds, using his voice, musical instruments, and any casual sound makers that come into his grasp. Stimulation of inner ear senses occurs most deliciously with swinging, rocking, twirling, hanging by the knees, somersaulting, riding fast, and being tossed high by daddy and other strong persons. Kinesthetic stimulation from muscle movements is also enjoyable. Experiences with taste and smell are interesting, especially when adults suggest, share, and talk about them.

When 4- and 5-year-olds were given tasks of shape discrimination, they used visual perception almost exclusively, even though they could also have used touch perception [1]. Instead of using their hands to gather additional information about the shapes they were matching, they used their hands to position the objects for visual regard. This finding was contrary to what might be expected from a common-sense viewpoint and also contrary to what has been found in Russian children, who matched shapes better after handling and viewing them rather than only viewing. The author suggests that the difference may be in the school systems, since Soviet schools encourage the use of touch in exploration and action.

A wide range of sensory experiences probably contributes to brain development, particularly during the preschool period. The connection between the two hemispheres of the brain is less complete than it will be after 7 or 8 years of age. In order to develop both sides of the brain fully during the time before much intercommunication occurs, it is recommended that children have abundant music, rhythmic exercises, movement exploration, art materials, and other right-hemisphere-related experiences, as well as those more pertinent to the left hemisphere, such as speaking, listening to speech, reading, and counting [15].

Thought Processes and Conceptual Development

The intellectual landmark of the end of infancy is the completion of the period of sensorimotor intelligence, a phase of cognitive development discussed in Chapter 3. At this point, the child has achieved two major feats, the control of his movements in space and the notion of object constancy. He realizes that an object continues to exist even when he does not perceive it and that it can move in space, which also is there when the child is not dealing with it.

Sensorimotor intelligence links successive perceptions and movements, with brief anticipations and memories. It does not take a large, sweeping view: "Sensorimotor intelligence acts like a slow-motion film, in which all pictures are seen in succession but without fusion, and so without the continuous vision necessary for understanding the whole" [70, pp. 120–121].

THE PERIOD OF PREOPERATIONAL THOUGHT

Representational thought is what makes the period of preoperational thought distinctly different from the sensorimotor period. Instead of confining his interactions to the here and now, the child can think about objects, people, and actions that are not present. He shows it first by deferred imitation and next by symbolic play or pretending [73, pp. 53–54]. Drawing or graphic representation is used some time after 2½ years. A fourth type of representation is a mental image, or internalized imitation. The fifth type is verbal representation, the use of words to represent objects and events.

Representational thought can be applied to the past, when the youngster acts upon an event that has happened, and to the future in the form of planning, which also appears as play. Both actions and objects are used in symbolic ways to serve representational thought. The child begins to use language at about the same time that he starts to use objects and actions in representational thought. Language quickly becomes a powerful tool of thought. Even so, imaginative and symbolic acts continue to be useful throughout life.

The period of *preoperational thought* ordinarily lasts from 18 months or 2 years to 7 or 8. During this time, the child is building mental structures that will eventually result in logical thinking or operations. This he does through his interactions with objects and people. The interaction takes the form of the two complementary processes, *assimilation* and *accommodation* [72, pp. 1–6]. The child assimilates by acting on the environment and fitting it into existing schemas. For instance, when first given a wagon or a kiddy car, the young child manipulates the wheels, using an examining schema that is already established. Further examination shows this toy to be different from his other toys and he adapts old schemas and develops new schemas for playing with it, thus accommodating to the wagon as he loads it, pulls and pushes it and unloads it, or as he propels the kiddy car. Through assimilation and accommodation, he learns the properties of toys and other objects, materials such as water, clay, and paint. He also learns ways of manipulating objects through "logico-mathematical experiences." By arranging, grouping, and counting his blocks, sticks, cars, or anything else, he is *operating* on them. Through repeated actions of this type, he internalizes these logico-mathematical experiences into concrete logical operations. While he is working his way through the period of preoperational thinking, his thought has certain characteristics that distinguish it from concrete logical operations, the period that is to follow.

Egocentrism. When a person acts egocentrically, she is unable to take the viewpoint or role of another person. Spatial role taking means realizing how a scene or object looks to the other person; conceptual role taking involves assessing the knowledge and thoughts of another. Moving away from an egocentric perspective is called *decentration,* since egocentrism means being *centered* on one's self.

Preschool children are quite egocentric when compared with older children and adults. Two-year-old Ricky offers his teddy bear to comfort his mother who is sick in bed. When Lydia, age 3, is shopping with her mother, she wants to buy her father a wagon for Christmas. They cannot take an adult perspective in anticipating thoughts and reactions in regard to teddy bears and wagons, but they could take the role of a parent in play. They could pretend to be mommy or daddy and go through motions and words that they have already perceived mommies and daddies using. Play is a mode in which the children explore the behavior of others without paying attention to the fact that the behavior is related to a different viewpoint.

Decentration occurs during the preschool years as the child acquires new cognitive skills and knowledge through which she can predict other people's perceptions, thoughts, and feelings. An investigation of conceptual role taking was carried out with children from 2 through 6 [60]. Each child left her mother and went with the experimenter into a room where she saw two videotapes. One showed a boy walking into a house while the child heard, "This boy is going into his grandmother's house. . . ." The other showed a boy walking up to his mother while the sound consisted of a request for a cookie. Next, the mother came in and the tapes were played again but without the sound. The examiner then asked the child questions about what her mother thought. "Does your mommy think the boy was going into the house?" "Does your mommy know whose house the boy was going into?" "How does she know?" "Did your mommy hear the same thing that you heard?" The child received a nonegocentric score if she realized that her mother knew that the boy went into the house and did not know whose house it was. The percentages responding egocentrically and nonegocentrically are given in Table 2–1. The table shows that nonegocentric responses increased steadily with age. Ability to justify answers also increased with age, but the shift was more sudden, with no children justifying at ages 2 and 3 and 40 per cent of the children doing so at age 4.

Spatial role taking was first investigated when Piaget and Inhelder asked children to show how a group of mountains would look from a different per-

Table 2-1.   Percentage at Each Year Giving Egocentric and Nonegocentric Responses and Justifications for Answers.

Age	Egocentric Responses	Nonegocentric Responses	Justification
2	100	0	0
3	95	5	0
4	35	65	40
5	10	90	60
6	0	100	90

SOURCE: Data from Tables 1 and 2 in D. G. Mossler, M. T. Greenberg, and R. S. Marvin. The early development of conceptual perspective-taking. In R. C. Smart and M. S. Smart (eds.) *Readings in child development and relationships.* New York: The Macmillan Publishing Co., 1977, pp. 176–181.

spective [72]. Children below 7 or 8 indicated their own point of view instead of that of a doll who faced another side of the mountains. After devising easier ways for children to indicate another viewpoint, American psychologists have found that children as young as 3 can take spatial roles under some circumstances. Grover, a character from "Sesame Street," drove his car along a road and stopped to look at scenes mounted on a turntable [8]. Children of 3 and 4 were asked to "move the turntable so that the fire engine looks the way Grover sees it." A nonegocentric response consisted of matching the scene to Grover's perception; an egocentric response was matching the scene to the child's own view. The scenes that Grover saw varied in difficulty. For the scenes containing toy objects, the children were right over 80 per cent of the time. For the scene with a wide variety of objects, 3-year-olds succeeded 79 per cent and 4-year-olds succeeded 93 per cent of the time. On Piaget and Inhelder's mountain scene, younger children gave 42 per cent correct responses and older children 67 per cent.

An analysis of the cognitive abilities underlying spatial role taking indicates two basic ones [63]. The child has to know that knowledge depends upon seeing, that what is hidden is not seen, and what is not hidden is seen. She must also suppress her own visual field while choosing the scene that the other person sees. A good beginning in the second ability had been achieved by the 3-year olds. Indications of the first ability were given by children 2 and younger when they were asked to show pictures to an adult [49]. At 18 months, they seemed to realize that the other person had to look at a picture to see it, but they kept the pictures in view of themselves also. By 2, most children turned the picture toward the adult even when they could not see it themselves.

Perceptual Salience. Perceptions dominate the young child's thinking. He is greatly influenced by what he sees, hears, or otherwise experiences at a given moment. Literally, seeing is believing. The static picture is what he believes. He does not pay attention to transformations or changes from one state to another. What he perceives at any one time is, however, only part of what a more mature person would perceive. Carolyn, a 2-year-old who remarked, "Choo-choo going fwimming," was beholding on the river a large object, followed by several similar, rectangular objects, that did in fact resemble a train. The pointed prow of the tug, the decks, the small size, the absence of wheels—all these features did not indicate to her that this object was not an engine, although they would have done so to an older child. If Carolyn saw these aspects of the tug, she ignored past experiences that would have been brought to bear on the situation by a more sophisticated observer. Nobody has seen a train moving itself on anything but a track. Carolyn's thinking was not flexible enough to watch the tug and barges, think of trains and how they run, compare this event with past observations of trains, and then come to a conclusion based on both present and past. Another illustration of the dominance of perception is the ease with which young children can be fooled by a magician. Although the older members of the audience reject the evidences of their senses because they reason on the basis of past experience, the preschool children really believe that the magician found his rabbit in the little boy's coat pocket and that the card flew out of the air into the magician's hand.

One of Piaget's famous experiments is done by pouring beads from one glass container to another glass, which is taller and thinner than the first. When asked whether there are more or fewer beads in the second glass, the child answers either that there are more, because the level of the beads has risen, or that there are fewer, because the glass is narrower. The child centers on *either* height or width more often on height, which is more salient [74]. In contrast, a child who had reached the next stage of thought, the period of concrete operations, would reason with respect to both relations and would deduce conservation. His perceptions would be placed in relation instead of giving rise to immediate reactions [70, pp. 130–131].

Perception becomes more flexible, "decentered," with increasing maturity. In their search for remembered objects, 5-year-olds were more able than 3-year-olds to ignore salient but irrelevant items [92].

Reasoning. Young children move from particular to particular rather than from general to particular. Piaget [71, p. 231] tells how Jacqueline, age 34 months, ill with fever, wanted oranges to eat. Her parents explained to her that the oranges were not ripe yet, they had not their yellow color and were not yet good to eat. She accepted the explanation until given some camomile tea, which was yellow. Then she said, "Camomile tea isn't green, its yellow already. . . . Give me some oranges!"

Thus, she reasoned that if camomile tea was yellow, the oranges must have become so. She went from one concrete instance to another, influenced by the way she wanted things to be.

Unsocialized Thinking. The young child feels no need to justify his conclusions and if he did, he would not be able to reconstruct his thought processes so as to show another person how he arrived at his conclusions. He takes little notice of how other people think, sometimes even ignoring what they say when he is talking. He begins to adjust his thinking to that of other people only as he becomes aware of himself as a thinker and as he grows in power to hold in mind several aspects of a situation at a time. Through years of interaction with other people, discussing, disagreeing, coming to agreements, the child gradually adopts the ground rules necessary for logical thinking.

GROWTH IN CONCEPTUALIZING

Most 2-year-olds can name pictures or drawings of familiar items, showing that they have inner representations of those objects. The child need not have seen a previous picture of the object in order to recognize what it depicts, thus showing that he has some sort of generalized representation, which might be considered a primitive concept. The Stanford–Binet Test shows that the preschool child's typical response to pictures is the naming of figures in them, whereas the child of 6 or 7 and 11 or 12 tells about actions as well and the child over 12 gives a theme. Thus, the conceptualizing of pictures develops from simple and concrete to abstract and complex.

The young child is hard at work organizing his experiences into concepts of classes, time, space, number, and causality. The fact that he does not quite make it until around 4 years is reflected in Piaget's term, *preconceptual thought,* which refers to the first half of the period of preoperational thought. The second half of this period, the stage of *intuitive thought,* is characterized by judgments being made on the basis of perceptions rather than on reason. He classifies more and uses more complex representations of thought than he does in the period of preconceptual thought.

Class Concepts. Even before the stage of preconceptual thought, children perceive certain similar or identical aspects in objects or in repeated events. One-year-olds will show a primitive kind of grouping behavior when presented with two sets of dissimilar objects, as did the infants who touched several clay balls in succession or several yellow cubes in succession [76]. Preconceptual children will group objects readily on a perceptual basis rather than according to any inclusive and exclusive categories. *Chaining* is a kind of grouping often employed by young children. Given blocks in various shapes, colors, and sizes, a child might put a red triangle next to a red cube, then add a blue cube, a long blue rod, a short blue rod, and a small green rectangle. Each object is related to the one beside it, but there is no overall relationship tying the collection together. Among 4- and 5-year-old Zambian children, about 20 per cent of grouping was of the chaining type [65].

Sensory, motor, and emotional experiences all enter into the early building of concepts. Young children often group together things that they have experienced together, as did the child who used *quack* to mean duck, water, and all other liquids and the child who used *afta* to mean drinking glass, pane of glass, window, and what was drunk out of the glass [96, p. 226]. The experience of the family group is often used in ordering objects that have no claim to family membership other than belonging in a category. For example, 2-year-old Dickie called two half dollars *daddy* and *mummy,* a quarter *Dickie,* and a dime *baby.* Children frequently take into account physical qualities such as heaviness, clumsiness, pliability, or prickliness, when naming objects. The name itself is thought to be part of the object, and language can express such qualities. Two children who made up a language used the word *bal* for *place.* The longer the vowel was held, the larger the place. *Bal* therefore meant village, *baal,* town, and *baaal,* city. The word *dudu* meant go. The speed with which it was spoken indicated how fast the going was [96, p. 261].

The first concepts are concrete, tied to definite objects of events. Through repeated experiences, especially those verbalized by other people in certain ways, the child develops abstract concepts. The concepts he builds will always be affected by the people around him, through the give and take of social living. For example, most children acquire the abstract concepts *red* and *black* through interactions with people who already have abstract terms for these concepts. How much more difficult, or even impossible, it is for a child to develop an abstract concept of red when *gab,* the word for red, is also the word for blood. Thus *red* and *blood* are forever tied together, as are *black* and *crow* in the word *kott-kott.* Even more concretely tied to perception is the Brazilian Indian word *tu ku eng,* which is used for any and all of these colors: emerald green, cinnabar red, and ultramarine blue. *Tu ku eng* is also a parrot that bears all three colors. Thus, green, red, and blue are not only bound up with the parrot but also with each other [96, pp. 234–241].

Perceptual salience is a key to much of the classifying of young children.

Many studies, beginning with one in 1929, have shown that preschool children are more likely to group objects on the basis of color rather than form [27]. For example, children are asked to choose from a group of red triangles and green circles the items that are like another item. The other item is either a green triangle or a red circle. Thus, the children are forced to match on the basis of either form or color. Table 2-2 shows proportions of children below and above 4.8 years classifying on the basis of form or color, as found in a recent study [32]. Research has shown that choosing color over form is more often done by younger children, deaf children, and children from disadvantaged groups and from preliterate cultures [27]. Such children may shift later to form-salience or may retain a preference for color. Formal schooling demands that a child pay attention to form in learning to read and write. The shift to form-preference may result from the requirements and pressures of a literate and technological culture.

Further research dealing with the use of categories shows that the salience of various concepts is related to age during the preschool years [47]. Children between 3½ and 6½ years of age were given systematic choices in how to group a collection of toys. It was possible to classify the toys in terms of color, size, number, form, analytic characteristics (such as having four wheels or two arms), or sex type (for girls or boys to play with). In general, the children found it easier to use color, number, form, and size for classifying toys than to use analytic concepts or sex type. There were age differences in the use of color, size, and form; with the younger children using color and size more easily than form and the older ones using form more easily than color and size. Many experiments have shown a developmental trend in the choice of complementary-based categories to similarity-based categories [18]. For example, when asked to choose what goes together from a collection of toy furniture and dolls, a 3-year-old would group a crib with a baby doll, while a 6-year-old would group crib, chair, and table. Younger children can be *taught* to use similarity-based categories, but their *spontaneous* groupings are more likely to be based on complementary categories. Such experiments have been criticized because the categories they use are not meaningful to young children [78]. Three-year-olds do not have a concept of furniture, a category that includes wide variety of objects. When tested with basic categories with which

Table 2-2. Percentages of Younger and Older Preschool Children Classifying by Color and Form.

Age	Color	Form
Under 4.8	61	39
Over 4.8	14	86

SOURCE: Data from G. A. Hale and L. E. T. Lipps. Stimulus matching and component selection: Alternative approaches to measuring children's attention to stimulus components. *Child Development*, 1974, **45**, 383–388.

they have had real experience, such as cats, fish, cars, and airplanes, three-year-olds, as well as older children, sorted on the basis of similarity. Developmental changes were seen only for sorting at superordinate levels, or higher levels of abstraction.

At levels of difficulty where spontaneous grouping is on complementary-based categories, children can be taught to use similarity-based categories [18]. Other experiments have also shown that young children can learn to group on dimensions other than those they choose spontaneously [100] and that they can solve more difficult problems when taught to use their conceptual abilities more efficiently [62].

When once a preschool child has sorted objects in terms of one particular classification, he finds it difficult to abandon that classification and sort them into another. The following experiment [35] demonstrates the gradual elaboration of classifying that takes place with growth. Children were given forms of several shapes and colors and told to put them into groups. The first step in ordering is to put the objects into groups of either form or color. The young child (78 per cent of 3-year-olds and 33 per cent of 4-year-olds) was unable to arrange the objects further even after the examiner set an example. In step 2, most 6-year-olds made subgroups by form after having grouped all the objects by color. In step 3, still another subgrouping was made. That is, after arranging the objects into colors, and into forms within the color groups, the child then ordered them according to size. Step 4, characteristic of the adult, involves taking more than one category into account at a time. In order to do this, the person has to abstract the categories completely. He has to be able to consider form, color, and size entirely apart from the objects in which he perceived them. This process is a freeing of thought from sensory perception. No child under 8 achieved it unaided. Helped by special training procedures, however, 4-year-olds classified on more than one dimension [64].

Time Concepts. The earliest experiences of time are most likely those of bodily rhythms, states that recur in regular patterns, such as hunger, eating, fullness. Interactions with the environment impose some patterns on bodily rhythms, calling them by such names as breakfast, nap time, and bath time. Other early experiences that form the basis of time perception include dealing with a succession of objects, such as filling a basket with blocks; taking part in an action that continues and then stops, such as pushing or pulling a wheeled toy; hearing sounds of varying lengths. These experiences, each a seriation of events, are one type of operation that is basic to the notion of time, according to Piaget [73, p. 198]. Events such as these constitute the order of temporal succession. A second type of experience basic to time concepts comes from temporal metrics, the repetitions of stimuli in patterns, such as music and dance, or even rhythms of patting that a parent might do to a child in arms. A third notion, that of *duration,* is necessary for mature time concepts. Duration involves appreciation of the intervals between events. In early childhood, time is not "an ever-rolling stream" but simply concrete events, embedded in activity. Time and space are not differentiated from each other. Having no overall, objective structure, time is largely the way that the preschool child feels it or wants it. To put it in Piaget's terms, the young child judges duration in terms of content, forgetting speed. Adults can appreciate this quality when they consider how long 10 seconds can be under the dentist's drill and how brief a hit Broadway show can be. Or, looking back at events such as your first formal dance or first trip alone, the vivid scene is as yesterday. Accepting the objective nature of time, the dental patient "knows" that the drilling was really only 10 seconds, the audience admits that the show lasted for 2½ hours, and the adult realizes that his solitary trip to Grandpa's was 10 years ago.

Time is structured differently by different cultures, groups, and individuals. A Balinese child must learn to orient himself within several simultaneously running calendars. An Eskimo gets a concept of night and day as varying dramatically from season to season, whereas to an Indonesian, night and day are very stable. Minute-conscious Americans are scheduled throughout the days, weeks, and years, equipped with abundant watches, clocks, timers, and calendars. The ages at which American children replace egocentric time concepts with objective ones are not necessarily those of other children in the world. In fact, in primitive time systems, nobody detaches time concepts from the concrete activities in which they are embedded, such as milking time, apple blossom time, or the year that a certain field was planted with yams. Emotional experiences may divide time into lucky and unlucky periods. Although Western civilizations have attained considerable objectification of time, there are still many time structures based on personal, emotional, and spiritual experiences—spring, holy days, vacation, mourning period, anniversaries. A child's concepts will be molded by the time concepts he encounters in other people—his family, friends, and teachers. As he checks his notions with theirs, he gradually changes his private, egocentric (self-referred) ones to generally held concepts.

Time concepts of children between 18 and 48 months were studied by both observation and questioning for two consecutive years in a nursery school [2]. All the children in the school were used both years, and all spontaneous verbalizations involving or implying time were recorded. The results show the trend of development in time concepts throughout the preschool period, although since the subjects ranged from high average to very superior intelligence, the age levels at which concepts occurred must be considered as applying to children of above average intelligence. Note, they do show the trend of development in time concepts from egocentric to objective:

18 months: Some sense of timing, but no words for time.

21 months: Uses *now*. Waits in response to *just a minute*. Sense of timing improved. May rock with another child, or sit and wait at the table.

2 years: Uses *going to* and *in a minute, now, today*. Waits in response to several words. Understands *have clay after juice*. Begins to use past tense of verbs.

30 months: Free use of several words implying past, present, and future, such as *morning, afternoon, some day, one day, tomorrow, last night*. More future words than past words.

3 years: Talks nearly as much about past and future as about the present. Duration: *all the time, all day, for two weeks*. Pretends to tell time. Much use of the word *time: what time? it's time, lunchtime*. Tells how old he is, what he will do tomorrow, what he will do at Christmas.

42 months: Past and future tenses used accurately. Complicated expressions of duration: *for a long time, for years, a whole week, in the meantime, two things at once*. Refinements in the use of time words: *it's almost time,*

a nice long time, on Fridays. Some confusion in expressing time of events:
"I'm not going to take a nap yesterday."
4 years: Broader concepts expressed by use of *month, next summer, last summer.* Seems to have clear understanding of sequence of daily events.*

Understanding of *yesterday* and *tomorrow* was traced in children from 2 through 4. The youngest had little comprehension of either term [34]. At 3, *yesterday* was understood in two ways, the usual one and also as a time other than today. *Tomorrow* was understood only as future, never as meaning *yesterday.* At 4, children understood both terms well.

Space Concepts. The young child's concepts of space, like his concepts of time, are derived from bodily experience. He gets sensations from within his body and from his interactions with the rest of the world. During the sensorimotor period, he looks, touches, mouths, and moves to build concepts of his body and other objects. During the period of preoperational thought, space is still egocentric, related to the child's body, his movements, and perceptions. Four-year-old Laura named a certain tree "the resting tree" because she often sat under its cool branches for a few minutes on her way home from kindergarten. The land where the "resting tree" was located was the "resting place," and the family who lived there was "the resting tree people."

Primitive languages contain many space words that refer to the body or its motion and location in space. So does everyday (nonscientific) English in such words and expressions as groundwork, sky-high, eye-level, handy, backside, neck and neck. When asking directions from the man in the street, how often does one get an answer such as, "Follow Elm Street for half a mile and then turn right onto Route 4?" Not very often. It is much more likely to be, "You know where the Mobil gas station is down past the cemetery? No? Well then, go to the second stoplight and turn kitty-corner to the Catholic Church. You can't miss it." *You can't miss it* is almost inevitable at the end of a set of directions so firmly rooted in concrete experience. The person giving such directions is doing it so much from an egocentric standpoint that he cannot imagine anyone finding the route less clear than it is in his own mind.

The ordering of space by preschool children has been studied in terms of their methods of dealing with columns and rows of pictures [28]. Children between 3 years 3 months and 6 years 3 months were tested in two sessions two weeks apart. The child was given a card with rows of pictures of 20 familiar objects and asked to name all the pictures and to report "I don't know" for unfamiliar ones. The order and direction used were noted. Responses were scored for organization, one point being given each time the picture named was adjacent to the one named previously. Scores increased very significantly with age and also increased with the same groups over a two-week period. Therefore, as children grew older, they applied more order to the way in which they dealt with objects in space, as though they realized increasingly that they could be more efficient if they organized their behavior.

* Reprinted by permission from L. B. Ames. The development of the sense of time in the young child. *Journal of Genetic Psychology,* 1946, **68,** 97–125.

EDWARD C. DEVEREUX

The ability to copy the order of the set of objects is first observable between 4 and 5 years of age. It is easier for a child to pile blocks in a certain order than it is for him to make a row that corresponds to a model [38]. In the pile, there is only one way to go, up. In making a row, one can add to the left or to the right. Even when frames were supplied in order that adding to the rows could be done in one direction only, the row constructed was still more difficult. The difference in ease of ordering may be connected with the space orientation of the body itself, up and down being an unchanging dimension, while left and right aspects of the environment change constantly.

The body is a reference point in judgments of up and down, left and right, near and far, and here and there. A preschool child also makes some *objective* space references, in which her own body and position are not used as orientation points. Kindergarten children were given tasks of arranging animals in a farm scene to match a display that had been rotated [75]. They were able to use unique features (a house and a barn) in placing animals in the correct quadrant. Without the aid of the house or barn, they were less likely to take account of the rotation and to persist as from their own point of view. An objective spatial judgment would be, "The horse goes beside the barn." An egocentric judgment would be, "The cow goes to this side of me and about as far away as I can reach." With cognitive development, children place larger amounts of spatial experience into objective reference systems, but even adults make frequent use of egocentric spatial orientation.

Children's use of spatial terms sometimes gives clues as to their understanding of spatial dimensions. Concepts of big, tall, and high were related and overlapping in 4- and 5-year-olds [56]. They were asked questions about large and small animals, which were placed on a table, and then placed one on a table and one on a box. When an elephant and a small turtle were both placed on the table, most children correctly chose the elephant when asked, "Which one is the big one?" When the turtle was moved to the top of a box while the child watched, the child picked the turtle as the big one. When the animals were presented with the elephant already on the table and the turtle on the box, children tended to answer correctly. Apparently the movement in an upward direction made the vertical dimension more salient. *Big* was estimated in terms of the top point. *Tall* and *high* were also judged by the top point. Thus, a definition that is really accurate for *high* was also applied to the dimensions of *big* and *tall*. This definition occurred in a particular context that added to the salience of the vertical dimension.

Quantity Concepts. Concepts of quantity may be numerical, but not necessarily so. *More or less* and *all, some,* or *none* refer to quantity, but not to numbers. A child can choose the dish with more ice cream in it, rather than the dish with less, even before she can respond differentially to the words *more* and *less*. *More* is understood earlier than *less*. In a sample of middle-class children, *less* was understood by 36 per cent of 3-year-olds and by 66 per cent of 4-year-olds [67]. The rest of the children treated *less* as though it meant *more*, giving the examiner the cup with more candy in it when they had been told to give her the cup with less.

A concept of *all* is built during the preschool years. The young child does not know whether a succession of objects that look alike are one and the same object or a series of objects. Jacqueline, age two and one-half, walking in the woods with her father, was looking for slugs (snails). Catching sight of one she commented, "There it is." Seeing another, several yards away, she cried, "There's the slug again." Piaget took her back to see the first one again and asked if the second was the same or another. She answered "yes" to both questions. Jacqueline had no concept of a class of slugs [71, p. 225]. A 2-year-old ordinarily has the concept of "another" when it is a case of wanting a cookie for each hand, or asking for more. The difference between cookies in the hands and slugs on Jacqueline's walk is that the two cookies are present at the same time, whereas the slugs were seen in succession.

A step beyond Jacqueline's dealing with a concept of slugs was shown by Ellen, at 3½. Looking up at the blue Michigan sky surrounding her, she asked, "Is our sky at camp joined onto our sky at home?"

Thus, Ellen showed that she realized that the sky in New York State and the sky in Michigan were either the same thing or of the same order of things. By asking, she was trying to determine whether there was one sky or more than one.

Adults often wonder why young children accept a succession of streetcorner Santa Clauses as Santa Claus. The reason is seen in the child's uncertainty as to whether similar objects constitute an individual or a class. Through experience and discussion, the child builds concepts of *one, some,* and *all*. At first, *all* means that he perceives in a given situation. The toddler, listening to his bedtime story about Sleepyboy taking off his clothing, gets up at the mention of Sleepyboy's shoes and points out the shoes of everyone in the family. This early form of generalization is a *plural concept.* It is less mature than the concept of *all shoes,* which begins at around 5.

Concepts of number, like concepts of space and time, are first derived from concrete experience. Evidence appears in certain words in which terms for numbers are fused with terms for objects. Werner [96, pp. 289–290] tells of cultures in which a different type of number name is used for each of seven classes of objects: indefinite and amorphous; long; round; flat; human beings; boats; and measures. He tells of a language in which ten baskets are *bola* and ten coconuts are *koro.* Partially fused, ten changes as the objects do. A step toward abstraction is shown in the language in which *lima,* the word for *hand,* is also the word for *five.* The use of the body as a natural number schema is found in primitive cultures and in children, and in an occasional college student. Number systems based on five or ten obviously have their roots in the human hand. Werner [96, p. 291] says, "At the beginning, no schema is an abstract form purely mathematical in significance; it is a material vessel in which the concrete fullness of objects is poured, as it were, to be measured."

A relationship has been shown, at least in retarded children, between the ability to articulate the fingers and the development of number concepts. Each child was asked to point, with eyes closed, to the finger touched by the examiner. A group showing high ability in number concepts made almost no errors, whereas a group with mathematical disability showed many errors [96, p. 296].

When a young child first begins to compare sets of items, he does not use numbers. The toddler does not have to count at all in order to choose the plate containing four cookies rather than the plate with two cookies. A configuration of objects, up to five or six, can be grasped perceptually without true number concepts being employed. A larger group may be seen as complete or not because every object is known as an individual. For instance, a 2-year-old (like the others) in a family of eight realizes that eldest brother is absent, not because he has counted and found only seven members present but because he does not see a certain individual who is often part of the family configuration.

When a child counts objects and tells accurately that there are seven apples or seven blocks, he has a concrete number concept, a more exact way of dealing with numbers of objects than does the child who discriminates on a perceptual basis. Counting or *numeration* was explored in nursery school children in Ontario [83]. Five mathematical tasks were given by means of cards with dots, each stimulus consisting of two sets of dots. To judge *magnitude,* the child was told to press the button under the bigger (or smaller) number of dots. For *equivalence,* the subject was to press the button over the picture with the same number of dots as the sample. To discriminate *quantity,* the child pressed the button over the picture with one, two or three dots. For numeral discrimination, numbers were to be pressed. *Numeration* required the child to press the button over the picture that had the number of dots that "went with the number." The numeration task was significantly harder than all the other tasks except equivalence. Thus, it was easier to discriminate numbers than to numerate. Magnitude, a relatively easy judgment to make, is a kind of ordering, while numeration involves more of an understanding of a number as a class. Numeration was found to be easier when all members of a set were the same than when they were different.

When young children are asked to judge items arranged in a line, or to compare two lines of items, they are likely to have difficulty in separating number from length. Piaget devised tests to demonstrate perceptual dominance in the judging of quantity [69]. For example, the child is given a number of flowers and the same number of vases and asked to place a flower in each vase. Then the examiner takes out the flowers and puts them in a bunch. He spreads out the vases and asks, "Are there more flowers or more vases?" The child under 7 or 8 usually says that there are more vases. If the vases are bunched up and flowers spread out, he is likely to say that there are more flowers. He bases his answer on the perception of the amount. The flowers, in a bunch, cover less area than the vases spread out. Therefore, he concludes that there are more vases. Instead of recalling his experience of matching flowers to vases, and reasoning that the quantities must be equal, he is dominated by what he sees.

Being able to count is no guarantee of being able to cope with a situation similar to the flowers test. Children between 5 and 9, all of whom could count beyond six, were asked to place a rubber doll in each of six little bathtubs, which were placed side by side [54]. Upon questioning, the child agreed that there were the same number of dolls and tubs. Then the experimenter asked him to remove the dolls and place them in a heap. Answers to the questions as to whether there were more dolls or more bathtubs usually brought the answer that there were more bathtubs.

An objective number concept involves knowing that the number of objects is the same, no matter how they are arranged. ...... = ::: = :...: The difference between 5- to 6-year-olds and 7- to 7½-year-olds in regard to this kind of understanding is demonstrated by this experiment [54]. Children were given two groups of four beans to represent eight sweets. Four sweets were to be eaten in midmorning and four more at teatime. Then two more sets of four were presented, and the children were told that these represented sweets to be eaten the following day, when only one was to be eaten in the morning and the remaining three would be eaten with the four teatime sweets. While the children watched, three sweets were taken from the group and added to the other group of four. Thus the children had in front of them two sets, one being 4 + 4 and the other 1 + 7. The experimenter then asked each child if he would eat the same number of sweets on each day. The younger children said "no" that 1 + 7 was either larger or smaller than 4 + 4. The older children gave the correct answer promptly. Questioning showed that they understood the equivalence of the sets and the compensation occurring in the change. The children under 7 demonstrated inability to weigh more than one factor at a time and their centering on what they first perceived. They compared either 1 or 7 with the 4s. The older children, having considerable freedom from perceptual dominance, could consider the several aspects of the situation in relation to one another.

Cardinal number concepts are built from putting objects into groups or classes and then abstracting out the number. Ordinal number concepts come from putting objects in series and then abstracting out the order. Classifying and seriation are therefore both essential activities in building number concepts. Below about 5 years a child cannot make a series of objects, as of dolls of increasing size, but between 5 and 6 he does so. At this point, he has great difficulty in finding the correct place for an object that has been omitted from the series, but at around 7 he can do this task easily. At 7 he is sufficiently freed from the perception of the dolls to conceive at the same time of the first doll being smaller than the second and the second smaller than the third. There is some evidence that children learn *ordination* earlier than *cardination* [9].

Causality Concepts. The idea of universal laws is absent in primitive and childish thinking. What explanations are given tend to be in concrete and personal terms. Egocentrism in regard to causality occurs at the same time and for the same reasons as egocentrism in concepts of space, time, and number.

The events of the outer world are closely linked with the child's inner world and his needs. During the preschool and school years, causality becomes less subjective. It can be followed through three stages of subjectivity. At first events are explained in terms of the child's own feelings and actions or in terms of people close to him or perhaps in terms of God. Although he does not consider all events to be caused by his own action, as he did in the sensorimotor period, he understands causes as forces resembling personal activity. "The peaches are growing on our tree, getting ready for us to eat." "The moon comes up because we need some light in the night." The next step toward maturity is to see natural events as caused by forces contained in themselves or by vague agents called *they*. "The radish seed knows it is supposed to make a radish." Increasing sophistication of thought decreases egocentrism, and the child begins to see causes as impersonal. For instance, heavy things sink and light thing float. Progress in understanding cause is from concrete toward abstract. At first, explanations are merely descriptions of events. QUESTION: "What makes a sailboat move?" PETER: "My daddy takes me out in our sailboat. Mummy goes and Terry goes. Daddy starts the motor and we go chug, chug, chug down the pond."

The idea of universal, impersonal causes is beyond even the stage of childhood thinking and is not achieved by naïve adults. The concept of chance is related to the concept of necessity. Both require some logical or formal thought. Young children's explanations tend to be diffuse and inconsistent. Several events are explained by several different causes instead of by a unifying cause. Piaget [69, p. 137] gives these accounts of conversations of an adult with two 5-year-old children, Col and Hei, dealing with the concept of floating:

> **Col:** Rowing boats stay on the water because they move.—**Adult:** And the big boats?—They stay on the water because they are heavy.
> **Adult:** Why does the boat (a toy) remain on the water?—**Hei:** It stays on top because it's heavy. . . . The rowing boats stay on top because they're big.—Fifteen days later Hei says, on the contrary, that boats stay "because they're not heavy." But comparing a pebble with a plank, Hei again says: "This pebble will go to the bottom because it isn't big enough, it's too thin." Finally Hei says that a stone goes to the bottom because "it's stronger" (than the wood.)—And the boats, why do they stay on top? Because the water is strong.

These children give different, and what look like conflicting, explanations of events that an adult would unify under universal laws of floating. The children are showing their inability to consider several factors at one time and their consequent inability to come to general conclusions.

Animism. When Becky, 6, and Nathan, 4, were examining a dead wasp, the following conversation took place.

NATHAN: Careful. It might come alive.
BECKY: It's dead.
NATHAN: It might come alive and sting us.
MOTHER: Could it come alive again after it's dead?
BECKY: No.
NATHAN: Maybe.
MOTHER: How could it come alive?
NATHAN: It would just wiggle around and wiggle around and then it would be alive.

Nathan's explanation was *animistic,* equating movement with life. Young children will say that clouds, moon, and fire are alive because they move, and because they are alive, they are conscious [69]. The wind knows that it blows. The sun knows that it moves. From an analysis of children's replies to questions about animism, physical causality, problem solving, and other skills and abilities, animism was not related to other kinds of causal thinking [5].

ACHIEVEMENTS IN THINKING DURING THE PREOPERATIONAL PERIOD

In all areas of thinking, the preschool child increases in speed and flexibility. Strongly dominated by perception and by his wishes in the early years, he moves toward greater control of his thinking. His earliest concepts of classes, space, numbers, time, and causes are rooted in concrete, personal experience, gradually becoming more objective and abstract as he has more experience, especially interactions with other people, who check his thoughts and conclusions.

Memory. The young child shows that she remembers by *doing* or acting out past experiences and representing them symbolically (making an action, object, or words stand for something else). When recalling an experience, the child is most likely to do so in terms of perceptions or sensory images. For example, five-year-olds used more sensory imagery and adults used more conceptual imagery in a test of remembering similar sentences [46]. Bruner [12, pp. 316–318] describes the process as *iconic representation,* meaning a mental picture or image. Older children and adults also use the three kinds of representation, *enactive, iconic,* and *symbolic.* As the preschool child matures she increases her coordination and integration of the different modes of representation.

Memories depend upon the context in which the experience occurred, the way in which experiences were processed in the first place, and processes of retrieval Selection of experience begins with what the child attends to and what she perceives. Then her performance is influenced by her modes of attending and searching, her level of conceptualizing, her capacities for extracting meaning, her awareness of strategies for memorizing, and her possession of strategies. As for awareness of memorizing and planfulness in trying to do so, the preschool child has little or none. Left to her own devices, memories are laid down quite spontaneously, as by-products of actions and experiences. She can, however, be helped to remember more than she does by her own spontaneous actions. A parent, teacher, older sibling, or psychological experimenter can improve the young child's memory by directing her attention, organizing material, and rehearsing in ways appropriate to the particular capacities of the child.

Capabilities. Children between the ages of 2 years, 9 months and 4 years, 4 months were tested for *recognition memory*. The experimenter showed the children small, attractive objects and later showed the same objects among a group of new ones. The younger children proved to be very capable in recognition memory, getting 81 per cent of the answers right. The older children did even better, with 92 per cent correct. The experiment demonstrated that before 3 years of age, children are already excellent in recognition memory, but that some development takes place during the next year and a half [68]. With children between 4 and 7, recognition memory for pictures was again found to increase with age. Steady increases in recognition were seen for both concrete and abstract pictures and concrete and abstract words, with concrete items being recognized more easily than abstract [10]. Another study on recognition of pictures and words showed 3-year-olds to be better in recognizing pictures than words [40].

A crucial development in recognition memory was found at 28 months, when children first recognized a stimulus that had changed since they last saw it. The transformation was from object to picture, as from a toy pig that had sat on top of the raisin reward, to a picture of a pig, placed on top of the raisin. Children over 28 months usually got the idea that the raisin was under the pig's picture; younger children did not. This experiment shows how memory performance depends upon the mental operations of the child. In this case, the essential action was to recognize the pig after it had undergone a change from toy to picture. The younger children could discriminate the toy pig from a toy horse and a toy cow, but did not see that a pig was a pig, even though transformed to a picture [86].

As everyone knows, *recall* is more difficult than recognition. The development of *recall memory* continues throughout childhood and adolescence. Preschool children can encode material to be remembered either as words or pictures and can switch from one mode to the other in retrieving. As might be expected, children were slower than adults on this task, especially in switching [91].

Aids to Memory. Even though the preschool child is not aware of himself as a thinker and memorizer, some of his spontaneous actions aid memorizing. Children as young as 3 labeled pictures when faced with a remembering task, but few below 3 did so [53]. Young children are notorious mimics, often repeating the words and actions of others. Although they are not rehearsing with a purpose in mind, a plan for remembering, they are performing the very actions that older children and adults do when they are trying to memorize [77]. Young children also frequently group objects in play. Even an infant will put a number of clothespins into a milk bottle or blocks into a basket. When an experimenter asked 108 2- to 4-year-olds to group colored shapes, only eight children made no response and the rest made groups of sorts, some even sorting on two dimensions [17].

Experiments have shown improvement in memory when adults help children in various ways. Training children to attend to relevant stimuli has been found helpful, since young children are usually not systematic in scanning and searching [92]. Labeling helped 4-year-olds, as well as older children, to recall pictures. In the same study, children 6 and older were also helped by grouping, but 4-year-olds were not [24]. Preschool children, as well as school-age children, recalled pictures better after both hearing and saying their names. The younger children were aided more by saying than by hearing [99]. Another experimenter found that when the names of pictures rhymed, 4-year-olds remembered the pictures better than when the names did not rhyme [51]. When words of similar meaning were grouped together, 3-year-olds remembered them better than words that were similar in sound or words that were not similar [52].

In schools for young children in China, repetition is used in singing, dancing, and going through the same routines. Enactive and iconic memories are thus stored along with symbolic memories, with different sensory modalities being activated [44]. The Montessori system also uses repetition in routines, as well as the child's own actions in concert with vivid sensory experiences in seeing, hearing, and touching. A parent gives help in remembering when he holds Jane or Jim on his lap and reads Mother Goose. The young child learns to repeat the verses just from hearing the rhyme and rhythm, seeing the pictures, and perhaps being rocked in the same tempo. Different cultures, schools, and families put their own particular emphases on memory aids for children.

Play

Play cuts across cognitive, imaginative, and motor activities, using them all and weaving them together. After a period of free play with a collection of objects, children were more able to respond to questions about the uses of the objects [16]. Through playful activity, it is thought, the children organized experiences and cognitive abilities in such a way that they could generate a variety of ideas. Play facilitated cognitive, imaginative, and adaptive behavior.

Sutton-Smith brings together three theories of play that explain its functions [88]. First, the child consolidates operations already developed in intelligent activity. (The same point could be made for motor activities being consolidated into smoother movements.) Second, play is used for exploring boundaries of competencies that are being developed. The child tries out all sorts of actions and combinations to find what he can do and what he cannot, what works and what does not. Third, competencies are combined into new organizations. In the discussion of imagination that follows, many of the activities are play, as well as imaginative behavior.

EDWARD C. DEVEREUX

Imagination

Adults look wistfully at young children's original interpretations of common-place events, their fresh, bright paintings, poetry, and freewheeling dramatics. Almost every adult has at least a fleeting memory of being that kind of person himself. "Every child an artist." "The magic years." "The golden years of child-hood." What happens to imagination?

Imagination takes many forms as it serves children in pleasure seeking, self-expression, exploration, problem solving, and integration of experience. Socio-dramatic play is described in the next chapter, as a contributor to social and emotional development. This section deals with the functions of imagination in its various contexts and forms.

IMAGINATION AS PART OF THE SENSE OF INITIATIVE

Having developed a firm sense of autonomy and a consequent concept of him-self as a person, the child wants to find out what he can *do*. To this end, he explores the world through his senses, through thinking and reasoning, and through imagination. In most situations, of course, these three instruments of exploration are combined. The essential part played by imagination, however, is probably least understood and appreciated. Through imagination, the young child tries on the roles of the important people in his world, the people who do things that he might some day do. Most vital of all are the roles of his parents, and these are the parts he plays first and most often, especially the part of the parent of the same sex. The child imagines being and/or replacing the parent of the same sex. In doing so, he imitates some of the parent's behavior and thinking, including his standards and goals. His own conscience develops through this activity, modeled upon the parent's, encouraged by his desire to be the parent. Gradually, through interaction with both parents, the youngster faces the facts that he can neither be nor replace his parent and that he himself can one day be a parent through growing up and behaving in grown-up ways. He is continually fascinated by the exploration of adult roles, which he does first and foremost through dramatic play, but also through literature and fantasy and even through dancing, painting, and other creative media.

Guilt is a necessary product of the developing sense of initiative, as the child changes from a simple pleasure-seeker to a complex self-regulator. Erikson [21, p. 256] expresses it thus:

> Here the most fateful split and transformation in the emotional power-house occurs, a split between potential human glory and potential total destruction. For here the child becomes forever divided in himself. The instinct fragments which before had enhanced the growth of his infantile body and mind now become divided into an infantile set which perpetuates the exuberance of growth potentials, and a parental set which supports and increases self-observation, self-guidance and self-punishment.

Through imagination, the child appeases and allays some of the conflicts that arise between these two parts of himself, the part that desires and the part that controls (the conscience). When his conscience punishes him too severely with guilt, he can ease the load through imagination. Not only does expression through some creative medium make him feel better; it is a way of solving problems. Imagination is also a powerful means of pushing aggressively out into the world and incorporating some of it into himself.

If life's problems are solved satisfactorily during the years when imagination predominates, then a residue of imaginative activity and a resource of initiative remain, to enliven, sparkle, inspire, and push throughout the rest of life. Such a person will get fresh ideas and will not be afraid to experiment with them. Even though he has attained objectivity, his thinking and feeling will be so flexible that he will be able to take off on flights of imagination. Both creativity and true recreation have their roots in imaginative play.

IMAGINATON AS A PART OF INTELLECTUAL DEVELOPMENT

In its simplest form, imagining consists of representing some part of outer reality by an inner image. Without the ability to use images as representations, man would forever stay in the sensorimotor stage of intellectual development. The first indications of imitative and imaginative play occur in babies during the final period of the sensorimotor stage, when the child imitates his own past actions in very simple, concrete ways. Thus, he shows that he has mental images of these actions. For instance, he pretends to go to sleep, curling up in the doll bed or on a pillow, shutting his eyes momentarily. He pretends to drink out of a cup and to eat from a plate. Thus, the first objects used for pretending are real pillows or cups. The pretending is in the use of them. The child makes one transformation. The next step in maturity of pretending is to pretend that another object is a pillow or a cup. For example, the child pretends to drink from a round block. He is making two transformations. Use of transformations in pretending was examined in children between 22 and 27 months [22]. The examiner encouraged a child first to use a cup to feed a horse, then to pretend feeding with objects that were neither horselike nor cuplike. As more transformations were required, there was a steady decrease in the number of children who were able to pretend. The experiment suggests that as children of this age mature, they grow more capable of subordinating the characteristics of the immediate environment to mental representations. When a toddler is playing in a sandbox, he may pretend to eat from a dish filled with sand and then take a real lick of sand. The action could be explained as requiring more difficult transformations than he was able to make. Development in pretending is rapid. By around 4, children sustain long episodes of pretend play that require many transformations.

Piaget stresses the role of symbolic games in development during the preconceptual period [70]. The transition from the sensorimotor period to preconceptual is marked by using symbolic patterns with new objects. Jacqueline, having pretended to sleep and pretended to cry, made her toys sleep and cry. Later she pretended to play with a cousin (who was not there) and then to be the cousin. Symbolic play represents experiences the child has had and the meaning that they have for him. It also can be what the child wants life to be. Egocentric, the child becomes submerged in action, loses awareness of himself as separate from the play, and lives in the role that he is dramatizing. The very act of living in that other role, however, leads him away from egocentrism, because it lets him see and feel how it is to be that other person or dog or airplane. As mental growth continues through the preconceptual stage, through symbolic play as well as other experiences, egocentrism gives way to objectivity. Piaget calls imaginative play "the purest form of egocentric and symbolic thought" [70, p. 127]. Symbols, he says, are needed as long as egocentric action prevails, since ready-made language is inadequate for the child's purposes. Language, being the product of society, cannot express all the experience and needs of the individual child, nor can the child master the language enough to serve him very flexibly.

TYPES OF IMAGINATIVE PLAY

The major forms of imaginative expression in early childhood are discussed in this section. Anyone who works with young children needs to know a great deal about the development and guidance of imagination. The following comments are intended only as an introduction to the topic.

Fantasy. Everyone does some thinking that is undirected, free, somewhat symbolic, and difficult or impossible to put into words. Fantasy serves pleasure rather than being directed toward reality or practical issues. Even so, it often produces solutions to problems. Sometimes it is called daydreaming. Fantasy, imaginative thinking, and symbolic thinking all refer essentially to this kind of behavior. Since people engaging in fantasy are not paying attention to the lesson that may be in progress, teachers have traditionally looked upon daydreaming with disfavor. Research in children's thinking shows, however, that fantasy has an essential role to play. Through her studies on imagination in Australian and English children, Griffiths [29] came to see fantasy and symbolic thinking as useful and adaptive ways of coping with life's problems. Instead of being a waste of time, a blank, or a pursuit of pleasure, imagination is a way of dealing with reality that is particularly appropriate for the young child. He can, of course, direct his thoughts to a limited extent, but this free-reining, personal, inner method of symbolic play is his natural medium of action. He makes objective contact with reality and then employs fantasy [29, p. 174].

> Like those simple animalculae that stretch out long pseudopodia into surrounding water in search of food, retiring afterward into a state of apparent passivity while digestion takes place, so does the child seek experience, and, having come into contact with reality in some form, retires within himself to understand and consolidate what he has acquired. He cannot tackle a problem all at once, immediately, even such problems as seem insignificant to us. This is surely the meaning of childhood; time is needed for adaptation.

Griffiths conducted a series of 20 interviews with each of 50 5-year-olds in situations where the child played freely with drawing materials and was encouraged to say anything he wished. Inkblots and an imagery test were used in addition to the recording of what the child said. For the first few days, comments were controlled and reality-adapted. After three or four days, nearly all children revealed evidence of fantasy. At first, items appeared scattered and chaotic in arrangement, but gradually the elements were linked, themes emerged, and the whole content became complex and closely knit. The whole was not static, but constantly developing in relation to the child's problems and experiences [29, pp. 14–31]. Through fantasy, the child moved from a personal, subjective, and egocentric point of view to a more socialized and objective attitude.

Fantasy appears in the spontaneous stories that children tell. A large number of stories, collected from preschool children, contributed to a study of fantasy [26]. Age trends showed increasing length, complexity, and expansion, along with increasing use of fantasy. A 2-year-old boy's story was: "Tractor fall down boom. Fall right down and bust his head off. And he run, run, run" [26, p. 31]. A typical story by 5-year-olds took from half a page to a page.

Sex differences were revealed. Boys seemed to be more intrusive and active and to use more themes of aggression, greater variety of characters, more objects of transportation, objects of nature, and other objects. Girls' stories were more intensive, detailed, involved with feeling, people, the domestic, the here and now. Compare the previous story of the 2-year-old with the following one from a 2-year-old girl: "Once upon a time there was a little girl and she hurt herself. And her mommy came here and she kissed her and made her better" [26, p. 39].

Sometimes one story will reveal progress in solution of emotional problems. Four-year-old Susan used the following tale with which to struggle symbolically with confusion, fear, good, and bad:

> Once Susan was in a theater seeing a grown-up movie. The lady who was giving the movie said, "Our magic fairy who is asleep will have to come out." And so the magic fairy woke up and came out. She chased everybody down the stairs and made everybody dance down the stairs. She chased me

down the stairs. When we went out, she spoke to each person as they went out the door and I do not know what she said to the other people, but she said this to me, "You did dance down the stairs but you did not like it." She said that she'd go back in the building and for me to stay there.

She chased me in front of the first car parked outside the theater. Then I started to run up across the bridge as quietly as I could. Then I just had time to sneak into a house and hide. When the good fairy came up, pat-a-pat, pat-a-pat, making a funny pat-a-pat, pat-a-pat, pat-a-pat noise. So I just had time to sneak up into my own house on Giles St. and lock the door when the good fairy came up and went ding-dong, ding-dong on my door bell. I would not open it or Mummy or Daddy or my sister, so the fairy could not get in.

Then the fairy went up and down, flying on top of my roof, for she thought that my house would burn down if she did. But it did not. There was a good fairy inside my house. And she, the good fairy, would not let my house burn down, for she took away the bad fairy's wand, and would not return it. So the bad fairy died, because fairies die when their wands are taken away. And so that was the end of the bad fairy and we all lived happily ever after.

Often the expression of fears and problems helps to minimize them. Adults know how much it helps to talk to a friend about a bad experience, past or anticipated. Young children often do not know exactly what is bothering them, or if they do, they cannot express it straightforwardly. To express it in a story or poem or in another artistic medium can relieve tension, clarify the trouble, and help the youngster to find solutions.

Sometimes hostility shows through the symbols, even when the comment is understood by all to be imaginary and not a real threat. This 5-year-old shows a certain flair for creative imagery, violent as his product is:

I'll push you out the window and you'll make a mess on the pavement and my Daddy will scrape you up with a knife and spread you on bread and eat you. Then he'll vomit you up.

Use of fantasy, estimated from interviews with preschool children, was correlated with scores on intelligence tests and creativity tests [39]. Both social and solitary fantasy were related to performance on the Peabody vocabulary test, but only social fantasy was related to the other measures.

Symbolism. The child's fears and problems are often symbolized by the toys he chooses and by the content of his imaginative games. Discovering an analogy between two objects and situations, he invests one as a symbol for the other. The story of 5-year-old Joyce illustrates this process [29, pp. 141–148]. Joyce and Dorothy were sisters whose father had died two years earlier. More recently, two neighbor children had died, one of them being their playmate, Dorothy L. Joyce sometimes went on errands for Dorothy L.'s mother, who called Joyce "my little girl" and sometimes acted as though Joyce had taken Dorothy L.'s place. Joyce was rivalrous with her sister Dorothy, a delicate child who received fussing and petting from their parents. Joyce had a china doll which was to her a little girl, and, after Dorothy L.'s death, a dead little girl. When telling the thoughts that came into her mind during a series of play interviews, Joyce disclosed that Dorothy L.'s mother had allowed her to see the dead child in her coffin, where "she was like a china doll." Shortly after this time, sister Dorothy became ill and had to go to the hospital. At this point, her daddy and Dorothy L. disappeared from Joyce's dreams and conversation. She became afraid of her china doll. Instead of taking it to bed with her, she put it on a chair. Waking in the night, she wanted to take the doll into bed, but was afraid that a mouse might get her. "They might get my dolly and get her eyes out with their claws."

Thus, Joyce pushed away the reality of her father's death and her sister's frightening disappearance, centering her fears upon an object, the doll, which she used to symbolize all these disturbing occurrences. The doll had formerly been a comforting object. She was still dealing with that object in the daytime, although not at night, when fears were most oppressive. Perhaps she was hanging onto the possibility of getting control of the whole terrifying situation through the doll, which served as such a powerful symbol.

Summarizing the functions of symbolic thinking or fantasy in the life of the child, Griffiths [29, p. 187] makes several points: Fantasy is the normal means of problem solving. Problems are attacked indirectly, often symbolically. The child is only vaguely aware of what he is trying to do. The problem is solved piecemeal, through a series of solutions. The process results in both acquisition of information and a change of attitude. The change of attitude is from personal and egocentric toward socialized and objective.

IMAGINARY COMPANIONS

Some young children create companions for themselves, often but not always, in the form of child playmates. The companion represents a creative act by the child who made it. Research on creative adolescents indicates that producers in literary fields were more likely than other people to have had imaginary companions during their childhoods [81].

Questionnaires about imaginary companions were completed by parents of 228 preschool children [55]. Equal percentages of boys and girls, 28 per cent of the total group, had one or more imaginary playmates. Firstborn children and children with younger siblings were more frequent among the children found to have imaginary companions, suggesting that loneliness may have prompted the creation. Further evidence for this notion is that children rarely played with imaginary companions when they had opportunities to play with real children. Outstanding characteristics of children with imaginary playmates were: they initiated more play on their own and engrossed themselves in it; they engaged in more different activities with household members; boys were more capable (than boys without imaginary playmates) of talking and interacting with adults. Half of the children had just one imaginary playmate; a quarter had two. Boys created companions in the ratio 3.5 boys to one girl; girls created 1.3 girls to one boy. Most of the parents (62 per cent) thought that the imaginary playmate was good for their child. Only 4 per cent of the parents thought that the playmate had a harmful effect.

HUMOR

Humor is an intellectual process that reduces anxiety. Young children usually laugh after experiencing heightened tension or arousal along with a judgment that the situation is safe or all right [79]. Three main types of humor were derived from observations of nursery school children's participation in humorous events [30]. The definition of humor events included surprising or unexpected events at which children smiled or laughed, and incongruous or inappropriate behavior that seemed to be intentional. The three main types of humor were *responsive, productive,* and *hostile.* Responsive humor included responses to events, people, statements, stories, songs, and animals. Examples were finding a "baby peanut" in a shell, someone's falling over a chair, and a funny story. Productive humor included silliness and clowning, teasing, word play, absurd creations, and displacement of injury to self-esteem. Hostile humor included humorous threats or attacks, making fun of someone else, and rebellion against authority. Productive humor was most common. Boys displayed more productive and hostile humor than girls; girls showed more responsive humor than boys. The most frequent type of responsive humor was response to events; the most frequent types of productive humor were silliness and absurdity. There was no evidence for a generalized trait that could be called sense of humor. In the nursery school, situations that elicited most productive humor were unstructured, such as free play and playing with blocks. Responsive humor occurred more often when the situation allowed for unexpected events.

What is funny to a preschool child is usually not very funny to an adult. Children's jokes include falling down, falling apart and growing together, getting lost and found, being hurt and getting well, toilet accidents or deliberate excretions, using inappropriate names, and saying forbidden words. Underlying such humor are children's envy of adult size, power, and privileges; worry over the wholeness and safety of their bodies; frightening aggressive impulses, and resentment of adult control in the face of their own striving for autonomy.

MUSIC AND DANCE

Creativity exists both in performance and in enjoying the music and dancing of others. In these areas, as in other parts of the preschool child's experience, exploration is vital. A rich environment offers opportunities to experiment with sound and gesture and with putting them together. Infants enjoy and respond to songs. By age 2, the child who has had some experience with singing will listen to others and will sing spontaneously as he plays. He likes action songs, in which he responds to words with gestures. He joins in with a few words as others sing. His first efforts to sing with a group will probably not be well coordinated, but they soon lead to his being able to follow along with others' singing. Next he sings alone. Soon he recognizes and asks for certain songs and recognizes various pieces of music [48, p. 377]. Creative expression flows when the few necessary facilities are present—a chance to listen; a chance to sing; the simplest of instruments to play; a group with whom to play, sing, and dance; experience to play, sing, and dance about. In a simpler society, a child can grow into the music and dance of his parents, watching, imitating, being taken through the motions, and joining in adult dances and music groups when he is sufficiently grown up. In complex Western culture, it often takes an adult with special skill and understanding to appreciate and facilitate the young child's creations in music and dance. Such a teacher develops the cognitive processes basic to the child's understanding and appreciation, as well as the feeling aspects [3, pp. 20–27]. As one student of the dance has said,

THE MERRILL-PALMER INSTITUTE. PHOTO BY DONNA J. HARRIS.

"A child cheerfully undertakes a multiple career as singer, instrumentalist, actor, and dancer. In what we call 'play,' he dramatizes poetry and makes it blood-brother to song" [57, p. 5].

In the machine age many children see little of rhythmic muscular activity that seems to them worth imitating. In contrast, primitive children experience the rhythms of weaving, grinding, and chopping. In a preschool day camp dancing grew out of the small happenings of every day: a Moon Time Dance when the

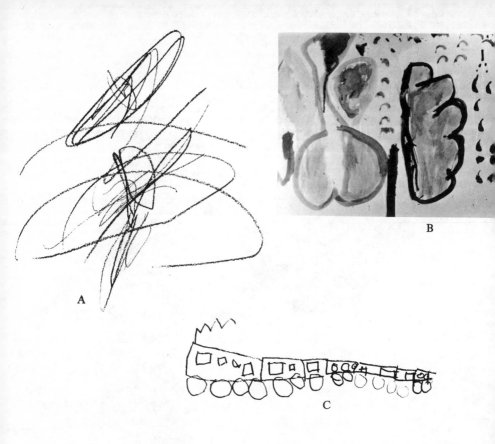

Figure 2-1. Development of graphic representation.
A. Scribble
B. Design
C. Pictorial, using circles and rectangles
D. Pictorial

Figure 2-2. Development of representation of human form between the ages of three and seven years.

children noticed the moon in the daytime sky, The Sunflower Dance, created by a 4-year-old and 2-year-old who found sunflowers, The Chocolate Sellers, dances of fears, of wonder of God, of cooking [19]. The teacher found that the higher the emotional content in the thought expressed, the more the child seemed to need rhythmic action to express it. With young children, there was rarely dancing without singing or rhythmic language.

With music, as well as dance, young children have potentiality for expression and enjoyment, perhaps even more than that of the average adult. It has been shown that music produces an emotional response in people and a more pronounced response in children than in adults, as measured by the galvanic skin response [101].

CREATIVE MATERIALS

Paint, clay, blocks, and other materials offer the same types of benefits that the child gets from fantasy, dramatic play, and creative language—increased understanding of the world and his relation to it, expression and understanding of his questions and problems, release of emotional tension, satisfaction from creating beauty and order. In fact, some of the most creative programs for children encourage the use of all forms of artistic expression and enjoyment in relation with one another. Emotionally disturbed children indicate in their artistic expression some of their malaise. Psychology students and professors, with no previous training in understanding children's art, were able to do significantly better than chance in matching paintings to personality descriptions [85]. The judges also separated the paintings of disturbed children from those of normal children. Since the judges could not tell how they did it, the investigators suggest an unidentified intuitive process at work.

When a child first encounters paint, clay, or any other new material, he has to explore it, to find out what it is like and what he can do with it. (Not only children. Watch an African graduate student in the first snowfall of the North American winter!) Set-up and limits are important here—"paint goes on the paper," "blocks are not to throw," "hold the saw this way."

In the graphic arts, a series of stages can be identified. The stages are illustrated in Figures 2-1 and 2-2. Each child goes through these stages at approximately these ages:

1. *Scribbling, from 1 to 3 years.* During the first quarter of the second year, a baby will make marks with a crayon on a paper, after a demonstration or encouragement to do so. By 18 months, he will scribble spontaneously. Even if paper and crayons are not given, 2-year-olds will make marks in the sand, on a sidewalk, or wall. The young child shows great interest in what he has made. He tries out different types of strokes and placements [41].
2. *Shape and design.* From 2 to 5 years. The child uses the lines that he has developed through his scribbling and makes shapes and designs from them. Even though he cannot write, the average kindergartner can tell printed characters from scribbling [25]. In a kindergarten of high socioeconomic status, 75 per cent of the children could distinguish cursive writing from scribbling. When children are making shapes and designs, they do so for the pleasure of

making them and not to represent something. A child develops his own style and preferences while discovering how to make more complex designs.

3. *Pictorial, from age 4 onward.* Now the child uses his lines, shapes, and designs to represent reality. Drawings of people are usually the first recognizable pictures. All over the world, children make their early drawings in the same ways. Their pictures of people, houses, trees, suns, boats, trains, and cars give little hint as to whether the young artists were American, Scottish, or Indonesian.

Language

Philosophers and scientists have long marveled over the origins of language in the species and in the individual. How can it be that every normal child growing up in a language environment learns to talk? The milestones of language acquisition follow a regular sequence that is linked in time with milestones of motor development [50]. Thus language, like motor development, has a strong maturational base. According to Chomsky, there is a universal grammar, or principles of language, that has evolved as part of human nature and is present in every human being [14]. The child uses these principles to learn his own language. This idea is consistent with the finding that infants are especially attuned to human sound patterns. Piaget and others believe that language development follows and depends upon conceptual development [7, 11, 73]. There is some difference of opinion as to whether children learn language largely through their own efforts or whether direct teaching plays an essential role. No matter where the emphasis lies, the child must hear language if he is to operate on it or be taught by it. In White's extensive study of competency, the best developing children were exposed to considerably more live language, directed toward the subject [97].

This little girl hears and produces language when she plays telephoning with her father.

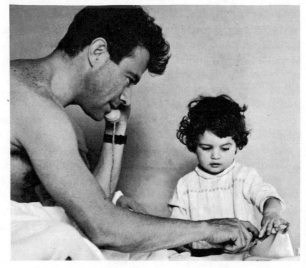

DALU JONES

Language is remarkable in that young children seem to learn it so easily although adults have difficulty in learning a foreign language and rarely, if ever, learn to speak it perfectly. Young children can even learn two or more languages perfectly. Another extraordinary feature of language is that any speaker can create a new sentence. And when one person says something different from all statements by previous speakers, an ordinary listener knows what he means. Language is creative; everyone uses language creatively. At the same time, language is governed by rules. The rules somehow allow for generating an infinite number of statements.

USES OF LANGUAGE

The ways in which children use language are discussed in reference to communications with others and to language used with the self.

Interpersonal Communication. Young children use gestures, such as pointing, for communicating, even when they are also able to use words. Gestures often work quite well when the object of the communication can be seen. Speech is needed when simply pointing to an object is not enough to express the meaning that the child wants to communicate [6].

When children first put words together, which they do at the end of the sensorimotor period, they talk about the sensorimotor world [11]. In a large number of languages studied by Brown, the first stage of utterance contains the same sorts of relations and propositions. That is, toddlers everywhere talk about the same subject matter. Examples include *that ball, more ball, all gone ball, Daddy chair, go store, big house,* and *Daddy hit.* Thus, they tell about things existing, disappearing, recurring, being owned or possessed, being located, and being acted upon.

As children develop during the years between infancy and school age, the meaning and content of the language change, keeping pace with the children's personal growth and developing knowledge and understanding of the world. The content, meaning, and purposes of spontaneous speech has been traced in 100 children between 2 and 5 in a nursery school setting [80]. Three groups of subjects were studied, advantaged white, advantaged black, and disadvantaged black. Analysis of 2,000 statements yielded nine categories of motives, grouped into personal, social, and other. Two-year-olds used these categories: *Reporting,* "I have new shoes."; "Look at the cement mixer."; *desire,* "Can I have some?"; *possession rights,* "That's my wagon."; "Me too."; "I have new shoes, too."; *learning statements,* "How does this go?"

Several age trends appeared. Younger children directed more comments to adults than did older children; older children directed more comments to other children than did younger children. The age trend, therefore, was to talk less to adults and more to other children. Self-differentiation increased with age, showing a marked increase at age 3, the time of onset of the sense of initiative in Erikson's scheme. At this point, children made many more ego-enhancing comments, including boasting, teasing, denigrating others, and assuming the teacher-role. "When I grow up, I'm going to be a pilot." "Look at my big house."

Social motives also change with age, with a marked change at 3 or 3½. Two-year-olds made many self-referring statements of an immature category. "Me too."

"I listen to Batman, too." Statements of joining and collaborating, showing more social maturity, increased with age. "Let's play house." "Give me some more, mommy; stop that, baby." By 4 or 5, children began to adapt their speech much more to the needs of the listener. Thus, the children's spontaneous remarks showed increasing verbal interaction with self–other differentiation.

Intrapersonal. Children often use language for noncommunicative purposes. Only 20 per cent of one child's comments were communicative when his speech was recorded in normal play situations between the ages of 21 and 27 months [13]. Language as a means of *self-control* is discussed in the next chapter. *Concept formation, problem solving,* and *memorizing* can also be carried on with the assistance of language. Other functions include *play* and *pleasure seeking.*

Psychologists are not agreed as to whether language is necessary for certain concept formations. However, there is evidence that language helps in discrimination learning problems. For example, in reversal-shift problems, a child learns to choose a certain color, shape, or size. Then the right answer is changed and he has to learn black instead of white, circle instead of triangle, or small instead of big. The shift is in the same dimension. Few children under 7 can make such a shift, but most children over 7 can do so [43]. The difference is thought to be in the use of verbal mediation. The older children say to themselves "Color is what counts. Now white is right instead of black."

Although children and nonhuman primates can form visual concepts without verbal labels, they seem to be unable to form temporal concepts without verbal labels [6]. For example, preschool children, not using labels, easily distinguished between one and two circles or other objects, but not between one and two flashes of light. Poor ability to deal with time sequences has also been found in older children with language deficiencies. It seems that visual imagery is stronger and more lasting than temporal imagery. Thus, verbal mediation would play a larger, more essential role in the formation of time concepts.

Verbal labeling was helpful to 3- and 4-year-olds in a memorizing task [66]. When lower-class children were helped to use a verbal strategy, they did better on the memory tasks.

Children play with sounds and words, creating beauty and pleasure for themselves and unintentionally delighting adults who overhear them. They are especially likely to play with words and sounds while in their cribs before going to sleep [85a]. Such was the case with Anthony, whose linguist mother recorded his presleep utterances [95]. Thus Anthony plays with sounds, ". . . in a pretty box . . . and cakes . . . what a sticks for cakes . . . for the click."

Ellen enjoys rhythm and imagery as she chants her moon song.

Crescent, crescent, crescent, crescent,
Crescent goes to sleep, crescent wakes up.
Ballie, ballie, ballie, ballie,
Ballie goes to sleep, ballie wakes up.

Jean creates a word picture to express her delight in a snowstorm.

The snowflakes are shaking hands.
It's like a white dress outside.

Receptive language, or hearing what others say, affords similar pleasures in sound play, rhythm, and imagery and equips children with devices to produce more pleasure for themselves. Children enjoy hearing the traditional nursery rhymes and the modern Dr. Seuss. They repeat satisfying passages, lingering over the intriguing bustard who only eats custard with sauce made of mustard. They sing songs and play records that give them pleasure through sound.

ACQUISITION OF LANGUAGE

A child starts with an inherited potential for acquiring language that is a part of human nature. Any normal newborn can learn any language. However, individuals are not all the same in the potential that they bring to language learning. Tests of language skills in fraternal and identical twins indicate the heritability of ability to paraphrase, memory storage, and talkativeness [23]. Other language skills, not sampled in this research, may well be heritable. (Heritability is discussed in Chapter 5.)

Rules of Language. In acquiring language, the child internalizes "a system of rules that relate sound and meaning in a particular way" [14]. The child cannot state the rules, any more than an older child can explain the rules for balancing a bicycle. She just operates according to the rules. Not even sophisticated adults can verbalize all the rules for speaking their own language correctly. Often a person knows that a statement is not exactly right and she can correct it but cannot state the rule that guided her.

Rules of language do not emerge all at once. Different rules are acquired at various stages of language development. The first rules are simple ones. Some of the first rules differ from those governing adult speech. The child modifies rules to be more like adult rules as she analyzes the language on more complex levels and as she has new experiences that require revision of the rules she already has. One of the early rules seems to be that the subject goes before the verb.

The first sentences have been called *telegraphic speech,* because they include only words carrying essential meaning. In comments such as "See doggie," "Mommy come home," and "Go car," only words carrying necessary information are used. However, these sentences can be understood, because the order of the words is correct. Even though the child reduces sentences to the barest essentials, he usually preserves the word order, an extremely important dimension of English grammar. When passive sentences are first encountered, they are often understood in terms of the order of an active sentence. For instance, 3-year-olds, when asked to show the picture indicating "the cat is chased by the dog," would point to the picture of the cat chasing the dog [4]. This finding indicates that syntax (order) is more important than form to the young child. This finding is not unexpected for speakers of English, a language in which syntax is very important. It is surprising, however, to find that Russian children also order their first two-word sentences strictly, even though Russian is a heavily inflected language, and word order is not so important as it is in English [84]. In fact, it seems to be universal that the subject precedes the object in the dominant actor-action form of a language.

When a rule is first grasped, it may be applied too widely. "I goed out and bringed my truck in." The rule is to make the past tense by adding *ed,* but there are exceptions! "He fixed it hisself." What could be more logical when all the other reflexive pronouns are made by combining the possessive pronoun with self? Myself. Yourself. Herself. In saying "hisself," the child is applying a rule and does not yet know about the exception. Likewise, the rule for forming plurals, the addition of *s,* is first applied to exceptional words, as well as regular ones, producing *mans, mouses,* and *gooses.*

Stages of Language Development. A useful concept in describing and studying language is the MLU, or mean length of utterance. The length of utterance, found by counting the number of morphemes, is the smallest unit of speech that conveys meaning. It may be a word or a part of a word, such as a prefix or suffix. *Eating* has two morphemes; *I want books* has four. The MLU is the average length of utterance. When the average length of utterance (MLU) is between one and two, occasional utterances are as long as seven morphemes [1]. In linguistic research, *stage* is defined by MLU. The first stage is the time when the MLU is between one and two. Four more stages are defined, by adding .50 increments to the MLU, starting with Stage 1 defined as MLU two. Children of the same MLU, no matter how different their ages, are similar in the grammatical forms they use.

Just as all children talk about the same experiences (sensorimotor) in Stage 1, so they form similar constructions. They first express two-term relations of occurrence, disappearance, recurrence, possession, location, and action. By putting two words in order, they can express all of these meanings. When the MLU reaches 1.50, three-term relations are expressed. The statement "Adam hit ball" looks as though two of the first type (two-term) had been strung together, with the one redundant word deleted [11]. Adam hit + (hit) ball = Adam hit ball. Four-term relations are used near the end of Stage 1.

Sequences in Stage 2 have been studied only for American children [11]. The addition of 14 functional morphemes occurs in an almost invariant sequence. These morphemes include noun and verb inflections, the copula *be,* the progressive auxiliary *be,* prepositions *in* and *on,* and articles *a* and *the.* These forms are acquired gradually.

A later sequence occurs in tag questions, which are not fully formed until after Stage 5, or even later [11]. *Won't you?* is a tag question in "You'll play with me, won't you?" "Henry likes to swim, doesn't he?" *Doesn't he* is a tag question. In order to ask such a question, the subject must be transformed into a pronoun and a negative constructed, which requires changing the order. All this takes considerable grammatical knowledge. Typical of many foreign speakers, a friend of ours always says, "Isn't it?" for a tag question, because the construction of a proper tag is beyond her grammatical competence.

Searching Meanings of Words. Although it is not hard to see how a child comes to connect concrete objects and actions with words that stand for them, other words must be much more difficult. The words *why* and *how* are examples of words that require high levels of abstraction [6]. How can the child find out what they mean? Interchanges with mature speakers are essential. It seems likely that the child learns the meaning of *why* by asking many *why* questions and *how* by repeatedly asking *how.* . . . By asking all sorts of questions using these terms, she learns what questions are acceptable and what are not. In response to "That's a nice fire," she asks "Why?". When the adult says, "I don't know why," the child learns that she did not use *why* adequately. So she tries it in another context. This explanation would suggest that when young children ask many questions, they are not necessarily looking for attention or even information, but for the meaning in language.

White pictures the young child as an active searcher for meaning, instigating many but not all interchanges with the mother [98]. The competent child turns often to his mother (or other adult or older child) who responds to his question or need of the moment, sometimes adding an interesting related idea. Thus a search for meaning and understanding includes using adults as resources.

Imitation. Children imitate the speech of their parents and others, including the investigators in a language study [42]. Imitation was most frequent when the MLU was two, more frequent than at MLUs of one and three. A comparison between the children's free speech and spontaneous imitations did include some grammatical features that had not previously been used in free speech. It could not be determined if the children could then use that grammatical feature as part of their own spontaneous speech. It may be that the imitation simply served to hold the utterance in the child's mind while she tried to form a hypothesis about the rule involved.

Practice. The repetitious utterances of young children, especially the recorded presleep utterances of Anthony and his brothers, give the impression that young children practice sounds, words, and grammar [95]. Some of Anthony's systematic manipulations of language resembled grammars and drills written for the study of a foreign language. The following excerpt is an exercise in noun substitution: "What color—what color blanket—what color mop—what color glass." Noun modifiers are explored in this sequence: "There's a hat—there's another—there's hat—there's another hat—that's a hat." A verb substitution pattern occurred thus: "Go get coffiee—go buy some coffee." Negatives are practiced: "Like it—don't like it—like it daddy." He holds a question-and-answer dialogue with himself: "There is the light—where is the light—here is the light." Some of Anthony's verbalizations have a large amount of sound play in them, such as: "Train— Anthony can see the plane—plane—plane—see bubble—bubble's here—bubbles —flowers—bed flowers." Sometimes he comments on his achievements: "One two three four—one two—one two three four—one two three—Anthony counting— good boy you—one two three."

Teaching. As the child responds to his mother's speech, the mother is aided in fitting her speech to what the child can use and understand [82]. Mothers' behavior as teachers of language was analyzed in 20 mother-child pairs, where children were between 2 and 5 years old [59]. Mothers' behavior was related to children's in terms of complexity, indicating that mothers knew very well what their children could understand and that they adjusted their own utterances to the capabilities of their children. Mothers' language behavior was related more to child's MLU than to his age. Mothers' mean length of utterance was closely related to

STANLEY SUMMER

Reaching the end of the preoperational period, this boy is beginning to coordinate sound, visual symbols, and motor coordination.

the child's, exceeding the child's MLU but not his maximal length. Thus, a mother pushed her child to the utmost of his capacity. Some mothers did more pushing to capacity than did others. Mothers' more complex forms of interaction increased as their children's did. More mature child responses included describing plans, past experiences, own acts, and objects or events. As these behaviors increased, so mothers increased in answering questions, guiding child's actions, giving explanations, and describing objects or events. Mothers often used the opportunities of the moment for teaching. Other studies, especially White's longitudinal ones, bear witness to the mother's important influence as a teacher of language [98].

Intellectual Achievements during the Preoperational Period

The outstanding intellectual achievement of the preschool child is "the co-ordination of knowledge constructed from perception and action with the vocal symbols of language in representational competence" [37]. During these years, the child moves from being dominated by perceptions and wishes to having greater control over thinking. Rooted in personal experiences, concepts of classes, space, numbers, time, and causes gradually become more objective as experience and interactions with others are used for checking conclusions.

Tests of Intelligence and Achievement

Many tests of intelligence have been invented, each according to the concept of intelligence defined by its creator. Binet, who with Simon, developed the first standardized intelligence tests, considered three different capacities as constituting intelligence—the ability to understand directions, to maintain a mental set, and to correct one's own errors [61, p. 349]. Terman [89], whose revisions of Binet's tests have had the greatest influence on modern intelligence testing, thought of intelligence as the ability to think abstractly and use abstract symbols in solving problems. Thorndike [90], who accepted a concept of intelligence as comprising problem solving through use of abstract symbols, defined three dimensions of intelligence: altitude, breadth, and speed. Altitude referred to the difficulty of the problem, the more intelligent person being able to solve the more difficult problem; breadth meant the number of tasks a person could do; speed, of course, referred to how fast problems were solved. Thorndike considered altitude the most important of the three attributes of intelligence. Guilford [31] thinks of intelligence as consisting of many different abilities, possibly 120, about 80 of which are already known. He stresses creativity as a component of intelligence. Wechsler believes that intelligence must be defined in terms of values, of effectiveness, and worthwhileness of what human beings do [94].

As our discussion of intelligence tests in the school-age section shows, many people today are rejecting the use of these tests, because their results have been used to the disadvantage of some groups and individuals. It is possible to use a different type of test that assesses the child's achievements in terms of criteria for school readiness [37]. Educational plans for a child can be made accurately through the use of such tests. However, intelligence tests are used widely in child development research. They can be used to derive useful information about growth and relationships without using the results in reference to individual children. Many studies would not be understandable unless the student had some knowledge of the meaning of IQ, MA, and so on. We, therefore, include a brief section on intelligence tests.

MEASUREMENT OF INTELLIGENCE

Many tests can be used with preschool children. The Stanford-Binet test, a direct descendant of the original intelligence test of Binet and Simon, yields a single mental-age score, from which the intelligence quotient is computed [89].

The Wechsler Intelligence Scale for Children yields verbal and nonverbal scores [93] The Stanford-Binet and the Wechsler can also be used at older ages. Tests designed for the preschool period, such as the Merrill-Palmer test [87] and the Gesell test [45], tend to interest young children more, because they have more manipulative materials and offer more sensory stimulation. The Peabody Picture Vocabulary Test is widely used for screening, since it can be given quickly and does not require the child to speak [20] The McCarthy Scales of Children's Abilities gives a general cognitive index and also scores for verbal, quantitative, perceptual-performance, memory, and motor development [58].

Mental age (MA) is a construct conceived by Binet. A child's MA is found by comparing his test performance with the average performance of a large number of children. Binet gave a large number of tests to a large number of children, found the ages at which most children passed each test, and arranged the tests in order of difficulty. This procedure is essentially the one that has been followed in constructing intelligence tests since then. To show how the MA is found, take, for example, a child who passes the items passed by the average 8-year-old. The child's MA is 8. If his chronological age (CA) is also 8, then he is like the average child of his age. If, however, his CA is 6 he has done more than the average. If his CA is 10, he has done less.

Figure 2-3. Distribution of IQs of children tested in the standardization of the Stanford-Binet Test.

SOURCE: L. M. Terman and M. A. Merrill. *Stanford-Binet intelligence scale*. Boston: Houghton Mifflin Company, 1960. L. M. Terman and M. A. Merrill. *Measuring intelligence*. Boston: Houghton Mifflin Company, 1937.

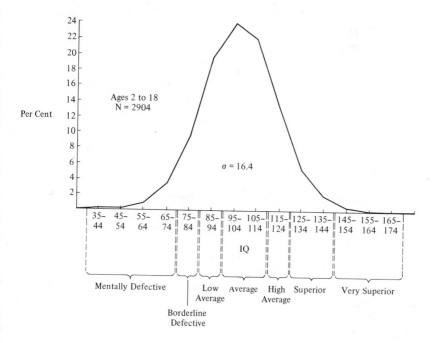

Intelligence quotient (IQ) is a construct originated by Stern, a German psychologist. IQ is a ratio of CA to MA, which has been found to be fairly constant. IQ is found by dividing MA by CA and multiplying by 100. 100MA/CA = IQ. Figure 2-3 shows the percentages of IQs occurring at different levels on the Stanford-Binet test.

IQ AS AN EXPRESSION OF RATE OF GROWTH

The intelligence quotient is a measuring of rate of growth in mental age, although the convention of multiplying by 100 obscures this fact. Tom, age 70 months, earns a score of 77 months of mental age. His average rate of mental growth throughout the whole of his 70 months is 1.1. For each month of CA he has achieved 1.1 month of MA. His IQ (100 × MA divided by CA) is 110. Margery, also age 70 months, earns a score of 63 months of mental age. Her mental growth has averaged .9 months for each month of CA. Her IQ is 90. If Tom and Margery continue to grow at their present rates, Tom's IQ will continue to be 110 and Margery's 90. Suppose, however, that each grows at the rate of one month of MA per month of CA for the coming year. Each will gain 12 months of MA. Tom's MA at the end of the year will be 89, his IQ, 108; Margery's MA will be 75, her IQ 91. The MA changes are large, but the IQ changes are small. At each test the resulting IQ expresses the average mental growth since birth.

IQ AS A MEASURE OF BRIGHTNESS

The common concept of IQ is as a measure of quality or strength of intelligence. The higher the IQ, the brighter the child and the more capable he is of doing good work at school. Tom, who has been growing at the rate of 1.1 months of mental age for each month of chronological age for 70 months, is brighter than Margery, who has been growing at an average rate of 0.9 MA months per chronological month. Jean, age 50 months, has been growing at the 1.1 rate and, therefore, has an IQ of 110. She is just as far above the average 50-month-old child as Tom is above the average child of 70 months. By the time Jean is 70 months old, if her mental growth continues at the same rate, her mental age will be 77 and her IQ will still be 110.

ERRORS OF MEASUREMENT

Errors are likely to affect any test through less-than-perfect presentation and scoring, through the subject's not performing at top capacity, and through poor conditions of testing, such as noise or discomforts. The standard error of measurement has been calculated for various ages and IQ ranges [89]. For practical purposes, *five* is the standard error. In interpreting any IQ, then, ±5 should be added to the figure. If Mary's measured IQ is 107, there are 68 chances in 100 that her "real" IQ lies between 102 and 112. There are 95 chances in 100 that Mary's IQ lies between 97 and 117.

The standard error must be used when comparing the IQs of two children and also when comparing two tests on one child. In the first case, the difference between IQs must be at least 10 before a real difference can be said to exist. When tests on the same child are compared, the difference between the two tests must be 10 or more before a real change in growth rate is indicated.

PREDICTING INTELLIGENCE

Tests done after age 3 are correlated with later tests, as shown by longitudinal studies in the United States and Sweden [36]. Data from two California studies shows correlation of 3-year tests with 5-year tests to be .58 for boys and .54 for girls. At ages 4 and 6, correlations were .60 for boys and .64 for girls. Tests done on the same children at adolescence and as adults in their 40s showed correlations in the .70s and .80s. Thus, intelligence tests have good predictive power for *groups,* and gain in power as children grow older. However, an *individual's* IQ cannot be predicted accurately. Radical changes in the environment produce large changes in IQ, especially if the events occur early in life. Class and ethnic differences in IQ have often been demonstrated. Present research is oriented to analyzing the specific reasons for these differences. For example, home environmental variables correlated with intelligence differently at different age levels and included a large number of characteristics [33]. This topic is discussed further in Chapter 4.

Summary

Cognitive development, language, and imagination are intimately related. Children seek sensory experience on which to operate, to enjoy, and to use in developmental processes.

The end of the period of sensorimotor development signals the beginning of the period of preoperational thought. The essential feature of this new period is representation by language. Actions and symbols also continue to serve representation. The child assimilates from the environment by fitting it into what he already knows. He accommodates by changing his schemas to fit aspects of the environment that cannot be assimilated. Egocentric in relation to both space and roles, the child progressively decenters with the acquisition of cognitive skills and knowledge. Perceptions dominate the young child's thinking, while little attention is paid to transformations. Thinking is unsocialized in that the child feels little pressure to square his thinking and conclusions with those of others.

In concept formation, development is from concrete to abstract. Concepts of class, time, space, quantity, number, and causality follow similar courses of development. Memory uses all available forms of representation: enactive, iconic, symbolic, and verbal. Recognition memory is excellent in preschool; recall memory improves throughout childhood and adolescence. Young children adopt some strategies to aid memory and make use of additional strategies offered to them. Strategies include labeling, rehearsing, grouping, and using a variety of sensory systems.

Play facilitates and integrates motor, cognitive, imaginative, creative, and social behaviors and abilities. Play also gives pleasure. Imagination, being an aspect of the developing sense of initiative, occurs in many different forms. Pretending and symbolism are early forms of representation. Fantasy, often pleasurable, is an important mode of dealing with emotions and problems in childhood. Some children create imaginary companions, probably as a solution to loneliness. Humor gives pleasure and reduces anxiety. Humor can be productive or hostile. Music and dance offer important modes of creativity and experience that differ from verbal and visual modes, enriching children's development. Creative materials give opportunities for sensory exploration and intellectual and emotional expression. Developmental sequences in their use have been identified.

Language emerges on a developmental timetable in all normal children in language environments. Human beings are especially sensitive to various features of language, seemingly extracting grammatical rules from what they hear. Language is used for communicating meaning to other people. Children talk about their own experiences, gradually differentiating self from others. Intrapersonal uses of language include self-control, concept formation, problem solving, memorizing, play, and pleasure seeking. Stages of language acquisition are defined by mean length of utterance (MLU), a measure that relates well to other measures of language development. Rules of grammar acquired early often fail to deal with irregularities. Children search for meaning in language, aided by responsive adults. Mothers fit their utterances to the level of language of their children. Children also imitate language and practice it.

Several intelligence tests can be used to measure IQs of young children. More specific tests may often be more useful than IQ tests for making plans for individual children. Intelligence tests are important research instruments.

References

1. Abravanel, E. How children combine vision and touch when perceiving the shape of objects. *Perception & Psychophysics*, 1972, **12**, 171–175.
2. Ames, L. B., and J. Learned. The development of verbalized space in the young child. *Journal of Genetic Psychology*, 1946, **68**, 97–125.
3. Aronoff, F. W. *Music and young children*. New York: Holt, Rinehart and Winston, Inc., 1969.
4. Bellugi-Klima, U. Language acquisition. Paper presented at the symposium, Cognitive studies and artificial intelligence research, Chicago: University of Chicago, 1969.
5. Berzonsky, M. D. A factor-analytic investigation of child animism. *Journal of Genetic Psychology*, 1973, **122**, 287–295.
6. Blank, M. Cognitive functions of language in the preschool years. *Developmental Psychology*, 1974, **10**, 229–245.
7. Bloom, L., P. Lightbown, and L. Hood. Structure and variation in child language. *Monographs of the Society for Research in Child Development*, 1975, **40**:2.
8. Borke, H. Piaget's mountains revisited: Changes in the egocentric landscape. *Developmental Psychology*, 1975, **11**, 240–243.
9. Brainerd, C. J., and M. Fraser. A further test of the ordinal theory of number development. *Journal of Genetic Psychology*, 1975, **127**, 21–33.
10. Brosnan, M. D., and K. N. Black. Developmental changes in memory processes for verbal and pictorial material. Paper presented at the meetings of the Society for Research in Child Development, Philadelphia, 1973.
11. Brown, R. Development of the first language in the human species. *American Psychologist*, 1973, **28**, 97–106.
12. Bruner, J. S. *Beyond the information given*. New York: W. W. Norton & Company, 1973.

13. Carlson, P., and M. Anisfeld. Some observations on the linguistic competence of a two-year-old child. *Child Development*, 1969, **40**, 569–575.
14. Chomsky, N. *Language and mind*. New York: Harcourt Brace & World, 1968.
15. Crinella, F. M., F. W. Beck, and J. W. Robinson. Unilateral dominance is not related to neuropsychological integrity. *Child Development*, 1971, **42**, 2033–2054.
16. Dansky, J. L., and I. W. Silverman. Play: A general facilitator of associative fluency. *Developmental Psychology*, 1975, **11**, 104.
17. Denney, N. W. Free classification in preschool children. *Child Development*, 1972, **43**, 116–1170.
18. Denney, N. W. Evidence for developmental changes in categorization criteria for children and adults. *Human Development*, 1974, **17**, 41–43.
19. Dixon, C. M. *High, wide and deep*. New York: The John Day Company, 1938.
20. Dunn, L. M. *Peabody Picture Vocabulary Test*. Minneapolis: American Guidance Service, 1959.
21. Erikson, E. H. *Childhood and society*. New York: W. W. Norton & Company, 1963.
22. Fein, G. A transformational analysis of pretending. *Developmental Psychology*, 1975, **11**, 291–296.
23. Fischer, K. Genetic contributions to individual differences in language acquisition. Paper presented at meetings of the Society for Research in Child Development, Philadelphia, 1973.
24. Furth, H. G., and N. A. Milgram. Labeling and grouping effects in the recall of pictures by children. *Child Development*, 1973, **44**, 511–518.
25. Gibson, E. J. The ontogeny of reading. *American Psychologist*, 1970, **25**, 136–143.
26. Goodenough, E. G., and E. Prelinger. *Children tell stories*. New York: International Universities Press, 1963.
27. Gotts, E. A. Some determinants of young children's attribute attending. *Merrill-Palmer Quarterly*, 1973, **19**, 261–273.
28. Gottschalk, J., M. P. Bryden, and M. S. Rabinovitch. Spacial organization of children's responses to a pictorial display. *Child Development*, 1964, **35**, 811–815.
29. Griffiths, R. *A study of imagination in early childhood*. London: Routledge and Kegan Paul, 1935.
30. Groch, A. S. Joking and appreciation of humor in nursery school children. *Child Development*, 1974, **45**, 1098–1102.
31. Guilford, J. P. Intelligence: 1965 model. *American Psychologist*, 1966, **21**, 20–26.
32. Hale, G. A. and L. E. T. Lipps. Stimulus matching and component selection: Alternative approaches to measuring children's attention to stimulus components. *Child Development*, 1974, **45**, 383–388.
33. Hanson, R. A. Consistency and stability of home environmental measures related to IQ. *Child Development*, 1975, **46**, 470–480.
34. Harner, L. Yesterday and tomorrow: Development of early understanding of the terms. *Developmental Psychology*, 1975, **11**:6, 864–865.
35. Hazlitt, V. Children's thinking. *British Journal of Psychology*, 1929, **30**, 20. Cited in Werner [96].
36. Honzik, M. P. Predicting IQ over the first four decades of the life span. Paper presented at meetings of the Society for Research in Child Development, Philadelphia, 1973.
37. Hunt, J. McV. and G. E. Kirk. Criterion-referenced tests of school readiness: A paradigm with illustrations. *Genetic Psychology Monographs*, 1974, **90**:1, 143–182.
38. Huttenlocher, J. Children's ability to order and orient objects. *Child Development*, 1967, **38**, 1169–1176.

39. Johnson, J. E. Relationship between fantasy play, creativity, and intelligence in preschool children. Paper presented at meetings of the American Psychological Association, Chicago, 1975.
40. Jones, H. R. The use of visual and verbal memory processes by three-year-old children. *Journal of Experimental Psychology,* 1973, **15,** 340–351.
41. Kellogg, R. and S. O'Dell. *The psychology of children's art.* New York: CRM-Random House, 1967.
42. Kemp, J. C. and P. S. Dale. Spontaneous imitations and free speech: A developmental comparison. Paper presented at meetings of the Society for Research in Child Development, Philadelphia, 1973.
43. Kendler, T. S. Development of mediating responses in children. In J. C. Wright and J. Kagan (eds.). Basic cognitive processes in children. *Monographs of the Society for Research in Child Development,* 1963, **28:**2, 33–52.
44. Kessen, W. et al. Children of China: Report of a visit. Paper presented at meetings of the American Psychological Association, New Orleans, 1974.
45. Knobloch, H., and B. Pasamanick. *Developmental Diagnosis* 3rd ed. New York: Harper & Row Publishers, Inc., 1974.
46. Kosslyn, S. M. and G. H. Bower. The role of imagery in sentence memory: A developmental study. *Child Development,* 1974, **45,** 30–38.
47. Lee, L. C. Concept utilization in preschool children. *Child Development,* 1965, **36,** 221–227.
48. Leeper, S. H., R. J. Dales, D. S. Skipper, and R. L. Witherspoon. *Good schools for young children.* New York: Macmillan Publishing Co., Inc., 1974.
49. Lempers, J. D., E. R. Flavell, and J. H. Flavell. The development in very young children of tacit knowledge concerning visual perception. Paper presented at meetings of the Society for Research in Child Development, Denver, 1975.
50. Lenneberg, E. H. *Biological foundations of language.* New York: John Wiley & Sons, Inc., 1967.
51. Locke, J. L. Phonetic mediation in four-year-old children. *Psychonomic Science,* 1971, **23,** 409.
52. Locke, J. L. and V. I. Locke. Recall of phonetically and semantically similar words by three-year-old children. *Psychonomic Science,* 1971, **24,** 189–190.
53. Loughlin, K. A. and M. W. Daehler. The effects of distraction and added perceptual cues on the delayed reaction of very young children. *Child Development,* 1973, **44,** 384–388.
54. Lovell, K. *The growth of basic mathematical and scientific concepts in children.* New York: Philosophical Library, Inc., 1961.
55. Manosevitz, M., N. Prentice, and F. Wilson. Individual and family correlates of imaginary companions in preschool children. *Developmental Psychology,* 1973, **8,** 72–79.
56. Matsaros, M. P. When is a high thing the big one? *Developmental Psychology,* 1974, **10,** 367–275.
57. Maynard, O. *Children and dance and music.* New York: Charles Scribner's, Sons, 1968.
58. McCarthy, D. *The McCarthy scales of children's abilities.* New York: Psychological Corporation, 1973.
59. Moerk, E. L. Verbal interaction between children and their mothers during the preschool years. *Developmental Psychology,* 1975, **11,** 788–794.
60. Mossler, D. G., M. T. Greenberg, and R. S. Marvin. The early development of conceptual perspective-taking. *Developmental Psychology,* 1976, **12,** 85–86.

61. Murphy, G. *An historical introduction to modern psychology*. New York: Harcourt Brace Jovanovich, Inc., 1930.
62. Nelson, K. E., and N. Earl. Information search by preschool children: Induced use of categories and category hierarchies. *Child Development*, 1973, **44,** 682–685.
63. O'Connor, M. Decentration revisited: A two-factor model for role-taking development in young children. Paper presented at meetings of the Society for Research in Child Development, Denver, 1975.
64. Odom, R. D., E. C. Astor, and J. G. Cunningham. Effects of perceptual salience on the matrix task performance of four- and six-year-old children. *Child Development*, 1975, **46,** 758–762.
65. Oknoji, M. W. The development of logical thinking in preschool Zambian children: A classification. *Journal of Genetic Psychology*, 1974, **125,** 247–255.
66. Oliveri, M. E. Interindividual and intraindividual communication in preschoolers: A social class comparison. Paper presented at meetings of the Society for Research in Child Development, Denver, 1975.
67. Palermo, D. S. Still more about the comprehension of less. *Developmental Psychology*, 1974, **10,** 827–829.
68. Perlmutter, M. and N. A. Myers. Recognition memory development in two- to four-year-olds. *Developmental Psychology*, 1974, **10,** 447–450.
69. Piaget, J. *The child's conception of physical causality*. London: Routledge and Kegan Paul, 1930.
70. Piaget, J. *The psychology of intelligence*. London: Routledge and Kegan Paul, 1950.
71. Piaget, J. *Play, dreams and imitation in childhood*. London: Wm. Heinemann, Limited 1951.
72. Piaget, J. and B. Inhelder. *The child's conception of space*. London: Routledge and Kegan Paul, 1958.
73. Piaget, J. and B. Inhelder. *The psychology of the child*. New York: Basic Books, Inc., 1969.
74. Poteat, B. W. and R. C. Hulsebus. The vertical dimension: A significant cue in the preschool child's concept of "bigger." *Psychonomic Science*, 1968, **12,** 369–370.
75. Pufall, P. B. Egocentrism in spatial thinking: It depends on your point of view. *Child Development*, 1975, **11,** 297–303.
76. Ricciuti, H. N. Objects grouping and selective ordering behavior in infants 12 to 24 months old. *Merrill-Palmer Quarterly*, 1965, **11,** 129–148.
77. Rogoff, B., N. Newcombe, and J. Kagan. Planfulness and recognition memory. *Child Development*, 1974, **45,** 972–977.
78. Rosch, E. and C. B. Mervis. Children's sorting: A reinterpretation based on the nature of abstraction in natural categories. In R. C. Smart and M. S. Smart. *Readings in child development and relationships*. New York: The Macmillan Co., 1977, pp. 140–148.
79. Rothbart, M. K. Laughter in young children. *Psychological Bulletin*, 1973, **80,** 247–256.
80. Schachter, F. F., K. Kishner, B. Klips, M. Friedrichs, and K. Saunders. Everyday preschool interpersonal speech usage: Methodological, developmental, and sociolinguistic studies. *Monographs of the Society for Research in Child Development*, 1974, **39:**3.
81. Schaefer, C. E. Imaginary companions and creative adolescents, *Developmental Psychology*, 1969, **1,** 747–749.

82. Seitz, S. and C. Stewart. Imitations and expansions: Some developmental aspects of mother-child communications. *Developmental Psychology,* 1975, **11,** 763–768.

83. Siegel, L. S. The development of the ability to understand numerical symbols. Paper presented at meetings of the Society for Research in Child Development, Philadelphia, 1973.

84. Slobin, D. L. The acquisition of Russian as a native language. In F. Smith and G. A. Miller (eds.). *The genesis of language.* Cambridge, Mass.: M.I.T. Press, 1966, pp. 129–148.

85. Smith, H. P. and S. W. Applefeld. Children's paintings and the projective expression of personality: An experimental investigation. *Journal of Genetic Psychology,* 1965, **107,** 289–293.

85a. Starr, S. and S. Eshleman. Contexts of language. Paper presented at meetings of the Society for Research in Child Development, Denver, 1975.

86. Steinberg, B. M. Information processing in the third year: Coding, memory, transfer. *Child Development,* 1974, **45,** 503–507.

87. Stutsman, R. *Scale of mental tests for preschool children.* New York: The World Publishing Company, 1930.

88. Sutton-Smith, B. The psychology of childlore: A theory of ludic models. Paper presented at meetings of the American Psychological Association, Chicago, 1975.

89. Terman, L. M. and M. A. Merrill. *Stanford-Binet intelligence scale.* Boston: Houghton Mifflin Company, 1960.

90. Thorndike, E. L. *The measurement of intelligence.* New York: Teachers College, Columbia University, 1926.

91. Tversky, B. Pictorial and verbal encoding in preschool children. *Developmental Psychology,* 1973, **8,** 149–153.

92. Vlietstra, A. G. and J. C. Wright. The effect of strategy training, stimulus saliency, and age on recognition in preschoolers. Paper presented at meetings of the American Psychological Association, Montreal, 1973.

93. Wechsler, D. *Wechsler intelligence scale for children.* New York: Psychological Corporation, 1949.

94. Wechsler, D. Intelligence defined and undefined: A relativistic appraisal. *American Psychologist,* 1975, **30,** 135–139.

95. Weir, R. H. *Language in the crib.* The Hague: Mouton & Company, 1962.

96. Werner, H. *Comparative psychology of mental development.* New York: International Universities Press, 1957.

97. White, B. L. Critical influences in the origins of competence. *Merrill-Palmer Quarterly,* 1975, 21.

98. White, B. L. and J. C. Watts. *Experience and environment: Major influences on the development of the young child.* Englewood Cliffs, N.J.: Prentice-Hall, Inc., 1973.

99. Yussen, S. R. and J. W. Santrock. Comparison of the retention of preschool and second-grade performers and observers under three verbalization conditions. *Child Development,* 1974, **45,** 821–824.

100. Zimmerman, B. J. Modification of young children's grouping strategies: The effects of modeling, verbalization, incentives, and age. *Child Development,* 1975, **46,** 758–762.

101. Zimny, G. H. and E. W. Weidenfeller. Effects of music upon GSR of children. *Child Development,* 1962, **33,** 891–896.

Readings in
Development in Cognition, Imagination, and Language

New studies question accepted beliefs about children's thinking, such as the principles on which children categorize and the conditions under which young children are egocentric. Child developmentalists have always maintained that play is essential for healthy development, but now research is clarifying the role of play in language and cognitive development. Similarly, parent-child interaction is known to be important for language development, but now the actual processes are being analyzed.

One approach to exploring children's cognitive behavior is to ask them to sort objects or pictures into groups. Eleanor Rosch and Carolyn B. Mervis maintain that there are natural categories, based on human experience in the world. They show how young children can use these categories as well as adults, and that only in superordinate classification does performance improve with age.

Spatial egocentrism means inability to differentiate between what one perceives from what another person perceives. Spatial egocentrism decreases as the child organizes space and his relationships within it. Peter B. Pufall explores these processes with kindergarten children, showing the gradual construction of spatial reference systems.

A child learns his mother-tongue largely from his mother. Do mothers have special qualifications as language teachers? Ernst L. Moerk studied mothers' utterances in relation to those of their children. He found that mothers adjusted their comments sensitively to the complexity of their children's utterances.

Children's Sorting: A Reinterpretation Based on the Nature of Abstraction in Natural Categories *

Eleanor Rosch and Carolyn B. Mervis
UNIVERSITY OF CALIFORNIA, BERKELEY AND CORNELL UNIVERSITY

Abstract

The previous developmental finding that young children do not group objects taxonomically (i.e., because they are the same kind of objects) was argued to be an artifact of the use of stimuli which are related only at a level of abstraction superordinate to the level at which basic structure exists in the real world. In the present studies, a total of 180 subjects at ages 3 years, 4 years, kindergarten, grades 1, 3, 5, and adult were divided into two groups, one of which was given an opportunity to sort sets of color pictures of common objects such as animals, vehicles, and clothing into groups at the hypothesized basic level of abstraction, the other of which was given the same pictures but in sets cross-cutting the basic level so that taxonomic sorting would necessarily be at the superordinate level. Experiment 1 was administered in the form of oddity problems, Experiment 2 with standard sorting procedures. Results were that subjects at all ages, in both designs, sorted the basic level groups taxonomically. The usual developmental trend was observed only for superordinate classifications. These results were not simply effects of vocabulary development. Implications for theories of categorization and of development were discussed.

There is a long tradition of sorting research in the developmental literature which indicates that young children and adults use different principles when classifying objects. Adults, when given instructions to "put together the things that go together" tend to put things together taxonomically (e.g., objects that belong to the same category); whereas, the younger the child, the more likely he is to sort on the basis of associations, stories, chains, and by means of other non-taxonomic criteria. A particularly well-known example of such a finding is given in Bruner, Olver, and Greenfield (1966); however, research of this nature spans over 30 years (for example, Annett, 1959; Garrettson, 1971; Goldman & Levine, 1963; Thompson, 1941). It is the contention of the studies to be reported here that most of the findings of this research tradition are artifacts of the items which have been used in the sorting studies; an error which has been due to an exclusive focus on cognitive developmental factors internal to the

Portions of this paper were presented at meetings of The Society for Research in Child Development, Denver, 1975. Printed by permission.

* This research was supported in part by a grant to the first author (under her former name Eleanor Rosch Heider) by the National Science Foundation GB-38245X, in part by a grant from the Grant Foundation, and in part by a grant from the National Institute of Mental Health 1 RO1 MH24316-01. Portions of this data were presented in a paper delivered at a meeting of the Society for Research in Child Development, Denver, 1975. We wish to thank Meriska Huynen and Carol Simpson for help in testing and the students and staff of the University of California nursery school and the Pacific Grove public schools for their kindly cooperation.

Carolyn Mervis is now at Cornell University. She was a National Science Foundation predoctoral fellow during performance of the research.

child and a neglect and lack of understanding of the actual structure of objects in the real world and of the reflection of that structure in psychological categories.

The developmental research in the sorting studies to be reported is based on a general theory of human categorization which has been elaborated in previous work (Rosch & Mervis, Note 1; Rosch, Mervis, Gray, & Simpson, Note 2). The basic argument of the theory is that categorizations which humans make of the concrete world are not arbitrary classes which the child must be taught to impose upon the environment in a rote manner; rather, the categories themselves have an internal rationale which renders them highly determined. Categories are structured because the real world is structured. Real-world attributes, unlike the sets often presented laboratory subjects, do not occur independently of each other; they occur in correlated (redundant) clusters. (For example, creatures with feathers are more likely also to have wings than creatures with fur.) Categorization occurs in order to reduce the infinite differences between stimuli to behaviorally and cognitively useful proportions; therefore, the basic category cuts in the world should be those which yield the most information for the least cognitive load. Basic categories should, thus, be the most inclusive categories which can follow the correlational structures perceived in the world.

In a series of converging experiments, we found that there is, in fact, a basic level of abstraction in adult human categorizations of concrete objects. Basic level objects were the most inclusive categories which were found to have the following properties: (a) Clusters of attributes occur which subjects agree are possessed by members of the category. For example, chairs (a basic level category) have seats, legs, you sit on them, etc., whereas, furniture (a superordinate) has virtually no common attributes, and kitchen chair (a subordinate) has basically the same attributes as chair. (b) Sets of common motor movements are made when using or interacting with objects of that type. This finding may be particularly important developmentally, since it means that basic level objects are the most inclusive categories for which a sensory motor schema (Piaget, 1952) can be formed. (c) Commonalities in the shape, and, thus, the overall look, of objects occur. (d) It is possible to recognize an average shape of an object of that class. (e) It is possible to form a concrete image of a typical member of the class (Rosch, Mervis, & Miller, Note 3).

In terms of developmental applications, basic level objects should be those first learned by means of visual perception and sensory motor interaction with the object and, thus, should be the first divisions of the world at which it might make sense to a child to put things together because they are the same type of thing. However, in *all* previous sorting studies, the possible taxonomic categories were invariably at the superordinate level; e.g., the child would have to put together a cat and a dog as animals rather than two cats as cats.

In our studies, subjects at each of the following ages—3 years, 4 years, kindergarten, grades 1, 3, and 5, and adult—were divided into two groups, one of which was given an opportunity to sort sets of color pictures of common objects such as animals, vehicles, clothing, and furniture into groups of basic level objects, the other of which was given the same pictures but in sets crosscutting the basic level so that taxonomic sorting would necessarily be at the usual superordinate level. The 3- and 4-year-olds received only two categories, and the task was administered in the form of oddity problems; the older groups received four categories, and the standard sorting task and instructions.

EXPERIMENT 1

While children below the age of 6 years may have difficulty understanding instructions in the standard sorting task (Bruner et al., 1966; Nash, Note 4), oddity problems can be comprehended at much younger ages (Gelman, 1972). Thus, in order to be able to include nursery school age children in our experimental design, the first experiment employed an oddity problem format.

METHODS.   SUBJECTS   Subjects were 40 nursery school children, 40 elementary school children, and 20 adults. The children included 20 3-year-olds, 20 4-year-olds, 10 kindergartners, 10 first graders, 10 third graders, and 10 fifth graders. In each age group, exactly half of the children were males and half females. Mean ages at the time of testing, for each age group respectively, were: 3 yr. 5 mo.; 4 yr. 7 mo.; 5 yr. 7 mo.; 6 yr. 5 mo.; 8 yr. 8 mo.; and 10 yr. 7 mo. The adult subjects (6 males, 14 females) were undergraduates who participated in the experiment for course credit. Socioeconomic status of the subjects was unknown.

STIMULI   Stimulus materials were color photographs of animals and vehicles. Four categories of animals—cats, dogs, butterflies, and fish—and four categories of vehicles—cars, trains, motorcycles, and airplanes—were used. Pictures were selected from a pool of 125–200 for each of the eight categories according to the procedure described in Rosch et al. (Note 2). Four pictures were used for each basic level category. Two sets of triads were used: one which could be correctly paired at the basic level, and one which could be correctly paired only at the superordinate level.

To prepare the basic-level triad set, four pairs of pictures from each basic level category were made yielding 16 pairs per superordinate. Pictures were paired with the restrictions that each of the four available pictures per basic-level category be used twice and that the two pictures in a pair not be the same color. The third member of the triad was chosen from the other superordinate category by the following procedure: there were four pairs of pictures within each basic level category. Each of the pairs was combined with one picture from each of the four different basic level pairs of the other superordinate. Thus, from the four pairs of cats, one pair was combined with a car, one with a truck, one with a motorcycle, and one with an airplane. The four pairs of fish were combined with a different car, truck, motorcycle, and airplane. This procedure was repeated for all eight categories, yielding 32 different triads.

To prepare the superordinate triad set, each picture from a basic level category was paired with one picture from each of the other basic level categories within the same superordinate. Thus, each car was paired with one train, one motorcycle, and one airplane. Again, the restriction was used that the two pictures in a pair not be the same color. This procedure yielded six sets of four pairs for each superordinate. Each pair was combined with one member from the other superordinate category according to the procedure described for basic level pairs. There were 48 triads in the superordinate set. For both the basic level and superordinate sets, all pictures were used an equal number of times.

PROCEDURE   For the two nursery school groups, triads were presented to the child, one at a time. The three pictures were put on the floor, and the child was told to put together (point to) "the two that are alike, that are the same kind of thing." After the child had gone through the entire set, the last six triads were shown to the child, one at a time. He was reminded which two pictures he had put together and was asked why they belonged together. If the child gave any reason other than a taxonomic one, he was asked if there were any other reason why the two pictures belonged together. Triads were presented in a different random order to each subject, and the order of pictures within triads were shuffled between subjects. Half the subjects in each age group (10 subjects) performed the task with the basic level set and half with the superordinate set. The nursery school children and the adults participated in the entire experiment as outlined above. Because a ceiling in correct sorting of both basic level and superordinate pairs had been reached by age four, and because a ceiling in giving taxonomic reasons for sorts for the basic level had also been reached by age four, the other subjects (elementary school children) were required to sort only six randomly chosen superordinate triads, for which they were asked to give the reason for their sort.

RESULTS AND DISCUSSION   The results were quite clear. At all age levels, basic level sorts were virtually perfect; for the 3-year-olds, the percent correct for basic level sorts was 99, and for 4 years and older, basic level sorts were perfect. Performance was considerably lower for the youngest age group, however, on sorts of the triads which could only be paired at the superordinate level: 3-year-olds, 55% correct; 4-year-olds, 96% correct.

There were no sex differences; data for both sexes were, therefore, combined in the analyses reported. A three-way Analysis of Variance (ANOVA) was performed on the pairing responses for the triads. Between-subject factors were Grade (3-year-olds, 4-year-olds, and adult) and Type of category (basic or superordinate). Category (animal or vehicle) was nested within Type of category. The dependent variable was per cent of correct responses. The effects of primary interest were that of Type of category and the interaction between Type and Grade. Our prediction that basic level sorts would be correct significantly more often than superordinate sorts was confirmed, $F(1, 54) = 26.58, p < .01$. Because a ceiling in performance on these simple triads had been reached essentially by age 4, a significant interaction could be expected between Type of category and Grade; that result was also obtained, $F(2, 54) = 18.54$, $p < .01$. These two results show that there do exist objects which even small children will classify in the same manner as adults. Basic level sorts are equally easy for all age groups; it is only superordinate level sorts which improve with age.

Not unexpectedly, the main effect of Grade was also significant: $F(2, 54) = 20.9, p < .01$. The effect of Category (animal or vehicle) was not significant— $F(1, 54) = .49$, ns.—and no interaction other than that between Type of category and Grade was significant. A Tukey test confirmed that 3-year-olds performed significantly worse than either 4-year-olds or adults, while there was no difference in performance between the latter two groups.

From the results of the sorting alone, it might be argued that the findings are simply a function of language development; that is, that children learn the names for basic level objects before those for superordinate categories, and that items are put together when the child knows they have the same name. Two pieces of evidence from the present study argue against such an interpretation.

Subjects' reasons for six of their sorts were obtained for all age levels. These reasons were classified into taxonomic reasons (giving the name of the two items placed together) and all other reasons such as giving attributes or autistic responses. To demonstrate the failure of naming to account for sorting results, results for percent of correct names for superordinate sorts are shown in Figure 1. Adults are omitted because they were perfect in both sorting and naming.

Two points are made clear by Figure 1. For all ages, correct sortings were superior to correct namings. (This was true also for the basic level names at the youngest age; correct sorts for 3-year-olds were 99%, correct names 65%; however, a ceiling was reached for basic level names by age 4). Since a difference

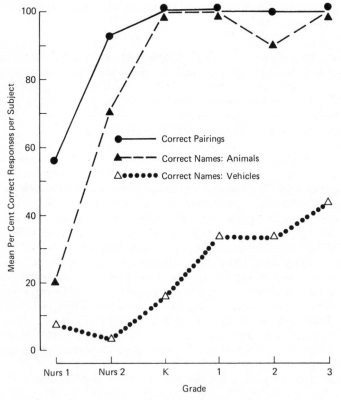

FIGURE 1.   *Correct sorting and correct reasons in the triads test.*

between sorting and naming could conceivably have been due partly to guessing (correct sorts could sometimes have been produced by chance but correct names had to be generated from an infinite set of linguistic responses), we compared correct names for the animal and vehicle categories. As already reported, there were no differences in percent of correct sorts between the animals and vehicles; however, as Figure 1 shows, animal pairs were named correctly far more often than vehicles at all age levels except the youngest, in which names for both were poor, and adults, in which names for both were perfect. The significance of this finding was tested by the Sign test (correct responses for animals versus vehicles for each child). Separate analyses were performed for each age level. The difference between animals and vehicles was not significant for the 3-year-olds or adults but was significant for all other age levels: 4-year-olds, $p < .035$; kindergarten, $p < .004$; grade 1, $p < .004$; grade 3, $p < .016$, grade 5, $p < .016$.

In summary: pictures of objects classifiable into basic level categories were classified in an adult taxononic manner by children at all ages, including 3-year-old children. Only the sorts of superordinate level objects showed the usual improvement with age. Evidence was presented that these results are not simply due to difference in knowledge of names for basic and superordinate level categories. Thus, our basic hypothesis concerning the effect of stimulus sets on sorting was confirmed.

EXPERIMENT 2

Experiment 1 used a simplified oddity problem format in order to create a meaningful task for 3- and 4-year-old children. However, all of the previous studies have used a different sorting procedure. In order to use a task directly comparable to that of previous studies, and in order to have a task difficult enough to show sorting differences for children older than 4 years, we performed a second study based on the same logic as Experiment 1, but using a standard sorting format.

METHODS.   SUBJECTS   Subjects were 64 children and 16 adults. The children were 16 kindergartners, 16 first graders, 16 third graders, and 16 fifth graders. In each group, exactly half the children were males and half females. Mean age at the time of test, for each group respectively, was: 5 yr. 7 mo.; 6 yr. 5 mo.; 8 yr. 4 mo.; and 10 yr. 7 mo. Adult subjects (6 males, 10 females) were undergraduates who participated in the experiment for course credit. Socioeconomic status of the subjects was unknown.

STIMULI   Stimulus materials were color photographs of clothing, furniture, people's faces, and vehicles. Four categories of each were used. They were: *clothing*—shoes, socks, shirts, pants; *furniture*—tables, chairs, beds, dressers; *people's faces*—men, women, young girls, infants; *vehicles*—cars, trains, motorcycles, airplanes. Pictures of items were chosen in the manner described in Experiment 1.

There were four sets of stimuli which could be sorted at the basic level and four sets which could only be sorted taxonomically into superordinate categories. Basic level sets consisted of one of the basic level categories from each of the four superordinates. For example, one subject might receive four shoes, four chairs, four men's faces, and four cars. Two subjects at each age level received each basic level set. To form the superordinate sets, each picture within the basic level sets was numbered arbitrarily 1, 2, 3, or 4. For a set, all of the like numbers were combined. For example, one subject received shoe 1, sock 1, shirt 1, pants 1, table 1, chair 1, car 1, etc. Two subjects at each age level received each superordinate level set.

PROCEDURES   The pictures in a set were shuffled and laid in front of the subject in random order. Instructions were: "Here are some pictures. (The experimenter called the child's attention to each picture by pointing to each in turn.) Put together the ones that go together, the ones that are the same kind of thing." The child was encouraged to include all of the pictures in his groupings. If his first sort was not taxonomic, the pictures were returned to a random order and he was asked if he could find another way to put them together. When the child had finished each sort to his satisfaction, he was asked why those pictures went together.

RESULTS AND DISCUSSION   A child was considered to have sorted taxonomically if either his first or second sort was broken into four groups of four pictures corresponding to the four categories built into the stimuli. The pattern of results was very similar to that obtained in Experiment 1. As in Experiment 1, there were no sex differences. For the basic level categories, all but one child in kindergarten and all but one child in the first grade sorted in an adult taxonomic fashion. For superordinate level sorts, however, only half of the children in each of those grades sorted taxonomically. All of the children in the older group (grades 3 and 5) and all of the adults sorted taxonomically for both basic level and superordinate sets. Because the results for kindergarten and first grade were identical, those two groups were combined for a χ^2 comparison of the difference between basic level and superordinate sorts. Results confirmed that for this group, basic level sets were sorted taxonomically significantly more than superordinate sets: $\chi^2 (1) = 3.64, p < .05$. Thus, as had been the case for the oddity problems of Experiment 1, children of all ages were virtually perfect when sorting the basic level stimuli, and only showed the usual developmental trend in sorting the superordinate level categories.

The children's reasons for their sorts were divided into taxonomic and non-taxonomic reasons following the procedures of Experiment 1. The comparison of taxonomic sorts and reasons are shown in Figure 2. The production of taxonomic reasons lagged behind taxonomic sorting responses. Separate χ^2 tests were performed for grades kindergarten and 1 and for grades 3 and 5 for the difference between the number of children giving taxonomic reasons versus the number giving taxonomic sorts. Both tests were significant: for the younger group, $\chi^2 (1) = 18.66, p < .001$; for the older group, $\chi^2 (1) = 3.79, p < .05$. In the present experiment, the probability of correct sorting by chance was extremely small (unlike the 1/3 correct guessing probability for the triads of Experiment 1). Thus, the difference between taxonomic sorts and taxonomic reasons indicates that the sorts were based on principles other than simple knowledge of the category names.

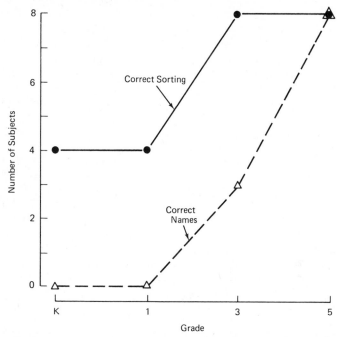

FIGURE 2.   *Correct sorting and correct reasons in the sorting task.*

In summary: for a traditional sorting task, as well as for the oddity problems of Experiment 1, it was shown that even kindergarten children sorted in an adult taxonomic manner when given categories which could be sorted at the basic level. Developmental changes in sorting occurred only for sets which could be grouped solely at the superordinate level.

GENERAL DISCUSSION   The general argument of the study has been that understanding the child's cognitive processes in classification can occur only within a general framework for understanding human categorization. Previous studies of children's sorting behavior have concluded that young children do not group objects because they are the same kind of object but use, as a basis of grouping, other connections between objects. However, these studies have used objects which we believe (Rosch & Mervis, Note 1; Rosch et al., Note 2) are not the same kind of thing for young children. In both of the present experiments, when children at very young ages (3 years for an oddity problem procedure, kindergarten for a sorting procedure) were presented with categories which previous research indicated mirrored the structure of the environment, items from those categories were classified in an adult taxonomic fashion. Only grouping into categories superordinate to these basic classifications demonstrated the usual developmental trends.

From these findings, we do not intend to argue that the logic of categorization does not change with age. The present research did not examine the meaning of categories as such to the child and the consequent logic of class inclusions. The studies do, however, suggest that classification by taxonomic identity (putting things together because they are the same kind of thing) is a far more primitive principle than has been supposed. Evidence that this is the case can also be derived from the very early occurrence of a stage in language development in which the child requests the names of things ("What that?") which is correlated with rapid development in the child's vocabulary of nouns (Brown, 1974). Evidence, somewhat more far afield, may be derived from the fact that stimulus generalization, a response which, by definition, treats non-identical stimuli as equivalent, is apparent in the earliest behavior patterns of infra-human organisms.

The results of the present study have both substantive and methodological implications. Substantively, the fact that basic level objects were sorted taxonomically at the earliest ages supports our claim for the primacy of categorizations at this level of abstraction. Furthermore, that our subjects did group taxonomically when given the right kind of objects indicates that grouping things by the kind of thing they are is a logically more primitive function developmentally than has been supposed. In terms of method, the study should serve as a general caution. Whenever classification tasks are used—for example, in memory research and cross-cultural investigations as well as in developmental studies—the cognitive operations of subjects cannot be considered apart from the nature and logic of the stimuli used.

Reference Notes

1. ROSCH, E. & MERVIS, C. B. *Basic objects in natural categories: I. Attributes and motor movements.* Manuscript submitted for publication, 1975.
2. ROSCH, E., MERVIS, C. B., GRAY, W., & SIMPSON, C. *Basic objects in natural categories: II. Shapes of objects.* Manuscript submitted for publication, 1975.
3. ROSCH, E., MERVIS, C. B., & MILLER, R. S. *Imagery of basic level, superordinate, and subordinate categories: A priming study.* Unpublished manuscript, 1975. (Available from the first author.)
4. NASH, S. C. The use of free recall to infer cognitive organization in three, four and five year olds. Unpublished MA thesis, University of Pennsylvania, 1973.

References

ANNETT, M. The classification of instances of four common class concepts by children and adults. *British Journal of Educational Psychology*, 1959, **29**, 223–236.
BROWN, R. *A first language.* Cambridge, Mass.: Harvard University Press, 1974.
BRUNER, J. S., OLVER, R. R., & GREENFIELD, P. M. *Studies in cognitive growth.* New York: Wiley, 1966.
GARRETTSON, J. Cognitive style and classification. *Journal of Genetic Psychology*, 1971, **119**, 79–87.
GELMAN, R. The nature and development of early number concepts. In H. Reese (Ed.) *Advances in child development and behavior.* (Vol. 7). New York: Academic Press, 1972.
GOLDMAN, A. E. & LEVINE, M. A development study of object-sorting. *Child Development*, 1963, **34**, 649–666.
PIAGET, J. *The origins of intelligence in children.* New York: International Universities Press, 1952.
THOMPSON, J. The ability of children of different grade levels to generalize on sorting tests. *Journal of Psychology*, 1941, **11**, 119–126.

Egocentrism in Spatial Thinking: It Depends on Your Point of View *

Peter B. Pufall
SMITH COLLEGE

Abstract

Sixty-three kindergarten children were tested on a spatial perspective task in which they had to copy the location and orientation of objects when the model and response spaces were aligned or one was rotated 90 degrees or 180 degrees. There were very few errors when the spaces were aligned, and there were significantly more errors on the 180 degrees than the 90-degree rotations. Egocentric responding dominated spatial responding on the 180 degrees but was infrequent on the 90-degree rotations. These findings are explained as due to the symmetry relations between space and self for each perspective difference.

An impediment to children's spatial thinking, and particularly spatial perspective taking, is its egocentricity. In general, egocentricity refers to the inability or failure to differentiate the subjective from the objective aspect of knowing. In the case of perspective taking, it is the failure to understand that perspective is relative, and this failure is evident when the child represents, in whole or in part, another perspective as identical to his own.

Although egocentricity is most frequently thought of as a property of preoperational thinking, it is clear from much of the reported literature that the preoperational child's thought is not exclusively egocentric (Fishbein, Lewis, & Keiffer, 1972; Laurendeau & Pinard, 1970; Piaget & Inhelder, 1956; Pufall & Shaw, 1973). Preoperational children do represent some aspects of space objectively while representing other aspects of the same space egocentrically. Moreover. egocentricity does not appear to be restricted to the preoperational period. Pufall and Shaw (1973) note that 10-year-old children not only reflected egocentricity in their spatial thinking but did so to a greater degree than the younger children for certain spatial layouts. In this same study it was clear that the 10-year-old children had achieved the level of operational thought. In contrast to younger children who preserved an isolated relation egocentrically, the older children organized large portions of space egocentrically. Thus, they did logically multiply spatial relations but failed to compensate for perspective difference.

Data such as these do not fit comfortably into a model of development which explains the shift away from egocentricity in terms of the development of abstract structures such as operational systems of logical multiplication.

These observations have led Pufall (Note 1) to distinguish two aspects of spatial thinking. One aspect is operative and deals with the development of structuring activities which constitute reference systems for organizing spatial

From *Developmental Psychology*, 1975, **11**, 297–303. Copyright © 1975 by The American Psychological Association. Reprinted by permission.

* The present research was supported by the Sloan Foundation. Thanks are due to Ann Pufall for help on data collection and Susan Lathrop for data analysis.

arrays and mapping perspectives into each other. Piaget and Inhelder's (1956) theoretical work specifying the development of infralogical structures gives one model of the development of the operative aspect of knowing. The more abstract operative systems act upon particular spaces and particular features within that space. The second aspect of spatial knowing, then, is the discrimination of distinctive features or relations such as parallel to. The empirical and theoretical work of the Gibsons (E. J. Gibson, 1969; J. J. Gibson, 1966) seems to be directed toward understanding this aspect of spatial knowing and its development.

Egocentric thought does not appear to fit comfortably as a property of either aspect of spatial thought. Egocentricity does not specify a structure or system but certainly can specify the relations to be structured; for example, the relations of right, left, near, and far can be multiplied into a two-dimensional system similar to a geographic system: far, far right, right, etc. Nor is egocentricity a property of an object to be discriminated since it is a relation between self and space. This relation is special because it does not change in functional importance as the child's structuring of space and discrimination of spatial features change.

Any theory of spatial thinking has to account for the development of organizational systems, discrimination of spatial properties, and the relation of these two to the functioning of egocentric thought. The latter problem involves specifying the conditions under which egocentric thought would function when perspectives need to be coordinated. If positions within a space were defined like squares in a patchwork quilt, each marked by topographically distinctive features, then positions would not be discriminated by relating them to other positions. As a consequence there would be few errors and no apparent egocentric involvement no matter what perspectives need to be coordinated. The more likely case in nature, and more interesting case to study, involves spaces in which positions have to be defined relationally because topographic features are repeated. Due to the repetition of features within a space, some perspectives would be more similar than others, and, of course, some egocentric descriptions of each perspective would be more similar.

The relation among perspective and egocentric description can be referred to as a symmetry relation. If perspective A and A' are symmetrical with respect to self, then one would expect the child, or even the adult, to describe the spatial relations egocentrically. In the limiting case, if the two perspectives are identical then positions of objects are frequently referred to as the far-right, far-left, etc., objects. Symmetry relations, in varying degrees, can be identified when there are perspective differences. For example, in the present study identical trees are located in one pair of diagonal quadrants and a barn and house are in the other diagonal pair. When the perspective differences are 180 degrees there is a symmetry with respect to the trees; there is a far-right tree and a near-left tree. When the perspective difference is 90 degrees there is no symmetry because the far-left tree now corresponds to the far-left house.

This analysis can be generalized to realizations intrinsic to space, for example, parallelness. The objects to be positioned were longer than they were wide and were often positioned so that they were parallel to a topographic property of the space. When there is no perspective difference or it is 180 degrees, the objects are not only parallel to that spatial feature but also continue to be parallel to an egocentric projection, for example, they project near to far. When the difference is 90 degrees, the parallel relation between the object and edge is preserved only if the relation to self is not. The symmetry relation in the first case might yield accurate positioning but the orientation of the object might be egocentric; that is, the child might preserve the orientation as looking toward him even though under a 180-degree transformation it should look away. If the asymmetric relation is preserved on the 90-degree perspective difference, then if there is an error of orientation it can not be egocentric.

In summary, the symmetry analysis predicts that egocentric functioning, rather than accuracy in spatial reasoning, is influenced by perspective difference, at least during the preoperational period. It is also assumed that the symmetry relations influence independently global and local descriptions of spatial relations. As a consequence the child might correctly discriminate what feature a position is adjacent to but egocentrically discriminate among those many positions about that feature.

METHOD

SUBJECTS   Sixty-three kindergarten children ranging in age from 5.5 to 6.0 years were tested. This age children were tested because they could be expected to express some degree of egocentricity and because they would not have mastered completely the perspective problem. The sample consisted of 30 girls and 33 boys; all attended parochial schools in Washington, D.C., and came from lower-middle- to middle-socioeconomic-status familes. All of the children were Caucasian.

MATERIALS   The basic equipment consisted of two 60 × 60 cm displays simulating a farm scene, two pairs of animals (lambs and rabbits), and a wooden screen 50 × 50 cm. Each landscape was divided into quadrants by a road running near to far and a stream running left to right. The stream ended in a pond on the right when a subject viewed it in its standard position. An object was located in the center of each quadrant: a house in the upper left, a tree in the upper right, a barn in the lower right, and a tree identical to the other tree in the lower left. Two objects, the trees, were repeated and also were symmetrical with no distinctive feature differentiating one side from another. Two objects were unique, the house and the barn, both in the sense of not being repeated but also in the sense that they were asymmetrical with distinctive features differentiating the four sides of each.

PROCEDURE   There were nine trials, three when the two displays were in the same orientation, three when one was rotated 90 degrees, and three when one was rotated 180 degrees. On each trial a screen was placed between the two displays. On the nonrotation trials the experimenter placed his animals on one display and then instructed the subject to place his animals on his display so that they were "in the same spot as mine [the experimenter's] and facing the same way as mine [the experimenter's]." On the rotation trials the experimenter rotated the display first and then placed his animals. On these trials the experimenter reminded the subject that the display had been rotated and to remember that fact when locating and orienting the animals. Another instruction used to sensitize the subject to the effects of rotation was to remind the subject that the two displays "should look the same when turned around again." After the subject had made his placements, the experimenter removed the screen and if necessary rerotated the display; then the experimenter pointed out whether or not the placements were correct.

Each child went through a two- or three-trial warm-up period, during which the child was familiarized with the instructions and the act of placing the animals. Corrections were made if necessary but they were needed infrequently.

PLACEMENT TYPES　There were six different placements, three for each animal. One placement by each tree (placement type: by a repeated feature), one placement by each building (placement type: by a unique feature), and two by the road (placement type: by an edge). The objects were oriented so that they were parallel to a side of the building or edge of the road. All six placements were approximately 1.88 cm from the adjacent object. On each trial the animals were located in adjacent quadrants. The placement types and perspective difference conditions were randomized with the following restrictions: On each trial two of the three placements were represented; the three perspective differences occurred within each block of three trials; and the same positions were not used on adjacent trials.

RESULTS

Placements were analyzed in terms of the relations to be preserved intrinsic to the space. As can be seen in Table 1, location and orientation were analyzed separately. Each of these was analyzed in terms of the type of feature (repeated, unique, or edge) next to which the placement was to be made. Location responses were scored in two ways. At a global level they were analyzed with respect to the "quadrant" in which the animal was located. And at a local level when placements were adjacent to either a repeated or unique feature, responses were scored in terms of their position "about a feature." This second measure was inappropriate when the animal was located next to the road. In those cases, switching from one side of the feature to the other involved

TABLE 1

Percentage of Error and Egocentric Responses

| | LOCATION | | | | | ORIENTATION | | |
| | Quadrant | | | About-a-Feature | | | | |
PERSPECTIVE DIFFERENCE	Repeated	Unique	Edge	Repeated	Unique	Repeated	Unique	Edge
90° Ego	8	0	24	37	2	43	4	13
Total	36	2	45	70	12	66	30	52
180° Ego	52	10	36	63	34	45	52	60
Total	53	11	51	79	37	74	66	63

changing quadrants as well. To score placements about a feature, the area around the feature was divided into four wedges with the feature at the center. As a consequence one position was correct, one preserved the egocentric relation, and two were incorrect for other reasons. Orientations were scored within a system similar to compass headings. The gaze of the animal was recorded as north, north-northeast, east, etc. One orientation was correct, one preserved egocentric relations, and six were incorrect for other reasons.

Table 1 contains the percentage of responses that were errors (total) and the percentage that were egocentric. Both percentages were based on all of the responses made by each child. As a consequence, when the two percentages are equal, it indicates that all errors were egocentric in kind. For example, children failed to discriminate a quadrant when it contained a repeated feature on 53% of the trials, and 52% of their responses were egocentric; therefore, 98% of the erroneous responses were egocentric.

There were very few location or orientation errors on the nonrotation trials: quadrant (1%); about a feature (1%); and orientation (5%). Obviously, these children could comprehend and duplicate the spatial relations when perspective was not a factor. Therefore, the errors in the two rotation conditions are due to the problem of compensating perspective differences. The subsequent analyses analyze performance on the 90-degree and 180-degree perspective difference problems. Due to the fact that the important contrasts are all within subjects, no overall analyses could be done. The differences in performance on the two rotation conditions were analyzed by a sign test.

The major questions asked in the present study were: (a) Does the type of spatial relation to be duplicated influence its discrimination? and (b) what influence does the degree of perspective difference have on performance? A visual appraisal of Table 1 indicates quite clearly that the type of placement as well as the degree of perspective to be compensated influence performance. In general, fewer errors are made when placements are adjacent to a unique feature and also when the smaller perspective difference is to be compensated. However, it is equally clear that there are interactions between types of placements and perspective differences. These interactions appear to be different for total versus egocentric errors. Consequently, each is reported separately and in turn.

TOTAL ERRORS   The children made the fewest errors discriminating quadrants when the placement was adjacent to a unique feature ($p < .01$). Errors on the other two placements did not differ significantly from each other. This pattern holds for both perspectives. The degree of perspective difference influences performance reliably only when the placement to be duplicated is by a repeated feature ($p < .01$). In that case children made fewer errors on the 90-degree perspective.

The type of placement also influenced discrimination performance about a feature. For both the 90-degree and 180-degree rotation, children made fewer errors when the placement was to be made by a unique feature ($p < .01$). Perspective difference influenced performance when placements were by a unique feature ($p < .01$) but not when they were by a repeated feature. In the latter case performance was poor on both perspectives.

Type of placement also influences orientation performance. On 90-degree perspective differences, children made significantly fewer errors of orientation when placements were to be made by a unique feature ($p < .01$), with no significant performance differences when placements were by a repeated feature or edge. There were no reliable differences in performance across placement types when the perspective difference was 180 degrees. Perspective difference had an effect only when placements were to be made adjacent to a unique feature. In that case children made fewer errors when the rotation was 90 degrees.

EGOCENTRIC ERRORS   Analyses of egocentric errors indicated reliable differences in discriminating quadrants among all placement types ($p < .01$) for both perspective differences. The children made fewer egocentric errors on 90-degree than 180-degree perspective differences when the placements were to be made adjacent to a repeated feature ($p < .01$) but the differences were not significant for placements in a quadrant by a unique feature or an edge.

The differences in performance in placing objects about a feature are significant for both perspective differences ($p < .01$). In each case children made fewer egocentric placements about a unique feature than they did about a repeated feature. The effect of perspective difference was significant for both placements by a unique and by a repeated feature ($p < .01$).

Egocentrism in orienting the animal was also affected by placement type and perspective difference. When perspective difference was 90 degrees, the differences in performance among placement types were significant ($p < .01$), but none of the differences were reliable when the rotation was 180 degrees. Differences in perspective influenced performance in orienting an object by a unique feature or an edge ($p < .01$) but not by a repeated feature. Children made very few egocentric errors on the 90-degree condition in the two former cases.

In the final set of analyses, performance on location and orientation was compared. Of the 63 children tested, 57 made more orientation than quadrant errors, and 59 made more orientation than about a feature errors. Similar results were found for egocentric errors; 53 children made more egocentric errors in orienting the animal than in locating it about a feature. In each case the distribution is significantly different from chance ($p < .01$).

DISCUSSION

In general, the data are consistent with the symmetry analyses suggested in the introduction; more specifically, the local symmetry relations were more important than the global ones. Children did make significantly more egocentric errors when the perspective difference was 180 degrees; however, their spatial thinking on the 180 degree trial was neither exclusively egocentric in this condition nor was it exclusively nonegocentric when the perspectives differed by 90 degrees.

The fact that children made fewer errors on 90-degree as compared to 180-degree differences and fewer location than orientation errors might be related to symmetry as well. Perhaps the assymmetry affords a disequilibrium that not only motivates the child to abandon an egocentric perspective but also to detect relations intrinsic to the space. The improvement was restricted to discriminating between the two trees and about the house or barn. The former suggests that the children coordinated spatial properties within a system. However, if such a system existed, it would be expected that the children would also better differentiate positions by an edge and positions about a tree, both of which are possible only if the positions are organized into a coordinate system. Perhaps it is more parsimonious to conclude that these children were at best more likely to detect distinctive features. This would account for the clear reduction in errors made about the unique features which were distinctively marked on all four sides and it also accounts for the discrimination between trees because one was by a pond while the other was not.

Orientation also seems to be influenced by local symmetry relations. In those cases where the animal was parallel to an edge or side of a building, the children conserved this relation (85%). When the perspective difference was 180 degrees, the parallel relation from both perspectives was symmetrical with respect to self, for example, the parallel lines projected along the near-far axis. Conserving parallelness was then consistent with egocentric thought on the 180-degree difference but not on the 90-degree difference. The tendency to conserve this relation accounts for the fact that children rarely oriented the animals egocentrically if the perspective difference was 90 degrees. However, when parallelness to any immediately adjacent feature was not an aspect of the orientation, perspective differences did not differentially affect how the animal was oriented. For both perspective differences, approximately 76% of the errors of orientation were egocentric.

The fact that perspective differences were significant for orientations by a unique feature is interesting and seems consistent with the equilibration hypothesis offered above. When there was asymmetry, the children would abandon an egocentric orientation and become more sensitive to spatial relations intrinsic to the space. In many cases they apparently detected the distinctive features which marked the sides of each building and projected the orientation towards them, for example, toward the silo. When there was symmetry the children were less likely to detect or use this information, probably because in this case the egocentric orientation appeared to be so similar to the objective orientation.

The most obvious difference in orientation and location performance was when placements were next to a unique feature. Children were much more likely to locate the animal on the correct side of that feature than to orient it correctly. Perhaps location was easier because the sides of these buildings differed in many ways; thus, location was redundantly marked, whereas orientation had to be projected onto a specific feature. The difficulty the children had detecting distinctive features toward which to orient the animal was reflected in the difficulty they had orienting the animals correctly by an edge. Another possibility was that orientation was initially not analyzed as having a direction but only as an angular relation between edges. Thus, children might accept conservation of an angular relation as a sufficient description of an orientation. This appears to be reasonable explanation for the children's efforts to orient the animal by an edge when the perspective was 90 degrees. They were correct on half of the trials, which is at chance level if they were randomly choosing direction but conserving the parallel relation with the appropriate edge. It is possible that both interpretations are valid. Perhaps the children's first level of analysis was to conserve the angular relation and the second level was to examine the features onto which the animal gazed. If distinctive features were nearby, the children were likely to use them, but if they were at some distance, they might not have been detected or used them. Nevertheless, even if they are proximate and detectable, their functional value depends on whether or not there was a symmetry relation between self and the two perspectives.

The symmetry hypothesis has been offered as an explanation for the dynamic relation among spatial reference systems (Pufall & Shaw, 1973). It follows from this hypothesis that objective and self-referential systems coexist in the young child's thought, and perhaps in thought at all levels of development. When the systems are asymmetric, the child is motivated to explore cognitively or act on the relations intrinsic to that particular space. Presumably, through such activity the pre-operational child not only differentiates topographic and projective spatial properties (E. J. Gibson, 1969; J. J. Gibson, 1966) but also abstracts or constructs operational systems of reference from actions of co-ordination applied to space.

The development of these two aspects of knowing marks the beginning of concrete operational thought. However, especially during the early operational thought, structuring activities are intimately linked with topographic cues. When topographic information is reduced, thus increasing symmetry among descriptions of surface features, there is increased egocentric thinking even among children as old as 10 years of age when they have to mentally transform a space (Pufall & Shaw, 1973). Egocentrism in this case reflects the operational level of thought as the child multiplies egocentric relations differentiating identical objects because they are far left, far right, etc. Older, but not younger, operational children perform almost errorlessly if they are given relatively brief experiences with this type of space, suggesting that they detect abstract spatial relations which reduce symmetry relations (Pufall, Note 1). Thus, during the concrete operational period, children learn to detect abstract spatial properties and this expanded sensitivity to distinctive features means that asymmetry would become more the rule than the exception.

Reference Note

PUFALL, P. B. Developmental relations between egocentrism and coordinate reference systems. In D. Shelton (Chair). *Development of spatial reference systems.* Symposium presented at the meeting of the Society for Research in Child Development Philadelphia, 1973.

References

FISHBEIN, H. D., LEWIS, S., & KEIFFER, K. Children's understanding of spatial relations: coordination of perspectives. *Developmental Psychology,* 1972, **7**, 21–33.

GIBSON, E. J. *Principles of perceptual learning and development.* New York: Appleton-Century-Crofts, 1969.

GIBSON, J. J. *The senses considered as perceptual systems.* Boston: Houghton-Mifflin, 1966.

INHELDER, B., & SINCLAIR, H. "Learning cognitive structures." In P. H. Mussen, J. Langer, M. Covington (Eds.) *Trends and Issues in Developmental Psychology.* New York: Holt, Rinehart and Winston, 1969.

LAURENDEAU, M., & PINARD, T. *The development of the concept of space in the child.* New York: International Universities Press, Inc. 1970.

PIAGET, J., & INHELDER, B. *The child's conception of space.* London: Routledge and Kegan Paul, 1956.

PUFALL, P. B., & SHAW, R. E. Analysis of the development of children's reference systems. *Cognitive Psychology,* 1973, 5, 151–175.

Verbal Interactions Between Children and Their Mothers During the Preschool Years

Ernst L. Moerk

CALIFORNIA STATE UNIVERSITY, FRESNO

Twenty children and their mothers were observed while interacting verbally in an unstructured situation. The 10 boys and girls ranged in age from around 2 to 5 years. Quantitative as well as categorical aspects of the interactions were analyzed. Both types of dependent variables were found to change with the age and the language level of the children. Close mutual adaptation of both partners for the quantitative as well as the qualitative dimension were demonstrated. The correlation patterns between the types of utterances allow the abstraction of a "primitive" and an advanced cluster of language-teaching/learning behaviors. The stability and generalizability of these trends were discussed in comparisons with other recent studies on this topic.

In contrast to previous assertions, recent evidence indicates that mothers provide language input highly suited for their preschool children (Snow, 1972; Drach, Note 1; Pfuderer, Note 2; Frank & Seegmiller, Note 3). It has also been reported that mothers adapt their language behavior to the capacities of their children as the children progress in their language skills (Phillips, 1973; Snow, 1972; Baldwin, Note 4). The detailed changes in the types of interactions and the possible consequences for language learning, however, have been only minimally explored (Moerk, 1974; Nelson, 1973; Baldwin, Note 4; Moerk, Note 5). Single suggestive findings on this topic have been reported: Slobin (1968) indicated that with increasing age of the child, the frequency of imitations and expansions declines. Shipley, Smith, and Gleitman (1969) also found a decline in imitation with increasing verbal maturity of the child. These early leads have recently been substantiated by Kemp and Dale (Note 6), Nelson (1973), and Bloom, Hood, and Lightbown (1974).

From *Developmental Psychology,* 1975, **11**, 788–794. Copyright © 1975 by The American Psychological Association. Reprinted by permission.

The existing evidence suggests several specific aspects of the verbal interactions between mothers and their children that need detailed study: (a) The influence of the age and language level of the child on types of verbal behavior of both members of the dyad has to be further explored. (b) The achievement of the calibration between mother and child has to be investigated. It appears that Moerk (1972) has to date made the only attempt to subject this topic to a detailed analysis. (c) The interrelationships between the various types of language behavior of children and their mothers have to be explored by means of contingency or correlational studies.

The present investigation is oriented toward these three aspects of dyadic interactions. Quantitative as well as categorical measures are included as dependent variables.

METHOD

SUBJECTS   The subjects were 10 girls and 10 boys with their mothers from normal middle-class homes. The ages of the girls ranged from 1 year 9 months to 5 years 0 months, and those of the boys from 2 years 4 months to 5 years 0 months. When the children were placed in rank order according to their ages, the modal difference between 2 adjacent children was 2 months. For both sexes there was one maximum difference of 12 months; between 2 boys there was also a minimal difference of 0 months. All three extremes appeared at the limits of the age range, the maximum difference at the upper age limit. English was the main language, although a second language was used in some homes and understood by the child. The 20 pairs were selected from over 30 dyads; length of protocol and normalcy of interaction were the selection criteria. Protocols with less than 100 utterances per member and those that provided evidence of tense and affected behavior were excluded. Observers were trained psychology students who had been previously acquainted with but were not related to the observed dyads. Each dyad had a different observer, who, as a familiar person, could blend unobtrusively into the behavior setting before he began the recording.

PROCEDURE   The design of the study is cross-sectional. Only one interaction of each mother–child pair, lasting 1 hour, was analyzed. The home was chosen as the setting for the observation and only mother–child interactions were analyzed. The behavior setting was described at the beginning of the observation, and whenever changes occurred they were recorded. Mothers and children followed their usual routines while their language interactions were tape recorded. The accompanying nonverbal behavior of both partners was recorded by the observers as completely as possible in written form, and both types of information were included in the transcribed protocols.

ANALYSIS OF DATA   The average length of utterance, in syllables, was calculated for each child as an index of his linguistic level. The utterances of both interaction partners were classified into categories according to their communicational functions. Only categories for which high interrater reliability of categorization could be obtained were used. The indices of reliability (Scott, 1955; Scott & Wertheimer, 1962) ranged from .76 to .93.

RESULTS AND DISCUSSION

Discussed first is the correlation between the age of the children and their mean utterance length, as well as the mutual adaptation of the verbal behavior of both partners in its quantitative aspect, as expressed by the length of utterances. A high correlation was found between the age of the child and his mean utterance length, $r(19) = .82, p < .01$. In contrast, the age of the child was not significantly related to measures of the mother's utterance length. A much better predictor of the mean length of the mother's utterances is the mean statement length of the child. The correlation between these two variables was highly significant, $r(19) = .69, p < .01$. Significant correlations were also found between the modal and maximum utterance length of both partners, $r(19) = .44, p < .05$ and $r(19) = .54, p < .01$; this also indicates that mothers and their children have developed congruence in specific aspects of interaction.

Correlations represent only relative similarity; the absolute differences between the obtained values could still be very great. These differences between the child's and mother's utterance length appear to be of special importance because the child has to analyze the mother's model in order to learn from it; these differences are reported in Figure 1.

The mean utterance length of the mother exceeds that of the child in all 20 dyads. Since the difference between the mean utterance length of both partners is small, the mother probably provides an optimal amount of incitement for the child to master this higher linguistic level. The mothers' mean utterance length increases less over the age span studied than does that of the children, which results in a decrease in the difference between the means. A comparison between the mothers' mean and the children's maximum provides evidence that the complexity of the mothers' utterances lies well within the range of competence of the child. When the curve of the mothers' maximum utterance length is considered, it is seen that almost all mothers maximally tax the capacities of their children. The only instance in which the maximum utterance length of the child exceeds that of the mother by two syllables is probably due to chance, since only a small number of interactions were sampled in 1 hour of observation. The high correlation between the mothers' and the children's maximum utterance length suggests that mothers are aware of sentence length as one aspect of their children's linguistic competence. The absolute difference between both maxima indicates, furthermore, that mothers know that the capacity to comprehend linguistic messages somewhat surpasses the capacity to produce them.

Large differences exist between the maximum, mean, and modal utterances of the mother. The differences between the mother's maximum length utterances and the child's mean and modal ones are even larger. Since the mother's maximum length utterances were usually comprehended by the child, the differences express the gap between the maximum performance potential and the average performance and between the performance in comprehension versus that in production, respectively. The impact of these discrepancies on the interactions of individual dyads and on the language acquisition of the child may be important. Figure 1 shows that despite the general age trend, large differences between individual dyads exist. Some mothers seem to be more prone than others to maximally tax the capacity of their children to process long sentences.

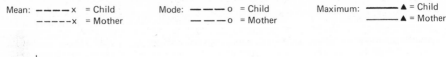

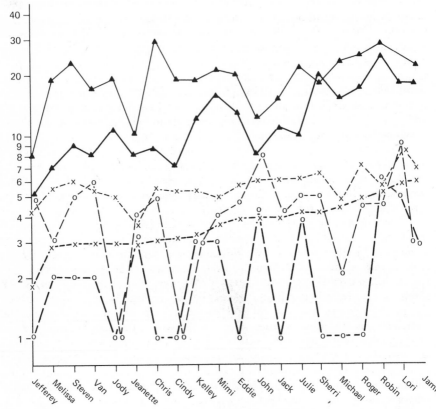

FIGURE 1.   *Changes in the measures of utterance length with increasing age of the child.*

The pattern of modal length statements, which is greatly subject to chance influences in small samples of interactions, is more irregular. Yet again, with one exception, the modal utterance length of the mothers is equal to or longer than that of their children.

More important than the quantitative aspects of language acquisition may be the changes in the type of interactions between mother and child when the child advances in age and language skills. Frequency counts of types of interaction were performed, and the raw frequencies were transformed into percentages of the total number of utterances of mother and child respectively. Since no significant differences between boys and girls were obtained, the data for both sexes were collapsed.

Eight categories for the verbal behavior of the mother and nine for that of the child could be reliably differentiated. Their mean frequencies and the standard deviations in percentages are presented after the label for each category. The mother's interactions fall into three larger content groups: (a) One group encompasses all those variables that represent a translation of objective/environmental/pictorial configurations into the verbal medium. These are: "Mother models from picture book" ($M = 5.02$, $SD = 6.68$); "mother describes an object or event" ($M = 5.41$, $SD = 3.86$); "mother describes her own acts" ($M = 1.03$, $SD = 1.04$); and "mother describes child's acts" ($M = 1.30$, $SD = 1.32$). (b) The next group, consisting of "mother gives corrective feedback" ($M = 4.18$, $SD = 4.83$) and "mother answers a question" ($M = 5.17$, $SD = 6.73$), deals with responses of the mother to verbal behavior of the child. (c) The third group, "mother guides child's action" ($M = 2.60$, $SD = 2.58$) and "mother gives an explanation" ($M = 3.54$, $SD = 2.54$), is somewhat in contrast to the first one because environmentals given are not translated into language, but language has to be translated into external or internal actions. The latter two categories are relatively sophisticated and their frequencies increase most with the age and language level of the child.

The nine categories of the child's verbal behavior seem to fall into four groups. "Child imitates" ($M = 5.54$, $SD = 6.99$) represents a special phenomenon and should probably be classified separately. The next three variables, "child asks a question" ($M = 9.62$, $SD = 6.88$), "child expresses a need" ($M = 10.81$, $SD = 5.97$), and "child answers a question" ($M = 16.98$, $SD = 9.02$), serve primarily as information exchange. The categories "child encodes from picture book" ($M = 8.34$, $SD = 11.39$), "child describes an object or event" ($M = 6.36$, $SD = 3.67$), and "child describes his own acts" ($M = 3.07$, $SD = 2.17$) parallel those of the mother in that external circumstances are translated into language. Finally, two categories, "child describes a past experience" ($M = 2.71$, $SD = 2.41$) and "child describes his plans" ($M = 3.43$, $SD = 2.88$), represent a translation of cognitive representations into the linguistic medium. The last two phenomena are more advanced cognitively, and their frequencies increase most distinctly with the linguistic level of the child.

This functional description of the categories suggests that these interactions could provide opportunities to teach and learn language. Moerk (1972) has provided some support for this suggestion. A summation of the means shows that approximately 25% of the mother's utterances and 65% of those of the child are accounted for by the above categorizations. With an average total of 300 and 200 utterances for mother and child, respectively, at least 75 and 130 utterances of the mother and the child, respectively, could be conductive to the teaching or the acquisition of language skills.

Changes in the form of interaction are more closely related to the mean statement length of the child than to his age or to the mean statement length of the mother. The discussion will, therefore, center on the correlation between the types of interaction and the mean statement length of the child. Four types of relationships can be distinguished:

1. An inverse relationship between the language level of the child and the frequency with which a type of interaction is used; this is expressed

in negative correlations. The correlations and regression equations used to predict the interactional category (Y) from the mean length of utterance of the child (X) are: "Mother models from picture book": $r(19) = -.61$, $p < .01$, $Y = 19.27 - 3.77 X$; "mother gives corrective feedback": $r(19) = -.61, p < .01, Y = 14.42 - 2.71 X$; "mother describes child's acts": $r = -.44, p < .05, Y = 3.34 - .54 X$; "child imitates": $r(19) = -.48$, $p < .05, Y = 17.45 - 3.15 X$; "child encodes from picture book": $r(19) = -.61, p < .01; Y = 32.80 - 6.47 X$.

2. A significant positive relationship between the mean utterance length of the child and the type of interaction is found in two instances. The same data are supplied as above. "Child describes a past experience": $r(19) = .57, p < .01, Y = -2.20 + 1.30 X$; "child describes his plans": $r(19) = .60, p < .01, Y = -2.66 + 1.61 X$. The correlation approaches significance in the case of "mother guides child's action": $r(19) = .39$, $.05 < p < .10, Y = -.92 + .93 X$.

3. The third group of interactional categories does not appear to be related to the level of the child's language. This independence is expressed in low and insignificant correlations.

4. Finally, the frequency of three interaction forms appears to be related curvilinearly to the age and mean utterance length of the child. Since this relationship is most distinct in regard to the age of the child, the correlation ratio, eta, in relation to age was computed. For "mother answers a question": $\eta(4, 15) = .64, p < .01$; for "child asks a question": $\eta(4, 15) = .66, p < .01$; and for "child answers a question": $\eta(4, 15) = .35$ (ns). These three correlation ratios are considerably higher than the corresponding correlation coefficients, $r = .29, .38$, and $-.21$, respectively; none of the latter reached significance.

A last aspect of the present analysis centers on the interrelation of the various forms of interaction. The complete correlation matrix is composed of three different submatrices: (a) the intercorrelations of the mother's forms of interaction; (b) the intercorrelations of interactional forms of the child; and (c) the correlations between the forms of interaction of the mother and those of the child as an expression of dyadic dynamics. Only the following three significant correlations were obtained between the interactional categories of mothers: Between "mother gives corrective feedback" and "mother describes child's acts," $r(19) = .59, p < .01$; between "mother answers a question" and "mother gives an explanation," $r(19) = .46, p < .05$; and between "mother guides child's action" and "mother gives an explanation," $r(19) = .55, p < .05$. These correlation patterns seem to represent a cognitive didactic interaction style of mothers.

The larger number of significant intercorrelations of the interactional behaviors of the child allow the abstraction of two clusters: (a) A cluster of "primitive" interactional forms, which are positively correlated with each other and negatively correlated with more mature forms. The following variables belong to this first cluster: "Child imitates" and "child encodes from picture books." (b) A cluster of more mature forms of interaction includes the variables "child describes his plans," "child describes a past experience," "child describes his own acts," and "child describes an object or event." The variables pertaining to the latter cluster are negatively correlated with those of the first cluster.

When the correlations between the forms of interaction of the mother and those of the child are inspected, the same dichotomy can be seen: the child's primitive forms, that is, imitation and encoding from picture books, are positively correlated with the mother's modeling from picture books and her corrective feedback. The correlations with imitation are: $r(19) = .77, p < .01$ and $r(19) = .44, p < .05$. Those with encoding from picture books are: $r(19) = .69, p < .01$ and $r(19) = .41, p < .10$. The child's use of picture books is also negatively correlated with the mother's more complex forms of interaction: "Mother gives an explanation," $r(19) = - .52, p < .01$, and "mother describes an object or event," $r(19) = - .47, p < .05$. On the other hand, the child's more mature forms of interaction are highly and significantly correlated with the mother's more sophisticated categories: "answers a question," "guides child's actions," "gives an explanation," and "describes an object or event." The correlation pattern between the primitive as well as the mature interactional forms of both partners again provides striking proof of the high level of calibration achieved between the partners even when the qualitative aspect of their interactions is considered.

In summary, the present findings are in accord with those of Pfuderer (Note 2), Moerk (1974, Note 5), Phillips (1973), and the reports of the group associated with Baldwin (Note 4) in indicating a gradual increase in the complexity of the speech of both mothers and children. All the authors affirm that the speech of the mother is always somewhat above that of the child in complexity, that is, the mother seems to "pace" the child's linguistic performance.

Similarities also appear between the few studies that deal with qualitative changes in interactions. Nelson (1973) reported the frequency of mothers' descriptions of objects to be around 7% while in the present study a mean of 5.41 and a standard deviation of 3.86 is found for this category. All researchers reported a decline in imitation with the language level of the child beginning around the age of 2 years. Nelson (1973) demonstrated that at the age of 2 years, the asking of questions by children is positively related to all language indices. The curvilinear relationship of question asking with age, as found in the present study, also suggests that question asking at this early age fulfills a productive function for language acquisition. A decline of this type of interaction from 26% at $2\frac{1}{2}$ years of age to 21% at age 5 was also reported by Baldwin (Note 4). These two reports are in conflict with Moerk's (1974) finding that question-asking behavior increases up to the age of 5 years. However, when Moerk (Note 5) reported data of a larger sample, he also found some indication of a decrease in this behavior when the children reached the highest level of language skills. Since all of the above-discussed studies included only a relatively small number of dyads, Seegmiller's (Note 7) observation may explain the differences. She indicated that wide differences between dyads exist in the amount of question–answer interaction. The same fact has also been observed in the present sample. Chance factors of sample selection may therefore account for the differences encountered in published reports.

Baldwin's (Note 4) conclusion that children progress from labeling to conversations about materials and activities is also supported by the present results. The more frequent descriptions of objects, events, and actions together with the steep increase in the discussion about past experiences and future plans represent the relevant evidence. In a related manner, Sigel (1971) discussed the "distancing function" of language, and Lewis (1973) and Morris (1938) offered some cognitive-evolutionary explanations for its development during early childhood.

Besides these specific points of correspondence, in all the relevant studies a close calibration between mother and child has been found for all channels of communication (Escalona, 1973). Accordingly, mothers seem to be discriminately, albeit perhaps without full awareness, involved in the language-teaching process. In all of the present protocols it was impressive to observe how "mothers frequently and opportunistically seized upon the present situations and materials to get in a bit of teaching" (Seegmiller, Note 7, p. 7). Since much teaching and learning can result from such interactions that continue over several years, the instructional activities of parents deserve closer attention in every attempt to explain first language acquisition.

Reference Notes

1. DRACH, K. M. The language of the parent: A pilot study. In K. Drach, B. Kobashigawa, C. Pfuderer, & D. Slobin (Eds.), *The structure of linguistic input to children* (Language-Behavior Research Laboratory, Working Paper 14). Unpublished manuscript, University of California, Berkeley, January 1969.
2. PFUDERER, C. Some suggestions for a syntactic characterization of baby-talk style. In K. Drach, B. Kobashigawa, C. Pfuderer, & D. Slobin (Eds.), *The structure of linguistic input to children* (Language-Behavior Research Laboratory, Working Paper 14). Unpublished manuscript, University of California, Berkeley, January 1969.
3. FRANK, S. M., & SEEGMILLER, M. S. *Children's language environment in free play situations.* Paper presented at the biennial meeting of the Society for Research in Child Development, Philadelphia, March 1973.
4. BALDWIN, C. P. *Comparison of mother–child interactions at different ages and in families of different educational level and ethnic backgrounds.* Paper presented at the biennial meeting of the Society for Research in Child Development, Philadelphia, March 1973.
5. MOERK, E. L. *Changes in verbal interactions of child–mother dyads with increasing language skills of the child.* Paper presented at the 20th International Congress of Psychology, Tokyo, Japan, August 1972.
6. KEMP, J. C., & DALE, P. S. *Spontaneous imitations and free speech: A developmental comparison.* Paper presented at the biennial meeting of the Society for Research in Child Development, Philadelphia, March 1973.
7. SEEGMILLER, B. *The norms and patterns of mother–child interaction in free play.* Paper presented at the biennial meeting of the Society for Research in Child Development, Philadelphia, March 1973.

References

BLOOM, L., HOOD, L., & LIGHTBOWN, P. Imitation in language development: If, when, and why. *Cognitive Psychology*, 1974, **6**, 380–420.
ESCALONA, S. K. Basic modes of social interaction: Their emergence and patterning during the first two years of life. *Merrill-Palmer Quarterly*, 1973, **19**, 205–232.

LEWIS, M. M. The beginning of reference to past and future in a child's speech. *The British Journal of Educational Psychology*, 1937, **7**, 39–56.

MOERK, E. L. Principles of dyadic interaction in language learning. *Merrill-Palmer Quarterly*, 1972, **18**, 229–257.

MOERK, E. L. Changes in verbal child–mother interactions with increasing language skills of the child. *Journal of Psycholinguistic Research*, 1974, **3**, 101–116.

MORRIS, C. W. Foundations of the theory of signs. In O. Neurath, R. Carnap, & C. W. Morris (Eds.), *International encyclopedia of unified science* (Vol. 1). Chicago: University of Chicago Press, 1938.

NELSON, K. Structure and strategy in learning to talk. *Monographs of the Society for Research in Child Development*, 1973, **38**, (1, 2, Whole No. 149).

PHILLIPS, J. R. Syntax and vocabulary of mother's speech to young children: Age and sex comparisons. *Child Development*, 1973, **44**, 182–185.

SCOTT, W. A. Reliability of content analysis. The case of nominal scale coding. *Public Opinion Quarterly*, 1955, **19**, 321–325.

SCOTT, W. A., & WERTHEIMER, M. *Introduction to psychological research*. New York: Wiley, 1962.

SHIPLEY, E. F., SMITH, C. S., & GLEITMAN, L. R. A study in the acquisition of language: Free response to commands. *Language*, 1969, **45**, 322–342.

SIGEL, I. Language of the disadvantaged: The distancing hypothesis. In C. Stendler-Lavatelli (Ed.), *Language training in early childhood education*. Urbana: University of Illinois Press, 1971.

SLOBIN, D. I. Imitation and grammatical development in children. In N. S. Endler, L. R. Boulter, & H. Osser (Eds.), *Contemporary issues in developmental psychology*. New York: Holt, Rinehart & Winston, 1968.

SNOW, C. E. Mother's speech to children learning language. *Child Development*, 1972, **43**, 549–565.

Chapter 3
Emotional and Social Development

THE MERRILL-PALMER INSTITUTE. PHOTO BY DONNA J. HARRIS.

The affective or feeling side of experience is a part of interactions with other people. Thus, social experience is closely linked with the development of emotions and self. Cognitive growth also influences emotional and social development. We may separate these aspects of development in order to discuss them, just as we might discuss first height and then weight, even though height and weight are closely related in physical growth.

Many of the child's social experiences are designed to shape his behavior in accordance with goals held by his family and their society. These experiences constitute *socialization*. Children try to control their parents' behavior, too, and often succeed in their efforts. Parents and children feel both love and hostility toward each other. Siblings and playmates also shape and influence one another.

Because the older infant and young preschool child are concerned with developing the sense of autonomy, they often resist a controlling parent. Problems of control may arouse hostility in parent and child. Then the sense of trust is involved. In developing the sense of initiative, the older preschool child may also challenge parental control. Excessive control can lead to stunted initiative. Parents are faced

153

with the problem of giving their children enough control and direction to socialize them adequately, while still giving enough opportunities for their children to develop themselves. The love and warmth of parent toward child determines the effects of the control exerted.

Love and Friendship

Happy feelings and positive interactions are now receiving the attention of researchers. There is active interest in finding out how to promote altruism and responsibility for group welfare rather than unrestrained self-interest.

As an infant, the child establishes bonds of attachment to parents, siblings, kin, and other people who offer care, interesting response, and stimulation. As the preschool child's social contacts expand, so can the number of people with whom he forms enduring bonds. He becomes attached to other children, his friends. Additional children form his peer group, in the neighborhood, day-care center, or nursery school.

INTERACTION WITH FRIENDS AND PEERS

When young children are friendly and involved with peers, they are likely to also be active, vigorous, assertive, expressive, aggressive, and not fearful or withdrawn [70]. Play is essential to children's learning and development. Play is influenced not only by the participants but by the conditions under which it takes place. Play may be nonsocial, as when two children engage in independent, separate activities. Or it can be social.

Social Play. Two essential features define social play [24]. The players alternate their behavior, each waiting in turn for the other to respond and fitting their response to the previous action. The play is nonliteral. The players know that it is "just pretend." For example, X and Y find a toy snake. X holds it up. Y, drawing back with an expression of alarm says "What's that?" X, laughing, says "It's a snake." Y then says "Do it again." They do it again.

There are definite patterns of interactions and repetitions, some with symmetrical turn taking. In one pattern, the second turn reproduces the rhythm, intonation, and volume of the first, as in X: "Bye, Mommy." Y: "Bye, Daddy." Three-year-olds tended to repeat these rounds more than 5-year-olds who created more complicated episodes. The fact that an interchange is play and not literal may be indicated by chanting or using a special voice, but often there are asides, such as "Let's pretend" or "I'll be the mommy and you be the baby." All sets of players showed that they recognized that a state of play was in force, that rules were mutually binding, and that both players could modify the theme of the play. The author suggests that one of the satisfactions of play is in eliciting and maintaining the responsive behavior of others. Each has the experience of control and being controlled, giving and taking. It is likely that basic social interaction patterns are thus acquired through social play.

Although the learning of social interaction involves some conflict, social play is usually positive in tone. Friendly behavior is much more frequent than is its opposite [44].

Sociodramatic Play. Children can pretend or make believe with or without other children. Below about 3 years of age, much pretending can be carried out just about as well alone, with occasional input from a parent. Between 3 and 5, children normally engage in more frequent, longer, more complex, and more social make-believe play. Through her research on the education of disadvantaged children in Israel, Sara Smilansky has defined sociodramatic play and has clarified its role in normal development and in compensatory education. She gives six essential elements of sociodramatic play [65].

1. Imitative role play. The child expresses a make-believe role in imitative acts and/or words.
2. Make-believe with objects. Actions or words are substituted for objects.
3. Make-believe in substituting words for acts and situations.
4. Persistence in the episode for at least ten minutes.
5. Interaction of at least two participants.
6. Verbal communication about the play.

The first four elements occur in dramatic play. The addition of the last two are essential for sociodramatic play.

Smilansky has observed that until about 3, a child imitates small pieces of his parents' (and other significant adults') behavior, expressing his identification with them through dramatic play. Thus, he irons as Mommy does or drives a tractor like Daddy. After 3, he begins to see that the thoughts, feelings, and actions he has been imitating are not merely single episodes but that they are also reactions to other people. Sociodramatic play is born of the understanding that people react to each other and interact with each other. The child needs other children, for now he wants to imitate both actions and reactions. He wants to reproduce the world as he understands it [65, p. 71].

Sociodramatic play was the setting for 65 per cent of the positive social reinforcement given by nursery school children to their peers, [11]. Thus, they interacted more in dramatic play than they did during involvement with art, music, table games, and such. In response to other children, children gave attention, approval, and submission. They were likely to initiate an exchange by offering affection, personal acceptance, and tokens. Dramatic play also facilitates the use of language, playful expression of anger and hostility, and the trying on of various roles. Thus, sociodramatic play is the arena in which children cooperatively work out their own interpretation and understanding of the social world and develop skills for dealing with social realities.

Inadequate sociodramatic play, then, might be expected to be found among children who are not dealing competently with the social demands that they face. Such was indeed the case among the disadvantaged children studied by Smilansky in Israel [65]. They did less role playing than the middle-class contrast group and engaged in more manipulative, repetitive, stereotyped activities with play equipment. Training in imaginative play was followed by increases in communication and decreases in aggression, hyperactivity, and passivity. Other experiments have shown positive effects of training in sociodramatic play upon problem solving and on comprehension of social roles and perspectives [21; 53a].

Improvement in imaginative play, concentration in play, and expression of positive feelings were seen in a group of New York working-class kindergarten children who received training in sociodramatic play [23]. After training, the children used "pretend voices" much more and simulated different sounds. They used equipment in more original ways. They engaged in more, longer, and more complex dialogues; did more labeling; and paid more attention to detail. Absorbed in their play, the children often resisted interruption. Within this group, comparisons were made between children who were predisposed to fantasy (high fantasy) and those with low tendencies to fantasize. The high-fantasy children were more likely to be only or eldest children and to have fewer siblings, more living space, and parents with more education and language facility. Mothers reported more closeness to high-fantasy children and more willingness to engage in imaginative activities with their children.

Understanding Others. In their sociodramatic and other imaginative play, children reveal their understanding of other people's behavior and feelings by the ways in which they play those roles. However, because it is difficult to measure spontaneous imaginative behavior or to experiment with it, researchers have sought other ways of testing children's perceptions of others. Stories or pictures or stories with pictures have been used as the bases of questions to the subject about how other people are feeling. In one such study, 40 per cent of the children showed that they understood how the story-child felt but that they themselves felt differently. In 17 per cent of the cases, children understood how the story-child felt and also felt the same emotion themselves [43]. The more similar the perceived person is to the subject, the more likely is the subject to understand the feelings of the person perceived [58]. For example, children identified affective states of like-sex characters better than they did characters of the opposite sex [14]. At the same time, brighter children did better than children of lower IQs in indicating how the story-children felt.

In order to communicate well, a person has to judge the effect of his words upon the listener, by taking the other's point of view. To understand the thinking of others is more difficult than to perceive their feelings. A method of testing such understanding is to have subjects describe stimuli that their listeners cannot see. Children of 4 and 7 were required to describe nonsense figures to listeners who gave verbal and nonverbal signs of not understanding [49]. Both groups reformulated their descriptions when asked to do so, but only the older children reformulated when listeners expressed their puzzlement nonverbally. Results suggest that between 4 and 7, children gain considerable ability to role-play the thinking of others.

Preferences in Friends. Young children have definite preferences in playmates. They can tell which children they like best and least. Observations in nursery schools reveal children playing consistently with liked peers. Degree of popularity can be assessed by sociometric methods adapted to young children. Instead of asking the child the names of his best friends, a useful technique is to show him a

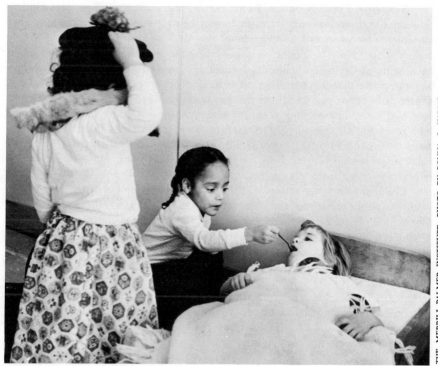

THE MERRILL-PALMER INSTITUTE. PHOTO BY DONNA J. HARRIS.

board mounted with photographs of all the children in his play group. He can then name or point to the one he likes to play with, the one he doesn't like to play with, one he would like to take home after school, and so on. Popularity scores can be derived from numbers of choices, and characteristics of low, high, and medium scorers can be studied.

High scorers on a picture-board sociometric test were found to be more likely than other children to use positive social reinforcement and to use it with a large number of children [27]. Positive social reinforcers were attention, approval, affection, acceptance, submission, and tokens. Low scorers (rejected children) were likely to give negative social reinforcement, which included noncompliance (refusing to submit or cooperate, ignoring overtures of others), interferences, such as taking property or disrupting activity, ridiculing, blaming, tattling, attacking, threatening, and demanding. Giving and receiving positive reinforcement were found to be reciprocal activities. That is, those who gave the most got the most. Four-year-olds gave more than 3-year-olds and also spread their reinforcements over a large number of recipients [11]. Boys gave more to boys and girls to girls.

Popular children sometimes use negative reinforcement with their peers. Other children seem to take into consideration the type of aggression used and the situation in which it occurs [44]. Peers are likely to tolerate provoked aggression directed toward an appropriate object, thus considering the intensity of the act and the degree of threat to the recipient.

Nonverbal Social Behavior. Facial expressions, posture, and gestures indicate emotional and motivational states in human beings, as well as in animals. Such movements act as signals to members of the same species. Nonverbal signals are organized into clusters. Young children show different clusters of signals in different situations. Crying and clinging, for instance, make up a cluster of signals that has immediate meaning for other persons. In order to examine peer interactions, approach behavior and facial expressions were observed and filmed in preschool girls and boys, approaching same-sex and opposite-sex peers [71]. Children of both sexes and all ages stayed farther away from and oriented their bodies farther away from children of the opposite sex. This finding is consistent with preschool children preferring to play with members of the same sex and giving more reinforcements to like-sex playmates.

Children sometimes act nonverbally as a group, taking cues from each other's gestures, facial expressions, and vocalizations. *Group glee* is a term used to describe a particular cluster of nonverbal signals used by a group of children [61]. Groups of children from 2 to 5 were videotaped in a school setting. Group glee consisted of joyful laughter or screaming often accompanied by intense physical action. Although glee usually spread through the group, it sometimes occurred in a burst, all at once. Glee was most likely to be shown by a group of seven to nine children that included both girls and boys. This study is of interest not only because of its focus on nonverbal group behavior but also because it deals with joy and happiness of children together. Anyone who has observed children has seen group glee, but few people have thought much about it.

Environmental Influences on Play. The physical setting determines much of how children play, in both obvious and subtle ways. Arrangements of space and toys may or may not offer opportunities for pretend play, cooperative block building, and moving freely. The nursery school teacher's knowledge and creativity are fully employed in setting the stage for play.

The effect of density on a group was explored by observing the same groups of six children each, in a large (265 square feet) and small (90 square feet) room [39]. In the high-density room, children spent more time in solitary play and less in interaction with each other. Boys showed more aggression than girls throughout, but were less aggressive in the small room than in the large one. It seemed as though children adjusted to overstimulation and likelihood of intrusion by cutting down on social interaction.

Sex differences in activity have often been noted, with boys playing more actively than girls. Differential activity level of boys and girls may be a result of social factors as much as of indoor-outdoor influences. When preschool children played alone, there were no differences in activity level between girls and boys, but when they played in groups, boys were much more active than girls [26]. Outdoors, boys were more active than girls. Since group play occurs more frequently outdoors, the excitement of the group is often or even usually added to the freedom of the outdoors.

The number of adults in the environment makes a difference in children's interactions with peers. Two studies in nursery schools showed that a high adult-child ratio was associated with low peer interaction [46, 51].

CARING FOR OTHERS

An important aspect of love is caring or giving care to others. When parents give care, it is often called *nurturance,* but when children give care, it is often called *sympathy, giving, helping,* or *altruism.*

Nurturance. Parents give care or nurture when they give food, clothing, shelter, and toys, when they express affection, pay attention, give comfort and help, and otherwise behave in ways that promote the growth, health, and well-being of their children. *Warmth* describes the emotional tone of nurturant behavior. Parents ordinarily give nurturance, some more than others. Grandparents, older siblings, and other kin are also sources of nurturance. Many adults feel nurturant toward all children, more in some cultures than in others. Erikson [18, p. 138] speaks of the sense of *generativity,* an essential of the mature personality. "Generativity is primarily the concern for establishing and guiding the next generation. . . ." A high degree of nurturance is involved in generativity.

There is a mutuality to nurturance, the other side of the coin being an acceptance of it. The love that a child feels for a parent has a large measure of this acceptance in it. He counts on the parent's nurturance, expecting it and accepting it as a continuing part of life. The development of the baby's sense of trust was in large part the result of the nurturance he received or, in Erikson's terms, of the strength of his parents' sense of generativity. Having learned to trust his family in this way, the child accepts love as the foundation of his world. Even when parental nurture is not very dependable, some of it is much better than none at all.

Nurturance in parents is vitally related to the socialization and development of children. Children are more likely to imitate nurturant models and to identify with them. Parental nurturance is correlated with children's moral development and prosocial behavior. It seems to be literally true that love begets love. Problem solving is also affected by nurturance. Preschool children, when faced with a complex puzzle task, did better under conditions of nurturance from an adult [15]. Highly dependent children were more affected by adult nurturance than were less dependent children. A relationship between nurturance and language development was seen in the interactions of language-delayed children with their mothers [74]. These mothers played and talked less, reasoned less, praised less, threatened more, and spoke critically of their children when they talked about them.

Altruism in Children. Evidence from anthropology and neurology indicates that there is an altruistic motive in human beings [32]. In other words, it is natural and human to be kind and helpful, as well as to be selfish and aggressive. Part of the hereditary equipment of each animal, including human beings, is concerned with self-preservation and part with species-preservation. Altruism, of course, promotes species-preservation. Children as young as 3, both American and Chinese, could tell the difference between happy and unhappy reactions as represented in stories [8]. Even in infancy, children react to others in ways that can be seen as sympathetic. Crying, while certainly serving self-preservation, seems to be a signal that causes a primitive sympathetic reaction in other infants and young children. In crying when a peer cries, the toddler may actually experience the distress

of the other child as though it were his own. As Hoffman [32] points out, the young child's limited cognitive development prevents him from fully realizing that it is another person who hurts. He tells of a year-old child who watched another child fall and cry, then looked as though she were going to cry, then put her thumb in her mouth and her head in her mother's lap. By around 2, the child realizes that the other person's feelings are independent of hers, but not different. She knows how others feel, although she is still limited in taking the role of the other. When feelings sympathetic distress, the child holds a goal of helping the other person and feels gratification when she succeeds. Hoffman suggests that intrinsic altruistic motivation would make it easy to instigate helping behavior in children. Indeed, this seems to be the experience of the Chinese, according to Sidel's reports on nursery schools in China [62].

Applying Mao's principles, the children learn to "care for each other, love and help each other" through example, stories, pictures, slides, songs, dance dramas, and actual helping. Teachers in China emphasize and expect positive, "good" behavior. If a child falls down, a teacher encourages another child to help him up. Children button each other's jackets. By 3 they are quite able to help each other. The Sidels saw many incidents of children sharing, none of pushing, grabbing, aggression, or hostile interaction between children.

Positive orientation in a group of United States parents also was associated with altruism in children [47]. Children were more generous to other children when parents emphasized doing or avoiding good than when they emphasized

EDWARD C. DEVEREUX

doing or avoiding bad. In an experiment with videotapes constructed from "Sesame Street" programs, increased amounts of socially valued behavior were shown by children who saw the tapes [38]. In behavior with peers, the subjects exceeded controls in number of cooperative strategies used, time spent in cooperative play while interacting socially, attempts to control by verbal means or demonstration rather than by physical means, success in control attempts, and display of positive rather than negative affect. Another experiment used television programs from "Misterogers' Neighborhood" and added training programs of verbal labeling and role playing [22]. Kindergarten children showed more helping behavior after seeing the programs and having training in role playing. Girls increased in helping when verbal labeling was added to role taking. Boys increased their helping behavior more than girls, but girls were more helpful in the first place. In an attempt to clarify the conditions under which United States children show concern for others, various conditions of nurturance, training, and modeling were explored [75]. The conclusion was that "the optimal condition for the development of sympathetic helpful behavior was one in which children observed an adult manifesting altruism at every level—in principle and in practice, both toward the child and toward others in distress." It remains to put this knowledge more into practice in North America.

Anger and Aggression

Anger is the distress that precedes or accompanies an attack on a frustrating situation. Diffuse and unproductive expressions of anger, such as crying, kicking, and throwing, are frequent in late infancy and the early part of the preschool period, when the child's desire for autonomy is strong and when he experiences many frustrations. *Aggression* is sometimes conceived as a controlled and productive attack on problems, resulting in increased knowledge, power, and/or status for the aggressor. In the latter context, the anger that accompanies aggression is a stirred-up, energized feeling that aids in problem solving and contributes to the development of the sense of initiative.

Hostile aggression is an attack on another person, often an attempt to hurt his self-esteem. Hostile aggression can be physical or verbal or both. *Instrumental* aggression is an attack oriented at securing an object, territory, or privilege.

When hostile aggression was explored in a sample of 101 societies throughout the world, considerable variation was found in the amounts of aggression shown [53]. The sex difference remained fairly constant, however. Boys tended to be more aggressive than girls. In no society were girls more aggressive than boys.

DEVELOPMENTAL ASPECTS OF AGGRESSION

Observations of preschool-, first- and second-grade children show age-related patterns of aggression [28]. Preschool children showed more incidents of aggression, indicating that aggression decreases with age. Preschool children's aggression was more often instrumental than hostile; they conflicted over toys and space. Aggression in older children was more often hostile than instrumental; they attacked each other's self-esteem. Boys were more aggressive than girls, but only in hostile aggression. There was no sex difference in instrumental aggression.

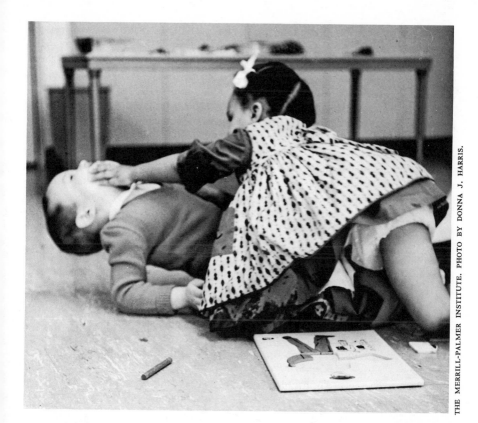

THE MERRILL-PALMER INSTITUTE. PHOTO BY DONNA J. HARRIS.

LEARNING AGGRESSIVE BEHAVIOR

Experiments by Bandura and his associates have shown that children readily imitate aggressive behavior shown to them by live models and by models in films, both human and cartoon [3]. Children reproduced in detail the attacks of an adult model on a large inflated doll. When one group of children saw a model rewarded for aggression and another saw the same model punished, the first group imitated the model and the second did not. Both groups expressed disapproval of the model's behavior, however, calling him mean, wicked, harsh, and bossy. Thus, even though the children considered aggressive behavior undesirable, they imitated what paid off. They made some attempts to justify their choice by calling the victim dumb and selfish. The children who had observed the punished model were then offered rewards for aggressive behavior. They promptly imitated what they had seen the model do, thus showing that they had learned the aggressive behavior, even though they had not performed it when they observed it.

When adults are permissive of aggressive behavior, children tend to act aggressively. Parents vary in how much aggression they permit, against whom they permit it, and how it may be expressed. A group of highly educated parents ranked aggression as high in a list of undesirable behavior. Only avoidance (being aloof, timid, and withdrawn) was less desirable [16]. Middle-class parents usually try to substitute verbal forms of aggression for physical, although they tend to feel that boys should be able to defend themselves by fighting "if necessary." Lower-class parents are more permissive of fighting and may actually encourage it in boys. Most parents discourage aggression against themselves but permitted and encouraged it against other people [4]. In punishing the child physically, parents are effectively demonstrating to the child how to act aggressively. Since they do not permit it toward themselves but encourage it toward others, the child learns how, when, and to whom to behave aggressively.

Applications of Research on Anger. Many of the studies mentioned indicate that the results of parental behavior are often unintentional. When one considers that what parents do in the first three years of life is likely to be reflected in children's behavior patterns, he is impressed with the complexity of parent–child relationships. Parental action springs from a wide variety of sources other than pure reason and self-control. Even so, a parent can consciously take some steps in order to make it easy for a preschool child to do the acceptable thing. Including the information derived from Goodenough's study of anger, itself derived from a number of research studies, the following list indicates conditions that discourage physical aggression and encourage the development of self-control:

1. The child is cared for on a flexible routine that provides food, rest, and activity before he is acutely and painfully in need of these things.
2. Parents and other caretakers answer his calls for help promptly.
3. The child is offered many opportunities to achieve and decide in approved ways.
4. Parents disapprove of hostile aggression and stop this behavior firmly.
5. Parents clearly express what behavior is permitted and what is not.
6. Physical punishment is avoided.
7. Television programs, films, and books showing aggression and violence are avoided.
8. An atmosphere of emotional warmth prevails in the home.

JEALOUSY AND RIVALRY

Jealousy is the angry feeling that results when a person is frustrated in his desire to be loved best; *rivalry* is the angry feeling that results when a person is frustrated in his desire to do best, to win or to place first. Very often an individual feels jealous and rivalrous toward the same person, although sometimes these emotions can be separated. A child is likely to feel jealous of the baby who displaces him as youngest in the family and to feel rivalrous with the older child, who is stronger and abler than he. Parents and children also feel jealousy and rivalry toward one another. The themes of jealousy and rivalry within the family flame in the most ancient literature. Cain and Oedipus symbolize some of the most disturbing situations existing in family life.

Jealousy of parents and the resolution of that jealousy make up the psychoanalytic story of the preschool period. The play age, the stage when the sense of initiative is developing, is the phallic stage in *psychoanalytic* terms. Almost every little boy says at least once, "Mummy, I'm going to marry you when I grow up," and every little girl has the equivalent plan for the future with her father. Wanting to be first in the affections of the opposite-sexed parent has as its corollary jealousy of the like-sexed parent. The like-sexed parent represents a powerful, full-blown picture of what the little child hopes to become, even the person who attracts and holds the other parent. As recognition of reality (that he cannot win over the powerful, wonderful parent) helps the boy to give up his attempts to be first with mother, he continues to try to grow more like his father. He identifies with him, feeling less jealous and more affectionate and sympathetic with him. He gains strength by joining with the father. A similar mechanism is thought to work through the girl's attempt to be first with her father.

Jealousy of siblings is usual in Western culture, in the typical small family, consisting of parents and children. "Let's send the baby back to the hospital" is the classic suggestion of the preschool child who has just lost his place as youngest in the family. Jealous actions include suggestions for getting rid of the baby and attacks on the baby (the most direct) and more devious attacks such as accidents and rough play, acting out aggression with toys, attacking the mother, whining, withdrawing, protesting extreme love and concern for the baby. Later on, jealousy takes such forms as bickering, fighting, teasing, and taking toys away.

Several decades ago, authorities who advised parents placed great emphasis on the value of preparing the child for a new baby. The hope was that jealousy would be eliminated if the young child understood the reproductive process and the characteristics of neonates, and if he realized that such a baby was about to enter the family. He was to "help" get clothes and equipment ready and to learn how to share in the baby's care. Attractive books with such titles as "Your New Baby" were read to the young child as preparation.

Modern experience has not shown any of these actions to be wrong or even useless. On the contrary, the most accepted authorities today still recommend them. Although we are not aware of studies definitively proving the worth of "preparing for the new baby," common sense and common experience show that the young child feels more loving and less jealous toward the baby who is introduced thus into his family. The difference today is that some jealousy and rivalry are regarded as inevitable in American culture—in fact, in most cultures. The reason for it is the same reason that the Book of Genesis puts forth in the story of Cain and Abel. Every child wants to be the best loved by his parents. The first child wants it most deeply, since he once was the only child and knew what it was like to have all the attention, company, endearments, and gifts.

It is possible that some decrease in indulgence would occur with increasing age of the child, but when it occurs along with the mother's pregnancy and the birth of a baby, it is easy to understand how the young child would hold the new baby responsible for the unhappy turn of events. In addition, the child sees the baby enjoying privileges he would like to have or which he is trying to give up, such as sucking a bottle, wetting his diapers, being carried and fondled, crying. One 5-year-old said: "Yes, I would like to change places with my baby brother. Then I could yell my head off and mamma would take care of nobody but me." Another commented, "Sometimes I wish I could tear magazines myself." When questioned about their relationships, 28 per cent of 360 5- and 6-year-olds said that they quarreled constantly with their sibs, 36 per cent reported a moderate amount of quarreling, and 36 per cent stated that they quarreled rarely [37]. When these children were asked if they would be happier without the sister or brother, about a third of them reported that they would. When the sib was an infant, especially of the same sex, there was less desire to be rid of him than when he was beyond infancy. Apparently infants disrupt their siblings' lives less than do older children. Second-born children, more than firstborns, wanted to be rid of the other children. The wider the age difference between sibs, the more the second-borns wanted to be rid of the firstborns. The second-borns' reasons were largely in terms of the behavior of the sibs themselves, such as, "He always socks me," "She likes to boss me too much," "Sometimes she wishes I were gone." When firstborn children wanted younger ones out of the way, their reasons were often in terms of parents' attitudes, especially favoritism toward the other child.

Children often express jealousy and rivalry in play and creative media. The following story by a 4-year-old illustrates imaginative expression of these emotions:

> You see, there was a little pussy and do you know, that the little pussy had to go to the bathroom so badly. He couldn't find a place to go. Finally he found a little girl and she said she'd take him into her house and he could go to the bathroom. The kitty said he'd like to be her pet. Where do you think he went to the toilet? In a pot. That little girl had him for a pet and was so nice to him. One day when the little girl's father came home, he brought a dog for a pet. But the dog was mean to the little kitty and hurt him *so* much. So the little girl didn't like the dog and she just had the kitty for a pet.

This little girl had a sturdy, aggressive toddler brother who knocked down her block buildings and spoiled her doll play. Still in diapers, he was a reminder of her rather recent achievements in toileting and other self-care. It seemed to us that the little girl, represented by the kitty, planned to ignore her little brother, represented by the doggie, as a way of coping with her jealousy and anger at him for intruding in her otherwise satisfactory life.

Reasons why parents behave in jealousy-inducing ways are to be found in the culture. In the small American family, there is not enough time and energy to go around after a new baby comes. In contrast, communes and the joint family system provide several adults who are responsive to all the young children. When a young child's mother is pregnant or busy with a new baby, the child still has the support and attention of people to whom he is attached. The young child's affection and desires for approval are focused less intensively on one or two persons. Therefore, one person cannot let him down so severely and even if his mother does disappoint him, aunts, uncles, and grandparents are ever ready to care for him and comfort him.

The materialistic and relativistic standards of American society have some bearing on the forms that jealousy and rivalry take. Parents' approval and resulting rewards often depend on how the child compares with his siblings, as well as with children outside the family. To look good and thereby be most approved and loved, he has to be better than someone else, often his brother or sister. If he were loved for himself and if his achievements were measured against his previous achievements, he would have less reason to be jealous of his siblings.

Applications of What Is Known About Jealousy and Rivalry. Jealousy and rivalry are so common in the American family as to be almost inevitable. These feelings can probably be minimized, if not eliminated, by some of the following procedures.

1. Preparing the young child for the birth of a sibling by telling him that the baby is coming, teaching him what babies are like, helping him to understand his own infancy, and assuring him of the parents' continued affection for him.
2. Understanding and accepting imaginative expression of jealousy and rivalry while firmly limiting direct expression.
3. Acceptance and appreciation of each child as an individual.
4. Avoidance of comparisons between children.
5. Avoidance of the use of competition to motivate siblings.

Fear

In infancy, fear has an innate basis in terms of stimuli that induce withdrawal. As the child interacts with his environment, he also learns to be afraid in certain

Entering a refugee camp, this child shows the fear that comes from threats to basic life processes. Hungry, thirsty, his body barely protected from the elements, he is probably suffering the most frightening situation— abandonment or separation from his mother or from the person who cared for him.

UNICEF PHOTO BY T. S. SATYAN

situations. The hereditary basis of fears continues to contribute to emotional behavior.

As a child grows up, he goes through age-related stages in regard to what frightens him and how he needs and uses his mother in coping with fears [9]. In early infancy, his mother soothes his fears by relieving distress. After the baby has become attached to his parents, fear of visual novelty occurs, as can be seen in reactions to strangers. Clinging and otherwise contacting the parent alleviates this type of fear and helps him to approach and explore strange objects. Pain and sudden intense stimuli continue to be frightening, as they were in infancy, and to be relieved through the parent or other familiar and nurturant people.

A close friend can have a reassuring and comforting effect on a child who is in a stressful situation, as shown in a study of 4- and 5-year-olds [57, 58]. Beginning in the preschool period and increasingly throughout the rest of childhood, increasing competence enables the child to cope with new situations without help from his mother or other adults.

SOURCES AND CONTENT OF FEARS

Like infants, preschool children can acquire fears through *conditioning*. Sometimes one painful experience is sufficient to establish a fear, as when a toddler comes to fear dogs by being pushed over, barked at, or bitten. Or a fear can be acquired by modeling, when another person is seen showing fear. Even a filmed reaction can have such an effect, as shown when preschool children watched a movie of a 5-year-old boy [69]. When his mother showed him a plastic Mickey Mouse, the child screamed and drew back, but when she offered him a plastic Donald Duck, he responded neutrally. After viewing the film, subjects avoided the Mickey Mouse toy more than the Donald Duck. A naturalistic example of modeling fears is that the fears of parents and children show a correspondence as to both kind and number [25]. In Britain, during World War II, children's reactions to air raids were greatly influenced by whether their parents showed calm attitudes or fearful ones [34].

Television has been found to contribute to fears in four- and five-year-old children [48]. Through measures of palmar sweating and through follow-up interviews, children were found to be frightened by violent cartoons and by violent human characters shown on television. A week later, the children remembered more details from the human violence film than from the cartoon violence or from the two nonviolent shows.

An overly demanding social situation puts the child into a position where he has no appropriate response at his command, causing him to attempt withdrawal. Johnny comes into the living room suddenly to find several strange adults there. Mother tells him to speak nicely to the ladies, but he is shy and silent. He could have spoken to old friends, or he could have spoken to the new ladies too had he been prepared ahead of time to expect strangers and to say something to them.

Imagination, initiative, and *conscience* contribute to fears at this time of life. Eager to explore and to try out new activities, the child tends to push beyond limits set by his parents. When his budding conscience tells him he is doing wrong, or that he wants to do wrong, he may create imaginative satisfactions, only to have those creations frighten him. He is especially likely to imagine animals that have powers he would like to have and to use, such as great strength for attacking other creatures, biting, kicking, or eating them. He may disguise his aggressive wishes quite elaborately, dreaming about such animals instead of telling stories about them or using them in dramatic play. The dream animals sometimes attack their creator, who feels guilty about his destructive wishes and thus suffers punishment. Dreams containing animals have been found to make up 61 per cent of the dreams of 4-year-olds, whereas at 5 and 6 the figure is only 39 per cent [68]. The proportion of animal dreams drops steadily with age, reaching a low of 7.5 per cent in adulthood. Fear of the dark may accompany the young child's fears of imaginary animals and bad dreams. When parents were questioned about the fears expressed by their children between birth and six years of age, the results showed a progressive decrease in fears that were responses to such tangible stimuli as objects, noises, falling, and strange people and an increase in fears of intangibles, such as imaginary creatures, darkness, being alone or abandoned, threat or danger of injury and harm [33].

The answers of 130 children to the question "What are things to be afraid of?" give information on the fears of children 5 years old and over [41]. Animals were mentioned most often, but less frequently as age increased. Eighty per cent of children were afraid of animals at age 5 and 6, 73 per cent at 7 and 8. Snakes were mentioned more often than any other animals. Then came lions, tigers, and bears. A third of children under 7 admitted to fear of the dark. Children rarely reported fear of the type that parents try to teach, such as fear of traffic, germs, and kidnappers.

An experimental study of children's fears confirmed the finding that expressed fear of tangible situations decreases with age throughout the preschool period [33, pp. 167–296]. Children were carefully observed when left alone, while walking across inclined boards that fell a distance of two inches, entering a dark room, meeting a peculiarly dressed stranger, walking across high boards, hearing a

Table 3-1. Fears Shown by Children Age Two to Six, in Several Experimental Situations.

	Percentage of Children Showing Fear			
Situation	24–35 Months	36–47 Months	48–59 Months	60–71 Months
1. Being left alone	12.1	15.6	7.0	0
2. Falling boards	24.2	8.9	0	0
3. Dark room	46.9	51.1	35.7	0
4. Strange person	31.3	22.2	7.1	0
5. High boards	35.5	35.6	7.1	0
6. Loud sound	22.6	20.0	14.3	0
7. Snake	34.8	55.6	42.9	30.8
8. Large dog	61.9	42.9	42.9	
Total	32.0	30.2	18.1	4.5

* SOURCE: Reprinted by permission from Arthur T. Jersild and Frances B. Holmes, Children's fears, *Child Development Monographs*, No. 20. New York: Bureau of Publications, Teachers College, Columbia University, 1935, Table 14, p. 237.

sudden loud sound, picking a toy out of a box containing a live snake, and being asked to pat a dog brought in on a leash. Their actions were judged as indicating fear or not. The percentage of children showing fear at four different age levels between 2 and 6 are shown in Table 3–1.

ANXIETY

Fear can be widespread and generalized, in contrast to being focused on a particular object or situation. When fear is widespread, generalized, and unfocused, it is called *anxiety*. The preschool child is likely to experience anxiety when separated for a long time from his mother, father, or main object of attachment.

The effects of partial and complete separation of toddlers from their mothers were explored with children between 16 and 27 months of age [29]. Two groups, carefully equated as to age and sex, were selected, one from each of two nurseries. All subjects were from intact families, without history of separation and with no indications that the children had been rejected. No subject had a sibling in the same nursery. The two nurseries were run identically, with one exception. In the first, the children stayed all day but went home at night; in the second, the children lived 24 hours a day in the nursery. The two groups did not differ in behavior for the first two days, but after that, the residential children showed more intense symptoms of anxiety. They sought relations with adults more intensely, sought affection more, cried more, did more thumb and finger sucking, lost sphincter control more often, and had more colds. The most striking difference was that the residential children showed more and greater hostility. This study indicates that although partial separation from parents is not necessarily destructive, *complete* separation is likely to be so.

Maternal employment is a tempting situation to fasten upon when searching for conditions causing anxiety in young children. Public opinion is often expressed against young mothers who hold jobs outside the home. A review of research on this topic concludes that maternal employment is too global a condition to use as a variable in investigating causes of children's behavior [67]. For example, 26 kindergarten children of fully employed mothers were matched in family factors, age, and sex with 26 kindergarten children whose mothers had never been employed during the lives of these children. No differences were found between the two groups on the nine personality characteristics investigated. A recent review concluded that if working parents interact frequently with their young children, the children's attachments are just as strong as those of children to parents who do not work outside the home. For normal personality and cognitive development of children of working mothers, substitute care must be stable and stimulating [18a].

It is sometimes held that when a parent leaves the family through divorce, death, or any other separation, a preschool child is likely to interpret the disruption as a result of his own unworthiness. Hence he would suffer a separation anxiety. Since fathers leave households more often than mothers, they are more likely than mothers to cause this kind of fear in preschool children.

APPLICATIONS OF RESEARCH ON FEAR AND ANXIETY

Although some fears are inevitable and even desirable (caution has survival value), children can learn to deal with frightening situations, and adults can help them to do so. Adults can also arrange and plan so as to prevent the development of extreme fears and anxiety. The following procedures are often valuable:

1. When the child is to be separated from the people to whom he is attached, make the transition gradual if possible.
2. At times of crisis, such as illness, keep the child with a person to whom he is attached.
3. Teach the child techniques for coping with situations in which he is inadequate.
4. Use modeling when possible for showing ways of coping and accepting objects and situations that the child fears.
5. Use conditioning when possible, to associate pleasure with a stimulus that has provoked fear.
6. Prepare the child for dealing constructively with situations that are about to come up. Talking, stories, and dramatic play are useful for this purpose.
7. Use the child's spontaneous expressions of fears, in fantasy, dreams, dramatic play, and artistic productions, to gain insight into what he fears and why he does so, in order to help him deal with the fears.
8. Never force a child into a situation he fears. Rather, minimizing the threat, such as by caging the animal that frightens him, encourage him to approach it in such a way that no harm occurs to him.
9. When a child is frightened by bad dreams, comfort him immediately, make sure that he wakens and agrees that the experience was a dream, not real, and put him back to bed, with a light if he wishes.

Discipline and Self-Control

North American parents carry the responsibilities of seeing that the children behave within certain limits, teaching them right from wrong and teaching them to control themselves according to what is considered right and wrong by their society. These responsibilities are heavy ones. Parents receive some help from the processes of normal growth. Cognitive development underlies the growth of moral judgment. Various emotional and social developmental processes result in children's wanting to be like their parents, wanting to please their parents, and wanting to relieve distress in other people. Parents receive little help from other people, however, in contrast to kibbutz parents, who share their responsibilities with the *metaplot* (caregivers) and Chinese parents, who are aided by grandparents and neighbors. Day-care centers, nursery schools, and comprehensive child development centers in North America give support to some parents in their efforts to socialize their young children.

The complexity of discipline is a result of its twofold purpose, obedience and self-control. Of the 2, obedience is probably simpler to achieve, although not easy. (For example, after an anxiety-provoking film, 3- to 5-year-olds obeyed a previously punishing adult, but after a neutral film, they were more obedient to a previously positive adult [10].) To achieve self-control, the child must develop conscience and moral judgment. By conscience, we mean an internalization of rules and principles that the child has made a part of himself and that he uses to make decisions about actions.

SEQUENCE OF BEHAVIORAL MORAL DEVELOPMENT

Because child–rearing methods strongly influence children's behavior, moral development differs in individual children and in different cultures. The sequence sketched here refers most clearly to middle-class children in the Western world.

Punishment-Reward Orientation Plus Primitive Altruism. The 2-year-old is often represented as a pure hedonist, seeking pleasure and avoiding punishment, and modifying her behavior as parents and others apply reinforcements. This picture is not wrong, but merely incomplete. We believe, along with Hoffman [32] and others [66], that infants and young children, as well as older children and adults, have a predisposition to cooperate with others.

At around 2, newly able to run, climb, feed herself, undress, talk, and so on, a child can find many gratifications and can cause disruptions in the household. With a strong desire for autonomy and an urge to explore, the young child often runs counter to what parents want her to do. If parents make full use of the child's basic altruism, there is little or no need for punishment. The first step is to arrange an environment in which the child has little opportunity to do wrong and can make choices that are right. A box of candy is not left on the coffee table. A washable surface is placed under places for painting, pasting, and water play. Then parents give clear directions on what to do, what not to do, what is right, and what is wrong. When stopping a child from one activity, parents give her something else to do. "No, Mother's scissors are too sharp for you to play with. Cut your paper with these children's scissors. There, that's right, cut with your scissors."

Praise, smiles, hugs, and gifts can act as reinforcements for "good" behavior. They also act as feedback that shows the child that she has pleased someone, probably a family member whom she loves. Signs of displeasure may function as punishment and feedback and as instigators of sympathetic distress reactions. Even infants cooperate more with mothers who are warm and responsive [66].

Obeys When Watched and Capable of Shame. As the child's sense of autonomy develops, according to Erikson, "His environment must back him up in his wish to 'stand on his own feet' lest he be overcome by that sense of having exposed himself prematurely and foolishly which we call shame . . ." [17, p. 85]. That is, shame comes from doing wrong too often, from causing too many disruptions and disasters while parents watch and punish or tell him he is bad. Or parents may even shame him as a method of control. In so doing, parents may promote in the child a secret determination to do what he wants, being careful not to get caught. "Shame is early expressed in an impulse to bury one's face, or to sink, right then and there, into the ground. But this, I think, is essentially rage turned against the self" [17, p. 252].

By around 3, children know many family rules and procedures that they will often follow if it is made easy for them to do so. They are in the process of internalizing rules, but have not gone very far with it. When a very attractive activity is forbidden, the child may need the presence of an authoritative person in order to inhibit a desired action. Ellen, just under 3, was fascinated by Lucy, a doll that belonged to Susan, age 5. Susan, knowing Ellen's passion for poking Lucy's blue glass eyes fringed with long black lashes, made a strict rule that Ellen was never to touch Lucy. One day Ellen came home from nursery school to behold Lucy sitting on the sofa. She fell on the doll with cries of joy, began to poke Lucy's eyes, and paused when her mother chided her, "Ellen, you know Susie doesn't want you to touch Lucy."

"But Mummy," Ellen said in hurt surprise, "Susie isn't here!"

The voice that commanded Ellen to inhibit her impulses toward Lucy was entirely external. When the voice was away at kindergarten, it simply wasn't there, and Ellen felt no restraint.

Internalization, Guilt, and Self-Control. When the child feels guilty over doing wrong or when he considers doing wrong, then he has achieved some internal controls. During the years between 3 and 6, some of the voice of society and family is taken into the child, internalized, made his own, and integrated with the rest of his personality. In this stage of development of the sense of initiative, many explorations and new activities are undertaken and even more are contemplated. Healthy growth requires a balance between initiative and restraint, strong enough internalized controls to regulate action but not too strong, so as to produce excess guilt and restriction.

From several of his studies, Hoffman concludes that children who control themselves through internalized means and who are independent of external punishment and rewards are likely to have mothers who often use inductive discipline [32]. By *inductive discipline,* he means explaining and drawing the child's attention to the consequences of his actions for other people. When children's moral orientation is based on fear of detection and punishment, they are more likely to have been disciplined by adults who asserted their power through physical force, material deprivation, or the threat of these.

Another factor is involved in achieving the balance between too much and too little internalized control. Parental warmth and confidence in the child influence her feelings about her parents and herself. She wants to please her parents and to be like them. If they believe that she can be good, do better next time, live up to their standards and improve as she grows, then the child can believe all this about herself. Parental firmness and consistency also contribute to the child's confidence and balance in the development of inner controls.

MORAL JUDGMENT

To know what is right or good involves making a moral judgment. Various cultures give concrete expression to the idea that a certain stage of mental maturity is necessary before the child can exercise either judgment or volition necessary for moral behavior. The Roman Catholic first communion, at age 7, is an example. So is the widespread assumption among tribal people that a child reaches the age of reason and responsibility at about 7. Six or 7 is the common age for starting school in earnest. The transition from preconceptual thought to the stage of concrete operations occurs at about the same time when changes occur in character. What precedes these changes?

The earliest judgments about what is good and bad come from what the parents impose in the way of rules and requirements. As a child comes to know the rules, *good,* to him, means following the rules and *bad* means not following them. Moral realism, according to Piaget [50, p. 106], has these features: (1) Any act that shows obedience to a rule or to an adult is good; a rule is not something thought of by a person, but rather something ready-made, which has been revealed to the adult and is now being imposed by him. (2) The letter rather than the spirit of the law shall be observed. (3) Acts are evaluated according to how well they keep to the rules rather than according to the motives that prompted them. Results, rather than intentions, are what count.

Moral realism is illustrated by 2-year-old Jacqueline Piaget, who had been told what would be the results of taking a laxative that her mother gave to her [50, pp. 177–191]. She nevertheless came close to tears and looked very distressed when she lost control of her sphincters. To Jacqueline, it was bad not to follow the rule about going to the toilet, even though her mother had explained that she was not responsible for the lapse. Another time, Jacqueline broke a fragile shell that Piaget had given her to play with. She was very upset over the breakage, even though her father tried to persuade her that it was not her fault.

By age 3 or 4, Piaget says, a child shows that he sees a difference between his own intentional breaking of rules and his unintentional breaches. He will plead "Not on purpose" to excuse himself. With the misdeeds of others, however, his attitude differs. Because of his egocentrism, his inability to see anything from someone else's point of view, the child does not understand that another person's breaking of rules could be "not on purpose." He judges the other person's acts by the results, since the results are all that he can perceive.

The next step in the development of moral judgment is to take account of other people's intentions. Cognitive control and flexibility are involved in seeing the other person's point of view. Ability to judge intentionality is correlated with role-taking ability [1] and reflectivity [56]. Even when intentions are taken into account, the outcome of an act is not ignored. Children between 4 and 18 were asked to evaluate actions that had either positive or negative outcomes and positive or negative intentions behind them. Figure 3-1 shows the extent to which younger children

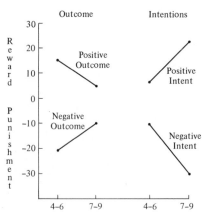

Figure 3-1. Age-related changes in evaluation of intentions and results of actions.

SOURCE: Adapted from B. Weiner and N. Peter. A cognitive developmental analysis of achievement and moral judgments. *Developmental Psychology,* 1973, **9**, 290–309.

(aged 4 to 6) and older children (aged 7 to 9) would give punishments for good and bad outcomes and intentions. Children changed in the direction of giving smaller rewards and punishments for outcome and larger for intentions. The age-related change in regard to intentions is greater than the change in regard to outcome [72].

MECHANISMS OF CONTROL

How do moral judgments and feelings of guilt become translated into action? *Volition,* or *willing to do,* is a step toward action. Moral action depends upon willing to do the right and good thing. Moral judgment of itself does not imply action. Everyone has had the experience of judging that an act was wrong and then doing it anyway, or judging that an act was good and failing to do it. Experiments on children's aggression (page 163) showed that children sometimes perform the very acts that they condemn verbally.

The idea of an age or stage of reason and responsibility comes into the topic of moral action, as well as moral judgment. Nobody expects a newborn baby to choose to do right or wrong, but almost everyone considers a 7-year-old to have some freedom of choice. The development of a sense of self gives conviction of freedom of choice. So do the experiences of temptation and guilt. The rightness and wrongness of the child's choices are strongly related to his experiences with parents and other socializing agents. Language is an important tool of volition.

Language. The language development that takes place during the preschool period is fundamental to voluntary behavior and hence to moral action. On the basis of his work with Russian children, Luria [40] traced four stages through which speech comes to exercise a regulating influence on behavior. A replication of Luria's study showed the same sequential development in Australian children [35].

1. At 18 months to 2 years, the *initiating function* can be seen. The toddler will clap his hands on command. Instructions will not change an activity that is underway, however. If you tell a child to take off his socks while he is putting them on, or to put rings on a bar while he is taking them off, he cannot change his actions. He only intensifies the efforts he is making.
2. At 3 to 4 years, the child can follow both initiating and inhibiting instructions. He can *wait* for a signal, after being told to do so. However, the initiating part of the instruction is stronger and often the child can inhibit only briefly. If he gets continuous verbal instruction, however, he can inhibit more easily.
3. At about 4 years, when the child's own speech is well developed, he can use it to *start and stop* his own actions. He can follow instructions as to using his own speech for voluntary acts.
4. External regulatory speech becomes internal. The child no longer says it out loud but to himself when he regulates his behavior.

In regard to moral behavior, language has another important function in addition to that of starting and stopping actions. Language is the means by which the child evaluates his actions. "I shouldn't have done that," the child says to himself, triggering feelings of guilt. There is widespread agreement that signs of guilt in

Table 3-2. Summary of Developmental Changes Basic to Moral Development.

Age	Moral Behavior	Cognitive and Volitional Behavior
	1. Obeys commands sometimes. Primitive altruism.	Cooperative with adult who cooperates with him.
	2. Obeys more commands. *Good* means following the rule or instruction.	Initiating function of speech. Verbalizes role of parent.
	3. Obeys when watched.	Inhibiting function of speech.
	4. Begins to internalize demands of parents.	Judges other people by acts, not intentions, but sees difference between his own intentions and unintentional breaking of rules.
	Some feelings of guilt.	Uses his own speech to initiate.
	6. Conscience fairly internalized. Definitely feels guilt.	Uses language to evaluate his actions.

children can be seen first at 4 or 5 years of age, the very time when children reach Luria's third stage in the use of speech to regulate behavior. "I shouldn't do that" is avoidance-mediating, anticipating an anxiety reaction. Talking to oneself is thus involved in feeling guilt and in avoiding guilt by means of controlling one's behavior. Since a certain stage of language development has to be reached before speech can regulate behavior, it follows that intellectual growth plays an essential role in moral behavior. Parents and other family members influence the child enormously in helping him to use language in organizing his mental processes and his behavior. Table 3-2 summarizes moral development in childhood.

The Self

An adult knows himself as both subject and object. He feels, he knows, he is; he can stand off and look at himself, his feelings, his actions, his relationships. As far as anyone knows, man is the only creature who can look at himself as an object. It is a viewpoint that begins as the infant distinguishes between his body and the rest of reality and which develops gradually, during the preschool period, as the child moves from preconceptual thought toward objectivity. Further elaboration of the self takes place throughout the whole period of development, perhaps throughout all of life.

The development of a sense of autonomy means that the child gets a clearer and clearer concept of himself as a person separate from other objects and other people, distinct in body and distinct in actions. With the growth of the sense of initiative, the child enlarges his concept of self by relating it to the world. Having made himself separate and distinct, he integrates his self-concept by trying on different roles (playing fireman, nurse, teacher), exploring, and expressing himself in various media. The self also develops as a masculine or feminine self.

PROBLEMS IN DEVELOPING SELF-CONCEPTS

Deprived Children. One of the outstanding characteristics of severely deprived children is a negative self-concept or even lack of self-concept. A child may not even realize that he is a person or that he has a name that distinguishes him from others. The conditions associated with positive self-concept or high self-esteem are often found lacking in the families of disadvantaged children. Conditions leading to high self-esteem are acceptance of the child, well-defined limits and values, and respect for the child's decision making within those limits. In very poor families, parents tend to be indecisive, disorganized, apathetic, and rejecting. Low in self-esteem themselves, they do not believe that they can control their own lives, let alone their children's. Though they may sometimes be warm and nurturant, they are more likely to try to give children immediate pleasure, through candy, money, toys, and clothes rather than to guide them to develop competency.

In comprehensive compensatory programs, parents are offered help in developing their own competence and self-esteem, as well as effective behavior in relation to their children [30]. Teachers try to show the child that he is a distinct individual, important because he is a person. The child is helped to establish self-confidence and self-esteem as he forms a clear and definite idea of himself. Teachers use many methods for promoting self-concepts. They provide mirrors, full length if possible, in places where children can easily look at themselves. They take pictures of the children, show them and discuss them. They may draw pictures or silhouettes of the children. Songs and games are made up to include the children's names. Feelings of autonomy and worthiness are stimulated by opportunities for successful decisions, achievement, and recognition. The teacher's respect for the individual child and her warm response to him are very basic in the development of his self-concept.

Minority Groups. Along with the realization that she is a separate and distinct person, the child takes an interest in how she is like other people and how she is different from them. By 3, children notice racial differences in appearance, such as skin color and differences in hair. When they ask their parents about such differences, the parents' answers help children to evaluate black, brown, and white skin, straight and curly hair, and other such attributes. Furthermore, the parents' answers show the child how to think of himself as a member of a particular ethnic group. Writing for black parents, Comer and Poussaint suggest what to say when a 3- or 4-year-old asks, "What is black?" "Am I black?" "Am I white?" The best answer, they say, is, "You are black like Mommy (or Daddy)" [13]. Because the parent is someone positive and important to the child, being like the parent will be seen as good if the parent shows enthusiasm about being black. Thus, the child begins to develop a positive racial identity and a concept of himself as worthwhile.

Negative self-concepts are indicated when children are slow to identify themselves as members of their own ethnic group and when they prefer members of the majority group to those of their own minority. Such has been the case in many studies of Afro-American children in the past, but there is evidence that growing black pride is helping black children to identify positively with blacks and to develop positive self-concepts [55]. Indian children seem to be in a worse position than black children, probably reflecting the low power possessed by their parents and their ethnic group. Chippewa Indian children from 3 to 10 showed lower self-evaluation and less accurate self-identification than any children previously studied [55].

Body Image Problems. Since the body is part of a person, the self-concept includes a body image, or concepts of the body—what it looks like, where it starts and stops, and what it can do. In the previous chapter, the section on movement education indicated the importance of giving children a variety of bodily experiences, encouraging them to use all their motor potential, and providing opportunities for exploring and defining space with their bodies. Body image grows clearer and stronger as a child gains control and expands sensory experiences. A child may be limited in growth of body image by all sorts of restrictive limits, such as illness, handicaps, lack of play space, lack of equipment, and lack of guidance and stimulation.

Another aspect of body image is evaluation in terms of beauty or attractiveness. As in so many aspects of self, a child gets many cues from parents and siblings, as to whether she is pretty and acceptable or ugly and unattractive. Cues are nonverbal as well as verbal. Clothing and grooming express what the mother or chief caregiver thinks of the child's worth and beauty. Clothing and grooming also set the stage for reactions of other people to the child's appearance. Jason, with his perpetually running nose and dirty face, receives fewer smiles and hugs than well-scrubbed, pink-cheeked Ben. The message Jason gets from many people is that he is not very attractive. Such messages are incorporated into his body image.

Acquisition of Gender-Related Behavior and Knowledge

There are differences in the ways in which females and males behave, as well as differences in what is expected of them. This topic is of great current interest and a generator of conflict between those who wish to change gender roles in the direction of freedom and those who see virtue in maintaining clear gender distinctions and restrictions. The topic is relevant to preschool children, because strong socialization influences are brought to bear upon them as they acquire their gender roles.

GENDER CONSTANCY

Part of self-development is coming to know oneself as female or male. *Gender identity* is a conviction of being female or male. There is general agreement that 3-year-olds know whether they are girls or boys. As early as 18 months, children are probably fairly firmly identified with one sex or the other [42, p. 13]. *Gender constancy* is a conviction that females remain females and males remain males throughout time and under different conditions. That is, gender constancy is conservation of gender.

Gender constancy was examined in children from 2 to 6, by means of interviews about dolls, photographs, and themselves [64]. A developmental sequence

Table 3-3.   Average Ages and Age Ranges at Four Stages of Gender Constancy.

Stage of Gender Constancy	Mean Age (months)	Age Range (months)
1. Inconsistent in identifying gender	34	26–39
2. Gender identity	47	35–62
3. Gender	53	36–68
4. Gender consistency	55	41–67

SOURCE: Data from R. G. Slaby and K. S. Frey. Development of gender constancy and selective attention to same-sex models. *Child Development*, 1975, **46,** 849–856.

was established, showing that gender identity is achieved before stability and stability before consistency. Questions testing gender identity include: Is this (doll) a girl or a boy?; Are you a girl or a boy? Gender stability is tapped by: When you were a baby, were you a girl or a boy?; When you grow up, will you be a mommy or a daddy? Questions concerning gender consistency included: (to boy) If you wore girls' clothes, would you be a girl or a boy?; Could you be a girl if you wanted to? Table 7-3 shows averages and age ranges at which children achieved the various levels of understanding of gender constancy.

SOURCES OF GENDER-ROLE PRESCRIPTIONS

To some extent, people think of the way things are as the way they ought to be, or as "natural." Existing behavioral differences are therefore the basis of some pressures for their continuance. But how do gender roles get made in the first place?

Girl-Boy Differences in Behavior. In the American research reported earlier in this chapter, boys have been found to be more active in group play and to show more hostile aggression, while girls have been seen to show more helping behavior in experimental situations. Whiting and Edwards studied stereotypes of sex differences by means of observations made in six cultures in North America, Asia, and Africa [73]. Results for preschool children are given here.

1. Dependency. Girls sought help and offered physical contact more than boys, consistent with the stereotype of girls being more dependent.
2. Sociability. Although the stereotype says that girls are more sociable, differences between girls and boys were not significant.
3. Passivity. There was no difference in proportions of self-instigated acts.
4. Nurturance. Boys and girls were equal in offering help and support. The stereotype holds that girls are more nurturant, and this was indeed true of school-age girls, but not in the preschool period.
5. Responsibility. Girls offered more responsible suggestions, as the stereotype predicts. However, the difference disappeared after the preschool period.
6. Dominance. Boys showed more egotistic dominance.
7. Aggression. Boys carried out more rough-and-tumble play and more verbal aggression.

Societal Socialization Pressures. As soon as a baby is identified as a girl or a boy, certain expectations and pressures begin to operate. Cultures throughout the world differ in their interpretations of gender-appropriate behavior, but there are certain consistencies. The majority of a sample of 110 cultures stressed achievement and self-reliance in boys and nurturance, obedience, and responsibility in

This nurturant father comforts his young son who has been hurt in rough and tumble play with older siblings. The little boy is learning that it is all right to express his feelings and to give and receive tenderness.

ROBERT J. IZZO

girls [5]. One possible explanation for this is that societies build upon the natural biological tendencies of each sex. Another possibility is that division of labor and work patterns are basic to socialization for gender-role behavior.

Comparing socialization practices in six cultures, Whiting and Edwards found greater pressure toward obedience in societies that required children to do infant care and animal husbandry [73]. They also found fewer differences between girls and boys in societies where both were required to take care of babies and do housework. Child care and housework are done in or near the house, in the company of women. When children are with adults, they are more likely to seek and offer help and to seek physical contact, attention, and friendly interaction, all of which are "feminine"-type behaviors. Infants tend to elicit help, support, and sociability, which are also "feminine." Interaction with peers is likely to produce the "masculine"-type behaviors of rough-and-tumble play and insulting interchanges. The boys who must work at home are, therefore, exposed to opportunities for "feminine" behavior rather than "masculine." Thus, gender-behavioral differences may be minimized or maximized according to societal conceptions of what is appropriate work for males and females.

Specific Socializers. Socialization pressures are applied by individuals living within a culture. Hospital personnel may attach pink or blue identification bracelets and comment on sweet, cute little girls and sturdy, "all-male" little boys. Parents and siblings react differently to boys and girls. Even when a change in gender assignment has been made in a baby, parents and siblings react differently to the same child whom they now consider a girl instead of a boy, or a boy instead of a girl [42]. In addition to parents, siblings and kin, toys, clothing, teachers, and the media function as gender-role socializers.

Parents' gender-role stereotypes or expectations were examined in 40 sets of parents of preschool children [2]. Parents were asked how they would react to certain behaviors in male and female children. The sample behaviors had been classified as illustrating feminine or masculine behavior. Female reactions included crying when left at school on first day, allowing a playmate to take her toys, and preferring art activities at school. Male reactions included not kissing parent goodnight, preferring large muscle activities, and disobedience at school. Both parents liked feminine behavior better in girls than in boys, encouraged it more often in girls, and thought it more important to encourage feminine behavior in girls rather than in boys. Also, mothers and fathers each liked and encouraged their own gender-typed behavior in both their sons and daughters. For example, fathers disliked their children's crying when left at school more than did mothers in both girls and boys. Thus, it can be seen that the gender of the parent, as well as the gender of the child, plays a part in the pressures exerted by parents upon the child.

Parents' attitudes and beliefs can also be seen in the way they set up their children's rooms and choose the toys and decorations for them. Among 48 girls and 48 boys under age 6, who had their own rooms, boys had more vehicles, educational art materials, sports equipment, toy animals, depots, machines, live animals, and military toys [52]. Girls had more dolls, doll houses, and domestic toys. Decorations in boys' rooms more often included animal motifs, while girls' rooms were decorated with flowers, lace, fringe, and ruffles. In a review of research on children's toy preferences and on the toys typed by adults as masculine or feminine, boys' toys are seen as clearly designated by adults and definitely chosen by boys [54]. Girls' toys, on the other hand, are toys that boys will not play with. Girls play with boys' toys, as well as girls'. An analysis of children's creative (measured by thinking up ways of changing the toy) responses indicated that boys' toys (typed masculine by adults) elicited more ideas from both girls and boys [54]. Boys' toys were more fun to play with and gave more opportunity for creativity and competency! No wonder girls want to play with boys' toys, too. Sex typing of toys thus implies more growth-promoting experiences for boys, as well as development of gender-role concepts for both sexes that represent feminine abilities and behavior as being inferior to masculine. For several years, psychologists measured children's gender-role preferences in terms of the toys they chose. It was considered healthy to be very clear in choosing toys and activities that had been typed as sex-appropriate. If competency and creativity are appropriate for women, then sticking to sex-typed feminine toys is not. In fact, freedom to choose from any and all toys would give more opportunities to both sexes. A similar point might be made for clothing, insofar as it restricts children or frees them to have a variety of experiences.

Observations of nursery school teachers have revealed them as behaving differentially to girls and boys. In one of the first of these studies, activities were classified as masculine or feminine according to whether boys and girls showed significant differences in choosing them [20]. In a similar study with 2-year-olds, a male teacher, and a female teacher, both teachers reinforced feminine behavior more than masculine behavior. However, the male teacher gave out a greater proportion of the rewards that were given for masculine behavior [19].

When verbal interaction was investigated in a preschool, teachers, all of whom were female, were found reinforcing feminine behavior in boys as well as in girls. Apparently, the behavior that they valued most was gender-appropriate for them. Another investigator found women teachers having more verbal interaction with boys, but giving more acknowledgements to the answers of girls [12]. In 15 preschool classes, again all with female teachers, boys received three times as many loud reprimands as girls [59]. When soliciting the teacher's attention, boys were more successful than girls, receiving more brief directions, more extended directions, and more extended conversations. When girls stayed close to the teacher, they got more attention than when they were farther away, but this difference did not exist for boys. These differences in responding to boys and girls could be expected to promote behavioral differences between the sexes. For example, the many loud reprimands might reinforce disruptive behavior in boys. The extended instructions on how to do things would promote independent problem solving. Girls were reinforced for staying close and got little impetus toward independent problem solving.

Television and children's books often show boys' activities as being more active, interesting, exciting, and important than girls' activities. Thus, both boys and girls are taught to value the male role more highly. Through efforts of human liberationists, some progress is being made to get the media to show that women and girls can lead important, exciting lives. The expressed vocational ambitions of preschool children still show that girls' ambitions are more restricted than boys'

[36]. Boys are more likely than girls to name a general adult role, while girls are more likely than boys to plan to be a parent. Boys apparently consider a wide range of occupations possible, but girls still tend to choose to be nurses or teachers.

PROCESSES OF LEARNING GENDER-ROLE BEHAVIOR

In the complex and important task of acquiring gender-role behavior, a child could be expected to use all of his resources for feeling, thinking, and learning. Parents dispense reinforcements with the aim of shaping their children's behavior toward the ideals that they hold for boys and girls. However, the gender of the child, and certain parental characteristics, determine the effects that those reinforcements will have. Highly masculine boys (as measured by a preference test) were likely to have decisive, dominant, powerful fathers who were warm and nurturant, giving their sons both rewards and punishments [6, 45]. Boys did not seem to be affected by the degree of masculinity of their fathers or by fathers who encouraged them to take part in masculine activities [45]. Girls high on femininity saw their mothers as being highly nurturant and powerful, but did not see their mothers as being more punishing than did girls who were low in femininity. Mothers of highly feminine girls were found to be high in self-acceptance but no higher in femininity than other mothers.

Parental nurturance influences the effectiveness of reinforcements. Nurturance and power also determine the extent to which the child will model his behavior on that of the parent. The feeling side of gender-role learning is important, but the child also thinks about it. Cognitive processes, as well as emotional ones, affect the child's observation of models. As children became more advanced in the four stages of gender constancy, they spent more time watching adult models [64]. Advanced boys watched the male model more than the female. Advanced girls tended to watch the female model more.

Parental Deprivation. Both girls and boys must learn what to expect of the other sex as they acquire their own gender roles. Both mothers and fathers contribute to the learnings of both boys and girls. The problem of father absence has been recognized for many years, since millions of children live only with their mothers. Very recently, mother absence has been increasing, but little is known about how children develop when only their fathers take care of them.

From a review of many studies of father absence, Biller concludes that father *availability* is very important in the masculine development of young boys [7]. (A father could be at home, and yet unavailable.) Age 5 seems to be a nodal point, before which father absence has the most profound effects. The first two years are even more critical than subsequent ones for what Biller terms *sex-role orientation,* which we interpret as gender identity, plus feelings of satisfaction concerning one's gender identity. Certain compensations can be made when fathers are absent or unavailable, as when a mother represents the father in a favorable light and encourages assertive, responsible behavior in her sons. Siblings and peers can help a boy to develop masculine behavior patterns. Father absence, especially during the preschool years, seems to affect boys more than girls.

What happens to families with preschool children when parents divorce? Parental behavior has been traced through a two-year period following the divorce [31]. Family disorganization develops during the first year, with reorganization taking place in the second year. At first, the mother is more restrictive, giving more commands, the child ignoring and resisting her. She becomes more effective and less authoritarian over the following two years. The father begins by being very indulgent and permissive and becomes more restrictive. The mother was able to function more positively with the children when the father had a positive relationship with the family and when other support systems interacted with the family, such as grandparents, siblings, friends, and/or a housekeeper.

Summary

Through socialization, parents and others shape children's behavior in accordance with the demands of society. Social interactions involve both feeling and thinking.

Interactions with friends take positive form in social play. Certain patterns and rules of interaction have been identified. Sociodramatic play is a complicated and sustained sort of make-believe involving several children, in which creative and cognitive development take place. Children use affective and cognitive processes in understanding other people. The ability to take the role of another increases during the preschool years.

Children like other children who give them positive reinforcement. Children reinforce like-sex peers more than peers of the opposite sex. Their nonverbal behavior indicates the same preference. Play behavior is influenced by environmental settings, including the amount and arrangement of space and the numbers of children and adults present.

Parents and children give care to each other in the form of nurturance, sympathy, giving, and helping. Parental nurturance affects the learning behavior of children in many ways. Children have altruistic impulses, as well as selfish ones. They react sympathetically to signals of distress emitted by other people. Altruistic behavior can be encouraged and taught.

Aggression in preschool children often occurs over toys and space. Boys and older children show more hostile aggression than girls and younger children. Hostile aggression can be reduced by planning the environment and routine, along with alternative opportunities, nurturance, and firm limits. Jealousy and rivalry occur most often in relation to siblings. They can be minimized by parents who plan, understand, accept, limit, and avoid comparisons and competitions. Fears are age-related, built upon an innate basis through experience with pain, strangeness, and observation. Anxiety is unfocused fear. Fears can be prevented and eliminated through prevention, reassurance, and teaching children to cope.

Discipline involves present compliance and future self-control. Moral development in the preschool period follows a predictable sequence of punishment-reward plus primitive hedonism, obeying when watched and feeling some shame, and internalization with guilt. Internalized children are likely to have mothers who use inductive discipline. Moral action involves willing to do right. Language aids the child in choosing a course of action. Moral judgment is involved in deciding whether an action is right or wrong. Moral realism means judging by results, not intentions. Judging intentionality is correlated with role taking and reflectivity.

With the development of the sense of autonomy, the child builds an increasingly clearer concept of himself as a distinct individual. The self develops through all sorts of play. Disadvantaged children may lack experiences necessary for development of a clear self-concept. Low self-esteem is often a problem with disadvantaged children and children from minority and ethnic groups. Body image, an aspect of self, is clarified through movement experiences and exploration, as well as by reactions of other people to the physical self.

Gender-role behavior is acquired as socialization pressures are brought to bear upon inherited potentials for action. The concept of gender constancy forms a developmental sequence of stages, gender identity, gender stability, and gender consistency. When the child achieves gender constancy, she knows that a person's gender remains the same, no matter what changes occur in time and circumstances. Gender-role prescriptions are cultural. Some consistency is seen throughout the world. Division of labor within a society prescribes some of the experiences through which children develop gender-typed behavior. Parents and siblings ordinarily exert the pressures required by the gender stereotypes of their culture. Toys offer and limit opportunities for developing behavioral patterns. Teachers dispense reinforcements dependent upon sex of teacher and sex of child. The media present sex-role stereotypes. Gender-role learning is strongly influenced by parental warmth and power. Parental absence and divorce affect children's learning and relationships.

References

1. Ambron, S. R. Role taking and moral judgment in five- and seven-year-olds. *Developmental Psychology*, 1975, **11**, 102.
2. Atkinson, J. and R. C. Endsley. Influence of sex of child and parent on parental reactions to hypothetical parent-child situations. Paper presented at meetings of the Society for Research in Child Development, Denver, 1975.
3. Bandura, A. The role of modeling processes in personality development. In W. W. Hartup and N. L. Smothergill (eds.). *The young child: Reviews of research.* Washington, D.C. National Association for the Education of Young Children, 1967, pp. 42–58.
4. Bandura, A. and R. Walters. Aggression. In H. W. Stevenson (ed.). *Child Psychology. The Sixty-second Yearbook of the National Society for the Study of Education.* Chicago: University of Chicago Press, 1963, pp. 364–415.
5. Barry, H., M. K. Bacon, and I. L. Child. A cross-cultural survey of some sex differences in socialization. *Journal of Abnormal and Social Psychology*, 1957, **55**, 327–332.
6. Biller, H. B. A multiaspect investigation of masculine development in kindergarten age boys. *Genetic Psychology Monographs*, 1968, **76**, 89–139.
7. Biller, H. B. *Paternal deprivation.* Lexington, Mass.: D. C. Heath & Co., 1974.
8. Borke, H. The development of empathy in Chinese and American children between three and six years of age: A cross-culture study. *Developmental Psychology*, 1973, **9**, 102–108.

9. Bronson, G. W. The development of fear in man and other animals. *Child Development,* 1968, **39,** 409–431.

10. Carlsmith, J. M., M. R. Lepper, and T. K. Landauer. Children's obedience to adult requests: Interactive effects of anxiety arousal and apparent punitiveness of adult. *Journal of Personality and Social Psychology,* 1974, **30,** 822–828.

11. Charlesworth, R. and W. W. Hartup. Positive social reinforcement in the nursery school peer group. *Child Development,* 1967, **38,** 993–1002.

12. Cherry, L. The preschool teacher-child dyad: Sex differences in verbal interaction. *Child Development,* 1975, **46,** 532–535.

13. Comer, J. P. and A. F. Poussaint. *Black child care.* New York: Simon & Schuster, Inc., 1975.

14. Deutsch, F. Effects of subject and story character on preschoolers' perceptions of affective responses and intrapersonal behavior in story sequences. *Developmental Psychology,* 1975, **11,** 112–113.

15. DiBartolo, R. and W. E. Vinacke. Adult nurturance and the preschool child. *Developmental Psychology,* 1969, **1,** 247–251.

16. Emmerich, W. The parental role: A functional-cognitive approach. *Monographs of the Society for Research in Child Development,* 1969, **34:**8.

17. Erikson, E. H. *Childhood and society.* 2nd ed. New York: W. W. Norton & Company, 1963.

18. Erikson, E. H., *Youth and crisis.* New York: W. W. Norton & Company, 1968.

18a. Etaugh, C. Effects of maternal employment on children: A review of recent research. *Merrill-Palmer Quarterly,* 1974, **20,** 71–98.

19. Etaugh, C., G. Collins, and A. Gerson. Reinforcement of sex-typed behaviors of two-year-old children in a nursery school setting. *Developmental Psychology,* 1975, **11, 255.**

20. Fagot, B. I. and G. R. Patterson. An in vivo analysis of reinforcing contingencies for sex-role behaviors in the preschool child. *Developmental Psychology,* 1969, **1,** 563–568.

21. Fink, R. S. The role of imaginative play in cognitive development. In J. Magary (ed.). *Piagetian theory and the helping professions.* Los Angeles: University of California Press, 1975.

22. Friedrich, L. K. and A. H. Stein. Prosocial television and young children: The effects of verbal labeling and role playing behavior on learning and behavior. *Child Development,* 1975, **46,** 27–38.

23. Freyberg, J. T. Increasing the imaginative play of urban disadvantaged kindergarten children through systematic training. In J. L. Singer (ed.). *The child's world of make-believe.* New York: Academic Press, 1973, 129–134.

24. Garvey, C. Some properties of social play. *Merrill-Palmer Quarterly.* 1974, **20,** 163–180.

25. Hagman, R. R. A study of the fears of children of preschool age. *Journal of Experimental Education,* 1932, **1,** 110–130.

26. Halverson, C. F. and M. F. Waldrop. The relations of mechanically recorded activity level to varieties of preschool play behavior. *Child Development,* 1973, **44,** 678–681.

27. Hartup, W. W., J. A. Glazer, and R. Charlesworth. Peer reinforcement and sociometric status. *Child Development,* 1967, **38,** 1017–1024.

28. Hartup, W. W. Aggression in childhood. *American Psychologist,* 1974, **29,** 336–341.

29. Heinicke, C. M. Some effects of separating two-year-old children from their mothers. *Human Relations,* 1956, **9,** 102–176.

30. Hess, R. D., I. Gordon, and D. Scheinfeld. Intervention in family life. In E. Grotberg (ed.). *Critical issues in research related to disadvantaged children.* Princeton, N.J.: Educational Testing Service, 1969.

31. Hetherington, E. M., M. Cox and R. Cox. Beyond father absence: Conceptualization of effects of divorce. In R. C. Smart and M. S. Smart (eds.) *Readings in child development and relationships.* New York: The Macmillan Co., 1977, pp. 195–204.

32. Hoffman, M. L. Developmental synthesis of affect and cognition and its implications for altruistic motivation. *Developmental Psychology,* 1975, **11,** 607–622.

33. Jersild, A. T. and F. B. Holmes. Children's fears. *Child Development Monographs, No. 20.* New York: Teachers College, Columbia University, 1935.

34. John, E. A study of the effects of evacuation and air raids on children of pre-school age. *British Journal of Educational Psychology,* 1941, **11,** 173–182.

35. Joynt, D. and B. Cambroune. Psycholinguistic development and the control of behavior. *British Journal of Educational Psychology,* 1968, **38,** 249–260.

36. Kirchner, E. P. and S. I. Vondracek. What do you want to be when you grow up? Vocational choice in children aged three to six. Paper presented at meetings of the Society for Research in Child Development, Philadelphia, 1973.

37. Koch, H. L. The relation of certain formal attributes of siblings to attitudes held toward each other and toward their parents. *Monographs of the Society for Research in Child Development,* 1960, **25:**4.

38. Leifer, A. D. How to encourage socially valued behavior. Paper presented at meetings of the Society for Research in Child Development, Denver, 1975.

39. Loo, C. M. Effects of spatial density on social behavior of children. Proceedings, 80th Annual Convention of the American Psychological Association, 1972, 101–102.

40. Luria, A. R. *The role of speech in the regulation of normal and abnormal behavior.* New York: Pergamon Press, Inc., 1961.

41. Maurer, A. What children fear. *Journal of Genetic Psychology,* 1965, **106,** 265–277.

42. Money, J. and A. A. Ehrhardt. *Man & woman, boy & girl.* Baltimore: Johns Hopkins University Press, 1972.

43. Mood, D., J. Johnson, and C. U. Shantz. Young children's understanding of the affective states of others. Paper presented at the Southeastern Regional Meeting of the Society for Research in Child Development, 1973.

44. Moore, S. B. Correlates of peer acceptance in nursery school children. *Young Children,* 1967, **22,** 281–297.

45. Mussen, P. and E. Rutherford. Parent-child relations and parental personality in relation to young children's sex-role preferences. *Child Development,* 1963, **34,** 225–246.

46. O'Connor, M. The nursery school environment. *Developmental Psychology,* 1975, **5,** 556–561.

47. Olejnik, A. B. and J. P. McKinney. Parental value orientation and generosity in children. *Developmental Psychology,* 1973, **8,** 311.

48. Osborn, D. K. and R. C. Endsley. Emotional reactions of young children to TV violence. *Child Development,* 1971, **42,** 321–331.

49. Peterson, C. L., F. W. Danner, and J. H. Flavell. Developmental changes in children's response to three indications of communicative failure. *Child Development,* 1972, **43,** 1463–1468.

50. Piaget, J. *The moral judgment of the child.* Glencoe, Ill.: The Free Press, 1960.

51. Reuter, G. and G. Yunik. Social interaction in nursery schools. *Developmental Psychology*, 1973, **9**, 319–325.

52. Rheingold, H. L. and K. V. Cook. The contents of boys' and girls' rooms as an index of parents' behavior. *Child Development*, 1975, **46**, 459–463.

53. Rohner, R. P. Sex differences in aggression: Phylogenetic and enculturation perspectives. Paper presented at meetings of the Society for Research in Child Development, Denver, 1975.

53a. Rosen, C. E. The effects of sociodramatic play on problem-solving behavior among culturally disadvantaged children. *Child Development*, 1974, **45**, 920–927.

54. Rosenfeld, E. F. The relationship of sex-typed toys to the development of competency and sex-role identification in children. Paper presented at meetings of the Society for Research in Child Development, Denver, 1975.

55. Rosenthal, B. G. Development of self-identification in relation to attitudes towards self in Chippewa Indians. *Genetic Psychology Monographs*, 1974, **90**, 43–141.

56. Schleifer, M. and V. A. Douglas. Moral judgments, behaviour and cognitive style in young children. *Canadian Journal of Behavioural Science*, 1973, **5**, 133–144.

57. Schwarz, J. C. Presence of an attached peer and security. Paper presented at the meetings of the Society for Research in Child Development, Santa Monica, Calif., 1969.

58. Schwarz, J. C. Effects of peer familiarity on the behavior of preschoolers in a novel situation. *Journal of Personality and Social Psychology*, 1972, **24**, 276–284.

59. Serbin, L. A., D. O'Leary, R. N. Kent, and I. J. Tonick. A comparison of teacher response to preacademic and problem behavior of boys and girls. *Child Development*, 1973, **44**, 796–804.

60. Shantz, C. U. Empathy in relation to social cognitive development. Paper presented at meetings of the American Psychological Association, New Orleans, 1974.

61. Sherman, L. W. An ecological study of glee in small groups of preschool children. *Child Development*, 1975, **46**, 53–61.

62. Sidel, R. *Women and child care in China*. Baltimore: Penguin Books, 1973.

63. Siegel, A. E., L. M. Stolz, E. A. Hitchcock, and J. M. Adamson. Dependence and independence in the children of working mothers. *Child Development*, 1959, **30**, 533–546.

64. Slaby, R. G. and K. S. Frey. Development of gender constancy and selective attention to same-sex models. *Child Development*, 1975, **46**, 849–856.

65. Smilansky, S. *The effects of sociodramatic play on disadvantaged preschool children*. New York: John Wiley & Sons, Inc., 1968.

66. Stayton, D. J., R. Hogan, and M. D. S. Ainsworth. Infant obedience and maternal behavior: The origins of socialization reconsidered. *Child Development*, 1971, **42**, 1057–1069.

67. Stolz, L. M. Effects of maternal employment on children: Evidence from research. *Child Development*, 1960, **31**, 749–782.

68. Van de Castle, R. L. His, hers and the children's. *Psychology Today*, 1970, **4:**1, 37–39.

69. Venn, J. R. and J. G. Short. Vicarious classical conditioning of emotional responses in nursery school children. *Journal of Personality and Social Psychology*, 1973, **28**, 249–255.

70. Waldrop, M. F. and C. F. Halverson. Intensive and extensive peer behavior: Longitudinal and cross-sectional analysis. *Child Development*, 1975, **46**, 19–26.

71. Wasserman, G. A. and D. N. Stern. Approach behaviors between preschool children: An ethological study. In R. C. Smart and M. S. Smart (eds.) *Readings*

in child development and relationships. New York: The Macmillan Co., 1977, pp. 167–176.

72. Weiner, B. and N. Peter. A cognitive-developmental analysis of achievement and moral judgments. *Developmental Psychology,* 1973, 9, 290–309.

73. Whiting, B. and C. P. Edwards. A cross-cultural analysis of sex differences in the behavior of children aged three through 11. *Journal of Social Psychology,* 1973, 91, 171–188.

74. Wulbert, M., S. Inglis, E. Kriegsmann, and B. Mills. Language delay and associated mother-child interactions. *Developmental Psychology,* 1975, 11, 61–70.

75. Yarrow, M. R., P. M. Scott, and C. A. Waxler. Learning concern for others. *Developmental Psychology,* 1973, 8, 240–260.

Readings in
Emotional and Social Development

Through interactions with other people, children acquire knowledge of others and of themselves and techniques for dealing with other people. Social interactions have a feeling side. Children learn to recognize and express their own emotions and to interpret and react to the emotions of others, using their cognitive resources as well as their emotions. Processes underlying social behavior are examined here.

Nonverbal communication occurs when one person reacts to another's nonverbal signals, such as facial expressions, posture, gestures, and distancing. Gail A. Wasserman and Daniel N. Stern analyzed the nonverbal signals given by preschool children as they approached a peer. Their behaviors indicated that children were aware of their own sex and that of the other child, since they made closer approaches to peers of their own sex. Nonverbal signals are thought to give more accurate information about children's attitudes toward peers than do their answers to questions.

Conceptual perspective-taking, or taking the point of view of another person, enables the first person to know or to make a good guess as to what the second person is thinking. Psychologists have paid a great deal of attention to the question of whether preschool children can take the point of view of another person. Piaget placed this ability in the stage of concrete operations, which begins at around 7 years of age. In the previous chapter, Pufall investigated children's ability to take another spatial perspective. Here Daniel G. Mossler, Mark T. Greenberg, and Robert S. Marvin have devised situations in which younger children can take the conceptual perspective of another.

Empathy refers to being able to perceive how another person is thinking and feeling, often with an emphasis on the feeling side. Helene Borke has investigated empathy in preschool children, both Chinese and American, and both middle-class and disadvantaged. Thus, she was able to test influences of culture and socioeconomic level in addition to showing age-level differences.

Social interaction is affected by individual differences in temperament, according to Jeannie L. Lewis. Rating children on nine dimensions of temperament, she related temperamental characteristics to social behavior at school and at home.

The family is, of course, the arena in which basic social-emotional interaction patterns are acquired. With the contemporary family changing as it is, the effects of new family forms upon children are relatively unknown. Therefore, an ongoing study at the University of Virginia is very important. A preliminary report of this research, by E. Mavis Hetherington, Martha Cox, and Roger Cox, gives insight into the impact of divorce on children, mothers, and fathers.

190

Approach Behaviors Between Preschool Children: An Ethological Study*

Gail A. Wasserman and Daniel N. Stern

NEW YORK HOSPITAL–CORNELL MEDICAL CENTER

The ethological approach to the study of nonverbal communication promises to further our understanding of interpersonal events. However, at this point, not enough is known about the development, in young children, of the components of nonverbal signal systems, such as distancing, postural orientation, facial expressions, and hand and head gestures.

Many aspects of the child's motivational state, such as fear, aggressiveness, affiliation and curiosity are communicated through these signal systems. Additionally, the child's differential use of such behaviors can serve as an index of the degree to which he differentiates such salient dimensions of his relationship to his peers as their sex as compared to his own, their dominance status, their familiarity, and their perceived aggressiveness, fearfulness, or friendliness. Accordingly, the study of these signal systems may provide us with new and powerful tools for examining various developmental issues related to normal and abnormal peer interactions.

This paper is part of an ongoing study of the ontogeny of such kinesic communications systems, as they operate in dyadic interactions. Previous work by Stern and Bender (1974) has documented the existence, in preschool children, of nonverbal signals which are organized into functionally meaningful clusters and are used differentially, depending on the situation in which the child finds himself. Specifically, Stern and Bender found consistent differences in the behavior of 3–5-year-old children approaching a strange adult. Depending upon the age and sex of the child and the degree of threat presented by the adult, children showed consistent differences in how close they would approach to the adult, the degree to which they oriented their faces and bodies away from the adult, and their usage of hand gestures, such as hand to mouth and hands behind back, as well as in their performances of facial expressions, particularly smiling and apprehensive mouth behaviors.

The current study extends these observations to peer interactions, rather than child–adult interactions, and examines nonverbal behavior between approaching peers, as a function of the child's age, sex, relative dominance-status, aggressiveness, and sex of the other interacting peer. We would also wish to document the presence of kinesic signals which are specific to sex related and dominance behaviors and to trace their emergence in the young child.

Presented at meetings of The Society for Research in Child Development, Denver, 1975. Printed by permission.

* The authors would like to express their appreciation to the following individuals and schools for their assistance in this research: Maryann Ford, Kathy Kappy Lewis, Larry Jordan, Andrea Consales, Helen Hall, Claire Jasinski, Miyako Namikawa, Margaret Pratesi; Mount Tom Country Day School, New Rochelle, N.Y.; Pengilly Day School, New Rochelle, N.Y.; Saxon Woods Country School, Mamaroneck, N.Y.; Ridge Street Country School, Portchester, N.Y.; Yonkers Jewish Community Center, Yonkers, N.Y.

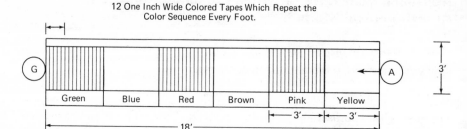

FIGURE 1.   *Approach carpet.*

Ss were 134 white 3–5-year-old children. Children from all the experiments I will describe are all middle-class preschoolers from the same suburban area. Children were met in their classroom by the experimenter and asked to participate in a study of how boys and girls walked. Children were brought, 4 at a time, 2 boys and 2 girls, to a familiar room in the school. Two children waited outside, while the other 2 entered the room. One child, whom we call the goal ("G"), was asked to stand on the end of a long rug, which was 18 feet long and 3 feet wide, and was marked with 12 different-colored, 1 inch wide strips of colored tape, which repeated the color sequence every foot. The second child, whom we call the approacher ("A"), was asked to stand at the other end of the

TABLE 1

ANOVA: Log of Approach Distance + 1, Peer Approaches

SOURCE	df	MS	F
Age (A)*	2	3.093	2.800
Sex (A)	1	.514	.465
Order	1	.067	.060
Age (A) × Sex (A)	2	.487	.441
Age (A) × Order	2	.951	.861
Sex (A) × Order	1	.625	.566
Age (A) × Sex (A) × Order	2	.211	.191
Error	122	1.105	
Sex (G)**	1	2.260	6.775†
Age × Sex (G)	2	.141	.423
Sex (A) × Sex (G)	1	.104	.312
Order × Sex (G)	1	.596	1.788
Age × Sex (A) × Sex (G)	2	.153	.458
Age × Order × Sex (G)	2	.332	.995
Sex (A) × Order × Sex (G)	1	.109	.325
Age × Sex (A) × Order × Sex (G)	2	.684	2.050
Error	122	.334	

* (A) = Approaching child.
** (G) = Goal child.
† $p < .025$.

rug. The experimenter then said, "Now, 'Johnny,' walk up to 'Susie,' and stop in front of her." A second experimenter scored the approach behavior. The approacher and goal then changed places, for a second run. Cycling in the waiting children, each child approached two other children of the same age as himself, one of the same sex, and one of the opposite sex. The order of approaches was counterbalanced.

TABLE 2

ANOVA: Angular Distance, Peer Approaches

SOURCE	df	MS	F
Age (A)*	2	1.282	.172
Sex (A)	1	6.794	.913
Order	1	2.318	.311
Age × Sex (A)	2	1.968	.264
Age × Order	2	7.943	1.067
Sex (A) × Order	1	4.409	.593
Age × Sex (A) × Order	2	8.320	1.118
Error	122	7.441	
Sex (G)**	1	7.469	6.179†
Age × Sex (G)	2	.701	.580
Sex (A) × Sex (G)	1	1.301	1.076
Order × Sex (G)	1	17.200	14.229††
Age × Sex (A) × Sex (G)	2	1.231	1.019
Age × Order × Sex (G)	2	.214	.177
Sex (A) × Order × Sex (G)	1	1.789	1.480
Age × Sex (A) × Order × Sex (G)	2	1.330	1.101
Error	122	1.209	

* (A) = Approaching child.
** (G) = Goal child.
† $p < .025$.
†† $p < .001$.

Two positional behaviors were recorded: 1) how close the approacher came to the goal ("approach distance"), and 2) the degree to which the approacher avoided directly facing or fully squaring off with the goal ("angular distance").

We expected that if dominance were one of the relevant dimensions of children's approach behavior, and if this dimension were more salient for boys, as some have suggested, then boys should stop further away from boys and should angle their bodies away more from boys.

Looking at the top half of Figure 2, which shows the graphs for approach distance, the upper right-hand figure indicates that children stop significantly further from opposite-sexed goals than from same-sexed goals. The bottom two figures are for angular distance, and as you can see from the graph on the right, children orient their bodies significantly further away from opposite-sexed goals than from same-sexed goals. There were, however, no differences as a function of the sex of either the approacher or the goal, rather, the relevant dimension was whether the goal was of the same or opposite sex as the approacher. As a

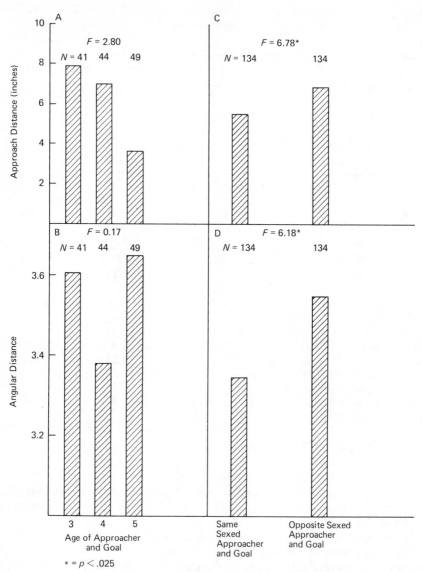

FIGURE 2.   *Approaches between children of the same age.*

footnote from the upper left-hand graph, you will notice that older children approach somewhat closer than younger children. This has been a consistent finding in our work, but it will not be commented upon further here. There are no age changes in angular distance.

Clearly, the major determinant of the approach behaviors here was not any hypothesized dominance related to sex, but rather a differentiation of the child's own sex relative to the sex of the goal child.

We then attempted to structure the situation so that the dominance–related aspects would be more salient for the child. We asked nursery school teachers to rank order the children in their classes by aggressivity. From each class list we picked the two most aggressive and the two least aggressive children. Taking each sex and classroom separately, then, every child both approached and served as the goal for two other children: one who ranked next to him on the class list and one from the other end of the scale with order counterbalanced. Here we had 26 boys and 28 girls.

Statistics for both approach distance and angular distance revealed no significant effect of either sex or aggressivity of approacher or goal. It would appear then, from these negative findings, that aggressiveness is not a component of the dominance relation, at least as measured by our approach situation.

Having ruled out aggressiveness, at least as reflected in teacher ratings, what other child characteristics might meaningfully be considered as components of dominance relations? The most obvious one, it seemed to us, would be age-status. This is likely to be a very salient dimension for young children, especially in a nursery school with age-graded classes, where issues such as which children take naps and who is taught to read, depend on which class a child is in.

Our next step, then, was to have 4-year-old children approach 3-, 4- and 5-year-olds of the same and opposite sex. On the first day of testing, subjects were asked to approach, one at a time, a 4-, a 3-, and a 5-year-old child, in that order, all of either the same or opposite sex. At a later session, between 1 and 4 weeks later, the child was asked to approach the 3 children of the remaining sex. The order 4, 3, 5 was chosen because we assumed that this would start off with a *known* peer, and only gradually work up to a less-known, higher status child. Here we used 8 4-year-olds of each sex as approachers, and 16 3-year-olds, 20 4-year-olds, and 15 5-year-olds as goals. Some of the 4-year-old goals were also used as approachers.

For this experiment, we videotaped the behavior of the approacher and the goal. The videotape record was later scored for a variety of facial expressions and hand gestures.

Once again, if dominance (as represented by the age or grade of the goal) were relevant here, we would expect more distancing and body aversion when children approach older goals than when they approach younger goals. Looking first at the two figures on the left of Figure 3, with the age of the goal plotted on the horizontal axis, we can see that there is no significant age of goal effect for either approach distance or angular distance. The most consistent finding was, again, as shown on the two figures on the right, that approachers of both sexes stopped further away from opposite-sexed goals and oriented their bodies more away from opposite-sexed goals than they did from same-sexed goals, regardless of age-status differentials. This is the same result we noted above.

Although we observed no sex differences per se in the positional behaviors studied, a finer analysis using the videotapes revealed some interesting sex differences in facial expressions and gestures of both the approacher and the goal. As seen in Figure 4, there was a trend for smiles to be more characteristic of approaches involving females, and for apprehensive mouth behaviors to be more characteristic of approaches involving males. This may perhaps be

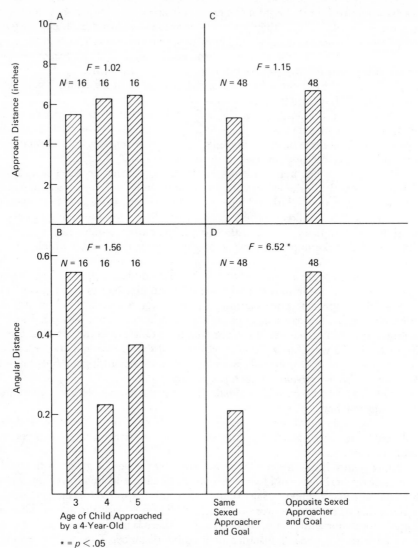

* = p < .05

FIGURE 3.   *Approaches of 4-year-old children to 3-, 4-, and 5-year-old children.*

evidence for some sort of dominance signaling between the boys, and possibly more affiliative behavior in the girls.

I don't have the time to discuss these differences further, but I do want to return to our major findings.

First, with the possible exception of our findings on facial expression, there is no evidence of dominance hierarchies based on sex, teacher ratings of aggressiveness, or on age-status within a year of the approacher's status. We do feel that our method of demonstrating dominance behavior is valid, because signs

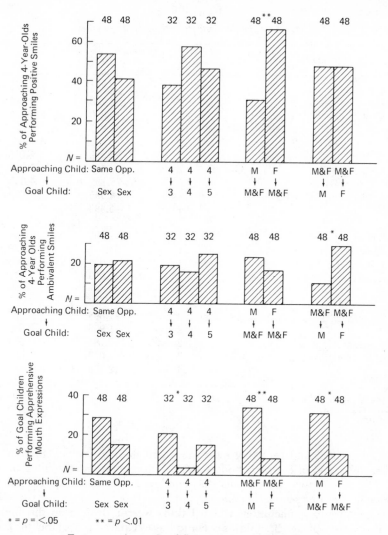

FIGURE 4.   *Sex differences in approach behaviors.*

and signals *are* components of dominance relations in adults, and we believe that the absence of any differences in these systems along the dimensions of sex, aggressiveness, or age-status means that such dominance relations are not yet present at the ages we have studied. This is in keeping with observations reported by Blurton-Jones (1967), in which he finds no evidence of a dominance hierarchy in children age 5 and younger. Further, Omark, Omark, and Edelman (1973), observing 4–8-year-olds, report very little relationship between observed dominance behavior on the playground and which child, of a pair, takes charge in solving a joint task. Who grabs toys, or who wins fights, may at this age very well be indications of some system other than that of a dominance hierarchy.

TABLE 3
ANOVA: Approach Distance, Age Status Differential

SOURCE	df	MS	F
Sex (A)*	1	2.344	.056
Order	1	162.760	3.882
Sex (A) × Order	1	10.010	.239
Error	12	41.927	
Age (G)**	2	5.469	1.015
Sex (A) × Age (G)	2	8.469	1.573
Order × Age (G)	2	26.135	4.853†
Sex (A) × Order × Age (G)	2	8.635	1.603
Error	24	5.385	
Sex (G)	1	14.260	.484
Sex (A) × Sex (G)	1	33.844	1.150
Order × Sex (G)	1	.094	.003
Sex (A) × Order × Sex (G)	1	270.010	9.171†
Error	12	29.441	
Age (G) × Sex (G)	2	11.698	.965
Sex (A) × Age (G) × Sex (G)	2	11.906	.982
Order × Age (G) × Sex (G)	2	6.781	.559
Sex(A) × Order × Age(G) × Sex(G)	2	1.073	.088
Error	24	12.128	

* (A) = Approaching child.
** (G) = Goal child.
† $p < .025$.

Our second, and probably most important finding, is that children stay further away and orient their bodies away from opposite-sexed children. This was true, in the two experiments that employed cross-sexed approaches, for approachers of *both sexes and at all ages*.

There are two conclusions which I think we can draw from this finding. The first is that by age 3, children seem to have acquired a sex label for themselves, and the second is that by age 3, children can discriminate the sex of their peers. The first finding is consistent with the work by Money (Money, Hampson & Hampson, 1957), and by Gesell (Gesell et al., 1940) on the acquisition of gender identity. It is usually assumed, however, that a correct assessment of other children's sex comes rather later than we have found it. At this age, the utilization of a nonverbal measurement such as we have reported, may prove more sensitive than direct questioning in assessing children's awareness of the sex of their peers.

Just as intriguing and perhaps more so, is that children consistently *avoid* children of the opposite sex. This is in keeping with findings that, in this age range, children direct more positive social reinforcement to same-sexed peers (Charlesworth and Hartup, 1967) and that they stay further from opposite-

TABLE 4

ANOVA: Angular Distance, Age Status Differential

SOURCE	df	MS	F
Sex (A)*	1	.094	.223
Order	1	1.760	4.190
Sex (A) × Order	1	.010	.025
Error	12	.420	
Age (G)**	2	.948	1.560
Sex (A) × Age (G)	2	1.156	1.903
Order × Age (G)	2	1.135	1.869
Sex (A) × Order × Age	2	.635	1.046
Error	24	.608	
Sex (G)	1	1.260	2.729
Sex (A) × Sex (G)	1	3.010	6.519†
Order × Sex (G)	1	.260	.564
Sex (A) × Order × Sex (G)	1	1.760	3.812
Error	12	.462	
Age (G) × Sex (G)	2	1.823	3.107
Sex (A) × Age (G) × Sex (G)	2	1.698	2.893
Order × Age (G) × Sex (G)	2	1.135	1.935
Sex(A) × Order × Age(G) × Sex(G)	2	.135	.231
Error	24	.587	

* (A) = Approaching child.
** (G) = Goal child.
† $p < .025$.

sexed peers in the playground (Langibis et al., 1973; Omark et al., 1973). This avoidance is not generally thought to begin until much later, in middle childhood, after which it becomes intense in preadolescence. In our study, however, there were quite a few instances in which the children verbally expressed their contempt for children of the opposite sex, so the intense avoidance may very well be present long before we would expect it.

From the ethological point of view, we consider these findings relevant to the origin and the ontogeny of the nonverbal signal systems regulating that very important sphere of human activity: interaction between the sexes. We are now planning to chart the development of these behaviors, as well as that of facial expressions and gestures, through middle childhood and adolescence, to observe and describe the changing signal systems which constitute inter-sex behavior.

References

BLURTON-JONES, N. in D. Morris (Ed.), *Primate Ethology*. London: Weidenfeld Nicholson, 1967. Pp. 347–368.

CHARLESWORTH, R. & HARTUP, W. W. Positive social reinforcement in the nursery school peer group. *Child Development*, 1967, **38**, 993–1002.

GESELL, A., HALVERSON, H. M., THOMPSON, H., ILG, F. L. COSINER, B. H., AMES, L. B., & AMATRUDA, C. S. *The first five years of life: A guide to the study of the preschool child.* New York: Harper & Row, 1940.

LANGIBIS, J. H., GOTTFRIED, N. W., & SEAY, B. The influence of sex of peer on the social behavior of preschool children. *Developmental Psychology*, 1973, 8, 93–98.

MONEY, J., HAMPSON, J., & HAMPSON, J. Imprinting and the establishment of gender role. *Archives of Neurology and Psychiatry* 1957, 77, 333–336.

OMARK, D. R., OMARK, M., & EDELMAN, M. Dominance hierarchies in young children. Paper presented at the International Congress of Anthropological and Ethnological Sciences, Chicago, 1973.

STERN, D. & BENDER, E. An ethological study of children approaching a strange adult: sex differences. In R. Friedman, R. Richart, & R. Vandewiele (Eds.) *Sex differences in behavior.* New York: Wiley, 1974. 233–258.

The Early Development of Conceptual Perspective-Taking

Daniel G. Mossler, Mark T. Greenberg, and Robert S. Marvin
UNIVERSITY OF VIRGINIA

Role-taking or perspective-taking refers to the " . . . process by which the individual somehow cognizes, apprehends, or grasps . . . certain attributes of the other person" (Flavell et al., 1968, p. 5). These attributes can include another persons' visual percepts, thoughts, desires, intentions, etc. The focus of this investigation was on conceptual rather than perceptual perspective-taking. Our aim was to find out when children correctly infer what another person *thinks* or *knows* rather than what another person *sees* or *hears*. Specifically, the purpose of this study was to determine the age at which children are able to engage in a simple form of conceptual perspective-taking.

The literature is unclear as to when children are first able to infer another person's state of knowledge. Some of the research has found that children younger than 7 years of age are not able to take another's perspective. Typically, young children respond egocentrically; they do not differentiate their viewpoint from another's viewpoint. For example, Flavell (Apple-dog story, 1968) and Chandler (Droodles task, 1973) used tasks in which the child had access to information not available to the other person, and in which the child was required to make an inference about the other's restricted conceptual viewpoint. They found children unable to engage in non-egocentric perspective-taking until ages 9 and 7, respectively. The younger children egocentrically inferred that the other person's knowledge of the story was the same as his own.

This body of research has been criticized for using complex stimuli and response demands which are beyond the capabilities of young children (Borke,

Presented at meetings of The Society for Research in Child Development, Denver, 1975. A brief report, titled "Conceptual Perspective-Taking in 2–6-Year-Old Children," appeared in *Developmental Psychology*, 1976, 12, 85–86. Printed by permission.

1971; Marvin, 1972). Thus, in these complex tasks, an egocentric response could indicate either a lack of perspective-taking skills, or a lack of some other cognitive skill required by the task. Using less complex stimuli and less complex response demands, a few studies have found evidence of basic perspective-taking abilities in children as young as three or four years of age. For example, Borke (1971) had children select a picture to match the affective state of a child in a story. She found that children as young as three years of age correctly anticipate the actor's feelings in certain simple contexts. Some of these studies have in turn been criticized on the grounds that they in fact may not be measuring perspective-taking. As Chandler states, "Non-egocentric thought, in the sense intended by Piaget (1956), is not simply a synonym for accurate social judgment but implies the ability to anticipate what someone else might think or feel precisely when these thoughts and feelings are different from one's own. Without this important qualification, egocentric and non-egocentric thought result in the same outcome and their measurement is hopelessly confounded" (1972, p. 105).

Therefore, to ensure that perspective-taking is required for correct performance, the task must be constructed such that the child's perspective is *demonstrably* different from that of the other. The task must contain a minimum amount of "shared cultural perspective." According to Chandler (1973) the term "shared cultural perspective" refers to the amount of shared knowledge between the subject and the other person. For example, a young child can accurately predict that a person at a birthday party will be happy. He need not engage in perspective-taking to correctly anticipate the other's feelings, since it is part of our shared knowledge that anyone at a birthday party (including the child himself) is probably happy.

Although Chandler presented this as an absolute quality, which is either absent or present, it is more useful to think of shared knowledge as a continuum along which perspective-taking situations may vary. Any such situation must involve a minimum of shared knowledge. Clearly, the child must attribute some shared qualities to the other person, i.e., that the other can think, that the other can hear, that the other can speak, and so on.

In a review of the social-cognition literature, Shantz (in press) concludes that the simpler the tasks are made, the earlier investigators are able to find evidence of these abilities. However, she questions whether these investigations are actually measuring perspective-taking or some other related abilities. In other words, the research which is most clearly measuring perspective-taking, by having demonstrably different viewpoints, is confounded with the use of complex stimuli and response demands. On the other hand, the research using stimuli and less complex response demands may not really be measuring perspective-taking at all.

These considerations are taken into account in this study. We investigated young children's abilities to engage in conceptual perspective-taking using a less complex variation of Flavell's privileged-information situation. While maintaining the requirement of demonstrably different viewpoints, we used short videotaped stories requiring the child to make a yes-no inference about the other's restricted viewpoint. To make the task as naturalistic as possible, the task was administered in the child's home using the mother as the other person.

Eighty middle-class children between the age of $2\frac{1}{2}$ and $6\frac{1}{2}$ years balanced for sex were used in this study. The subjects included 10 2-year-olds ($\bar{X} = 2:8$), 20 3-year-olds ($\bar{X} = 3:5\frac{1}{2}$), 20 4-year-olds ($\bar{X} = 4:6$) 20 5-year-olds ($\bar{X} = 5:6$), and 10 6-year-olds ($\bar{X} = 6:4$).

The children were presented with two videotaped stories containing one or two bits of information. In one story, the videotape showed a boy walking into a house; the audio stated, "This boy is going into his grandmother's house." In the second story, the videotape showed a boy getting up from a table and walking up to his mother; the audio contained his direct request for a cookie. The order of presentation of the stories was counterbalanced. The actual procedure was as follows.

The experimenter spent 20–30 minutes playing with the child and showing him the equipment. Then the experimenter told the child that they were going to play a T.V. game. The experimenter asked the mother to wait in the other room. With the mother out of the room, the child was shown one of the stories. He was then questioned to make sure that he understood and knew the correct bit of information about the story. Interestingly, when asked "What happened on the T.V. ?", most children said, "It went off!" The child was then asked, "Was the boy going into the house?" and "Whose house was the boy going into?"

The experimenter then went into the other room and brought back the mother. The child was told; "Now you and mommy are going to watch the story again, but this time I am going to turn the sound down." The experimenter made sure that the child watched as he turned the sound down. The child and the mother were then shown the same story without the audio portion. The experimenter then said to the child, "Now I am going to ask you some questions about what your *mommy* thinks." The child was questioned about his mother's knowledge of both the audio and video portions of the story. With respect to the grandmother story, the child was asked; "Does your mommy think the boy was going into a house?" and "Does your mommy know whose house the boy was going into?" The child was then asked to justify his response. "How does your mommy know that?" or "How come she doesn't know?" The same full procedure was repeated for the second story. At the end of the questioning procedure for the last story, the child was asked. "Did your mommy see the same thing that you saw?" and "Did your mommy hear the same thing that you heard?"

The child's responses were coded as either egocentric or non-egocentric on the following basis. A child was given a non-egocentric score for the grandmother–house story if he realized that his mother knew the boy went into a house (yes), but that she did not know whose house (no). For the cookie story, a child was given a non-egocentric score if he realized that his mommy knew the boy was sitting at a table (yes), but that his mother did not know what the boy asked for (no). For the last set of questions, a child was given a non-egocentric score if he realized that his mother saw the same thing that he saw (yes), but that she did not hear the same thing that he heard (no). The justifications were scored as correct if the child said that his mother did not know because either the sound was turned down, or she was out of the room.

Since the questions were highly correlated (Tetrachoric coefficients .90–.93), they were collapsed across to give one overall egocentric or non-egocentric score. If the child answered none or only one of the three questions non-egocentrically, he was scored as egocentric. If however, the child answered either two or three of the questions non-egocentrically, he received a non-egocentric overall score. Additionally, a child received a justified or unjustified overall score depending on whether or not he answered a greater than chance proportion of the justifications correctly.

A five by two chi-square analysis was performed on both the perspective-taking questions and the justifications. With respect to the perspective-taking questions, a chi-square value of 50.72, p < .001 demonstrated that children of different ages performed differentially on the task.

None of the 2-year-olds performed non-egocentrically.[1] Only one of the 20 3-year-olds answered two or more questions non-egocentrically. However, 13 of the 4-year-olds and 18 of the 5-year-olds responded in a non-egocentric fashion. All of the 6-year-olds responded non-egocentrically. Thus the major age difference in this task was at 4 years of age, with more than half of the 4-year-olds answering in a non-egocentric fashion.

Age trend with respect to the justifications was somewhat different. A chi-square value of 34.55, p < .001 indicated that children responded differently depending on their age. None of the 2- or 3-year-olds correctly justified his answer. Eight of the 20 4-year-olds responded correctly as did 12 of the 20 5-year-olds. Nine of the 10 6-year-olds justified their responses correctly. Thus, the shift for veridical performance on the perspective-taking questions was more rapid and complete compared to the shift for correct performance on the justifications.

Since we used a simplified task with minimal memory constraints and minimal response demands, we can be more confident that a failure to perspective-take was not due to the task complexity. On the other hand, we have constructed a situation with demonstrably different perspectives between the child and his mother. Therefore we can be more certain that a child who is characterized as non-egocentric has some basic perspective-taking skills.

The results of this study indicate that a majority of children as young as four years of age are able to make inferences about another's conceptual points of view, i.e., about another's thoughts or states of knowledge. Obviously in any

TABLE 1

Responses to Perspective-Taking Questions and Justification Questions

	AGE IN YEARS					
RESPONSES	2	3	4	5	6	
Egocentric	10	19	7	2	0	$\chi^2 = 50.72; p < .001$
Non-egocentric	0	1	13	18	10	
Unjustified	10	20	12	8	1	$\chi^2 = 34.55; p < .001$
Justified	0	0	8	12	9	

[1] Six of the 10 2-year-olds were administered only one videotape sequence as they could not follow the task at all.

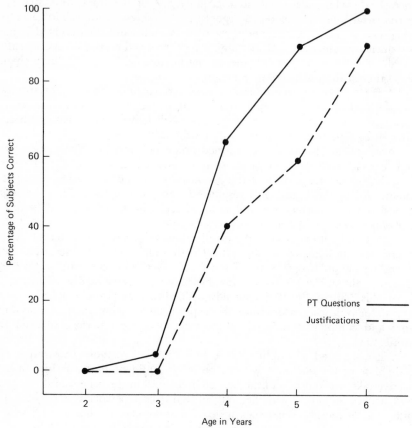

FIGURE 1. *Responses to audio-visual task.*

situation there are a wide variety of cues that children can use as a basis for making inferences about others' perspectives. These cues may be, among others, spatial, temporal, verbal, or non-verbal, or they may be purely situational. In our research we are currently attempting to isolate the kinds of cues that children use in this particular perspective-taking situation. The kinds of questions we are concerned with are: Do children use a multiplicity of cues? Does the reliance on any one type of cue change with age? What are the first cues used by children in perspective-taking?

In concluding, we would like to examine the results of this study in the light of certain aspects of Piaget's theory. Piaget (1956) described perspective-taking as a concrete operational ability which involves reversibility and co-ordination of perspectives. According to Piaget, these abilities are typically unavailable to children younger than 7 years of age.

However, Piaget describes the sub-period between 4 and 7 years of age as the "intuitive period." Children in this subperiod periodically decenter and show a gradual co-ordination of representative relations.

Almost all of our 4-, 5- and 6-year-old children could be so characterized. A further problem is that the ability to perform correctly on a perspective-taking task does not in and of itself constitute concrete operations. The hallmark of concrete operations is the formation of highly organized representational cognitive structures which are reversible, and are integrated with other, similar, structures. With reference to the difference in results between correct perspective-taking and correct justification, it appears that a majority of the 4-year-olds in this sample, and almost all of the 5- and 6-year-olds in this sample, possess at least the ability to engage in reversible representational operations, and further that a majority of these children are able to integrate their perspective-taking into a justified, explanatory framework. There is, however, a sizable minority of 4- and 5-year-olds who do not integrate their perspective-taking into a justified explanatory framework. This suggests two things: first that operational reversibility may be a necessary, but not sufficient, criterion for concrete operations; second, that the criterion of numerous operations being organized *together* may be a more valid criterion. In other words, it may be necessary to reassess our notions of the intuitive and concrete operational periods, and of the transition from one to the other.

References

BORKE, H. Interpersonal perception of young children: Egocentrism or empathy? *Developmental Psychology*, 1971, 5, 263–269.

CHANDLER, M. J., and GREENSPAN, S. Ersatz egocentrism: A reply to H. Borke. *Developmental Psychology*, 1972, 7, 104–106.

CHANDLER, M. J. Role-theory and developmental research. Paper presented at the American Psychological Association, Montreal, 1973.

FLAVELL, J. H., BOTKIN, P. T., FRY, C. L., WRIGHT, J. W., and JARVIS, P. E. *The Development of Role-Taking and Communication Skills in Children*. New York: John Wiley & Sons, 1968.

MARVIN, R. S. Attachment- exploratory- and communicative-behavior of 2, 3, and 4-year-old children. Unpublished Ph.D. Dissertation, University of Chicago, 1972.

PIAGET, J. *The Psychology of Intelligence*. London: Routledge and Kegan Paul, 1950.

PIAGET, J. and INHELDER, B. *The Child's Conception of Space*. London: Routledge & Kegan Paul, 1956.

SHANTZ, C. U. The development of social cognition. In *Review of Child Development Research*, Vol. 5, in press.

The Development of Empathy in Chinese and American Children Between Three and Six Years of Age : A Cross-Culture Study *

Helene Borke

CARNEGIE-MELLON UNIVERSITY

A series of social interaction situations representing the four emotions of happy, afraid, sad, and angry were administered to 288 American children and 288 Chinese children. Twenty-four girls and 24 boys, half from middle-class families and half from disadvantaged families, were tested at 6-month intervals between 3 and 6 years of age. Children from both cultural groups exhibited similar overall trends in their ability to recognize other people's emotional responses. By 3 years of age, the majority of American and Chinese children could differentiate between happy and unhappy reactions in other people. Perception of afraid, sad, and angry feelings developed somewhat later and appeared to be influenced by social learning. This cross-cultural study confirms the results of a previous investigation that very young children are capable of empathic responses. The awareness of other people's feelings by young children from very different cultural backgrounds suggests that empathy may be a basic human characteristic related to social adaptation.

Empathy in its most advanced stage is the ability to perceive the world from the perspective of the other. Although awareness of another person's view point is essential for effective interpersonal communication, very little is known about the early development of empathic ability. Until recently, most of the available evidence suggested that young children are primarily egocentric and that sociocentric thinking seldom appears before early adolescence (Burns & Cavey, 1957; Chandler & Greenspan, 1972; Flapan, 1968; Flavell, Botkin, & Fry, 1968; Freud, 1965; Gollin, 1958, Piaget, 1926, 1928, 1967; Werner, 1948).

In two previous papers (Borke, 1971, 1972), the present author questioned the conclusion that young children are egocentric and unable to take another person's perspective. Data from an earlier study (Borke, 1971) indicated that by 3 years of age children are capable of differentiating between happy and un-happy responses in other people and can recognize social situations associated with these responses. An alternate hypothesis was proposed that the development of empathy is a continuous process which proceeds through a series of hier-archical stages closely related to cognitive development. Empathy is manifested in very young children as a conscious awareness that other people have feelings which are different from their own and culminates during adolescence in what Piaget describes as truly relativistic thinking, thinking that involves the ability

From *Developmental Psychology*, 1973, **9**, 102–108. Copyright © 1973 by The American Psychological Association. Reprinted by permission.

* The author would like to thank Hwang Chien-hou, Chairman of the Psychology Department, National Taiwan Normal University, and Sarah Su, Professor of Child Development, National Taiwan Normal University, for their help in collecting the data for this study and for the valuable insights they provided on the early socialization of Chinese children. This investigation was supported by United States Public Health Service Grant MH 17778–01.

to put oneself in another person's place and see the world through that person's eyes.

Since the original research was based on a small sample of middle-class American children (Borke, 1971), the effects of cultural and social class variables were not investigated. A cross-cultural study which controlled for social class differences was conducted to provide information about (a) the relationship between the development of empathic ability and specific social class and cultural influences and (b) the universality of development of empathic awareness. The study compared very young Chinese and American children. Both the Chinese and American cultures emphasize the central importance of the family, but in each of these societies socialization occurs within the context of very different cultural traditions. The Chinese family encourages mutual dependence and social conformity, whereas the American family stresses self-reliance, and individual freedom (Murphy & Murphy, 1968).

METHOD

Several steps were taken to insure that the instrument employed to measure empathy would be as free as possible of cultural bias. First, American kindergarten children in the United States and Chinese kindergarten children in Taiwan were asked to describe the kinds of situations that might make them feel happy, afraid, sad, or angry. The children's spontaneous comments were tape recorded and categorized. Responses common to both groups were used as the basis for constructing two sets of stories: (a) stories describing general situations that might make a child feel happy, afraid, sad, or angry and (b) stories describing situations in which the child being tested does something that might cause another child to feel happy, afraid, sad, or angry.

These two sets of stories were then administered to 87 Chinese and 96 American second graders. The children were asked to indicate how another individual might feel in each situation by selecting one of four stylized faces depicting the emotions of happy, afraid, sad, or angry. Ekman, Sorenson, and Friesen's (1969) study, indicating pancultural elements in the identification of emotions from facial expressions, provided the research basis for presenting the stylized faces. A chi-square analysis was used to determine which stories had responses that differed from a random-classification pattern. The four stories which showed the highest agreement among children's responses in both cultural groups were selected for each of the affective categories (i.e., happy, afraid, sad, and angry). Also selected were four situations which showed high agreement among children's responses in one cultural group but not in the other and three situations which showed high variability of responses for the children in both cultural groups.

The final set of 23 stories was administered to 288 Chinese and 288 American children. Half of the children in each group were from middle-class families and half were from disadvantaged families. The children were also equally divided between the two sexes. Twelve girls and 12 boys from similar socioeconomic and cultural backgrounds were tested for each 6-month interval between 3 and 6 years of age (i.e., 3–3.5, 3.5–4, 4–4.5, 4.5–5, 5–5.5, 5.5–6).

The 3- to 5-year-old American and Chinese middle-class children who participated in this study all attended private nursery schools. The children in the 5- to 6-year old range were selected from public school kindergartens in predominantly middle-class neighborhoods. The American 3- to 5-year-old children in the disadvantaged group attended either Head Start or child care programs supported by federal funds. The 5- to 6-year-old American youngsters went to kindergartens in the same elementary schools that provided the educational programs for the younger children. The Chinese preschool children described as lower class attended special workers' preschools supported by the government. The 5- to 6-year-old Chinese youngsters were selected from schools located in working-class neighborhoods.

The task was administered individually to the children in their schools. The American children were tested by graduate students under the supervision of the principal investigator; the Chinese children were tested by college psychology majors in their senior year. Sarah Su, Professor of Child Development, National Taiwan Normal University, translated the test materials, established liasons with the cooperating schools, and supervised the students who did the testing.

The testing procedure used by all of the examiners consisted of first asking the children to identify drawings of faces representing the four basic emotions of happy, afraid, sad, and angry. After helping the children identify each of the faces, the examiners presented the first set of stories. Each story in this set was accompanied by a picture of a child with a blank face engaged in the described activity. The children were asked to complete the pictures by selecting the face that best showed how the child in the story felt. The faces were presented in random order, and with each presentation the examiners again identified the emotions for the youngsters. The same procedure was followed for the second set of stories involving peer interactions except that a single picture of a youngster standing was used for all of the stories.

RESULTS

Chinese and American children between 3 and 6 years of age were compared for number of correct perceptions of happy, afraid, sad, or angry social situations. An analysis of variance design was used to evaluate the relative effects of six variables: sex, status, nationality, age, emotion, and test part. Five of the six variables, sex, status, nationality, age, and emotion, contributed significantly to the variance ($p < .01$). There were no significant differences between the two test parts. The first-order interactions significant at the .01 level were status and emotion, nationality and emotion, nationality and age, and emotion and age. The significant second-order interactions were status, nationality, and emotion; and status, nationality, and age (see Table 1).

American and Chinese children demonstrated similar overall trends in their ability to identify happy, afraid, sad, and angry situation (see Table 2). Recognition of these four types of emotional situations generally increased with age (see Figure 1). Perceptions of happy situations showed only a small increment since by 3 to 3.5 years of age over 90% of the American and Chinese middle- and lower-class children perceived the happy situations correctly (see Tables 3 and 4).

TABLE 1

Analysis of Variance Comparing Effects of Sex, Socio-economic Status, Nationality, Test Part, Emotion, and Age on the Ability to Perceive Other People's Feelings in Social Situations

SOURCE	df	MS	F
Sex (A)	1	3.84	9.86**
Status (B)	1	13.24	34.02**
Nationality (C)	1	5.49	14.10**
Test part (D)	1	.76	1.94
Emotion (E)	3	177.65	456.43**
Age (F)	5	15.91	40.87**
A × B	1	.16	.41
A × C	1	.05	.13
A × D	1	.01	.01
A × E	3	.27	.71
A × F	5	.38	.97
B × C	1	1.42	3.66
B × D	1	1.64	4.22
B × E	3	1.97	5.06**
B × F	5	1.11	2.86
C × D	1	.14	.35
C × E	3	1.65	4.23**
C × F	5	2.06	5.30**
D × E	3	1.23	3.16
D × F	5	.08	.21
E × F	15	3.82	9.81**
A × F × C*	1	1.42	3.66
B × C × E	3	8.25	21.19**
B × C × F	5	1.20	3.07**
Residual	4533	.39	
Total	4607		

* Only three-way interactions with mean squares substantially above those for the higher-order interactions were included. The remaining were pooled into the residual term.
** $p < .01$.

Identification of fearful situations showed the greatest improvement with age. Recognition of fearful situations increased from an average of 50% correct responses between 3 and 3.5 years of age to over 90% correct responses by age 5 (see Figure 1). There was considerable variation in the younger children's ability to recognize fearful situations. Seventy percent of the Chinese middle-class children correctly identified the afraid situations as early as 3 to 3.5 years of age, as compared with only 40% of the American middle-class children in this youngest age group. The American middle- and lower-class children caught up with the Chinese middle-class youngsters by age 4 to 4.5, but the Chinese lower-class children remained behind in their ability to recognize fearful situations until 5.5 to 6 years of age (see Tables 3 and 4).

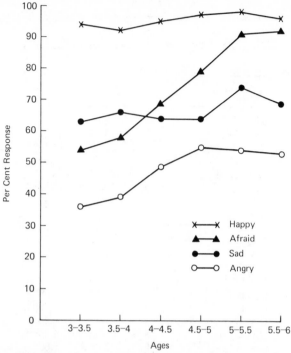

FIGURE 1.   *Percentage of correct responses of American and Chinese children at various age levels to social interaction situations.*

The children's recognition of sad situations appeared to increase only slightly with age (see Figure 1). The apparent lack of improvement in the children's accuracy of perception of sad situations stemmed from cultural and social class differences which cancelled each other out when the data from the American and Chinese children were combined. In the youngest age group, 3 to 3.5 years, middle-class and lower-class Chinese children correctly identified

TABLE 2

Percentage of Correct Responses by American and Chinese Children to Social Interaction Situations

NATIONALITY	SOCIAL CLASS	INTERACTION SITUATION			
		Happy	Afraid	Sad	Angry
American	Middle	96	73	79	51
	Lower	97	75	58	54
	Average	96	74	69	53
Chinese	Middle	96	80	66	51
	Lower	93	68	70	36
	Average	95	74	68	44

TABLE 3

Percentage of Correct Responses by Middle- and Lower-Class American Children at Various Age Levels to Social Interaction Situations

| | SOCIAL INTERACTION SITUATION | | | | | | | |
| | Happy | | Afraid | | Sad | | Angry | |
AGE	Middle Class	Lower Class	Middle Class	Lower Class	Middle Class	Lower Class	Middle Class	Lower Class
3.0–3.5	93	97	40	52	57	52	32	47
3.5–4.0	91	96	48	63	78	52	40	48
4.0–4.5	97	97	71	74	77	52	57	52
4.5–5.0	97	97	84	78	84	53	65	62
5.0–5.5	98	98	96	93	88	74	60	54
5.5–6.0	99	95	97	91	88	63	53	59

67% and 76%, respectively, of the sad situations as compared with American middle-class and lower-class youngsters of the same age who recognized the sad situations only slightly more than 50% of the time. At the older age levels, American middle-class children showed a dramatic improvement in their ability to identify sad situations reaching 88% accuracy by 6 years. The Chinese children, in contrast, showed a slight decrease with age in the accuracy of their perception of sad situation (see Tables 3 and 4).

Chinese and American children consistently perceived angry responses less accurately than any of the other emotions (see Figure 1). There was, however, a significant increase with age in the children's ability to identify angry situations. The Chinese lower-class children had more difficulty recognizing the angry

TABLE 4

Percentage of Correct Responses by Middle- and Lower-Class Chinese Children at Various Age Levels to Social Interaction Situations

| | SOCIAL INTERACTION SITUATION | | | | | | | |
| | Happy | | Afraid | | Sad | | Angry | |
AGE	Middle Class	Lower Class	Middle Class	Lower Class	Middle Class	Lower Class	Middle Class	Lower Class
3.0–3.5	96	91	70	54	67	76	38	27
3.5–4.0	93	90	68	52	76	84	40	28
4.0–4.5	94	91	75	52	69	55	51	38
4.5–5.0	98	96	83	71	61	62	58	38
5.0–5.5	96	99	94	82	53	79	62	42
5.5–6.0	96	94	87	94	67	59	57	44

situations than the children in any of the other groups (see Tables 3 and 4).

In both cultures, girls were more accurate than boys in their ability to perceive social situations ($\bar{X} = 1.44$ for girls and 1.39 for boys). There were no significant interactions between sex and any of the other variables (i.e., nationality, status, age, or emotion). Separate analyses of the four emotions—happy, afraid, sad, and angry—also showed no significant differences between girls and boys.

DISCUSSION

A comparison of very young American and Chinese children revealed basic similarities between the two groups in the early development of empathic awareness. Chinese and American children by 3 to 3.5 years of age were able to differentiate easily between social situations which evoke happy and unhappy responses in other people. These results are consistent with the findings reported in a previous study (Borke, 1971) and provide further evidence that the capacity for social sensitivity and empathic awareness develops at a very early age.

Recognition of afraid, sad, and angry emotions appeared to be influenced to a considerable extent by the interaction of social class and cultural factors. Chinese middle-class youngsters between 3 and 3.5 years of age were far more accurate in identifying fearful situations than Chinese lower-class children or American middle- or lower-class children in the same age range. This increased awareness of fearful situations by very young Chinese middle-class children may reflect the overprotective tendencies of Chinese middle-class parents, who frequently set limits on their youngsters' active exploratory behavior because they are afraid the children will hurt themselves. American middle-class children between 3 and 3.5 years of age experienced the greatest difficulty recognizing fearful situations. This finding would be consistent with the attitudes of American middle-class parents, who encourage active play and self-reliance in their young children and tend to minimize the possibility of danger or getting hurt. The rapid increase with age in the ability of American middle-class children to recognize fearful situations supports the results of a previous study (Borke, 1971). In this earlier paper, it was suggested that as middle-class American children grow older, they learn about situations which evoke fear responses through exposure to books and television as well as their own experiences. Interestingly enough, the Chinese lower-class children, for whom books and television are least accessible, lagged behind the other youngsters in their recognition of fearful situations.

The ability of Chinese middle-class and lower-class youngsters between 3 and 4 years of age to recognize sad situations more accurately than American middle- or lower-class children of the same age possibly reflects the emphasis within the Chinese culture on feeling "shameful" or "losing face." The American middle-class children showed a considerable increase with age in their ability to recognize sad situations. This trend was also observed in previous studies (Borke, 1971; Borke & Su, 1972) and may be related to the greater social acceptability of feeling sad between 4 and 7 years of age when American middle-class children, more so than the children in any of the other three groups, are actively engaged in the task of developing inner controls over their unacceptable feelings.

American and Chinese children at all age levels had the greatest difficulty identifying angry situations. Since young children certainly experience anger, these results suggest that in both the American and Chinese societies children become aware of the unacceptability of expressing angry feelings at a very early age. The greater inability of lower-class Chinese children to perceive angry responses in others as compared with middle-class Chinese children and middle-class and lower-class American children may be related to the extreme subservience expected of lower-class individuals in the Chinese society. The socialization of lower-class Chinese children to accept this role apparently begins quite early.

An analysis of the children's incorrect responses to the sad and angry situations indicated that the majority of American and Chinese youngsters gave "angry" as their alternate response to sad situations and "sad" as their alternate response to angry situations. Only 10% of all incorrect responses to the sad and angry situations fell in other categories. The children's inability to differentiate sharply between sad and angry situations also occurred in a previous study (Borke, 1971). At that time, three possible explanations were suggested: (a) ambiguity in the stories selected, (b) stronger conflict associated with feeling sad and, especially, angry in our society as compared with feeling happy or afraid, (c) individual differences in responding to frustration, with some people having a greater tendency to react with anger and others to react by feeling sad.

Although in the present study every effort was made to select situations which the majority of the children in both cultural groups would perceive as predominantly sad or angry, there was still considerable overlap in the perception of these two emotions. The cumulative evidence from this and previous investigations (Borke, 1971; Borke & Su, 1972) suggests that any situation which has the potential for either a sad or angry response generally has the potential for both (i.e., an individual might initially feel sad because someone close was leaving but later experience anger over the frustration caused by the separation). The greater difficulty experienced by the children from both cultural backgrounds in identifying angry situations as compared to happy, afraid, and sad situations supports the possibility that stronger conflict is associated with feeling angry in both the American and Chinese societies. There was also evidence that some individuals respond to frustration primarily by feeling angry and others by feeling sad. Twenty-four percent of the American and Chinese children gave "sad" as their primary response to all of the sad and angry stories and 7% gave "angry" as their primary response. This indicates that almost one third of the youngsters had a previously established set which influenced their perception of sad and angry situations. The multiplicity of factors operating in the perception of sad and angry responses suggests that the ability to differentiate between sad and angry reactions in other people is a considerably more complex process than the identification of happy or fear responses.

The relationship of empathic ability to sex differences has been considered in a number of studies. The results are contradictory with some researchers reporting differences (Dimitrovsky, 1964; Gollin, 1958) and other finding no difference (Borke, 1971; Feshback & Roe, 1968; Rothenberg, 1970; Walton 1936). In the present study, sex differences appeared as a significant variable but contributed the least to the overall variance. One possible conclusion is that any significant relationship which might exist between empathic ability and sex is very small and can easily be affected by slight variations in the populations from which the samples are drawn.

This cross-cultural research supports the results of previous studies showing that very young children are capable of empathic awareness. The ability to differentiate between happy and unhappy responses in other people appears to be well established in both Chinese and American youngsters by 3 years of age. Some of the social class and cultural differences in the children's perceptions of fearful, sad, and angry reactions seem to indicate that social learning is an important factor in the ability to recognize other people's feelings. The presence of empathic awareness in young children from very different cultural backgrounds suggests that empathy may well be a basic human characteristic related to social adaptation.

References

BORKE, H. Interpersonal perception of young children: Egocentrism or empathy? *Developmental Psychology*, 1971, 5, 263–269.

BORKE, H. Chandler and Greenspan's "ersatz egocentrism": A rejoinder. *Developmental Psychology*, 1972, 7, 107–109.

BORKE, H., & SU, S. Perception of emotional responses to social interactions by Chinese and American children. *Journal of Cross Cultural Psychology*, 1972, 3, 309–314.

BURNS, N., & CAVEY, L. Age differences in empathic ability among children. *Canadian Journal of Psychology*, 1957, 11, 227–230.

CHANDLER, M. J., & GREENSPAN, S. Ersatz egocentrism: A reply to H. Borke. *Developmental Psychology*, 1972, 7, 104–106.

DIMITROVSKY, L. The ability to identify the emotional meanings of vocal expressions at successive age levels. In J. R. Davitz (Ed.), *The communication of emotional meaning*. New York: McGraw-Hill, 1964.

EKMAN, P., SORENSON, E. R., & FRIESEN, W. V. Pan-cultural elements in facial displays of emotion. *Science*, 1969, 164, 80–88.

FESHBACH, N. D., & ROE, K. Empathy in six and seven year olds. *Child Development*, 1968, 39, 133–145.

FLAPAN, D. *Children's understanding of social interaction*. New York: Teachers College Press, 1968.

FLAVELL, J. H., BOTKIN, P. T., & FRY, C. L., JR. *The development of role-taking and communication skills in young children*. New York: Wiley, 1968.

FREUD, A. *Normality and pathology in childhood*. New York: International Universities Press, 1965.

GOLLIN, E. S. Organizational characteristics of social judgment: A developmental investigation. *Journal of Personality*, 1958, 26, 139–154.

MURPHY, G., & MURPHY, L. B. *Asian psychology*. New York: Basic Books, 1968.

PIAGET, J. *The language and thought of the child*. New York: Harcourt-Brace, 1926.

PIAGET, J. *Judgment and reasoning in the child*. New York: Harcourt-Brace, 1928.

PIAGET, J. *Six psychological studies*. New York: Random House, 1967.

ROTHENBERG, B. Children's social sensitivity and the relationship to interpersonal competence, intrapersonal comfort, and intellectual level. *Developmental Psychology*, 1970, 2, 335–350.

WALTON, W. E. Empathic responses in children. *Psychological Monographs*, 1936, **48**(1, Whole No. 213).

WERNER, H. *Comparative psychology of mental development.* New York: International Universities Press, 1958.

The Relation of Individual Temperament to Initial Social Behavior

Jeannie L. Lewis
THE OHIO STATE UNIVERSITY

Though the area of peer relations has been considered important for social adjustment, it has rarely been an area for research into individual differences—particularly in its very early stages. I conducted, in 1973, an exploratory study to search for a relation between a child's behavioral individuality or temperament in the home setting and his initial adjustment to peers in a pre-school setting.

Individual temperament, the "how" of behavior—as conceptualized by the research team of Thomas, Chess, and Birch—has been found to relate to the development of pathology, match between parent and child, and style of school performance (Thomas, Chess, and Birch, 1963, 1968; Gordon and Thomas, 1967; Ross, 1966). Thomas, Chess, and Birch distinguished the "difficult" pattern of behavior (predominantly non-adaptable, intense, and tending to withdraw from novelty) which was found to antedate the development of behavior disorders. The "slow-to-warm-up" child (low in activity level, intensity, with withdrawal tendency) typically took some time to adapt to new experiences. Thus, temperamental characteristics have been found significant for the child's capacity to adapt to environmental changes and the quality of his reactions to novelty and stress. I expected individual differences in the child's style of behavior to be evident in the manner with which he adapted to the pre-school peer group—as a novel and potentially stressful setting. This study was also expected to shed light on cross-setting continuities and discontinuities in behavior, as well as what forms of social behavior prove to be meaningful psychological variables.

My subjects were fourteen children enrolled in Montessori pre-schools in the Columbus, Ohio, area. They ranged from 2 years 5 months to 3 years 10 months of age and were of upper-middle class background. Only three of the fourteen had had previous structured group experience—in short-term day care programs. From interviews with their mothers, I gathered data on each child's typical behavior in a variety of areas at home, within the concurrent six-month

Paper presented as part of the Symposium "Nature and Development of Early Peer Relations," Meetings of the American Psychological Association, New Orleans, 1974. Printed by permission.

period. According to the guidelines of Thomas, Chess, and Birch (1963), this material could be rated along the nine dimensions of temperament—activity level, rhythmicity, approach/withdrawal, adaptability, intensity, threshold, mood quality, distractibility, and persistence. I wanted to preserve the continuous nature of temperament, and so used the percent of ratings at one extreme of each dimension as the final score for each child. This had been done in a project related to the original Thomas, Chess, and Birch project (Terestman, 1964).

The three classrooms in which the subjects were enrolled had a teacher/child ratio of about 15/2. The observational data were collected after each child had attended pre-school for about two weeks. Data were taken for thirty-minute periods on four separate days during free play periods. Data consisted of time samplings (15 second intervals) of the social behavior of each individual subject—social distance and nature of activity. Through event sampling within these intervals, any social behaviors in visual, physical, and verbal modes were recorded. The visual behaviors included looking and watching. Physical behaviors recorded were approaches and actions toward other children (including giving, touching, pushing, taking). Verbal behavior included talking and play noises. To record these behaviors I chose to use a symbol system similar to that used by Blurton-Jones and other ethological researchers who have studied and catalogued pattern of children's social behavior (Blurton-Jones, 1972; McGrew, 1972; Leach, 1972). Each of the classes of behavior mentioned was given a 2–3 letter symbol and a notation as the object of the behavior (child or teacher). As an example, an approach to a child would be recorded "Apr-C." In the data analysis, behaviors toward children and teachers were separated. An average percent-time score for all these classes of behavior was derived for each subject. Also noted were expressions of positive mood and duration of continuous activity with materials.

It was possible, in looking at the results, to get an idea which classes of behavior might be meaningful psychological variables. I felt that the visual behaviors, in view of their lack of positive relationships to either temperament or other social behavior, plus the difficulty in recording them, were less crucial. Social distance (isolation versus proximity) proved to be highly related to both temperament and other behavioral variables, and was quite easy to record via time-sampling.

Three dimensions of temperament were found to be especially significant in relation to social behavior. These were activity level, approach/withdrawal tendency, and sensory threshold. The high activity level child, in addition to showing a great deal of physical activity, was also socially active toward both children and teachers. Children high on approach tendency were similarly attracted and active toward social objects. It seemed in general that the "easy" temperament characteristics (approach orientation, adaptability, and positive mood) were associated with high social proximity. The sensitive, low threshold child, conversely, tended toward isolation, social and physical restraint.

Physical activity level and approach tendency were found to be highly correlated across home and school setting. Distractibility at home was associated with many variations in activity and generally erratic social contact in pre-school. Regularity and persistence at home were associated with stable, constructive activity and a high level of verbal communication in the peer group. Expressions of positive mood showed a not quite significant correlation across settings. However, persistence at home was not related to a tendency to persevere in activities at school. Neither adaptability, intensity, or mood were found to be related to the classes of social behavior. It is likely that if qualitative measures of behavior had been chosen—such as the intensity of behavioral reactions, from mild to strong—these dimensions might have been found more significant.

The findings showed that individual characteristics of the child influence the nature of early social behavior, aside from previously researched factors of age, sex, and previous pre-school experience. The relations of temperament to competent, precocious behavior complement the volume of findings relating temperament to pathology.

The child's style of behavior may influence both his immediate reaction to novel setting and social objects, as well as the nature of past experiences he has accumulated. For example, the very active child is likely to have sought and experienced a multitude of social contacts in the past (probably building his level of social skill), as well as exhibiting a great deal of current energy and mobility in initial response to the pre-school setting. The vulnerability of the low threshold child to massive, novel stimulation may have restricted the extent of his past social experience, as well as currently fostering a reaction of withdrawal to block out overwhelming input.

Earlier research has focused on energy or activity level and sensitivity threshold as characteristics important in adaptation. These characteristics act to determine the magnitude of behavioral output, the processing of input, and individual tolerance level. This exploratory study suggests in addition that the typical direction of behavior (approach versus withdrawal) may be a further adaptive factor.

These results could also be looked at in terms of individual differences that predispose to precocity in social development. Edward Mueller (of this symposium) has proposed that early social contacts are object-centered—that interest in play objects may be the initial social attractants. If so, then high activity level or approach-oriented children could be expected to accumulate in greater quantity and intensity the experiences with materials that induce social interaction with peers. They would achieve social competence earlier and with less need for intervention or warm-up than the more inactive, withdrawn children.

So these results have implications for the theoretical contribution of individual differences to the course of social development. On the practical side, an understanding of temperamental contributions to social adjustment could help parents and educators to anticipate a child's reaction to the pre-school experience and aid in treatment.

Clearly this study must be interpreted and generalized cautiously in light of small sample size, limitations in the measures, and restricted social class range of the subjects. It is also possible that the special Montessori setting had an influence on the findings, as some emphasis on independent activity was apparent in the approach. It would be interesting to have follow-up information on the adaptation of the more sensitive, withdrawn children to determine whether their behavior reflected reactions to novelty or a more lasting style of social restraint. Though the sensitive child was weak on social participation, it did not appear that he was completely uninvolved. Sensitivity was associated with a great deal of watching behavior. Thus, these children in their own way appeared to be absorbing with interest what was happening around them. They were usually responsive to social overtures made by others, but took little initiative themselves. It seems likely that the focus on initiated behavior in this study (as opposed to social responsiveness) has given a rather one-sided picture of the sensitive child's social competence.

A larger sample size would permit a clearer look at possible sex differences in the pattern of results, as well as the effects of age and previous group experience.

This exploratory study has found that individual differences in the style of behavior have an impact upon the child's initial adaptation to a peer group. At the same time that many advances are being made in the general knowledge of early social development, the study of individual differences may illuminate some of the bases for such changes for emerging patterns of adjustment.

References

BLURTON-JONES, N., Categories of child-child interaction, in Blurton-Jones (ed.), *Ethological Studies of Child Behaviour*, Cambridge University Press, London, 1972, pp. 97–128.

GORDON, E. and THOMAS, A. Children's behavioral style and the teacher's appraisal of their intelligence, *Journal of School Psychology*, (5) #4, 1967, pp. 292–300.

LEACH, G. M., A comparison of the social behavior of some normal and problem children, in N. Blurton-Jones (ed.), *Ethological Studies of Child Behaviour*, Cambridge University Press, London, 1972.

McGREW, W. C., Aspects of social development in nursery school children with emphasis on introduction to the group, in N. Blurton-Jones (ed)., *Ethological Studies of Child Behaviour*, Cambridge University Press, London, 1972, pp. 129–156.

ROSS, D. C., Poor school achievement; a psychiatric study and classification, *Clinical Pediatrics*, (5), #2, 1966, pp. 109–117.

TERESTMAN, N., Consistency and change in mood quality and intensity studied as aspects of temperament in preschool children, unpublished doctoral dissertation, Columbia University, 1963.

THOMAS, A., CHESS, S., and BIRCH, H., *Behavioral Individuality in Early Childhood*, New York University Press, New York, 1963.

THOMAS, A., CHESS, S., and BIRCH, H., *Temperament and the Development of Behavior Disorders in Children*, New York University Press, New York, 1968.

Beyond Father Absence: Conceptualization of Effects of Divorce

E. Mavis Hetherington, Martha Cox, and Roger Cox
UNIVERSITY OF VIRGINIA

It may seem rather odd that the first paper on a symposium on fathers is dealing with fathers who are absent rather than present. However, I believe a fruitful way of studying the role of the father and the impact of the father on mothers and children is to examine changes in family interaction and functioning following a divorce in which the mother has been granted custody of the child.

If you examine the literature on father absence carefully you will be struck by how little we know of factors that mediate differences found between children with absent or present fathers. We tend to rely very heavily on explanations based on modeling. How can children, particularly boys, be expected to exhibit normal cognitive and social development or sex-role typing or self-control, if they don't have the field independent, quantitative, problem solving, instrumental, self-controlled, masculine model of the father to imitate?

Undoubtedly the lack of a male model is an important factor in the development of children. However there may be less direct but equally powerful ways in which father absence effects children.

Following a divorce in which custody has been granted to the mother, the mother–child relationship may become more intense and salient. The father is infrequently present to moderate or mediate in the interaction. The mother must most of the time take over parenting roles assumed by both the mother and father in intact families, and this often imposes considerable stress on the mother. There are fewer time outs in the parenting game in one-parent families.

In addition to pressures associated with lack of paternal support in child rearing following divorce, the divorced mother has other stresses to cope with. The lack of the paternal support system is also felt in economic needs, needs for intimacy and sexual gratification, restrictions in social and recreational activities and contacts with adults. How she copes with these stresses will impact on the development of the child.

It would be just as unfortunate to view the effects of father absence solely in terms of the effects of absence of a father on mothers and their related effects on children, as it is to lean too heavily on modeling as an explanation for these effects. Divorce affects the whole family system and the functioning and interactions of the members within that system. To get a true picture of the impact of divorce, its effects on the divorced father living out of the home and on the mother and children must be examined. Because of time limitations, I am going to restrict my presentation today to a discussion of changes in functioning of mothers and fathers following divorce. I am not going to present any of our

Paper presented as part of the Symposium "Beyond Father Absence: Conceptualizations of Father Effects," Society for Research in Child Development, Denver, 1975. Printed by permission.

findings on changes in the behavior of children following divorce although this was a main focus of our project.

The findings I am going to report today are part of a two-year longitudinal study of the impact of divorce on family functioning and the development of children. The goals of the study were first to examine the response to the family crisis of divorce, and patterns of reorganization of the family over the two-year period following divorce. It was assumed that the family system would go through a period of disorganization immediately after the divorce, followed by recovery, reorganization, and eventual attainment of a new pattern of equilibrium. The second goal was to examine the characteristics of family members that contributed to variations in family processes. The third goal was to examine the effects of variations in family interaction and structure on the development of children.

The original sample was composed of 36 white, middle-class boys and 36 girls and their divorced parents from homes in which custody had been granted to the mother, and the same number of children and parents from intact homes. The final sample was 24 families in each of the groups, a total of 96 families. Sample attrition was largely due to remarriage in the divorced families, to families or a parent leaving the area, and to eight families who no longer wished to participate in the study. Families with stepparents were excluded, since one of the interests in the investigation was seeing how mothers and children functioned in father absent homes and how their functioning might be related to deviant or nondeviant behavior in children. In the analyses to be presented today, families were randomly dropped from groups to maintain equal sizes in groups.

When a reduction in sample size occurs from 144 families to 96 families, one immediately becomes concerned about bias in the sample. On demographic characteristics such as age, religion, education, income, occupation, family size, and maternal employment there were no differences between subjects who dropped out or were excluded from the sample and those who remained. In addition when a family was no longer included in the study, a comparative analysis was done of their interaction patterns and those of the continuing families. Some differences in these groups will be noted in the course of this presentation. In general, there were few differences in parent-child interactions in families who did or did not remain in the study. However, there were some differences in the characteristics of parents who remarried and how they viewed themselves and their lives.

The study used a multimethod, multimeasure approach to the investigation of family interaction. The measures used in the study are presented in the first table. The parents and children were administered these measures at two months, one year, and two years following divorce.

In this presentation I am going to restrict my discussion mainly to the findings based on parent interviews and the observations of the parent and child in a structured interaction situation in the laboratory, although I will occasionally refer to related findings on other measures. Therefore only these two procedures will be presented in detail.

As was found by Baumrind using some similar measures, the parent-child interaction patterns in the home observations and in the free play and labora-

TABLE 1

PARENT MEASURES	CHILD MEASURES
Interview	Unstructured observations in the home
Unstructured observations in the home	Observations of free play
Observations of free play with parent	with parent and child in the
and child in the laboratory	laboratory
Observations in structured task	Observations on structured task
situation with child	situation with parent
Diary record	Observation in nursery school
Personality measures:	Peer nomination
State-Trait Anxiety Inventory	Teacher ratings
CPI Masculinity-Femininity Scale	Problem checklist
Draw a Person	It Test
Personal Adjustment Scale	Draw a Person
(Adjective Checklist)	
Socialization Scale CPI	
Rotter I-E Scale	

tory sessions were remarkably congruent. For example, parents who were nurturant, who made high use of positive or negative sanctions, or who had good control over their children tended to be so across situations. Children who were compliant, oppositional, or affiliative also tended to maintain these behaviors across situations.

Parents were interviewed separately on a structured parent interview schedule designed to assess discipline practices and the relationship with the child; support systems outside the family household system; social, emotional, and heterosexual relationships; quality of the relationship with the spouse; economic stress; family disorganization; satisfaction and happiness; and attitudes toward the self. The interviews were tape recorded. Each of the categories listed in Table 2 were rated on scales by two judges. In some cases the category involved the rating of only a single 5- or 7-point scale. In others it represents a composite score of several ratings on a group of subscales. Interjudge reliabilities ranged from .69 to .95 with a mean of .82. The interviews were derived and modified from those of Baumrind, Sears, Rau, and Alpert, Becker, Martin and Hetherington, and others.

Each parent was observed separately interacting with the child in the laboratory in a half-hour free-play situation and in a half-hour structured situation involving puzzles, block building, bead stringing, and sorting tasks. The interaction sessions with the mother or father were on different days, separated by a period of about a month. Half of the children interacted with the mother first and half with the father first. Behavior was coded in the categories in Table 3. The coding procedure was similar to that used by Patterson and his colleagues where the observation period is divided into 30-second intervals and an average of about five behavior sequences of interactions between the subject and other family members were coded in the 30-second interval. Two raters

TABLE 2

Control of child	Economic stress
Maturity demands of child	Family disorganization
Communication with child	Problems in running household
Nurturance of child	Relationship with spouse
Permissiveness-restrictiveness with child	Emotional support in personal matters
Negative sanctions with child	Immediate support system
Positive sanctions with child	Social life and activities
Reinforcement of child for sex-typed behaviors	Contact with adults
	Intimate relations
Paternal availability	Sexuality
Maternal availability	Number of dates
Paternal face-to-face interaction with child	Happiness and satisfaction
	Competence as a parent
Maternal face-to-face interaction with child	Competence as a male/female
	Self-esteem
Quality of spouse's relationship with the child	Satisfaction with employment
	Conflict preceding divorce
Agreement in treatment of the child	Tension preceding divorce
Emotional support in child rearing from spouse	

rated all sessions. Interjudge agreement on individual responses averaged .83 per cent.

A repeated measures analysis of variance involving test session (two months, one year, two years), sex of subject, sex of parent, and family composition (divorced versus intact) was performed for each measure on the interview and structured interaction tasks. In addition, correlational analyses of all variables within and across subgroups was performed.

What kind of stresses are likely to be experienced by members of a divorced couple? How might these be related to parent–child relations?

Greater economic stress in divorced couples was apparent in our sample. Although the average income of the divorced families was equal to that of the intact families, the economic problems associated with maintaining two households for divorced couples led to more financial concerns and limitations in purchasing practices in divorced couples. It has been suggested by Herzog and Sudia that many of the deleterious effects of father absence on children could be eliminated if economic stability was provided for mothers with no husband in the home. However, in our study the number of significant correlations was not above chance between income or reported feelings of economic stress and parents' reported or observed interactions with their children or with behavior of the child in nursery school. It may be that in our middle-class sample with an average family income of about $22,000 the range is not great enough to detect the effects of economic stress. In a lower-class sample, the greater extremes of economic duress might be associated with variations in parent-child interaction or the development of the child.

A second area in which stresses are experienced by divorced couples are in social life and in meaningful, intimate interpersonal relationships. Divorced

TABLE 3
Interaction Coding

PARENT BEHAVIOR	CHILD BEHAVIOR
Command (positive)	Opposition
Command (negative)	Aversive opposition
Question	Compliance
Nonverbal intrusion	Dependency
Ignore	Negative demands (whining, complaining,
Affiliate (interact)	angry tone)
Positive sanctions	Aggression (tantrum, destructiveness)
Negative sanctions	Requests
Reasoning and explanation	Affiliate
Encourages	Self-manipulation
Dependency	Sustained play
Indulgence	Ignore
Opposition	
Compliance	
Encourages independence	

adults often complain that socializing in our culture is organized around couples and being a single adult, particularly a single woman with children, limits recreational opportunities. Both the interview findings presented in Table 4 and the diary records kept by parents indicate that social life is more restricted in divorced couples and that this effect initially is most marked for women. Divorced men go through a period of active social life one year after divorce; however by two years the social activities of divorced fathers have declined. Divorced mothers report having significantly less contact with adults than do the other parents and often commented on their sense of being locked into a child's world. This was less true of working than nonworking mothers.

Heterosexual relations play a particularly important role in the happiness and attitudes toward the self of both married and divorced adults. Happiness, self-esteem, and feelings of competence in heterosexual behavior increased steadily over the two year period for divorced males and females, but they are not as high even in the second year as those for married couples. It should be noted, however, that the subjects who later remarried and were shifted from this study of divorce and father absence to a stepparent study scored as high on happiness, although lower on self-esteem and feelings of competence, as did parents in intact families. Frequency of sexual intercourse was lower for divorced parents than married couples at two months, higher at one year, and about the same frequency at two years. Divorced males particularly seemed to show a peak of sexual activity and a pattern of dating a variety of women in the first year following divorce. However the stereotyped image of the happy, swinging single life was not altogether accurate. One of our sets of interview ratings attempted to measure intimacy in relationship. Intimacy referred to love in the Sullivanian sense of valuing the welfare of the other as much as one's own, of a deep concern and willingness to make sacrifices for the other, and strong

TABLE 4

Mean Ratings of Parental Variables of Intact and Divorced Couples of Preschool Children

VARIABLES AND TIME AFTER DIVORCE	INTACT		DIVORCED	
	Father	Mother	Father	Mother
Social life and recreation				
Two months	21.60	20.98	14.21	12.27
One year	21.85	21.17	22.25	15.56
Two years	21.13	21.17	16.96	16.94
Family disorganization				
Two months	15.73	13.17	23.83	20.31
One year	15.15	12.96	22.60	22.85
Two years	15.29	12.75	19.19	17.56
Parental control				
Two months	31.7	30.6	21.7	19.3
One year	29.9	30.6	18.6	15.3
Two years	30.7	30.0	24.0	23.3
Positive sanctions				
Two months	6.00	7.35	7.90	5.42
One year	6.04	7.29	7.63	4.42
Two years	5.96	7.23	4.88	6.08

attachment and desire to be near the other person. Intimacy in relationships showed strong positive correlations with happiness, self-esteem, and feelings of competence in heterosexual relations for both divorced and married men and women. Table 5 shows that in the divorced but not in the married sample if subjects were divided into those above and below the median in terms of intimacy in relationships, happiness correlated negatively with frequency of intercourse in the low intimacy group and positively in the high intimacy group. The same pattern held for self-esteem. This was true for both divorced males

TABLE 5

Correlations Between Frequency of Sexual Intercourse and Happiness in High and Low Intimacy Divorced Groups

	HIGH INTIMACY		LOW INTIMACY	
	Male (N = 24)	Female (N = 24)	Male (N = 24)	Female (N = 24)
Two months	+ .40*	+ .43*	− .09 (n.s.)	− .42*
One year	+ .49**	+ .47**	− .41*	− .46*
Two years	+ .54**	+ .52**	− .48**	− .57**

*$p < .05$.
**$p < .01$.

and females. The only nonsignificant correlation was for low intimacy males immediately following divorce. Many males but few females were pleased at the increased opportunity for sexual experiences with a variety of partners immediately following divorce. However, by the end of the first year both divorced men and women were expressing a want for intimacy and a lack of satisfaction in casual sexual encounters. Women expressed particularly intense feelings about frequent casual sexual encounters, often talking of feelings of desperation, overwhelming depression, and low self-esteem following such exchanges.

Thus far we have been focusing mainly on changes in the divorced partners in the two years following divorce. We will now look at differences in family functioning and in parent–child interactions as measured both in the interview and in direct observations in the structured interaction situation.

One of the sets of interview scales was family disorganization, which dealt with the degree of structure in proscribed household roles, problems in coping with routine household tasks, and the regularity and scheduling of events. The fathers' scales dealt with similar problems but focused on those in his life and household. It can be seen in Table 4 that the households of the divorced mothers and fathers were always more disorganized than those of intact families, although this disorganization was most marked in the first year following divorce and had significantly decreased by the second year. Children of divorced parents were more likely to get pick-up meals at irregular times. Divorced mothers and their children were less likely to eat dinner together. Bedtimes were more erratic, and the children were read to less before bedtime and were more likely to arrive at nursery school late. These results were found both in interviews and in the structured parental diaries.

The interaction patterns between divorced parents and children differed significantly from those in intact families on almost every variable studied in the interview, and on most of the parallel measures in the structured interaction situation. On these measures the differences were greatest during the first year and a process of re-equilibration seemed to be taking place by the end of the second year, particularly in mother–child relationships. Some of the findings for fathers must be interpreted in view of the fact that divorced fathers become increasingly less available to their children over the course of the two year period. Although at two months divorced fathers are having almost as much face-to-face interaction with their children as are fathers in intact homes who, as has been demonstrated in Biller's work, are often highly unavailable to their children, this interaction declines rapidly. At two months, about one quarter of the divorced parents even reported that fathers in their eagerness to maximize visitation rights were having more face-to-face contact with their children than they had before the divorce.

Because of time limitations the results of the parent–child interactions cannot be presented in detail. However I will try to summarize some of the more important findings and present a few tables to give the flavor of the results. In almost all of the parent–child relations data I am going to present there were significant third or fourth order interactions. The tables I will present will be the highest level interaction for those variables. I will present mainly tables from the interview data but the findings dealing with parallel variables from the observational data are similar.

TABLE 6

Mean Ratings of Parental Variables of Intact and Divorced Couples with Preschool Boys and Girls

VARIABLES AND TIME AFTER DIVORCE	INTACT				DIVORCED			
	Girl		Boy		Girl		Boy	
	Father	Mother	Father	Mother	Father	Mother	Father	Mother
Maturity demands								
Two months	26.6	31.4	32.8	32.2	17.8	19.9	18.4	20.0
One year	25.8	31.0	33.2	32.3	13.0	14.8	16.3	13.7
Two years	26.3	31.9	33.3	33.0	20.9	24.1	28.7	24.7
Communication								
Two months	15.0	17.1	14.9	17.3	11.3	11.1	10.7	9.0
One year	15.5	17.5	15.3	18.1	11.7	9.8	9.8	11.9
Two years	15.5	18.3	16.0	18.7	12.0	15.9	8.3	12.9
Nurturance								
Two months	33.1	33.4	30.3	32.8	32.0	29.5	31.5	25.7
One year	33.0	32.9	30.6	32.5	29.4	24.3	22.0	23.6
Two years	33.2	32.1	30.3	32.3	24.6	30.9	25.7	27.1
Consistency								
Two months	20.1	19.7	18.4	18.3	14.3	15.8	13.0	12.7
One year	20.1	20.0	19.3	18.5	10.7	11.0	10.5	9.9
Two years	20.2	20.5	20.0	20.0	17.5	17.8	14.1	16.6
Negative sanctions								
Two months	15.13	10.54	17.08	14.00	8.29	18.71	10.33	20.38
One year	14.88	10.71	18.00	13.67	8.46	22.88	13.29	24.04
Two years	14.67	10.29	18.71	12.88	13.13	15.38	15.50	17.75

It can be seen in Table 6 that divorced parents make fewer maturity demands on their children. Although this changes over the two years after divorce, they are demanding less self-sufficient, autonomous, and mature behavior of their children than are parents in intact families. Note the curvilinear shape of the function over time which can be seen particularly for mothers.

Table 6 shows that divorced parents communicate less well with their children. That is, they are less likely to solicit the child's opinion and to use reasoning and explanation than are the parents in intact families. This effect is more marked with boys than with girls.

In Table 6 it can be seen that there is a steady decline in nurturance of divorced fathers with their children. For divorced mothers there is a marked drop by the end of the first year which we assume is a period of reorganization and a marked increase by the end of the second year as the family re-equilibrates.

On Table 6 we also see that divorced parents are less consistent than parents in intact families with the most marked decline in consistency occurring at the end of the first year and increased consistency in the second year.

Table 4 shows that the lack of consistency is reflected in the lack of control divorced parents have over their children. Again we see the increase in control following the drop in the first year. This same pattern was obtained when the per cent of parental commands to which the child complied was examined in the structured interaction situation. For divorced parents its lowest point was at one year with a marked increase in successful commands at two years.

Table 4 shows that the lack of control in the divorced parents seems to be associated with very different patterns of relating to the child for mothers and fathers. The divorced mother tries to control the child by being more restrictive and giving more commands which the child ignores or resists. The divorced father wants his contacts with his children to be as happy as possible. He begins by initially being extremely permissive and indulgent with his children and becoming increasingly restrictive over the two year period, although he is never as restrictive as fathers in intact homes. The divorced mother uses more negative sanctions than the divorced father does or than parents in intact families do. However by the second year her use of negative sanctions is declining as the divorced father's is increasing. In a parallel fashion, Table 4 shows that the divorced mother's use of positive sanctions increases after the first year as the divorced father's decreases. The "every day is Christmas" behavior of the divorced father declines with time. The divorced mother decreases her futile attempts at authoritarian control and becomes more effective in dealing with her child over the two year period. Effectiveness in dealing with the child is related to support in child rearing from the spouse and agreement with the spouse in disciplining the child in both divorced and intact families. When support and agreement occurred between divorced couples, the disruption in family functioning appeared to be less extreme and the re-stabilizing of family functioning occurred earlier, by the end of the first year.

When there was agreement in child rearing, a positive attitude toward the spouse, low conflict between the divorced parents, and when the father was emotionally mature as measured by the CPI socialization scale and the Personal Adjustment Scale of the Adjective Checklist, frequency of father's contact with the child was associated with more positive mother–child interactions. When there was disagreement and inconsistency in attitudes toward the child, and conflict and ill will between the divorced parents, or when the father was poorly adjusted, frequent visitation was associated with poor mother–child functioning and disruptions in the children's behavior. Emotional maturity in the mother was also found to be related to her adequacy in coping with stresses in her new single life and relations with children.

Other support systems such as that of grandparents, brothers and sisters, close friends, or a competent housekeeper also were related to the mother's effectiveness in interacting with the child in divorced but not in intact families. However they were not as salient as a continued positive relationship of the ex-husband with the family.

In summary, when a father leaves the home following divorce the family system is in a state of disequilibrium. Disorganization and disrupted family functioning seem to peak at one year and be re-stabilizing by two years following the divorce. Stresses in family functioning following divorce are reflected not only in parent–child relations but in the changes in life-style, emotional distress, and changes in attitudes toward the self of the divorced couple. These changes in the parents may be mediating factors in changes in the child's behavior. A want for intimacy seems to be a pervasive desire for both males and females and the attainment of intimate relations seems to be associated with positive adjustment and coping behavior.

Since this study only lasted two years, it is impossible to state whether the re-stabilizing process in the divorced family had reached an asymptote and was largely completed at two years or whether this readjustment would continue over a longer period of time until it would ultimately more closely resemble that in intact families.

Chapter 4
Supports for the Development of Children

The previous three chapters have indicated many ways in which parents mediate the impact of the environment upon their children, influencing all areas of children's growth. Parents themselves are growing persons, with needs and problems. A well-developing parent can contribute more to healthy child development than can a stagnating or stunted parent. When middle-class groups are compared with economically deprived groups, the more privileged children usually rank higher in health, growth, nutritional status, self-esteem, achievement motivation, impulse control, intelligence, and language development. Analyses of parental behavior usually show middle-class parents providing more of the care, guidance, stimulation, and teaching that make it possible for their children to develop well. Middle-class children, therefore, are more likely to do well in school, to develop personality characteristics favorable to success, to learn technologies of the culture, and to achieve economic affluence or at least comfort. Socioeconomic status is thus self-perpetuating, with the average poor parent unable to teach children the values and behavior patterns that would let them break out of the cycle.

Parents have to learn how to be parents, building specific behavior patterns

229

on a few inherited response patterns. In nonindustrial societies, parents teach their children how to be parents, and other family and community members assist with the lessons. In North America, social change is so rapid that the child-rearing methods of one generation are outdated by the time parents become grandparents. Furthermore, North American children have few opportunities to care for younger children. When young people become parents, many of them know next to nothing about how to feel and behave as parents.

The job of child-rearing is a large one. In most cultures, the responsibility is shared; parents do not have to do it all. One of the ways in which parents are helped and supported is by being taught the skills required. Children and adolescents learn something about parenting before they become parents, and more about it while on the job. Other ways of supporting parents and families include actual help in caring for children and educating them.

Poor Children and Their Families

The people who have the least adequate supports for development are the poor, 27 per cent of white families and 52 per cent of black ones, if we take as the poverty line an income one quarter below the national median income [7]. Over two thirds of poor people are white, less than one third are black. About half of children in low-income families live in families headed by a woman. Black children are six times more likely than white ones to live in poor, one-parent families. Poor people are more likely than people with adequate incomes to start childbearing earlier, to have more children, to space their children more closely, to bear children out of wedlock, and to have more unwanted children. Added to these burdens are bad health, miserable housing, inadequate food and clothing, and exposure to violence. Solutions to the problems of the poor go far beyond aid in rearing their children, since economic and political actions are needed. However, contributions can be made by education and child development programs.

EDUCATIONAL DEPRIVATION

The culture of poverty includes restrictions that affect every member of the family in every aspect of life and development. By about 2 years of age, the child is missing more and more experiences basic to the type of intellectual growth required for participation in the mainstream of culture. Living in a crowded, noisy home, he learns to ignore sounds, since few of them have any relevance for him. When people speak to him, they tend to speak in single words or in short sentences, often in commands. He may be late to discover that everything has a name. Lacking this powerful piece of knowledge, he is slow to seek out names, lags in adding to vocabulary, and hence drops farther and farther behind the average child in thinking as well as in talking and understanding language. His family may speak an English dialect that is unfamiliar to the teacher. Comprehending him with difficulty, the teacher considers the child's speech inaccurate phonetically and gramatically. The child then has trouble understanding the teacher, because she talks in longer, more complicated sentences than he has heard, she sounds her words differently, she uses words he does not know, and she talks about things, places, and events that he has never experienced.

Very poor homes, in contrast to middle-class homes, offer young children few toys and play materials. Children may not have the visual and tactile stimulation that comes from play with color cones, blocks, nests of cubes, puzzles, paints, clay, crayons, and paper. They lack the emotional satisfactions of cuddly toys and the imaginative and social possibilities of dolls, housekeeping equipment, costumes, and transportation toys. Their motor development is not encouraged, as it would be through the use of climbing apparatus, tricycles, and large building materials. Nature is not seen as orderly, beautiful, and wondrous, since nature is hardly seen at all. Preschool children in slum areas rarely go more than a few blocks from home. A woman who grew up in a slum recalls that as a child, the only beauty she saw was in the sky.

Upon entering first grade, educationally deprived children are at a severe disadvantage in many ways, but most seriously in the main job of the beginner in school, learning to read. In contrast to children from more educated families, they are more personal and concrete, more dependent on action and context, and lacking in the skills of linguistic analysis and synthesis [6]. Disadvantaged children differ from middle-class children in what the teacher's words mean to them, in what they know about themselves. First grade is baffling to those who lack meaningful experiences with language and ideas, toys and places, people and other living things. Unable to cope with reading and other school activities, the educationally deprived child falls farther behind in second grade and still farther behind as he grows older. He feels hopeless and defeated. Intellectually and educationally retarded, he is a problem to the school and to himself.

New behavior can be learned. Opportunities can be opened. Child development research has identified some of the parent-child interactions associated with good and poor development. Although group differences favor the middle class, well-developing and poorly developing children and parents exist at all socioeconomic levels [42]. Even when parents and children get along quite well, there is often room for improvement. Almost all parents could learn to understand their children better, to make better provisions for growth, to interact with children more effectively, and to enjoy parenting more. This chapter is concerned with ways of supporting, teaching, and helping parents and young children to function more adequately and to develop optimally. Most families need support systems. Some also need compensatory or therapeutic programs that try to overcome the effects of deprivations, faulty development, injuries, and social disorganization.

Goals for Development and Behavior

Who should set goals for children? This question is philosophical and political. In China and the Soviet Union the state has an overall policy, implemented by citizens, including parents. Parents are not solely responsible for the guidance of their children. If parents do a bad job in the eyes of neighbors and teachers, they are helped to change their attitudes and their child-rearing methods. In the 1960s, when North Americans became concerned about compensating for deficits in the children of the poor, the prevailing notion was that child development specialists could properly set goals for health, physical development, intellectual development, social growth, and education. The idea was challenged by representatives of the poor, who believed that the poor parents knew what they wanted and should be given the resources for carrying on their own programs. A presently emerging notion is that children should speak for themselves as far as possible and that child advocates should promote the well-being of children when their interests are being neglected or negated. The various points of view are represented in existing programs for children and parents.

A child development specialist can set up goals for the development of children without insisting that any particular child or parent adopt them. This, in effect, is what many program directors do. The adoption and application of specific goals can still be left up to the parent or to the parent and teacher, in cooperation. An example of clear goals can be seen in White's Harvard Preschool Project. Through extensive observation and analysis, in which parents collaborated, White and his associates have identified competent behavior in young children and their parents, with the purpose of learning how to promote the development of competence. Their analysis has resulted in the following list of competencies achieved by successful 6-year-olds and by some children as young as 3 years [42].

Social abilities
1. Getting and keeping adults' attention in socially acceptable ways.
2. Using adults as resources.
3. Expressing both affection and hostility to both adults and peers.
4. Leading, following, and competing with peers.
5. Showing pride in his accomplishments.
6. Taking part in adult role behavior or otherwise expressing a desire to grow up.

Nonsocial abilities
1. Linguistic: grammatical capacity, vocabulary, articulation, extensive use of expressed language.
2. Intellectual: sensing dissonance, anticipation of consequences, ability to deal with abstractions, such as numbers, letters, rules, taking the perspective of another person, making interesting associations.
3. Executive: planning and carrying out multistepped activities, using resources effectively.
4. Attentional: maintaining attention to a proximal task while simultaneously monitoring peripheral events.

This list of competencies makes realistic goals for intellectual, linguistic, social, emotional, and self-development. We add the following goals for physical development.

1. Regular, consistent growth in which height and weight are consistent with each other.
2. Body well balanced, at rest and in motion; free and varied body movements.
3. Body well nourished; adequate intake of nutrients; good appetite.

4. Adequate functioning of all bodily systems.
5. Sleep-rest cycles supply sufficient rest and activity.
6. Signs of positive health present: clear skin, bright eyes, shiny hair, firm muscles, abundant energy, lack of tension.
7. Absence of disease but if ill, quick recovery.
8. Continually adding and refining motor skills.

THE COMPETENT PARENT

Competent parents, of course, promote and facilitate all of these competencies in their children. By listing various goals, processes, and functions, we may have made it look as though a good parent would pay attention to intellectual development at one time, social development at another, and to physical development at some other time. In practice, parents work toward many goals at the same moment. The following incident, recorded just as it happened, occurred in the space of 15 minutes. At the right is an analysis of the mother's behavior.

SCENE: A doctor's office.

Caring for child's health.

CHARACTERS: Tess, age 25 months. Her mother.

MOTHER: What have you got in your hand? Show me and I'll show you where you can put it so that you won't lose it. There! You have a little pocket where you can keep it. Put it in there. There. You can feel it through the material. See? Put your hand on it here. Feel it. It's round and hard.

Monitoring. Aware of safety.
Anticipates. Prevents loss of object.
Makes use of resources at hand.
Respects autonomy.
Gives clear directions.
Facilitates tactile discrimination.

Labels shape and texture.

(Tess and her mother are looking at a book. A year-old baby comes and looks at it, too.)

MOTHER: Give him this one. It has a hard cover.

Promotes awareness of other child.
Implies characteristic of infants.

TESS: He took mine.

MOTHER: Then you take his. You trade. (Tess and her mother look at the book.)

Teaches social skill.

MOTHER: See the twins. Two little girls exactly the same. Twins. That's a skeleton. That's what people look like inside, only no skin and no muscles.

Gives information.
Repeats key word.
Gives information. Ties it to what child knows about subject

TESS: You sit in this chair.

MOTHER: I can't sit there. The chair's too little. It's for little people.

Promotes concepts of size and space relations.

(Tess plays with the humidifier.)

MOTHER: That's a machine. Leave it alone, please. (She goes over to it.) It's a humidifier. See? There's water in the bottom. It makes the air moist. It keeps the air from being dry.

Sets limits firmly but politely.
Teaches new word. Describes object. Explains function. Restates function.

MOTHER: The doctor is looking at the baby now. He's going to look at you. (Shows book again.) See. This is what he's going to do to you. He's going to look in your ear.

Turns child's attention to next event. Mother anticipates.
Prepares child to accept new experience that could provoke fear.

This competent mother taught brief lessons in sensory discrimination, concept formation, language acquisition, heredity, anatomy, physics, and social skills. She operated within the limiting confines of a waiting room full of people, respecting her child's immaturity and autonomy and yet restraining her from being bothersome and destructive. She accomplished her main goal, getting medical care for Tess, and prepared Tess to accept the doctor's ministrations confidently.

At the other extreme is a mother who takes her child to the doctor's office, places him on a chair, and says, "You sit there and be good. If you don't, I'll tell the doctor on you and he'll fix you." An example in the middle is the mother who gives her child a toy or two, settles herself with a magazine and answers his questions in a word or two, while continuing to read.

From his experiences in identifying and studying competent preschool children and their mothers, White draws some conclusions about the important characteristics and practices of primary caretakers [42, pp. 240–244].

Successful mothers tended to be busy, highly energetic people who were neither depressed, angry, nor unhappy. They enjoyed their young children and liked spending time with them. Rarely were they meticulous housekeepers, but rather designers of environments for learning, in which young children could find safe, interesting things to do. Acting as consultants rather than directors, they were usually but not always available for help or to share an idea. Most of the interactions are instigated by the child, but occasionally by the mother. The mother's response was often more than an answer, including an idea or suggestion that took the child further along in what he had started. Setting sensible limits firmly, successful mothers were not afraid to say *no* or to tell the child to wait for a moment. Such mothers strengthen their children's intrinsic motivation to learn and give them an orientation toward tasks.

The Teaching of Parenting

Through Head Start, begun in 1965, the federal government stepped up its efforts to teach parents. Home Start, initiated in 1972, by the Office of Child Development, extented the teaching of parenting by home visitors. Some states, such as Minnesota, have invested in parent and family education programs that give sound support to parents as primary educators of children. Preparental education is a vital part of the Education for Parenthood Program of the Office of Child Development. The Exploring Childhood Program offers both classroom and field work. Relatively few schools have the program at present. Some high schools, of course, have their own programs of parent education. When a panel of 55 North American family life educators were queried about programs in the 40 states and five provinces they represented, 35 of the panelists were able to find one or more programs taught by qualified family life teachers [20a]. Questions to 44 of these teachers revealed only six of them receiving any federal support for parent education and only one engaged in the *Exploring Childhood* program.

Parenting skills are taught in some high schools, in many nursery schools and as integral parts of many child development programs. Some communities offer education in parenting and family living.

In Grand Rapids, Michigan, Wyoming Graet Community Education runs the Parent and Child Living Center [43]. Although oriented to parents of preschool children, the Center accepts all adults who wish to learn about child growth and development, family management, home care and repair, personal growth and development. The program is free to participants and offers high school credit to those who want it. Bringing their young children with them, parents meet in small groups for about two hours a week. At other times, they meet in groups of adults for half a day, while their children are cared for elsewhere.

The Wayne-Westland (Michigan) Community School District offers the Sparkey program to parents and their children from birth to five years. Parents go to workshop sessions and also receive help and instructions in the home. Parents participate in classes for 4- and 5-year olds in schools and in the homes of "paraparents," who receive in-service training. Programs are carried on for parents whose children have special needs.

These two examples indicate ways in which many parents are learning the skills and understanding that they need for bringing up children. Unfortunately, many other parents have not yet been touched by such programs.

Monitoring of Health, Growth, and Development

Ever since 1911, about 95 per cent of New Zealand infants have received care from the Plunket Society, otherwise known as the Royal New Zealand Society for the Health of Women and Children. The society is supported by voluntary means, supplemented with some government funds. A specially trained Plunket nurse calls on the new mother and baby in the home for the first few weeks and sees them in her neighborhood office after that, until the child is 5 years old. The nurse weighs and measures the child, taking not only height but chest and head circumference as well; she plots these measurements on a graph and watches the pattern of the child's growth. She tests and observes the child's sensory functioning, posture, language development, and behavioral normalcy. Starting with her first days as a parent, the mother builds a relationship with the nurse. The mother asks questions, receives information and advice, and shares insights and worries with the nurse. The mother can telephone the nurse if she needs help between visits and can schedule extra visits as required. During the days that I (MSS) made house rounds and office visits with a Plunket nurse, she gave psychological support to a new mother who had suffered severe depressions after previous births. She discussed nutrition, outdoor exercise, and arrangement of living space with a teenage single mother. In the neighborhood office, an eye examination by a doctor was recommended for a 3-year-old. A postural defect was found in another child. Several mothers discussed illnesses and doctor's recommendations, the nurse helping them to understand anything that had puzzled them.

Preschool Part-Day Programs

The first nursery schools, started in England in the 1900s, gave a great deal of physical care and in many ways, resembled what today is called day care. The early nursery schools gave child-rearing support to poor families. Although play and learning were recognized as important, the daily program also included baths, meals, naps, and outdoor exercise. Maria Montessori, whose materials and techniques are still used today, started a school for poor children in Rome in 1907. Although she emphasized mental development and mutual aid between children, she also provided food and taught cleanliness and order. The kindergarten, with its emphasis on education rather than physical care, had German origins.

The North American nursery school has always served the middle-class and sometimes the lower socioeconomic groups. During the Great Depression, the United States government supported nursery schools for children of the poor. In the 1960s, Head Start again offered nursery schools to poor people. In these two eras, physical development and nutrition received some attention, with the recognition that economically deprived children needed physical compensations. When serving the middle class, however, nursery schools have emphasized education, often minimizing attention to physical development and rarely involving parents to any great extent. Parents tend to see nursery schools as supplements to the education they provide at home and as enjoyable places where children develop socially.

Many different kinds of nursery school programs have been developed, especially during the past decade. There is much overlap in program and functions, since all are designed to be good for children. Starting with the traditional nursery school, we briefly describe the main types of programs on the current scene.

THE TRADITIONAL NURSERY SCHOOL

In calling it *traditional,* we do not mean that the basic type of nursery school is out of date. Although there are variations on this model and extreme departures from it, whole-child approach is as sound as ever for promoting balanced development of mind, body, and self, and for building social relationships. The basic nursery school also provides a foundation from which programs can be built in order to meet special needs.

In traditional nursery schools, the child is treated as a whole person who grows through differentiation and integration of body, personality, and intellect. Provisions for play, health, and growth are carefully planned and maintained. Social growth is promoted by arrangements that facilitate cooperative play, and guidance that gives insight into motivations and feelings of oneself and others. Equipment and program are attuned to the stages of personality growth that dominate the preschool years.

Building the Sense of Autonomy. The miniature world, which strikes the casual visitor as so cute, is child-sized in order that the child can *do the utmost for himself.* He hangs his snowsuit on the hook that is just the right height; his feet touch the floor when he sits on the toilet. The child-sized world is arranged in such a way that its occupants can *make many decisions for themselves,* decisions that turn out to be right. A child selects a puzzle from the puzzle rack and puts it back

A traditional nursery school. The children seen here have chosen to play with table games. The doll corner and dress-up center are in the background.

before he takes another. An easel with fresh paper, paints, and brushes invites him to paint, standing on a floor protector that keeps a spill from being a disaster. The housekeeping corner is full of equipment that children can manage—doll clothes with wide armholes and big buttons, a low bed in which children can snuggle with dolls, a sturdy, stable ironing board with small iron, unbreakable dishes and a place to wash them, grown-up purses, shoes, and hats, for easy dressing up.

The teachers appreciate what it means to young children to be independent successfully, to make decisions that turn out well and to feel worthwhile in what they do. In addition to encouraging and facilitating such behavior, teachers also know what not to do, never to use shaming as a way of controlling behavior, never at any age, but especially at this time of life, since doubt and shame undermine the growth of autonomy. Neither is competition used as an incentive, since it too would threaten the child's growing sense of autonomy.

Discipline in the nursery school is not quite the same as the discipline that many students and parents have known in their lives. It is easier to understand in terms of the sense of autonomy. The teacher sets limits on what the child may decide for himself and what he may do. She makes the limits clear and sticks to them firmly, giving him freedom within them. She does not say, "Wouldn't you like to come indoors now?" She says, "Now it's time to go indoors." She does not say, "Nice little boys don't grab toys from little girls." She says, "Dilly is using the doll carriage now, Tommy. You may have it when she is finished. Could you use the rocking bed now?" Thus a choice really is a choice and a direction is definite. The teacher understands that the children will often test the limits she sets, as part of their growing up. Because the child knows she respects and accepts him as a person, because he trusts her, he can usually accept the limits she sets for him. Because he likes her and wants to be like her, he often wants to do what he perceives she wants. Thus, discipline in the nursery school is carefully planned and carried out in such ways that children can grow in autonomy through successful deciding and doing [28, pp. 313–331].

Motivational and intellectual aspects of growth are involved in building initiative and imagination. The nursery school's stress on creative activities is one of its most vital ways of contributing to preschool growth. Not only is creativity valuable in itself now and in the future but imagination is more than a supplement to controlled thought during the preschool years. The young child solves through imaginative processes many problems that he cannot handle by controlled thinking.

Setting him free within comfortable limits, the nursery school invites the child to reach out into his world, to explore it vigorously and curiously, to imagine himself in a multitude of roles, to create a variety of beauty. All of this magic is implicit in the combination of children, raw materials, space, some carefully chosen equipment, and teachers who love children and know a great deal about them. Dramatic play requires only a few simple props, but it needs a push at the right moment and hands off at other moments. The skillful teacher will suggest straight-

This nursery school child is exploring ways of using paint.

ROGER MEROLA

ening the corner block before the whole post office tumbles down. She is quick to produce paper that will do for letters for the postman to carry. She suggests that Ronnie could be a customer at the stamp window after he has hung on the fringes unable to get into the game.

Managing paints, clay, paste, and such is so simple that first-time observers often see the teacher doing nothing. It takes real understanding of initiative and imagination, however, to let children create freely, often by keeping quiet and doing nothing. Teachers never "fix up" children's products. They accept them. They never draw models to be copied. They never tell children what to make with materials. They don't say, "What is it?" They listen to what the child spontaneously says about his creations. They show that they realize it meant something to him to do what he did.

Initiative and imagination are stimulated by books, stories, music, trips, pets, plants, and visitors with special messages for children. Such experiences provide ideas that are worked over in dramatic play and creative efforts with materials.

Perhaps it is in the area of initiative and imagination where the nursery school supplements the home most generously. What home can provide such a constant flow of fingerpaint and play dough? What mother can arrange for a group of peers for daily playmates or be on hand constantly to supervise dramatic play constructively? Or to play the piano for a group of elephants who turn into butterflies? Or to take children to see a hive of bees working behind glass? Or to arrange for her child to find out how a pipe organ works? Or to have his teeth cleaned with a group of his friends, attending the dental hygiene clinic after a child-oriented introduction?

Facilitating Intellectual Development. The tremendously rich environment of the nursery school offers never-ending opportunities. The child constantly perceives, integrates his perceptions, and integrates sensory experience with verbal. Toys and materials are readily available for handling in addition to looking, a condition that stimulates richness in thinking about objects [12]. Since most preschool children think preconceptually and intuitively, a nursery school curriculum is designed to give them problems that they are capable of solving. Through building with blocks, they learn that two of these equal one of those and that a square can be divided into two triangles. Counting may result from figuring out how many blocks to bring from this shelf and how many from that, when blocks are kept sorted according to size and shape. Counting happens in many situations that have real meaning—two cookies for each child at snack time, time before lunch for singing three songs. How many children go home with Peggy's mother? The workbench is a place for dealing with linear measure, roughly, of course, in terms of *longer* or *shorter than* or *about the same size as*. The sink is for learning about volume, if you are allowed to pour water back and forth instead of just washing your hands. Useful equipment includes containers graduated as to size and another series of similar size but different shapes. Clay, sand, and mud offer chances to experiment (loosely speaking, not scientifically) with size, shape, and volume. So do many other materials found in nursery schools offer opportunities for development of the schemas of cognition—pegs and pegboards, puzzles, shoes to lace, matching games, color sorting games, musical instruments, records, and books.

ROGER MEROLA

Language is a vital part of the curriculum. The teacher is a model of clear, pleasantly toned, noncolloquial speech. Skilled in understanding baby talk, she replies in speech that the child comes to imitate. She encourages children to talk, to tell her and other children about their experiences and feelings. New words and concepts come from books, stories, songs, and the many planned new experiences of nursery school. The beautiful books and satisfying storytimes make children look forward eagerly to learning to read to themselves. Here is preparation for reading —good speech, something to talk about, a love of books. Here also is intellectual development taking place through language, when children communicate with others and acquire verbal symbols with which to think.

Concepts of *time* are part of preschool endeavors, even though young children do not handle chronology very objectively. Many of their comments and questions and much of their play shows efforts to straighten out their ideas of time and to understand how life changes. Although children make barely a beginning in comprehending the historic past by 8 years of age, preschool children often have an interest in the sweeping changes in life that have occurred with the passage of time. Before they are interested in or able to tell minutes by the clock, they hear about dinosaurs, horse and buggies, steam locomotives. Through play, conversation, and thought, children arrange these past events and phenomena into a very rough historical concept. In India we found that relatively uneducated people would often tell us, "It happened in ancient times," meaning that it happened before

Independence. It could have occurred any time between 3000 B.C. and A.D. 1947. "Ancient times" is probably the way children think of the past before they have had the rigors of history lessons brought to bear upon them. The history lessons will be richer in meaning if they come after the past has content for the children, even though it is content without much chronology.

Nursery schools usually have a policy of including parents, encouraging them to visit, to discuss their children, and to take part in parents' meetings. In actual practice, parent participation often falls far short of what the nursery school teachers consider ideal.

COOPERATIVE NURSERY SCHOOLS

Parents are teachers and participants with professional teachers in cooperative nursery schools. The price of admission usually includes a certain amount of work to be done by either or both parents. Parents learn from the head teacher, a trained professional, while on the job and in sessions of training, planning, and evaluation. Many parents have learned to set up environments in which children are free to choose and to learn. Parents have learned new methods of discipline that better help their children to achieve self-control and consideration for others. They have learned ways of stimulating cognitive, imaginative, and social growth. Thus, cooperating parents are likely to continue at home the same sorts of opportunities for growth that their children enjoy at school. Cooperative nursery schools involve fathers as well as mothers, sometimes for traditional male skills of building, repairing equipment, and teaching carpentry, sometimes as teachers who bring variety and breadth to a female-dominated world.

The New Zealand *Play Centres* are cooperative nursery schools with some important differences. They have a long tradition of being run and supported entirely by parents. A few professionals give consultation and training. Although the government now gives considerable support, parents still raise substantial sums of money and plan budgets and policies. They make and improvise much of the equipment. Parents, almost entirely mothers, learn to be teachers by taking a regular series of steps in participation and training. A supervisor is a mother who has gone through the long apprenticeship and course of study. To many mothers, the Play Centres have been an avenue to a world broader than the home afforded, to social contacts, learning, and self-esteem. All of this is in addition to the primary goal of being a better mother and teacher. For Maori women, who were quite restricted from broad social participation, Play Centres have opened opportunities for freedom, self-expression, and self-esteem. Children benefit when their mothers feel good about themselves. Mothers' self-attitudes affect the values and behaviors that they teach.

COGNITIVELY ORIENTED PRESCHOOLS

Intellectual development is a prime goal of these schools. Often, but not always, Piaget's theory forms the basis of cognitively oriented preschools. Kamii, who was formerly the curriculum director of the Ypsilanti program, maintains that when teachers use Piagetian concepts, they try to promote the development of intelligence as an organized whole, rather than as a fragmented list of skills [20].

Piagetian-based programs are designed to facilitate children's search for knowledge and acquisition of concepts through their own activities.

Kamii, Weikart, and their associates in Ypsilanti have carried on program development and research for over a decade. Other examples of Piagetian programs include those at the universities of Wisconsin, Windsor, and Waterloo [3, 29]. Lesson plans and materials have been designed within these programs. Packages of materials and teacher guides are also available commercially [21]. The Waterloo program is described as having three main areas of development, social emotional, cognitive, and psychomotor [29]. The first area includes interpersonal relations, self-concept, and self-management. Three classes of knowledge are included under cognitive development, logico-mathematical, social, and physical. Psychomotor development includes large and small muscle development and all sorts of coordinations. The curriculum consists of prepared lesson plans that the teacher chooses to fit the stage of development of the child, aiming to present material that is challenging, but not too far beyond the child so as to be discouraging. An example of a lesson is the teaching of *same and different*. The materials are sets of items with two the same and one different. Starting with two identical dolls, the teacher explains that they are twins who want to receive the same birthday presents. The children then choose two identical objects, place them in one box for the twins' presents, and place the odd object in another box. Over 60 such lessons are available to teachers to use in the Waterloo program.

The earliest Piagetian preschools were created as compensatory programs, in order to prepare educationally deprived children for school. At present, the programs are available to affluent children as well, because they help *all* children to develop their intelligence. The Ypsilanti-Perry Preschool Project, conducted by Weikart and his associates in the early 1960s, included three types of nursery school. They were Piagetian, traditional, and language-focused. Perhaps the most important results of research done to date is the finding that the children who attended the preschool derived clear and lasting benefits [40]. Five years after their preschool experience ended, the experimental children from all three types of program were doing better in school than the control children, who did not go to nursery school. In spite of the differences between the programs, measurable effects on the children were very similar. In the Wisconsin project, also, a Piagetian group was compared with a traditional nursery school group [3]. Measured differences were negligible. It seems that children can make good use of different pathways to intellectual growth and success at school. Probably the differences in results have not yet been measured adequately.

Is cognitive development really influenced by attendance in a program that has cognitive development as its aim? An analysis of 227 studies leads to the conclusion that childhood education makes a significant contribution to the development of intelligence in 3- to 5-year-old children from lower socioeconomic levels [35]. In fact, the author said, the impact is profound. The Stanford-Binet test, Peabody Picture Vocabulary Test, and Illinois Test of Psycholinguistic Abilities all showed clear and significant differences between children who had attended cognitively stimulating programs for at least seven to nine months, as compared with children who had not had such experiences.

BEHAVIOR MODIFICATION PROGRAMS

All schools, of course, use reinforcement to encourage desirable behavior and to eliminate undesirable actions. Some programs are based heavily on the *systematic* use of reinforcement, with behavior shaping as a goal. A *positive reinforcement,* commonly known as reward, is an occurrence following an event and increasing the chances of the event's recurring. A *negative reinforcement* decreases the chances of recurrence of the event that it follows. *Shaping* is done by breaking down the steps leading to the desired behavior into small steps. Each step is taught by reinforcement, the whole action being learned gradually.

Behavior modification has been used very successfully in helping children to acquire skills that they lack and in eliminating other actions [37]. Socially isolated children have learned to approach others and to play with them. Silent children have learned to speak more. Inactive children have learned to go to the climbing equipment and use it. Sometimes sufficient reinforcement occurs when teachers watch, smile, and speak when the child moves toward the climbing bars, for example, and turn away when the child goes in the opposite direction.

A reinforcement-based preschool program is the language-learning program of Bereiter and Englemann, which has now been modified into a reading program [19]. The Bereiter-Englemann method has been used in many preschools, including the one in Ypsilanti. The essence of the program is a highly structured curriculum, presented in small steps that are reinforced promptly. This method has been very successful in teaching the specified responses to children who were defined as deficient in language or culturally deprived. Similar methods have also been used successfully in the elementary school, increasing children's academic performance. In some programs, parents are instructed in the systematic use of reinforcement.

Critics of behavior modification usually admit the usefulness of reinforcement in certain situations, especially social ones. They worry about the fragmentation of learning and about intrinsic (self) motivation being depressed by extrinsic rewards (reinforcements). There is evidence that when children engage in an activity for which they expect and receive a reward, they later show less interest in the activity than they show in an activity for which a reward was neither expected nor given [16].

MENTAL HEALTH AND AFFECTIVE PROGRAMS

A variety of programs are based on concern for feelings, self-concepts, and interpersonal relationships. Different theories and practices are represented by different programs, including behavior shaping and decision making [23].

An example of a clearly stated and productive program is the preventive mental health program at the Hahnemann Medical College in Philadelphia [33]. The aim in this program is to teach children how to think, not what to think, and to learn a style of problem solving that employs thought and language in coping with everyday situations. Teachers use games and dialogues to teach three levels of language and thinking. First-level concepts are *and, or,* and *not; same–different; happy–sad–mad; some–all; if–then.* Second, children learn that different people feel differently, that feelings change, and that they can find out things by listening,

The teacher listens carefully to what the children are saying and asks them questions that lead them on in thinking and perception.

watching, and asking. Third-level concepts (solutions) are attained through inter-personal problem-solving thinking. After a child thinks of a solution, the teacher asks, "What might happen next?" Children think of many different possibilities. Further questions lead children to evaluate solutions in terms of their consequences. The cognitive training program increased children's ability to find solutions to inter-personal problems and possible outcomes. Greatest gains in problem solving and in social behavior were made by impulsive and inhibited children, in contrast to the best adjusted children. Thus, the program was found to be most helpful to the children who most needed help. Children of low and of high IQ were benefited. Thus, behavior was favorably affected by the learning of cognitive problem-solving skills.

PROGRAMS FOR HANDICAPPED CHILDREN

Some traditional nursery schools admit one or two handicapped children into groups of normal children. The handicapped children are helped to make as much use of the program as they can, while the normal children have opportunities to give care and to increase their understanding. At Monash University in Australia, Marie Neal founded a preschool program in which half the children were normal and half had many types of handicaps. Teachers were especially trained to step in

These twins need walkers to support them while moving around. They attend a nursery school for normal children that includes a few children with handicaps.

ROGER MEROLA

with assistance at crucial moments, enabling a handicapped child to take the next step toward a goal. We were told that the half-and-half proportion worked very well.

In 1969 at the University of Minnesota, the Research, Development and Demonstration Center in Education of Handicapped Children was founded [24]. The staff identify children with linguistic handicaps as well as infants and young children who show likelihood of developing such handicaps. The staff develop, apply, and evaluate methods and materials to help children overcome their handicaps. Then, of course, the staff make their findings and methods available for use in other settings. Much of the work in this program has been done with deaf and retarded children.

Sometimes parents band together to create programs for their handicapped children. Nursery schools for mentally retarded children are the result of such an association. Not only do such schools help the children; they also help the parents. Parents of handicapped children carry many burdens. They have the extra caregiving required, but they may have some feelings of self-reproach over having a handicapped child. They have the very real worry of how the child will get along as an adult in the world. If these parents and their children can take part in an appropriate school, they can share their problems with each other and with their children's teachers can learn easier and better ways of caregiving and teaching. All can achieve a greater sense of worthiness and belonging.

Children's activities are enriched when parent education programs show mothers how to provide for creative experiences at home. These children gathered pine cones, sticks, and leaves and then painted them.

PARENT-INVOLVEMENT AND HOME-TEACHING PROGRAMS

Parent education has always played some part in preschool programs, but recently, there have been more efforts to develop and use the abilities of parents as teachers. Fathers, as well as mothers, are now recognized as important influences on children's development. The significance of fathers was first demonstrated by research on father absence. Biller has reviewed research, including many of his own studies, to show that fathers affect children, especially boys, in all areas of life, including cognitive development [2]. Further research has specified some of the actual teaching behavior of fathers, as well as mothers. Programs have been developed with such research as a base, trying to help parents to acquire more effective teaching methods. So far, the recipients of these efforts have been mostly mothers. Before describing programs, we discuss some of the research that has given rise to programs.

Parents as Teachers. A classic study by Hess and Shipman examined mothers' language and teaching style [18]. Black mothers and their preschool children were drawn from four socioeconomic levels, interviewed at home, and then brought to the laboratory for testing and observation. The mothers' patterns of language are of special interest here. The middle-class mothers talked a great deal *more* to their children, in answering questions and instructing them on the tasks set up by the experimenters. The upper-middle-class mothers' verbal output was almost twice as great as that of mothers in the two lowest groups. Quality was different, as well as quantity. Mothers in the highest group were more likely to use abstract words, complex syntactic structures, unusual phrases, and, in general, an elaborate code. Thus, these mothers led their children to manipulate the environment symbolically, to recognize subtle differences in language, and to use language in thinking. Through use of language, they encouraged children to anticipate what would happen as a result of this or that action, and to delay action while deciding. Contrasting teaching styles can be seen in the following examples of mothers teaching their children to sort toys:

> MOTHER I: All right, Susan, this board is the place where we put the little toys; first of all you're supposed to learn how to place them according to color. Can you do that? The things that are all the same color, you put in the same section; in the second section, put another group of colors, and in the third section, you put the last group of colors. Can you do that? Or would you like to see me do it first?
> CHILD I: I want to do it.
> MOTHER II: Now, I'll take them all off the board; now you put them all back on the board. What are these?
> CHILD II: A truck.
> MOTHER II: All right, just put them right here; put the other one right here; all right, put the other one there.
> MOTHER III: I've got some chairs and cars, do you want to play the game? (No response) O.K. What's this?
> CHILD III: A wagon?
> MOTHER III: Hm?
> CHILD III: A wagon?
> MOTHER III: This is not a wagon. What's this?

The middle-class children performed much better than the working-class children on the sorting tests and also verbalized the bases on which they were sorted. They also reflected more before answering. Planning was much more evident in the middle-class mothers and children, whereas in both verbal and motor behavior, the working-class mothers and children tended to act out of context, without meaning, without anticipation. For instance, a mother would silently watch her child make an error and then punish him. The other mother would anticipate the error, warn the child to be careful, to avoid the mistake, and to consider the important cues before making a decision.

Social class differences in language and teaching style have been confirmed by other studies, showing middle-class mothers using more complex, elaborated speech patterns, more instruction, less physical intrusion, and less negative feedback [1]. Middle-class mothers were more likely to react sensitively to each child as a unique individual.

Using some of the techniques from Hess and Shipman with fathers and their 5-year-old sons, significant behavior differences were found between professional and nonprofessional fathers. The former used more complete sentences and more verbal rewards. They also did more teaching beyond the task instructions [9].

Observed parental behavior was related to cognitive measures in children. Mothers were observed with sons and daughters in lower-class families [26]. Mothers' nurturance was positively related to girls' IQ and to their motivation to achieve while taking the test. Mothers' behavior was not correlated with boys' achievement and motivation. In a study of similar variables in fathers and their young sons and daughters from four socioeconomic levels, paternal nurturance was positively related to sons' IQ and motivation, but not to daughters' [10a]. Fathers' restrictiveness was negatively related to cognitive measures. Class differences were seen in the behaviors that correlated with cognitive competence. Higher level fathers gave more positive response and cognitive stimulation. The observations also showed that fathers treated daughters differently from sons, apparently giving them "mixed messages" through ambivalent behavior toward them. The fathers' behavior may well strengthen the daughter's tendency to model herself on her mother, and thus minimize the father's influence.

Studies such as these indicate parental behaviors that are helpful to children's cognitive development. Programs can be constructed so as to teach these behaviors to parents and oriented to groups whose children tend to have slow or inadequate cognitive development. Such programs have had considerable success. Parents usually seem willing and able to learn procedures that will help their children. Home teaching, usually a sharing by teacher and mother, is carried on successfully in many programs, especially with infants. Examples of preschool programs follow.

Begun in 1959 at Peabody College in Tennessee, the Early Training Project was planned to develop cognitive skills in educationally deprived children [15]. Experimental groups gained in IQ and maintained higher levels than control groups for three years after the end of the intervention program. The intervention began as a summer preschool, followed by a year-round program of weekly home visits by a teacher who worked with the child and the mother. The children in this group had three summers of nursery school, and three winters of teacher visits. Another group had two years of summer school and teacher visits for the remainder of the time. By having one control group in the same community and another in a town 60 miles away, the investigators were able to measure the diffusion of the intervention program to relatives and friends of the families in the program. They found solid evidence of diffusion to relatives and friends and also to children in the same family, especially to younger siblings close to the ages of the children in the program. Younger siblings of experimental children tested significantly higher over a two-year period than did younger siblings of control children. It seems reasonable that changes made in the mother benefited the younger siblings as well as the children to whom the program was directed. It is also reasonable that one way of maintaining IQ gains is to involve mothers in the educational process. When mothers learn how to teach their children and when they experience the rewards from it, then they are likely to exert steady and lasting influence on their children's intellectual development. In fact, when children had no nursery school, educated, involved mothers had a greater stimulating effect than similar mothers did on children who were attending preschools [14].

Already mentioned in reference to Piagetian programs, the Ypsilanti-Perry

Preschool Project began in 1962 to include mothers in the education of their children [40]. During the first two years of the project, mothers were mostly observers, but by the third year, mothers were included more as participants. Eventually, the mother was regarded as "a major partner in the education of her young child." Thus, the staff and researchers gradually became more and more convinced of the great potentialities of mothers as teachers. The data showed definite positive effects of mothers' active participation. Also, the results indicated greatest effects upon the children who had been judged most in need of help.

Parents were also brought into the mental health program of the Hahneman Medical College, in which children learned to find cognitive solutions to interpersonal problems [34]. Mothers of black, inner-city 4-year-olds learned to transmit problem-solving skills to their children. The mothers were taught games and modes of conversing that helped their children to learn the skills. Examples are given of typical dialogues before and after this training.

Before	*After*
CHILD: Mommy, Tommy hit me.	C: Mommy, Tommy hit me.
MOTHER: Hit him back.	M: Why did he hit you?
CHILD: But I'm afraid.	C: I don't know.
MOTHER: You have to learn to defend yourself.	M: He might have hit you because. . . .
CHILD: O.K., Mommy.	C: He was mad.
	M: Why was he mad?
	C: 'Cause I took his truck.
	M: Is that why he hit you?
	C: Yep.
	M: Grabbing is one way to get that truck. Can you think of something different to do so he won't hit you?
	C: I could tell him I'd play just a little while.
	M: That's a different idea.

Thus the mother gained information and helped the child to think of causes and alternatives for action. This program is outstanding in that it teaches mothers and children more powerful ways of using their intelligence to solve important problems of living. It stands in contrast to the many programs that use IQs and school achievement as chief criteria for judging their worth.

Mental Health. In another nursery school project focused on mental health, teachers established close, cooperative working relationships with parents, in order to help children to cope better with emotional and developmental disturbances [36]. In addition to the regular teaching methods of the nursery school, teachers paid special attention to fantasies, play communications, defensive reactions, and maladaptive coping of children. They shared their observations, hypotheses, and efforts with parents in frequent conferences. Parents and teachers helped each other to gain insights and confidence in their attempts to help the child cope better with problems of living and developing. Examples of such problems are death, illness, separation from parents, marital disruption, sibling rivalry, privacy, and nudity.

Social-emotional benefits and positive mental health have also been reported in school-age children who were part of a mother-child home program in verbal interaction [22]. The IQs of the experimental children were also higher. In this program, intellectual and socioemotional factors were seen as interacting and influential in the child's being able to succeed in school.

Television. Another approach to educating young children is through television. In this area, too, the potential of parents as educators is recognized. The Appalachia Educational Laboratory in Charleston, West Virginia, for children from ages 3 to 5 designs a program, "Around the Bend" [13]. At the end of each half hour, a communication is addressed to the parents, interpreting and recommending the follow-up activities. A television viewing guide with suggestions for activities is sent to the parents weekly. Parents who accept, and 95 per cent do, receive a weekly visit from a trained local paraprofessional, who shows them how to set up and carry on relevant activities with their children. Measured results of the program have been impressive. Children who have completed the program do just as well on tests given in first grade as do children who have been to kindergarten. Children of low socioeconomic status gained as much as children of middle and high status. Children who tested low in intelligence gained more than children who tested higher. Thus, the parent involvement overcame some of the drawbacks of programs such as "Sesame Street" that showed greater gains for more advantaged children. Presumably, better educated parents would do more follow-up on their own. With the Appalachia program, disadvantaged parents were helped to implement the television program, which they did successfully. When a half-day of kindergarten attendance was added to the combination of viewing "Around the Bend" plus the home visitor, children did even better, especially in measures of social behavior.

BILINGUAL PROGRAMS

When children do not speak English well, they are at a disadvantage in the regular public school. Often other ethnic differences add problems to the language burden carried by children from minority groups. Children may be disadvantaged by their learning styles and by responses to work demands that do not match the styles and responses of middle-class white children. Children acquire their mother tongue and their attitudes toward work and learning from their families, in the home. When children experience failure and inadequacy at school, they develop low self-esteem and perhaps poor concepts of their family and culture. Therefore, preschool programs have been designed to prepare children whose English is inadequate for entering the public schools. The dilemma posed by ethnic learning styles and values remains difficult. For example, North American Indian children usually come from cultures that value harmony and cooperation [26]. Competition, individuality, aggression, and regimentation are disapproved. If the ideal of cultural pluralism is to be maintained in ethnic education, then Indian children will learn within their own frame of reference.

Many different ways of teaching English to young children have been tried [25]. Many difficulties have been encountered in motivating children to learn a second language. One successful program has included parents, through the realization that parents are not only effective teachers but also that not including them makes a split in the child's world [17]. The program followed the already established method of beginning the teaching of cognitive skills in the mother tongue, which was Spanish for some children and English for others. The other language was used in informal activities and personal interactions. Members of the community were trained as teachers. While children were in school, adults who wished to do so attended English classes. Trained volunteers from the community worked in children's and adult's classes. Health and social services were provided. Teachers went into the homes to train *parents,* not children. Parents learned specific activities and child development principles from the home teachers and then taught the specific activities to their children. All children gained greatly in achievement measures related to school success. Those who were taught entirely at home with a weekly home lesson for the mother did as well as those who had a five-day-a-week school program plus a monthly home lesson. Mothers reported satisfaction and showed more willingness to telephone the teacher and to come to school. Teachers found the mothers more cooperative.

A bilingual nursery school gives advantages to the English-speaking children who learn the other language, as well as to the children who come with another language and add English. In addition to the obvious advantage of being able to communicate with another group of people, cognitive flexibility is greater in bilinguals than in monolinguals. When 4- to 6-year-old Head Start children were tested for their understanding of object constancy, naming objects and using names in sentences, bilingual children were found to be superior on all measures. An analysis of their performances makes clear the advantage that the bilingual child has. Bilinguals did much better in switching labels assigned to objects, such as calling a cup a plate. The subject was asked which object was really a cup and which was called a cup. Bilinguals did better also in using regular labels in sentences and using nonsense labels in sentences. These results suggest greater flexibility in the bilingual and, more specifically, suggest that the bilingual child may be more aware that there are different ways of saying the same thing and that the name is assigned rather than an intrinsic part of the object [11].

Day Care

Day care means care of children during the time when their parents need to have their children cared for. Although some nursery schools do just that, their aim is not to give supplementary child care services to parents, but to teach children and facilitate their development. Usually nursery school programs are provided for part of a day. The government-run nursery schools in the 1940s were care centers as well as nursery schools, in that they provided care while mothers worked at jobs. As it is now conceived, day care includes the services of a good nursery school plus other services. Formerly, day care usually meant a program in which children's physical and safety needs were met. The old type of day care is called *custodial,* whereas the new kind is called *developmental* or *quality.* Physical and safety needs are just as important as they ever were. Quality day care includes giving children good food, planning adequate activity-rest cycles, designing a safe environment, keeping a steady, optimal temperature indoors, keeping children clean and comfortably clothed, and providing supervision indoors and out. Quality day care also includes cognitive stimulation; opportunities for motor development; guided social experiences; encouragement of all types of creativity; and assistance in developing self-esteem, responsibility, and cooperation.

THE NEED FOR DAY CARE

Children need care. When parents are not available, someone else must give care. One-parent families are likely to need day care if they have preschool children. About 8.9 per cent of Canadian families and 11.6 per cent of United States families are one-parent families [30, 38]. Although most one-parent families are headed by women, an increasing number of fathers are taking care of their children singlehandedly. When mothers have jobs outside the home, they need day care for their young children. Among women with preschool and schoolchildren in the United States, about half work outside the home [8]. The number of these children has been estimated at four and a half million [41]. Another group of mothers who need day care for their children are those who are studying and training for jobs. And then there are women who are at home but who need relief from steady child care for reasons of their own health or temperament, or of their children's special problems and handicaps. Actually, it is unlikely that any person can stand unrelieved responsibility for young children. If a parent has no partner, friends, or relatives who will take over the caregiving function for a few hours a day, then she needs a play group, nursery school, or day care.

TYPES OF DAY CARE

Although day-care centers may come to mind first when day care is mentioned, the greatest number of children are given care in homes. There are four main settings in which day care is given [8].

In-Home. The caregiver performs either in her home or in the home of the child. Often she cooks, cleans, and does other sorts of homemaking along with child care. She may be a relative or a friend. Since in-home care is not licensed, standards and supervision are up to the parent purchasing the service.

Family Day Care. The caregiver provides care in her home for more than one child, and as many as six children. This setting may be much like a family, offering a close relationship between child and caregiver. Some changes in the physical setting of a home are usually necessary, in order to provide an environment that meets children's needs. Family day care may be licensed and supervised. In both Canada and the United States, many communities offer training and assistance to family day-care givers. A description of the training and supervision of one such program can be found in a report on the Associated Day Care Service of Philadelphia [39]. The Child Care Coordinating Council of Wayne County, Michigan, publishes a newsletter that details the multitudinous efforts and interactions of staff, parents, and volunteers in providing a variety of child care services [5].

This licensed family day care program serves three children. The mother who runs the program has had a course and receives supervision from a specialist in child development.

Family Group Care. Similar to family day care, but involving seven to 12 children, family group care requires more than one caregiver and considerable changes to the physical arrangements of most homes.

Day-Care Centers. A day-care facility is planned and arranged entirely for the care of children. It may be built especially for the purpose. It looks more like a school than a home, although often there are attempts to arrange it in a homelike style. With more personnel and more formal organization, it may be less flexible in meeting needs. However, the day-care center is more likely to have better trained staff, specialists more available, a more structured curriculum, more and better space and equipment, and more opportunities for social interaction among the children. In China, day-care centers are often attached to factories and other places where mothers work. The children pictured here are at the nursery of the Institute for Biological Products in Peking. In North America, day-care centers are more often located in relation to neighborhoods and homes.

EFFECTS ON CHILDREN

Research yields conflicting results as to the behavioral effects of day care on young children. At Johns Hopkins University, middle-class children were assessed by means of the "strange situation," a method described in an earlier chapter [4]. Two groups of day-care children, ages 2 and 3 years, were compared with children being reared at home. Day-care children interacted less with their mothers across a distance, cried more during separation, and showed more oral behavior and stranger-avoidance. When reunited with the mother, they showed more avoidance and resistance. The 2-year-olds showed more avoidance behavior than the 3-year-olds. The latter showed more anxious, ambivalent behavior and more distress at

VICTOR W. SIDEL

Lunch time at the nursery of the Institute for Biological Products in Peking. The mothers of these children, or perhaps the fathers, work in the Institute.

separation, whereas in the home-reared group, 3-year-olds showed less of these behaviors than did 2-year-olds. At Syracuse University, day-care children were rated on emotional reactions in the center, although not with their mothers [31]. Half of the subjects had started day care at from 5 to 22 months of age, while the other half had just started. The groups were equated for age, sex, race, parental occupation and education, and included both middle-class and lower-class children. The early starters showed more positive affect when beginning day care and remained happier throughout the fifth week. Further studies on these children showed the early starters to be more active motorically and less cooperative with adults [32]. A comparable study in Kansas showed more favorable results. Early starters were higher in peer cooperation, problem solving, planfulness, and ability to abstract. They tended to cooperate more with adults [22a].

Conflicting results from the few available studies suggest that very little is known about the effects of day care on children, either now or later. Although much is known about kibbutz children and Soviet children, conclusions about day care drawn from these cultural settings are not directly applicable to North America. There are many differences other than day versus home care. Another unknown is the difference between day-care children and children who have been left alone or in the care of young siblings or very inadequate adults. It stands to reason that day care is enormously better for a young child than minimal or no care at home. There is much to learn and to practice in regard to making connections between children's lives at home and in day care. If day care is to be a real supplement to the family, it must be thoroughly integrated with the home.

Comprehensive Programs

One particular program has been comprehensive in terms of the numbers of children affected, the numbers of units operated, and the scope of its goals and methods. Another type of program is comprehensive in the sense that it attempts to promote the total health and development of the child.

Begun in 1965 as a compensatory program for deprived children, Head Start has taken many forms. Originally conceived for the improvement of children's health, physical development, self-esteem, social relationships, and family welfare, Head Start has produced preschool programs of all theoretical persuasions, both nursery schools and day-care programs. The majority of evaluations of Head Start have concentrated on intellectual measures and ignored the contributions to health and social development that were made. The earliest evaluations, comparing intellectual measures at the beginning and end of the first summer, showed an average gain of three and one-half months of mental age during a six- or eight-week program [19]. A later analysis was based on two years of data collection in year-round programs. Assessments were made of motivation, feelings of adequacy, and other behaviors in addition to IQ, which was found to show a mean gain of 4.5 points. A subsequent study considered different types of programs, teachers, and children, yielding some indications of best fits. When a sample of Head Start children reached grades 1, 2 and 3, tests showed them significantly higher than non-Head Start graduates in intelligence and arithmetic achievement [10].

A carefully designed study assessed the cognitive, motivational and perceptual effects of 14 Head Start classes [23a]. Children were studied at the time that the programs were carried on and during a three-year follow-up period. Four different types of programs were included: traditional, Montessori, Bereiter-Englemann, and Darcee. (The last one combined an emphasis on aptitudes and attitudes.) The programs that emphasized cognitive learning had greater immediate impact, but over the four years, the stable effects occurred in noncognitive areas. Boys who had Montessori programs were, at the end of second grade, highest of all groups in IQ, curiosity, ratings on ambition, and achievement in reading and mathematics. The Bereiter-Englemann program produced the highest achievement and IQs during the preschool period. Thereafter, IQ declined steadily, an average of 11 points, and boys' reading achievement was lowest for the four groups in grade 2. Boys seemed to profit more than girls from the programs. Further study seems to be needed in regard to sex differences in reactions to the programs. Consistency of preschool and later programs was found to be important, as might be expected. One of the general conclusions drawn from this study was that raising IQ is not a desirable goal for a prekindergarten program.

AN IDEAL PROGRAM

Ideally, mothers, fathers, and teachers are colleagues in facilitating the balanced development of the child. Cognitive growth is stimulated by experiences that challenge, but not at the expense of the child's social-emotional growth and a growing sense of self. Children receive medical, dental, and nutritional care that promote health, not just care in case of illness. Parents share their problems, excitements, joys, and sorrows with other adults—teachers, parents, and citizens. The loneliness of parenthood is dissipated and its burdens lightened because people care about other people's children and all people invest themselves in the next generation. Yes, this program is a dream, but why not reach toward it?

Summary

Parents are developing persons whose competence affects the growth and competence of their children. Poor parents have the least adequate supports for the development of themselves and their children. The burdens of poverty afflict all family members. Educational deprivation results in children who are at a disadvantage when they enter school.

Goal setting raises philosophical questions. Who should set goals for children? White's list of competencies for 3- to 6-year-olds provides a picture of a competent child who can do well in meeting life's challenges. Competent parents also have distinguishing characteristics.

Parental behavior is learned; only a few response patterns are inherited. Supports for children and parents include programs that monitor health, growth and development, nursery schools, and day care. In all such programs, parental learning is an important aspect.

There are many types of preschools. The traditional nursery school is concerned with all-around development. Such schools provide for physical, personality and social development, along with intellectual. Many other types begin with this base and add a specialized interest. Cooperative nursery schools have parents as teachers as well as professional teachers. In these schools, parents often gain in competence and self-esteem. Cognitively oriented nursery schools have intellectual development as their prime goal, but in good schools, intellectual development is broadly conceived as interlocking with other aspects of growth. Piaget's theory forms the conceptual base of many or most cognitively oriented nursery schools. Behavior modification programs use systematic reinforcement to promote the acquisition of desired behavior patterns. Language development has often been a goal of behavior modification programs. Mental health programs place feelings, self-concepts, and interpersonal relationships in high priority. A cognitive training program has increased children's ability to solve interpersonal problems.

Research has shown the powerful influence of parents' teaching style on cognitive development. For this reason, and for social and motivational reasons as well, parent participation is an essential part of a variety of programs, including cognitive, mental health, television-based, and bilingual programs. Bilingual programs are helpful not only to children whose mother tongue is not English but also to the English-speaking participants. Bilingualism promotes cognitive flexibility.

Day care that is merely custodial is not acceptable. Developmental or quality day care includes an educational program along with meeting the child's physical needs, promoting his physical and motor development, and keeping him safe and secure. Many families need day care as a supplement to what they can offer their children. Although single parents and working mothers have outstanding needs, all parents need relief from constant child-caring responsibility. Varieties of day care include in-home, family day care, family group care, and day-care centers. The effects of day care on children have not yet been clarified by research. There are some indications of differences between children who have had day care and those who have been cared for by their mothers at home.

References

1. Bee, H. L. et al. Social class differences in maternal teaching strategies and speech patterns. *Developmental Psychology,* 1969, **1,** 726–734.
2. Biller, H. B. *Paternal deprivation.* Lexington, Mass.: D. C. Heath & Company, 1974.
3. Bingham-Newman, A. M., R. A. Saunders, and F. H. Hooper. Logical operations instruction in the preschool. Final report—Hatch Research Project 142–1769, July 1st, 1971, to August 30th, 1974. Madison: University of Wisconsin, 1975 (mimeo).
4. Blehar, M. C. Anxious attachment and defensive reactions associated with day care. *Child Development,* 1974, **45,** 683–692.
5. Brown, S. L. (ed.). *Wayne County 4C Coordinator,* 71 E. Ferry, Detroit.
6. Bruner, J. S. *Poverty and childhood.* Detroit: Merrill-Palmer Institute, 1970.
7. Chilman, C. S. Families in poverty in the early 1970s: Rates, associated factors, some implications. *Journal of Marriage and the family,* 1975, **37,** 49–60.
8. Cohen, D. J. Day Care 3: Serving preschool children. U.S. Dept. HEW, Office of Human Development, Office of Child Development, DHEW Publication No, (OHD) 74–1057, 1974. Washington, D.C.: U.S. Government Printing Office, 1974.
9. Deal, T. N. and L. L. Montgomery. Techniques fathers use in teaching their young sons. Paper presented at meetings of the Society for Research in Child Development, Minneapolis, 1971.
10. Emanuel, J. M. and E. L. Sagan. The intelligence, reading achievement, and arithmetic achievement scores of Head Start attendees compared to Head Start non-attendees in the first, second and third grades. *Training School Bulletin,* 1974, 110–132.
10a. Epstein, A. S. and N. Radin. Motivational components related to father behavior and cognitive functioning in preschoolers. *Child Development,* 1975, **46,** 831–839.
11. Feldman, C. and M. Shen. Some language-related cognitive advantages of bilingual five-year-olds. *Journal of Genetic Psychology,* 1971, **118,** 235–244.
12. Goodnow, J. J. Effects of active handling, illustrated by uses for objects. *Child Development,* 1969, **40,** 202–212.
13. Gotts, E. E. Speech at the University of Rhode Island, December 2, 1975.
14. Gray, S. W. *Selected longitudinal studies of compensatory education—A look from the inside.* Nashville, Tenn.: Demonstration and Research Center in Early Education, George Peabody College for Teachers, 1969.
15. Gray, S. W. and R. A. Klaus. The early training project: A seventh-year report. *Child Development,* 1970, **41,** 909–924.
16. Greene, D., and M. Lepper. Effects of extrinsic rewards on children's subsequent intrinsic interest. *Child Development,* 1974, **45,** 1141–1145.
17. Hahn, J., and V. Dunstan. The child's whole world: A bilingual preschool that includes parent training in the home. *Young Children,* 1975, **30,** 281–288.
18. Hess, R. D., and V. C. Shipman. Early experiences and the socialization of cognitive modes in children. *Child Development,* 1965, **36,** 869–886.

19. Horowitz, F. D., and L. Y. Paden. The effectiveness of environmental intervention programs. In B. M. Caldwell and H. N. Ricciuti (eds.). *Review of Child Development Research, vol. 3*, Chicago: University of Chicago Press, 1973.

20. Kamii, C. One intelligence indivisible. *Young Children*, 1975, **30**, 228–238.

20a. Kerckhoff, R. K., and M. Habig. Parent education as provided by secondary schools. *Family Coordinator*, 1976, **25**, 127–130.

21. Lavatelli, C. S. *Piaget's theory applied to an early childhood curriculum*. Boston: American Science & Engineering, 1970.

22. Levenstein, P. VIP children reach school. Last chapter. Paper presented at meetings of the Society for Research in Child Development, Denver, 1975.

22a. Macrae, J .W. and E. Herbert-Jackson. Are behavioral effects of infant day care program specific? *Developmental Psychology*, 1976, **12**, 269–270.

23. Martorella, P. H. Selected early childhood affective learning programs: An analysis of theories, structure, and consistency. *Young Children*, 1975, **30**, 289–301.

23a. Miller, L. B., and J. L. Dyer. Four preschool programs: Their dimensions and effects. *Monographs of the Society for Research in Child Development*, 1975, **40:** 5 and 6.

24. Moores, D. F. Research, development and demonstration center in education of handicapped children. *Annual Report 1973–74*. Minneapolis: University of Minnesota, 1974.

25. Nedler, S. Explorations in teaching English as a second language. *Young Children*, 1975, **30**, 480–488.

26. Nimnicht, G. P., and J. A. Johnson. *Beyond "Compensatory Education": A new approach to educating children*. San Francisco: Far West Laboratory for Educational Research and Development, 1973.

27. Radin, N. Observed maternal behavior with four-year-old boys and girls in lower-class families. *Child Development*, 1974, **45**, 1126–1131.

28. Read, K. H. *The nursery school*, 5th ed. Philadelphia: W. B. Saunders Company, 1971.

29. Rubin, K. H. Piaget in the preschool: From theory to practice. *Orbit*, 1974, **5**, 4–8.

30. Schlesinger, B. The one-parent family in Canada: Some recent findings and recommendations. *Family Coordinator*, 1973, **22**, 305–309.

31. Schwarz, J. C., G. Krolick, and R. G. Strickland. Effects of early day care experience on adjustment to a new environment. *American Journal of Orthopsychiatry*, 1973, **43**, 340–346.

32. Schwarz, J. C., R. G. Strickland, and G. Krolick. Infant day care: Behavioral effects at preschool age. *Developmental Psychology*, 1974, **10**, 502–506.

33. Shure, M. B., and G. Spivack. A preventive mental health program for four-year-old Head Start children. Paper presented at meetings of the Society for Research in Child Development, Philadelphia, 1973.

34. Shure, M. B., and G. Spivack. Training mothers to help their children. Paper presented at meetings of the Society for Research in Child Development, Denver, 1975.

35. Steele, C. Early childhood education—Does it make a difference? *Texas Tech Journal of Education*, 1974, **1**, 9–25.

36. Stein, M., E. Beyer, and D. Ronald. Beyond benevolence—The mental health role of the preschool teacher. *Young Children*, 1975, **30**, 358–372.

37. Stolz, S. B., L. A. Wienckowski, and B. S. Brown. Behavior modification: A perspective on critical issues. *American Psychologist*, 1975, **30**, 1027–1048.

38. Sudia, C. E. An updating and comment on the United States scene. *Family Coordinator*, 1973, **22**, 309–311.

39. Sulby, A. B., and A. Diodati. Family day care: No longer day care's neglected child. *Young Children,* 1975, **30,** 239–247.

40. Weikart, D. P. Parent involvement processes and results of the High/Scope Foundation's projects. Paper presented at meetings of the Society for Research in Child Development, Denver, 1975.

41. Westinghouse Learning Corporation. Day care survey: 1970. Report to the Office of Economic Opportunity, April, 1971.

42. White, B. L., and J. C. Watts. *Experience and environment. vol. 1. Major influences on the development of the young child.* Englewood Cliffs, N.J.: Prentice-Hall, Inc., 1973.

43. Wyoming Graet Community Education. *The parent and child living center.* Grand Rapids, Michigan, (undated).

Readings in
Supports for the Development of Young Children

The educational experiences of young children have far-reaching influences upon them. An objective of research is to specify the particular effects of different kinds of experience on cognitive, social, and personal development. This chapter samples a variety of educational influences, a theory and its application, a special program of education for a special kind of subgroup, and the use of television.

Although an excerpt from Piaget's work is included elsewhere in this book, we believe that students can also profit from interpretations of Piaget. Millie Almy's writings have introduced many teachers and students to Piaget's thinking. Almy has helped teachers to make Piaget a basic part of their teaching. Her recent article, "Piaget in Action," is a very lucid account of what Piaget's theory and findings have to offer to the education of young children.

Minority groups exist in almost all nations. In addition to possessing different customs and cultural values, they often speak a different language. How shall the children of minority groups be educated into the mainstream without damage to their self-esteem and ability to learn? Connie R. Sasse reviews research and describes and explains bilingual education with special reference to Mexican-Americans. She brings out the fact that social, legal, and judicial issues are involved in bringing about equality of educational opportunity through bilingual education. Thus, the child is seen as influenced not only by his family and school but by the whole of society.

Dorothy G. Singer and Jerome L. Singer are well known for their work on children's imagination. When they undertook to investigate the impact of television on children, they were especially interested in how television might contribute positively to socialization. The research reported here involves effects on imaginative play.

260

Piaget in Action

Millie Almy
UNIVERSITY OF CALIFORNIA, BERKELEY

As word about Piaget has spread, psychologists, teachers, and others have tried to accommodate to ideas that often run counter to the behaviorist tradition in which most of us were brought up. Not surprisingly, we have assimilated Piaget's concepts to our own cognitive structures in ways that have often distorted and changed the concepts. It should also be noted that Piaget, although not altering the basic grand design of the theory that he began to sketch some fifty years ago, has explored new problems, made discoveries, modified some of his views, and strengthened others. Meanwhile investigators have conducted research, some of which is strongly supportive of the theory and expands on it, and some of which calls certain elements into question. Perhaps one can say that the theory is dynamic and does not stand still for the educator who wishes to put it to use in the classroom. Despite this, I think certain elements of the theory are basic and can provide some guidance to teachers.

Educators often identify Piaget as a learning theorist. This is an example of the way we tend to assimilate new ideas to old structures. Piaget's basic concern is not with learning (that is with changes in behavior that cannot be attributed to maturation) but rather with the development of knowledge. Accordingly, he cannot be identified with the majority of psychologists who have influenced American education.

Once the educator grasps the fact that Piaget's concern is with knowledge, or with knowing, and not with learning, the further distinctions that Piaget makes may only gradually be understood. For example, *physical knowledge*, knowledge that can be inferred directly from observation of the physical world, differs from *logico-mathematical knowledge*, knowledge that individuals construct from their own actions on the physical world. Again, it may be some time before the distinctions between *figurative* and *operative knowledge* become clear. *Figurative knowing* is static and tied to immediate perception. *Operative knowing* transcends the immediately given and can deal systematically and logically with transformations. It is the latter kind of knowing that, for Piaget, marks the mature intelligence, and in the long run enables the individual to deal more and more effectively not only with physical knowledge but with social and moral knowledge as well.

Whatever difficulty many educators have had with the different kinds of knowledge postulated by Piaget, most have, I think, had less trouble accommodating to the idea that the mature intelligence evolves through a series of stages, and that the thinking of the child differs from that of the adult, not merely in the quantity of concepts available but qualitatively as well. Even here, however, there is evidence that the theory has been assimilated to the traditional

Reprinted by permission from *Young Children*, Vol. XXXI, No. 2 (January 1976). Copyright © 1975, National Association for the Education of Young Children, 1834 Connecticut Avenue, N.W., Washington, D.C. 20069.

ways of schooling. Piaget's research has undoubtedly more often been used to determine the sequence in which concepts should be presented to children than to determine the nature of the classroom experience the children should have. In other words, educators have more often called on Piaget to determine *what* children should be taught rather than *how* they should be taught. It is the *how* that is most important if we are to see Piaget truly in action in the classroom.

Out of the hundreds of articles and books Piaget has written, only a few deal with matters of education. These suggest that the *how* is to be derived from an understanding of the factors that are involved in the child's transitions from the sensorimotor period of infancy to the concrete-operational thinking of childhood and finally to the formal operations that characterize the thinking of the mature adult.

Piaget identifies four factors that contribute to these transitions. The first three—maturation, action on the physical environment, and social interaction—are all involved in the fourth—the process of equilibration or self-regulation.

The fact that maturation is one factor influencing the way the child's knowledge develops does not imply, as many psychologists and educators have assumed, that Piaget espouses an emerging curriculum dictated only by the current interests and capabilities of the child. It does suggest, however, that certain kinds of curricular activities are more appropriate for certain ages than for others.

As Piaget has put it,

> We must recognize the existence of a process of mental development; that all intellectual material is not invariably assimilable at all ages; that we should take into account the particular interests and needs of each stage. It also means . . . that environment can play a decisive role in the development of the mind; that the thought contents of the ages at which they occur are not immutably fixed; that sound method can therefore increase the students' efficiency and even accelerate their spiritual growth without making it any less sound. (Piaget, 1966, p. vi).

Just as the recognition of the factor of maturation does not mean a curriculum that is tied to what the child can do today, so an emphasis on the child's action on the physical environment does not mean a curriculum that is only manipulative. The child grows in understanding of the world by testing the ways it responds to investigations and by observing the effects the child's own actions have. Such manipulation is essential in developing real comprehension. I am convinced that the reason most children are as intelligent as they are in the all too prevalent "look and say" curriculum found in most kindergartens and first grades and in too many preschools comes from the fact that they do actively explore their environment when they are outside the four walls of the classroom. On the other hand, children left entirely to their own devices miss many opportunities to derive fuller meaning from their experience. Social interaction is essential to move an ordinary experience with the physical environment to what Hans Furth calls "higher level" thinking.

The teacher who sees that the child who has just observed that "big" things float soon has an encounter with a big thing that sinks, contributes to the child's development, even if not a word is said. But words may also facilitate development, as when the teacher, having observed an older child arranging and rearranging a set of cubes in different patterns, inquires as to what the child found out through the manipulations. The teacher in the traditional classroom spends much time *telling* children about the world and then questioning them to see whether they have remembered what they have been told. Piagetian theory seems to call for a teacher who listens more than she or he tells and whose questions are designed to promote reflection and further inquiry on the part of the child.

Piagetian theory also emphasizes the importance of the child's interaction with other children. As children confront the beliefs of those who see things differently, as they adapt their wishes to others or vice versa in ongoing socio-dramatic play, as they contest with each other in structured games, they become less egocentric and better able to take other viewpoints.

The influence on the child's development of maturation, of experiences with physical objects, peers, and adults, are all subsumed under the process of *equilibrium* or *self-regulation*. This aspect of Piaget's theory has given both psychologists and educators difficulty. The process, Piaget maintains, is continuous with other organic functions. To American psychologists who have been trained to think more like physicists than biologists this concept has seemed incomprehensible. To the educator who has come to think of schooling as a process in which a competent teacher moves a group of children from one grade level to the next, proving the accomplishment by the results of achievement tests, the concept has been anathema.

Essentially, equilibration, from the viewpoint of the child, is a "do-it-yourself" process. A child may need much or little physical experience or confrontation with peers or questioning by teachers in order to accommodate existing cognitive structures to a new idea, and the way that idea is assimilated depends on what the child already knows or believes considering his or her own life history. Piaget does not suggest that because it is the child who is ultimately in control of his or her own cognitive development the teacher is thereby freed from responsibility. But he does caution with regard to logico-mathematical structures, "Children have real understanding only of that which they invent themselves, and each time that we try to teach them something too quickly we keep them from reinventing it themselves" (1966, p. vi).

As I reflect on the complexities of Piaget's theory, I wonder not that so few teachers have tried to put it in action but rather that so many are doing so. When they do, they opt to focus not on behavior which is readily observable, but on development which can only be inferred. They choose to have classrooms that are filled with a variety of objects and for children who are actively engaged with them, rather than tidy classrooms where pencil, paper, and workbooks can be neatly stored and children sit quietly in their seats. Their classrooms will inevitably hum with conversation and discussion. The essential difference between their classroom and others, however, lies not so much in the ways they appear or sound as in the teacher's awareness of the ways each child thinks and the provisions made to support and facilitate that thinking. Such provision goes beyond the narrowly cognitive and takes into account each child's concerns and interests as well.

How do teachers who want to put Piaget's theory into action go about it? Furth says that teachers prefer to begin trying certain activities with children rather than getting into the theory. I suspect that is generally, although not always, true. But what activities? The answer to this, I presume, depends not only on the teacher's personal intellectual predilections, but also on which of the many interpreters of Piaget's theory he or she encounters. Some interpreters stay close to the theory and rely on it almost to the exclusion of other developmental theories. Others are more eclectic, calling, for example, on Erikson and Werner for further illumination of psychological processes and on Dewey and Whitehead for amplification of the pedagogical. Some interpreters believe that a good place for teachers to start is with the tasks that Piaget has posed children. Some have even incorporated such tasks into the curriculum. For others, as for some of my colleagues at the University of California, Berkeley, the tasks are a means of getting the teacher tuned in to the thought of children. In their program, student teachers, whether destined to teach at the early childhood, elementary, or secondary levels, conduct Piagetian interviews with children at all the levels.

To put Piagetian concepts into action requires, above all else, a thinking teacher. He or she looks beyond the child's verbalizations and manipulations and tries to understand what they mean to the child. This way of looking at and thinking about children is far from easy. It adds, however, a new and satisfying dimension to teaching.

References

PIAGET, J. *Science of Education and the Psychology of the Child.* New York: Orion Press, 1970.

PIAGET, J. Foreword to *Young Children's Thinking* by Millie Almy and others. New York: Teachers College Press, 1966.

Bilingual Education in the Southwest : Past, Present, and Future

Connie R. Sasse
TEXAS TECH UNIVERSITY

In February 1974, the U.S. Commission on Civil Rights issued the sixth and final report of its Mexican American Education Study. Entitled *Toward Quality Education For Mexican Americans*, the report identifies three basic principles that provide a focus for improving the education of Chicano students.

1. The language, history, and culture of Mexican Americans should be incorporated as inherent and integral parts of the educational process.
2. Mexican Americans should be fully represented in decision-making positions that determine or influence educational policies and practices.

From *Texas Tech Journal of Education*, 1974, **1**, 65–83. Reprinted by permission.

3. All levels of government—local, State, and Federal—should reorder their budget priorities to provide the funds needed to implement the recommendations enumerated in this chapter (1974, p. 187).

A number of specific recommendations covering curriculum, student assignment, teacher education, counseling, and Title VI are included to support the three basic principles identified above. One specific recommendation concerning curriculum is that "state legislatures should enact legislation requiring districts to establish bilingual education or other curricular approaches designed to impart English language skills to non-English-speaking students while incorporating into the curriculum the children's native language, culture, and history. These programs should be instituted for each group of students whose primary language is other than English, and who constitute five percent of the enrollment or number more than 20 in a given school" (1974, p. 204).

The U.S. Commission on Civil Rights is a temporary, independent, bipartisan agency established by Congress that has power only to recommend courses of action; thus, it has no power to enforce compliance with its recommendations. Under these circumstances, the purpose of this paper is to assess the probability of the above specific recommendation being implemented in the public schools of the Southwest. To accomplish this, I intend to review the background and current status of bilingual education, outline the rationale for bilingual education, discuss research findings relevant to the benefits of bilingual education, and summarize the legal status of bilingual education—both legislative and judicial aspects. Finally, I will attempt to predict the conditions under which the above recommendation could be implemented.

WHAT IS BILINGUAL EDUCATION   Bilingualism is the ability of an individual to use, primarily to understand and speak, two languages. Bilinguals may be classified according to their skill in two languages along a more or less infinite scale, with some bilinguals having one dominant and one secondary language, while others are reasonably balanced in two languages. Some bilinguals switch easily from one language to another, whereas others find it extremely difficult and confusing to do so. In many cases, children entering the public school system are considered bilingual when in fact they are monolingual in their mother tongue.

If there is some ambiguity in the literature over the definition of who is a bilingual, there is less confusion (at least in the professionals' minds) over what constitutes bilingual education. Most authors in the field use the definition of bilingual education found in the Draft Guidelines to the Bilingual Education Program under Title VII of the Elementary and Secondary Education Act. The guidelines (Andersson and Boyer, 1970, vol. 2, p. 8) state that "bilingual education is instruction in two languages and the use of those two languages as mediums of instruction for any part of or all of the school curriculum. Study of the history and culture associated with a student's mother tongue is considered an integral part of bilingual education."

In amplifying this definition, Benítez (1971, p. 500) suggested that in order to be considered truly bilingual, an English-Spanish program must contain four basic areas: (1) English language skills, (2) Spanish language skills, (3) subject matter (mathematics, science, social studies), and (4) culture of both target groups. He further emphasized that in a bilingual program English must be taught as a second language, but that teaching English as a second language (ESL) does not automatically assure a bilingual program, because to be truly bilingual the program must also be bicultural.

There is a very curious paradox associated with the development of bilingual education in our country. Throughout the course of history, in this country and abroad, the ability to speak two or more languages has been a mark of the educated man, an elitist, if you will. Many dollars are spent to develop language programs at the secondary or postsecondary level, yet the schools seemingly make conscious efforts to force all elementary students to be monolingual. Gaarder (1965) contended that bilingualism can be either a great asset or a great liability, depending upon the education the child receives in both languages. In our public schools millions of children have been damaged or cheated or both by well-intentioned but ill-informed educational policies that have made their bilingualism an ugly disadvantage (Nedler, 1971). Yet, at the same time, we honor and respect the educated diplomat who is at ease conserving in another language.

RATIONALE FOR BILINGUAL EDUCATION   The public conscience has gradually become sensitive to the predicament of the minority population, and new theoretical models have been developed and implemented, so that educational leaders have come to the point of view that initial school experiences should capitalize on the child's home language and culture. While granting that a person living in a society, the language and culture of which differ from his own, must be equipped to participate meaningfully in the mainstream of that society, it should not be necessary for him to sacrifice his rich native language and culture to achieve such participation (Board of Regents of New York Department of Education, 1972, p. 144).

The child's mother tongue is not only an essential part of his sense of identity, it is an important aspect of his self-image and his sense of dignity about himself and his family. Schools can, and should, maintain and strengthen the sense of identity that a non-English-speaking child brings to school, and should build on that sense of identity to give the child skills that will enable him to function in the mainstream society. It appears that young children have an impressive capacity to learn, and especially in the case of language learning, children learn the sound system, the vocabulary, and the basic structure of a language more easily and better than do adults or adolescents. Moreover, considerable evidence indicates that initial learning through a child's non-English home language does not hinder the learning of English or of other school subjects. In addition, as Andersson and Boyer (1970, vol 1, p. 49) pointed out, bilingual education holds the promise of helping to harmonize various ethnic elements in a community into a mutually respectful and creative pluralistic society.

With this solid rationale for bilingual education, it is interesting to speculate why it has taken so many years for bilingual education to become accepted and promoted. There are perhaps two reasons why it has taken so long to overcome the traditional monolingual instructional approach to non-English-speaking children: ambiguities in the evaluation of bilingualism and the misdirection of bilingual programs in the schools.

Although there is a long history of research investigating and evaluating bilingual education, much of it has been contradictory or inconclusive. Because children taught in their native language could not be shown to have marked improvement in English language skills, it was felt that there was little use to "waste time" on instruction in the mother tongue when the schools' goal was to bring the students to proficiency in English. It has only been within the past few years under the impetus of the humanistic education movement that educators have begun to consider the affective aspects of instruction in the mother tongue. In fact, a number of authors (Andersson and Boyer, 1970; Herbert, 1972; John and Horner, 1971; Levenson, 1972) have suggested that an improved self-concept, a sense of adequacy, and a cultural identity are perhaps the most important outcomes of bilingual education for the non-English-speaking child.

The second background factor that has hindered the development of bilingual-bicultural programs as defined above has been the concept of compensatory education as remediation for perceived inequality of educational opportunity according to Arciniega (1973, p. 178). Although the goal of equal educational opportunity has long been espoused by most people, there are two differing views of what constitutes equality (see Figure 1). The "equal-access-to-schooling" view, the more traditional, contends that equal educational opportunity is said to be attained when it can be demonstrated that different segments of the population have a roughly equal opportunity to compete for the benefits of the educational system. In contrast, the "equal benefits" view focuses on the distribution of the results or benefits of the system. In other words, equality of opportunity exists only when the range of achievement is approximately the same for the various groups being served by the system.

Traditionally, and especially during the 1960's and the era of the "culturally deprived," educators have viewed minorities (whether racial, ethnic, or economic) in terms of deprivation. They assumed that the implementation of education to "make up the deficit" would bring about equality of educational opportunity. The limitations of this model, the experiences with compensatory education in the 1960's, and the emergence of minority professionals have led to the development of an alternate scheme for achieving equality of educational opportunity.

Instead of being perceived as deficiencies, cultural differences are perceived as strengths to be enhanced and promoted. These strengths serve as a base for the Culturally Democratic Learning Systems Approach. The implementation of this model theoretically results in the elimination of institutional racism, cultural bias, and discrimination in the schools and leads to equality of educational opportunity through the equal benefit view. Programs of bilingual-bicultural education as described above clearly fit this emerging model.

Another way of comparing the two approaches to bilingual education is through *cultural assimilation versus cultural pluralism* models. The traditional aim has been assimilation, centering almost exclusively on methods to insure that students would be assimilated into the English language culture as rapidly as possible. If the native language was used as a medium of instruction, it was used

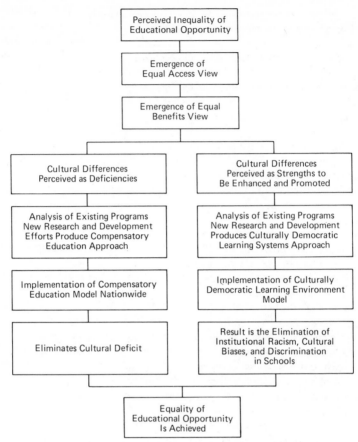

F I G U R E 1.   *Schematic of alternative responses to the equal benefits view.* (From Arciniega, 1973.)

only as a bridge to English—one to be crossed as rapidly as possible and then destroyed (Kjolseth, 1973, p. 13).

The pluralistic model includes instruction in both English and non-English with each language receiving equal time and equal treatment. The developmental trend of the program is toward maintenance of both languages. In the assimilation model the ethnic language is being exploited, whereas in the pluralistic model the ethnic language is being cultivated (Kjolseth, 1973, p. 16). Again, bilingual-bicultural education fits the pluralistic model.

P A S T A N D P R E S E N T S T A T U S O F B I L I N G U A L E D U C A T I O N   The existence of bilingual education in the United States falls into two separate and distinct eras. The first began in 1840 with German and English being the languages in which instruction was given. This era lasted until 1919 when all German instruction in elementary schools and almost all in secondary schools was eliminated as a result of World War I hysteria. From 1920 until 1963, bilingual education essentially disappeared from the United States. The modern era in bilingual education commenced in 1963 when the Coral Way Elementary School in Miami, Florida, offered a choice between the traditional all-English program and a bilingual program that included instruction in Spanish by experienced Cuban teachers.

Although bilingual education holds promise for both English-speaking and non-English-speaking students, full bilingual programs as defined earlier are seldom found. The Southwest is the geographical region of the country with the largest concentration of Spanish-speaking people, which should make it fertile ground for bilingual programs in Spanish and English; however, they are infrequently initiated. Only 6.5 percent of the Southwest's schools have bilingual programs and these are reaching only 2.7 percent of the Mexican-American school population—only one student out of nearly 40 (Uranga, 1973, p. 166).

In more narrowly conceived programs based on the compensatory approach to bilingualism, English as a second language (ESL) is taught with the objective of making non-English speakers more competent in English. In these transitional programs, no effort is made to present related cultural material. Although considered a less desirable program than full bilingual education, only an estimated 5.5 percent of the Mexican-American students in the Southwest receive some kind of instruction in ESL (Uranga, 1973, p. 166).

Even more narrowly conceived than ESL are the remedial reading programs offered in some schools. Using a strictly monolingual approach, remedial reading has been much more accepted than either bilingual education or ESL. More than half of the Southwest's schools offer remedial reading courses, yet only 10.7 percent of Chicano students are enrolled in these classes (Uranga, 1973, p. 167).

It is obvious that current programs are simply not adequate to meet the needs of Mexican-American youth. Only 2.7 percent of all Mexican-American youth are enrolled in programs that have been identified as truly bilingual. Another 16.2 percent are receiving instruction in narrowly conceived ESL or remedial reading programs, which leaves 81.1 percent of all Chicano students with no access to programs that might facilitate their school performance and achievement.

RESEARCH ON BILINGUALISM AND BILINGUAL EDUCATION

Regarding bilingual education, Fishman (1965, p. 227) noted that few behavioral science fields have been plowed as frequently, and fewer yet have produced more contradictory findings, than the relationships among bilingualism, intelligence, and language learning. The controversy and contradictory claims are not surprising in an area with political overtones that make it difficult for researchers to be objective, inasmuch as their research can affect the lives of a number of people (Turner, 1973, p. xiii). Furthermore, many contradictory findings in the literature frequently stem from differences in methods of investigation and the difficulty of separating the alleged language handicap from educational retardation, cultural and socioeconomic conditions, emotional concomitants, or any combination of the above factors (Darcy, 1963, p. 259). In general, however, the early work in this country found that bilingual students were handicapped in terms of intellectual functioning. In a review of research on Spanish-English bilinguals in the Southwest and in New York City from 1950 to 1960, Darcy (1963) found that bilingual subjects received lower but inconsistent scores on verbal and nonverbal group and individual intelligence tests. However, she reported that when bilinguals and monolinguals were matched for socioeconomic status their mean scores on a nonverbal test of intelligence did not differ significantly.

One study during this early period in bilingual research that did find bilingualism to be an advantage was conducted by Malherbe (reported in Zintz, 1969, p. 399) concerning bilingualism in South Africa. Malherbe tested about 18,000 students who had been educated in three types of secondary schools. One group was educated in English-speaking schools, another in Afrikaans-speaking schools, and a relatively small, third group was educated in Afrikaans-English bilingual schools. The data showed a small but statistically significant advantage in favor of the bilingual school in regard to language attainment in both English and Afrikaans at all intelligence levels.

Despite Malherbe's findings, in the early 1960's, the prevailing attitude was that bilingual students were mentally disadvantaged. This myth was shattered in 1962 by Peal and Lambert in their classic study of 10-year-old school children from six French schools in Montreal, Canada. Balanced bilingual children were compared with monolingual children on intelligence, attitude, and achievement. The samples were matched on socioeconomic class, sex, and age. One strength of this study over many of the previous ones was that tests standardized in the native language were used. Moreover, data were collected from several assessment devices rather than one or two. Peal and Lambert found that French and English-speaking bilinguals performed significantly better than French-speaking monolinguals on both verbal and nonverbal intelligence tests, and appeared to have a greater mental flexibility, a superiority in concept formation, and a more diversified set of mental abilities. The bilingual students were found to be further ahead in school than the monolinguals, and they achieved at a significantly higher level than did their classmates in English study, as might be expected, and in school work in general. The monolinguals saw their own group (French-Canadians) as being superior, whereas the bilinguals held more favorable attitudes towards the English than towards the French.

Modiano (1968, pp. 34–43) studied three tribal areas in the Mexican highlands. Students who were native speakers of two of the indigenous languages of Mexico were studied in 26 schools. An equal number (13) of Federal and State schools were matched on demographic data with bilingual schools of the National Indian Institute. In the Federal and State schools, reading was taught in the national language, Spanish, whereas in the Indian Institute Schools, reading was first taught through the vernacular prior to instruction in Spanish The purpose of the study was to determine which group of schools produced the greater measure of literacy (specifically, greater reading comprehension) in Spanish. In all three tribal areas, a significantly larger ($P = .001$) proportion of students from the bilingual schools were selected by their teachers as being "able to understand what they read in Spanish," than were selected from the all-Spanish State and Federal schools. In addition, in each tribal area, students who had first learned to read in their mother tongue read with greater comprehension in Spanish (as measured by standardized tests) than did those who had received all reading instruction in Spanish.

In the area of Spanish-English bilingualism, a project in the El Paso Public Schools found that Mexican-American first grade students receiving instruction in both Spanish and English scored as well on English language proficiency tests as the control groups, which were instructed in English only. And, their proficiency in Spanish was far superior to that of the students who were taught monolingually (Olstad, 1973, p. 52).

A similar project involving 4,000 children in the San Antonio Independent School District found that children receiving instruction in both Spanish and English made more gains in English vocabulary and grammar than did children in the English-only program. Children receiving bilingual instruction tested higher in English proficiency. They also made greater gains in IQ (as measured by the Goodenough-Harris Draw-a-Man Test) than did those in the English-only program (Olstad, 1973, pp. 52–53).

In another project (Bates, 1970, pp. 77–78), first grade children participated in a bilingual program in which the bilingual teacher worked for two hours daily with each class, with half the time spent in instruction in Spanish and half in English. The instruction for the remainder of the day was in English. There was no significant difference in mean gain in English verbal ability between the total experimental group and the total comparative group; thus the time spent on Spanish language development in the bilingual program had not penalized the pupils in English verbal ability. The Mexican-American pupils in both groups had a greater mean gain than the Anglo-American pupils; they began and ended with less English verbal proficiency than the Anglo-American pupils, however.

Politzer and Ramírez (1973, p. 60) obtained speech samples from Mexican-American children who attended a monolingual school ($N = 67$) and Mexican-American children attending a bilingual school ($N = 59$) in the same school district. The children watched a silent movie and then audiotaped the story of the movie. The errors from standard English were counted and categorized. Politzer and Ramírez found that the spoken English of Mexican-American children who had spent approximately three years in a bilingual program was no worse than that spoken by the children who had been instructed for three years in a monolingual program. In addition, they found that bilingual education and the use of Spanish at school had positive effects on Mexican-American children's attitudes toward Spanish and toward their Mexican-American background.

In another study Hickey (1972, pp. 25–26) hypothesized that some of the widely used tools for measurement of intelligence and verbal learning ability were functionally ineffective with Mexican-American bilinguals. His study focused specifically on structural and functional differences in the language that could affect test scores. Hickey tested 100 monolingual (Anglo-American) and 100 bilingual (Mexican-American) Head Start students with the Peabody Picture Vocabulary Test (PPVT). He found that 20 percent of the PPVT consists of words ending in "ing" and that the Mexican-American children consistently missed these items. He found that there were no sex differences in the scores, and that the "ing" words were the only differences between the two groups. Accordingly, Hickey modified the PPVT to eliminate the "ing" endings; he then tested 30 students from each lingual group and found no differences between the monolingual and bilingual students.

The final research reported in this review is that of Lambert and Tucker in a six-year longitudinal bilingual study in Canada (Lambert and Tucker, 1972; D'Anglejan and Tucker, 1971). In 1965, a group of English-speaking Canadians enrolled their first-grade children in an experimental class taught only in French except for two half-hour periods daily in English language arts. These children were matched with two control groups, one taught in English and the other in French, in nearby neighborhoods. Children were assessed for intelligence; socioeconomic status and parental attitudes toward French-Canadian people and culture were matched. Each spring of the study, the experimental and control classes were given a battery of tests to assess their intellectual and cognitive development and attitudinal status. Approximately 100 different measures were administered to all children each year.

After six years, the program has not resulted in any intellectual confusion or retardation among the subjects. In fact, the experimental children performed as well as the control groups in mathematics tests via English and French, indicating that they had no difficulty in using their mathematical concepts acquired via French when called upon to work in English. There was no evidence of a lag in English language skills, either active or passive, when the experimental children were compared with the control group of monolingually instructed English-speaking children. The productive skills in French of the experimental children were not equal to those of the French-speaking control class, their speech tending to be less fluent and to contain more grammatical errors than that of native-speaking children. However, they had attained French language skills that the researchers judged to be far beyond the level that they would have attained through traditional second language teaching methods—and at no cost to their English language ability.

Another interesting result emerged from assessment of the children's attitudes toward their own and other ethnolinguistic groups. The product of this program appeared to be essentially a new type of individual (neither exclusively English nor French), who possessed a sensitivity and a positive outlook toward both ethnolinguistic groups.

LEGAL STATUS OF BILINGUAL EDUCATION

As recently as the mid-1960's, 21 states, including California, New York, Pennsylvania, and Texas, had laws requiring that all public school instruction be in English. In seven states, including Texas, a teacher risked criminal penalties or the revocation of his license if he taught bilingually.

FEDERAL LEGISLATION   In the mid 1960's Chicanos in the Southwest and members of other groups mounted a widespread campaign for bilingual-bicultural education, which culminated in 1967 when bills were introduced in

Congress to amend the Elementary and Secondary Education Act of 1965 to provide for bilingual education programs. On 2 January 1968, President Lyndon B. Johnson signed into law the Bilingual Education Act, Title VII of the Elementary and Secondary Education Act of 1965 as amended in 1967. The Act begins with this declaration of policy:

> In recognition of the special educational needs of the large numbers of children of limited English speaking ability in the United States, Congress hereby declares it to be the policy of the United States to provide financial assistance to local educational agencies to develop and carry out new and imaginative elementary and secondary school programs designed to meet these special educational needs. For the purpose of this title, "children of limited English-speaking ability" means children who come from environments where the dominant language is other than English. (As cited in Andersson and Boyer, 1970, vol. 2, p. 1)

Programs under the Bilingual Education Act are intended primarily for children of limited English-speaking ability between the ages of three and 18, and English-speaking children are expected to have an opportunity to learn the non-English mother tongue of their classmates. Another feature of the Act is the poverty clause, which restricts grants to school districts "having a high concentration of such children from families (A) with incomes below $3,000 per year, or (B) receiving payments under a program of aid to families with dependent children under a state plan approved under Title IV of the Social Security Act."

The original authorization for the bill was $400 million, to be spent over a period of six years; however, only $117 million of that money has been spent. The authorization for fiscal year 1973 was $135 million, but after much haggling between the administration and Congress, the actual expenditure was approximately $35 million, which supported 213 projects in 32 states and territories and involved 19 languages other than English. Of the estimated 100,222 students enrolled in Title VII projects, 91,138 are in Spanish-English bilingual programs.

There has been a steady decline in the number of new proposals received for funding under the Bilingual Education Act. In 1970, 315 proposals were received in the Bilingual Education Programs Branch of the U.S. Office of Education. In 1971, 195 were received, and in 1972, only 150 new proposals were received (Andersson, 1971, p. 435).

In 1972, the Emergency School Aid Act reserved 4 percent of its total appropriation for bilingual education, which made $9 million available to fund 40 projects in 1973. The ESAA program does not stipulate that the children come from impoverished backgrounds, but communities seeking ESAA funds must be under a comprehensive desegregation plan acceptable to the Office for Civil Rights (Wright, 1973, p. 184).

There are a number of other federal laws that make provisions for bilingual education. The Education Professions Development Act (now incorporated into the National Center for Improvement of Educational Systems) has funds available for training bilingual teachers and counselors. Bilingual projects are authorized for migrant education (Title I—Migrant, ESEA) and Indian education (Indian Education Act of 1972). Other funds are available through the Ethnic Heritage Program (Title IX of ESEA), and through the Head Start and Follow Through programs of the Economic Opportunity Act (Wright, 1973, p. 184).

It may be that the federal laws governing bilingual education will soon be changed. Both Senator Joseph Montoya and Senator Edward Kennedy have bills pending that would revise current federal programs. However, even if Congress makes changes in bilingual education legislation, the effects on non-English-speaking children will be slight unless more money is appropriated (Wright, 1973, p. 185).

STATE LEGISLATION   In 1971, Massachusetts became the first state to *require* school districts to provide bilingual programs for children whose first language is not English. The Massachusetts Transitional Bilingual Act calls for the use of both a child's native language and English as mediums of instruction and for the teaching of history and culture associated with a child's native language. It authorizes state expenditures of up to $4 million a year to help districts meet the costs of bilingual programs exceeding the average per pupil expenditure in the district as a whole (Kobrick, 1972b, p. 56).

Although the Massachusets statute requires school districts to provide bilingual programs, participation by the children and their parents is voluntary. The major weakness of the statute is that it is silent on whether English-speaking children may be enrolled in bilingual programs. Therefore, it does not contain safeguards against the isolation of minority children in such programs (Kobrick, 1972b, p. 57).

Other states, such as Pennsylvania, mandate bilingual education without providing the necessary funds, or provide funds without compelling bilingual instruction, as do New Mexico, New York, and Washington. Within the past year, Texas passed legislation that established bilingual education as state policy for non-English-speaking students and budgeted $700,000 for 1973 and $2 million for 1974, after which the funds will come from general education monies. California appropriated $5 million in 1972 for an experimental two-year program. One unusual aspect of the California law is that at least one-third of a class must be proficient in English in order to insure that the class is actually bilingual. Louisiana recently has established a program to preserve the French-speaking heritage of its Cajun population (Wright, 1973, p. 185).

JUDICIAL ACTION   Although the number of cases that have been tried in the courts concerning bilingual education has been small, the impact of these cases has been felt widely, and will continue to be felt if others take advantage of the precedents that have been set.

In the case of Serna versus Portales Municipal Schools (351 F. Supp. 1279, 1972), a class action suit, it was asserted that the school district had discriminated against Spanish-surnamed students by failing to provide learning opportunities that satisfied both their educational and social needs. The plaintiffs claimed deprivation of due process and equal protection guaranteed by the Fourteenth Amendment to the United States Constitution and of their statutory rights under Title VI of the Civil Rights Act of 1964, specifically Section 601.

The court ruled that the Spanish-surnamed children did not in fact have equal educational opportunity and that a violation of their constitutional right to equal protection existed. The Portales school district was ordered to reassess and enlarge its program directed to the specialized needs of its Spanish-surnamed students in all four elementary schools and to recruit and hire more qualified Spanish-speaking teachers and teacher aides in each of the district's schools. In a similar case against the school district of San Felipe Del Rio, Texas, the district judge ruled that bilingual programs must be instituted to accommodate the needs of the Mexican-American students.

The most recent judicial decision came on 21 January 1974, when the Supreme Court of the United States ruled on the case of Lau versus Nicols (U.S. 94 S. Ct. 786, 1974). This case concerned the failure of the San Francisco school system to provide English language instruction to approximately 1800 students of Chinese ancestry who do not speak English. It was claimed that this denied them a meaningful opportunity to participate in the public educational program and thus violated Section 601 of the Civil Rights Act of 1964, which bans discrimination based "on the ground of race, color, or national origin," in "any program or activity receiving federal financial assistance," and the implementing regulations of the Department of Health, Education, and Welfare. The original decision had gone against the plaintiffs in the U.S. District Court for the Northern District of California and in the United States Court of Appeals for the Ninth Circuit.

In reversing the decision of the lower courts in Lau versus Nichols, the Supreme Court noted that it seemed obvious that the Chinese-speaking minority received from the school system fewer benefits than did the English-speaking majority. In 1970, HEW issued clarifying guidelines for the implementing regulations of the Civil Rights Act of 1964. In part, these stated:

> Where inability to speak and understand the English language excludes national origin-minority group children from effective participation in the educational program offered by a school district, the district must take affirmative steps to rectify the language deficiency in order to open its instructional program to these students. (Lau versus Nichols, p. 789)

Because the San Francisco school district had agreed to comply with Title VI of the Civil Rights Act of 1964 as part of its contractual agreement in receiving federal monies, the Court used this agreement as a basis for its landmark decision.

SUMMARY AND IMPLICATIONS—THE CASE FOR IMPLEMENTATION OF BILINGUAL EDUCATION FOR MEXICAN-AMERICAN STUDENTS

The intent of this paper has been to survey the evidence available, and then attempt to predict the probability of bilingual education being incorporated into the schools of the Southwest that serve Mexican-Americans, whose native tongue is Spanish.

Although a number of highly respected educators feel that bilingual education for both English-speaking and Spanish-speaking students would be a valuable direction for schools to take, it is doubtful that this type of program will ever attain anything but limited availability in the Southwest. Whereas Lambert's longitudinal study in Canada provides evidence that English-speaking children would not suffer in terms of their English language skills if they enrolled in a program in which instruction was in Spanish, and in fact, would gain fluency in Spanish as well as a favorable attitude toward Spanish and the Spanish culture, it is not likely that this evidence will be considered. It seems that the majority of Americans are so ethnocentric that they would see little value in being fluent in another language and comfortable in another culture. The change in attitude that would be required for all pupils to be enrolled in bilingual programs is simply too great for this alternative to be viable for large numbers of people at this time.

Regarding bilingual education for Spanish-speaking students, the prospects appear more promising. Although researchers have not been able to demonstrate conclusively that a Mexican-American child can become literate in English best by first becoming literate in Spanish, research shows that instruction in Spanish does not retard English language skills. In addition, a number of authors have pointed out that the affective aspects of instruction in the mother tongue are tremendously important in the development of self-concept, self-esteem, and a sense of adequacy in Mexican-American students.

Another promising sign has been the change in the attitude of both educators and the public over the last decade. As recently as 1967, it was illegal to give bilingual instruction in a number of states, whereas today many states have legislation supporting or mandating bilingual education.

Of course, the most important event relating to the future of bilingual education was the Supreme Court decision in Lau versus Nichols that failure to provide a child who does not speak English with English language instruction is clearly a violation of the 1964 Civil Rights Act. Even though the court did not prescribe what type of program should be instituted to remedy the situation, it clearly stated that some type of special program must be provided for non-English-speaking students, and that school districts have an affirmative duty to rectify the language deficiencies of non-English-speaking students in order to open the instructional program to these students.

There are still obvious obstacles to be overcome. Many communities doubt that the maintenance of non-English languages is desirable. It is possible that some individuals could even misinterpret Lambert's longitudinal data to support their contention that Mexican-American children would do as well to attend English-speaking schools, inasmuch as the Lambert experiment involved a home/school language switch. However, the Lambert experiment was conducted under conditions that are not directly generalizable to the Southwest. The province of Quebec contains approximately a 1:1 ratio of English and French-speaking citizens. The experiment was designed to support the maintenance of the weaker language (French), that is, the one most likely to be lost. From the perspective of the maintenance of the weakest language, the Lambert data would support the maintenance of Spanish in the Southwest through bilingual programs.

Another obstacle is the lack of qualified teachers. A survey cited by Light (1972) of teachers of English as a second language found that such teachers are almost totally unprepared for their work. In a sample of elementary and secondary school teachers, it was found that 91 percent had no practice teaching in ESL. Eighty-five percent had no formal study in methods of teaching ESL, while 80 percent had no formal training in English syntax. Sixty-five percent had no training in general linguistics. Teacher preparation institutions are only beginning to realise that new and better programs are urgently needed to educate qualified teachers in the numbers required. In these days of the over-supply of teachers, it may be that the shortage of qualified bilingual teachers will end due to the laws of supply and demand, but it is likely that it will be a number of years before there is any appreciable number of certified bilingual teachers. In fact, recent California Legislation (Wright, 1973, p. 185) excuses bilingual teachers from certification—which may be an indicator of the measures necessary to create a cadre of bilingual teachers. Along with the lack of qualified teachers, there is a lack of adequate materials, and an oversupply of inadequate evaluation methods and instruments.

With all the problems attendant to a widespread initiation of bilingual education, it appears that Lau versus Nichols has opened the door. Given the reluctance of the educational system to move itself and the lag between edu-cational theory and school practice, it may be that those who stand to benefit most from bilingual programs will have to force the issue. Minority language speakers, primarily Spanish-speaking in the Southwest, who are unable to get bilingual programs established will have to be willing to take the issue to the courts. A school district under court order to provide some type of special instruction for non-English-speaking students will be in no position to delay initiation of a program. In the Southwest, it will be up to Mexican-Americans to provide this legal impetus, if necessary, and to be in positions on the local, state, and national levels to have input into the kind of programs established.

It seems ironic that legally the stage is set for minorities to demand full bilingual programs, yet many of the programs that are evolving with the label "bilingual" are half-way measures that at best can be considered transitional programs. It appears that only as Mexican-Americans in the Southwest gain the political power necessary to have access to the decision-making process, and only as they are willing to use the legal tools available to them, will bilingual-bicultural programs be established to meet the needs of all students.

References

ABRAHAMS, ROGER D., and TROIKE, RUDOLPH C. (Eds.), *Language and Cultural Diversity in American Education*. Englewood Cliffs, New Jersey: Prentice-Hall, Inc., 1972.

ANDERSSON, THEODORE. "Bilingual Education: The American Experience." *The Modern Language Journal* 55 (November 1971), 427–437.

ANDERSSON, THEODORE, and BOYER, MILDRED. *Bilingual Schooling in the United States*. 2 vols. Washington, D.C.: U.S. Government Printing Office, 1970.

ARCENIEGA, TOMÁS A. "The Myth of the Compensatory Education Model in Education of Chicanos." In Garza, Rudolph O. de la; Kruszewski, Anthony; and Arceniega, Tomás A. (Eds.), *Chicanos and Native Americans*. Englewood Cliffs, New Jersey: Prentice-Hall, Inc., 1973, pp. 173–183.

BATES, ENID BUSWELL. "The Effects of One Experimental Bilingual Program on Verbal Ability and Vocabulary of First Grade Pupils." Unpublished doctoral dissertation, Texas Tech University, 1970.

BENÍTEZ, MARIO. "Bilingual Education: The What, the How, and the How Far." *Hispania* 54 (September 1971), 499–503.

Board of Regents of New York State Department of Education. "Emphasis on Bilingual Education." *Intellect* 101 (December 1972), 144–145.

CARLISLE, JOHN. "A Closer Look at the Bilingual Classroom." *Hispania* 56 (May 1973), 406–408.

CARROW, ELIZABETH, "Comprehension of English and Spanish by Preschool Mexican-American Children." *Modern Language Journal* 55 (May 1971), 299–305.

CROSS, WILLIAM C., and BRIDGEWATER, MIKE. "Toward Bicultural Education for the Southwestern Mexican-American." *Education* 94 (September/October 1973), 18–22.

D'ANGLEJAN, ALISON, and TUCKER, G. R. "Academic Report: The St. Lambert Program of Home-School Language Switch." *Modern Language Journal* 55 (February 1971), 99–101.

DARCY, NATALIE T. "Bilingualism and the Measurement of Intelligence: Review of a Decade of Research." *The Journal of Genetic Psychology* 103 (1963), 259–282.

FISHMAN, JOSHUA. "The Status and Prospects of Bilingualism in The United States." *Modern Language Journal* 49 (March 1965), 143–155.

GAARDER, A. BRUCE. "Teaching the Bilingual Child: Research, Development, and Policy." In *Bilingualism and the Bilingual Child, A Symposium*. Reprinted from *The Modern Language Journal* 47 (March and April 1965), 165–175.

GARZA, RUDOLPH O. DE LA; KRUSZEWSKI, Z. ANTHONY; and ARCENIEGA, TOMÁS A. *Chicanos and Native Americans*. Englewood Cliffs, New Jersey: Prentice-Hall, Inc., 1973.

GUERRA, MANUEL H. "Educating Chicano Children and Youth." *Phi Delta Kappan* 53 (January 1972), 313–314.

HERBERT, CHARLES E. JR. "The Bilingual Child's Right To Read." *Claremont Reading Conference Yearbook* 36 (1972), 51–58.

HICKEY, TOM. "Bilingualism and the Measurement of Intelligence and Verbal Learning Ability." *Exceptional Children* 39 (September 1972), 24–28.

IANCO-WORRALL, ANITA D. "Bilingualism and Cognitive Development." *Child Development* 43 (December 1972), 1390.

JOHN, VERA P., and HORNER, VIVIAN M. *Early Childhood Bilingual Education*. New York: Modern Language Association of America, 1971.

KJOLSETH, ROLF. "Bilingual Education Programs in the United States: For Assimilation or Pluralism?" In Turner, Paul R. (Ed.), *Bilingualism in The Southwest*. Tucson, Arizona: The University of Arizona Press, 1973, pp. 3–28.

KOBRICK, JEFFREY. "A Model Act Providing for Transitional Bilingual Education Programs in Public Schools." *Harvard Journal of Legislation* 9 (January 1972a), 260–300.

KOBRICK, JEFFREY W. "The Compelling Case for Bilingual Education." *Saturday Review* 55 (April 29, 1972b), 54–58.

LAMBERT, WALLACE E., and TUCKER, G. RICHARD. *Bilingual Education of Children*. Rowley, Massachusetts: Newbury House Publishers, Inc., 1972.

Lau versus Nichols, 94 S. Ct. 786 (1974).

LEVENSON, STANLEY, "Spanish and Portuguese in the Elementary Schools." *Hispania* 55 (May 1972), 314–319.

LIGHT, RICHARD L. "On Language Arts and Minority Group Children." In Abrahams, Roger D., and Troike, Rudolph C. (Eds.), *Language and Cultural Diversity in American Education*. Englewood Cliffs, New Jersey: Prentice-Hall, Inc. 1972, pp. 9–15.

MODIANO, NANCY. "National or Mother Language in Beginning Reading: A Comparative Study." *Research in the Teaching of English* 2 (April 1968), 32–43.

NEDLER, SHARI. "Language, the Vehicle; Culture, the Content." *Journal of Research and Development in Education* 4 (Summer 1971), 3–8.

OLSTAD, CHARLES. "The Local Colloquial in The Classroom." In Turner, Paul R. (Ed.), *Bilingualism in the Southwest*. Tucson, Arizona: The University of Arizona Press, 1973, pp. 51–66.

PEAL, ELIZABETH, and LAMBERT, WALLACE E. "The Relation of Bilingualism to Intelligence." *Psychological Monographs* 76 (1962) Whole No. 546.

POLITZER, ROBERT, and RAMÍREZ, A. G. "An Error Analysis of the Spoken English of Mexican-American Pupils in a Bilingual School and a Monolingual School." *Language Learning* 23 (June 1973), 39–61.

Serna versus Portales Municipal Schools, 351 F. Supp. 1279 (1972).

STENT, MADELON D.; HAZARD, WILLIAM R.; and RIVLIN, HARRY N. *Cultural Pluralism in Education: A Mandate For Change.* New York: Appleton-Century-Crofts, 1973.

TUCKER, G. R., and D'ANGLEJAN, ALISON D. "Some Thoughts Concerning Bilingual Education Programs." *Modern Language Journal* 55 (December 1971), 491–493.

TURNER, PAUL R. (Ed.), *Bilingualism in the Southwest.* Tucson, Arizona: The University of Arizona Press, 1973.

URANGA, SUSAN NAVARRO. "The Study of Mexican-American Education in the Southwest: Implications of Research by the Civil Rights Commission." In Garza, Rudolph O. de la; Kruszewski, Z. Anthony; and Arceniega, Tomás A. (Eds.), *Chicanos and Native Americans.* Englewood Cliffs, New Jersey: Prentice-Hall, Inc., 1973, pp. 161–172.

U.S. Commission on Civil Rights. *Toward Quality Education for Mexican Americans.* Report VI: Mexican American Education Study. Washington D.C.: U.S. Government Printing Office, 1974.

WRIGHT, LAWRENCE. "The Bilingual Education Movement at the Crossroads." *Phi Delta Kappan* 55 (November 1973), 183–186.

ZINTZ, MILES V. *Education Across Cultures.* Dubuque, Iowa: Kendall/Hunt Publishing Company, 1969.

Family Television Viewing Habits and the Spontaneous Play of Pre-School Children *

Dorothy G. Singer and Jerome L. Singer
UNIVERSITY OF BRIDGEPORT AND YALE UNIVERSITY

In most families in this country and, increasingly, throughout the world, it can probably be said that television is indeed very much a member of the family. Surveys suggest that in most homes where there are young children, from toddlers to early adolescents, the television set is on much of the time during the day and well into the night and is viewed with different degrees of concentration by all members of the family. Like an imaginary companion, "Big Brother," it is there providing stimulation and talking to the smallest child in a way that has never been a part of human experience before. Viewed from this vantage point, it seems almost a national disgrace that so little attention has been paid by appropriate governmental or private agencies to the direct impact of the

From *American Journal of Orthopsychiatry*, 1976, 46, 496–502. Copyright © 1976 the American Orthopsychiatric Association, Inc. Reproduced by permission.

* This research was supported in part by the Yale Child Study Center, the Yale Institute of Social and Policy Studies and Family Communications, Inc.

television set on the socialization of children. The major thrust of formal research until fairly recently has been to examine possible influences of television upon overt aggressive behavior. The relevant reviews of this literature (Singer, 1971; Murray, 1973) show that exposure to aggressive material on television will have the effect of increasing the level of aggression in children, particularly those already showing tendencies toward overt aggressive behavior. The serious implications of such findings are clear but have not yet been fully faced by either the networks or various mental health agencies. If only 20 per cent or 30 per cent of all pre-school children show a predisposition to aggressive behavior in the sense of being inclined to direct physical attacks on other children, the extensive exposure of such children to the large amounts of direct violence on television, whether in cartoons or live form, is likely to generate a sizable upsurge in the occurrence of acts of overt violence by these children in the short run at the very least. This certainly constitutes a national mental health problem and one that calls for serious attention. We should like also to point out more subtle and as yet relatively little studied effects of aggressive material on television. The spate of detective and police shows on television, while generally representing the side of law and order, almost always end up with the good guys shooting the bad guys to death. Obviously the writers' intentions are merely to wind the story up quickly and dramatically but the message in many subtle ways is being communicated to the vast millions viewing that it's okay for the police to shoot down "alleged perpetrators" rather than go through all the trouble of arresting them and bringing them to trial.

Our primary concern in the present paper is to examine more extensively possible ways in which the television medium may be put to use for what might be termed pro-social or constructive social goals as part of the overall socialization process. The presentation here represents essentially a case report on a two-month experience with the children and parents of a day care center in a small industrial city in Connecticut with the subsequent follow-ups carried on over almost a year as part of consultation to the parents of the center. The major focus of our intervention was the study of spontaneous imaginative play shown by the children during the course of the free-play periods in the day care center. The position we took and which will not be detailed here at length was that while all children show a certain amount of pretend or make-believe or socio-dramatic play as an inevitable part of cognitive growth, what Piaget called ludic symbolism, there are interesting differences in the extent to which children engage in such games and interesting consequences for children of the differences in predisposition to imaginative play. For example, a study carried out by Biblow (Singer & Singer, 1973) indicated that children already predisposed to make-believe and fantasy play showed less likelihood of aggressive behavior when frustrated and also after viewing an aggressive television show. Children more predisposed to aggressive play were somewhat inclined to increase the level of aggression following the exposure to the aggresive TV presentation.

The major thrust of our research study was to examine the ways in which exposure to a children's television show, specifically "Misterogers' Neighborhood," would enhance the spontaneous imaginative play of children after several weeks of exposure and would also perhaps increase the level of positive emotionality in the course of play. Briefly, the formal experiment itself which has been extensively described elsewhere (Singer & Singer, 1974) involved a comparison of control group with children watching "Misterogers" daily for two weeks in a group, a second group watching the same program but with an adult serving as a kind of intermediary and translator, and the third group which viewed no television but was provided with a live adult teacher who engaged in a variety of make-believe exercises with the children. The results of this study indicated pretty clearly that exposure to the live adult model had the largest impact on increasing the spontaneousness of the behavior of the children as measured in post-experimental free play periods. Exposure to the "Misterogers" show with the adult intermediary showed the next largest increment, while mere exposure to the television show alone (particularly since the show is slanted at the individual child and there were fifteen viewers in the group) led to only more small increments in make-believe play. By comparison, the control group children showed, if anything, a drop in the occurrence of make-believe play over a six-week period.

In order to carry out this investigation, we felt that it was important to involve ourselves and our staff of eight raters who were unfamiliar with the experimental hypothesis as fully as possible with the school and its director to establish a sense of rapport and to provide the parents with as much opportunity for informed consent concerning their children's participation in the study. This, therefore, included regular meetings with the parents before, during and subsequent to the experimental phase of the study. These meetings afforded us the opportunity to obtain data by the use of questionnaires on television viewing habits and on personal attitudes towards sex role in child rearing and towards the personal and social self-worth on the part of the parents.

While we do have more formal statistical data, our approach in this presentation will be concerned with the general qualitative indications that emerge from our contact with approximately seventy parents whose children attended the day care center. The families involved were all in their twenties and thirties and might be classified best as American-ethnics. That is, they represented persons working in blue-collar or lower level white-collar positions with strong sub-cultural ties to Italian, Ukrainian, Polish, and Irish backgrounds. In most cases the mothers worked at least part time and viewed the day care center as an absolute necessity. Following are some of the more general outcomes that emerged from the questionnaire responses describing children's and family television favorites and extent of viewing. Our data also included self-ratings on child-rearing attitudes, sex role, and a particularly interesting measure of personal and social self-worth, an adjective checklist based on the work of Carlson and Levy (1968).

The general indications were that these families tended to view by far the most popular television shows such as "All in the Family," "I Love Lucy," and the various popular detective/police shows such as "Mannix," "Kung Fu," and so on. A typical family pattern involved the children's viewing of television in the late afternoon on return from school and staying up relatively late so that many of the children viewed a number of the prime time more aggressive television shows, generally in the company of their parents. One mother who by many standards would seem to have been more educated nevertheless reported gleefully how much she enjoyed watching "Creature Features," a monster movie show, with her four-year-old. Because of the nature of the location of the city, educational television was not easily available and so most of the parents and children have never seen "Misterogers" nor "Sesame Street," although they had heard a little bit about these shows, and, as our research went on, parents quickly began to at least say the right things about the value of this type of programming. It seemed quite clear initially that the major import of our survey and interview with the parents was how little thought or attention these basically well-intended and responsible parents paid to the content or extent of television viewing by their children.

When we divided the groups into those whose children showed a greater amount of spontaneous imaginative play compared with those whose children showed the low median scores on spontaneous make-believe play, we found interesting differences both in the mothers' self-reports of style and the quality of television programming viewed in the family. On the self-worth checklist, for example, the mothers of those children who showed more imaginative spontaneous make-believe play tended to significantly more often rate themselves high in Personal Self-worth rather than Social Self-worth. They rated themselves higher on traits such as "ambition," "confidence," "creative," "energetic," "fair-minded," or "idealistic." The mothers of the children who showed significantly less spontaneous imaginative play were more likely to have rated themselves high on variables such as "attractive," "compassionate," "considerate," "cooperative," "friendly," "generous." If we then looked at the television viewing patterns, we found that the parents of the less imaginative children reported both the child's favorite programs and their own as involving aggressive or violent components. Programs such as "Daktari," "Hogan's Heroes," "Kung Fu," and "Gunsmoke" were more likely to be the favorite viewing of both parents and children where the mothers reported higher Social rather than Personal Self-worth scores and also where the children shared lower spontaneous imaginative play.

In other words, there seemed to be a general configuration that emerged in our admittedly small but fairly intensively studied sample. Mothers whose self-orientation was built around major emphasis on independence, thoughtful or internally oriented values tended in some subtle way to communicate this pattern to their children. As other researches we have carried out suggest mothers foster make-believe play through storytelling, and through allowing the children privacy. In addition, such mothers tended to take a more active role in monitoring the TV viewing habits of the children and placed greater emphasis on programming that was less likely to be directly aggressive or violent. Parents whose Self-worth orientation was built more around their relationship to others tended to be less supportive or fostering of imaginative play in their children and also tended to be less concerned about the quality of programming that children viewed or about the likelihood of the children's exposure to aggressive content.

The second phase of our investigation involved watching the children more directly in their response to various of the "Misterogers" programs to see if we could get some clue as to the kinds of materials that particularly held the children's attention. Viewing in a group as large as fifteen is not the ideal situation for the "Misterogers" program, quite frankly. "Misterogers" himself talks directly to the individual child, one presumably viewing alone or with one or two others in a home atmosphere. At the day care center, the groups of fifteen were naturally more restless and less able to concentrate at the slow pace of a program like the "Misterogers" one. Nevertheless the level of concentration was moderately high for three and four year olds for all of the programs. Particularly effective were programs that involved make-believe animals and puppets. What seemed clear was that the building of tension and indeed even moderate aggression as in the "Jack in the Beanstalk" puppet show that took up part of one of the programs will hold attention, produce positive emotional reactions that can be easily recorded, and will reduce the likelihood of overt aggressive behavior in the children. For groups as large as this, the more low-keyed programs such as the one that dealt with books and reading while stimulating a good deal of imaginative play in the children during the program itself failed to hold their attention to the set and in that sense was somewhat less accessible for this type of large audience. Our experience based on analysis of the pattern of the children's behavior as observed by raters during each of the programs used suggests that there are distinct advantages to the use of television with an available adult intermediary as part of day care or nursery facilities provided that the viewing groups are limited to perhaps no more than six and ideally three or four. In settings such as those with the adult initially present and then gradually phasing himself or herself out the gentle message of "Misterogers" and the stimulating quality of his Neighborhood of Make-Believe for imaginative play seems decidedly to be an important positive way in which television can have an impact.

A final phase of this modest form of community intervention included the establishment of parent groups that met through the following year under the direction of one of the authors. What emerged amongst other things from these group meetings with parents was the sense that modestly educated young parents are eager for help in learning how to use the television medium more effectively. They're not always sure that they can control the set. The inevitable family fights over viewing of sports activities necessarily emerge. Nevertheless there seems to be considerable interest in the possibility that help might be forthcoming in deciding on what might be the most appropriate types of television shows for various age levels of children. Parents also needed help with facing some of their own social attitudes. For example, the low-keyed gentlemanly "Misterogers" was perceived by many women and particularly those who took a strongly traditional feminine orientation on one of the scales we employed of sex-role identification as being perhaps too "effeminate"; they felt it wasn't a good idea to expose their sons to this type of programming. It was clear that parents need help in understanding the difference between homosexuality and gentle humanity. For this group of parents anything that smacked of homosexuality was terribly distressing and it required some help for them to see that whatever their prejudices might be they were irrelevant to the quiet and thoughtful approach that "Misterogers" took to the children. But it became quite clear to us in the course of the study that even relatively "liberated" women were inclined to feel that their sons would be in some way distorted in their growth if they were not exposed to vigorously active or aggressive male figures on television. Perhaps one implication of our experience with this group around the "Misterogers" show was that if women's liberation is to become a reality in the more ideal sense, women are going to have to pay more attention to accepting the gentleness in their own sons and to preparing them for more of the tenderness and sensitivity that in the past has been so exclusively emphasized for women.

IMPLICATIONS

The general implications of our experience in this particular mixture of formal experiment with community intervention on a small scale has led to some important directions in which we feel research ought to go in the future. We believe that it is quite feasible to study the ongoing viewing patterns of children to a variety of programming and to rate the children by the use of trained observers on a variety of affective reactions as well as indications of degree of concentration and overt aggressiveness. We believe it is desirable to compare the pattern of viewing and enjoyment of particular programs with response to other programs and also to examine the subsequent outcomes in spontaneous play behavior of persistent viewing of a variety of programs. One obvious question we have has to do with the differential impact of shows such as "Misterogers" with more popular and better known "Sesame Street." There seems little question that the quick cut and lively theatricality of "Sesame Street" may hold children's attention more, particularly if viewed in groups. What remains to be studied more extensively is the degree to which the "message" whether cognitive or attitudinal is grasped by the child. Recent studies of the use of the Fat Albert spots by children indicated that techniques are available for evaluating the degree to which the particular pro-social message may be grasped by a youthful audience. It would seem that little by little psychologists will have to take the trouble to evaluate the socialization impact of widely viewed programs and use this information to feed back suggestions both to parents and producers.

Another implication that grew clearly out of our contact with the parents in the group was the desirability of building into either regular clinical or educational facilities or to consultation programs for parents of children in nursery schools, kindergartens or day care centers some regular systems of obtaining information on parents' viewing habits and then feeding back to the parents suggestions on approaches to monitoring the TV, to viewing the television closely with children and serving as intermediaries or translators. Parents also need to learn methods of clearly limiting the children's exposure. Many parents were genuinely surprised to realize that allowing children to view late night shows might actually increase the possibility of nightmares or overt aggressive behaviors for some of them. Once confronted with some of the research evidence in this connection or with the reasonable alternatives available, parents seemed only too eager to rethink their approach to the children's viewing habits.

One of our theoretical hypotheses that as yet bears more intensive testing has to do with the possibility that children who have been encouraged to develop more extensive imaginative play tendencies are likely to be less influenced by negative content and more capable of integrating pro-social messages perceived from television. It remains to be seen whether this hypothesis can be supported in more formal research, but it appears to us that there is a whole variety of questions of this kind that need to be asked about the interaction of predispositional variables, general parental atmosphere and the response to specific pro-social types of television content (see Appendix).

In conclusion, our position based on this and related experience in observing pre-school children and their response to teaching and television viewing is that there is still a tremendous opportunity for increasing the scope and flexibility of socio-dramatic and imaginative play in most children. Television provides both an exciting viewing situation and interesting and elaborate content which can later be incorporated by children into make-believe play. The problem is that what tends to get incorporated by many children are the more violent aspects of the television content since those are so much the focus of the adult oriented programming to which we found so many really young children exposed. Our position is that interesting and elaborate make-believe themes using both realistic and puppet or fantasy characters abound in life and these can be used in programming or in direct make-believe training for children so that they can be incorporated into the play behavior of the children subsequently. Such imaginative play along with some of the other pro-social kinds of exposure such as the cooperativeness or positive alternatives to aggression in frustration situations that have been dealt with by Stein and Friedrich (1973) seem to us important parts of socialization for all children. Rather than approaching television which is clearly here to stay as a member of our family with negative attitudes either of censorship or helpless scorn, we believe that it is up to psychologists to examine the parameters of the child's imaginative capacities and then find ways in which systematic viewing with adult help can enhance growth possibilities in a variety of constructive areas.

References

CARLSON, R. & LEVY, N. A brief method for assessing social-personal orientation. *Psychological Reports*, 1968, **23**, 911–913.

CBS/Broadcast Group. A study of messages received by children who viewed an episode of "Fat Albert and the Cosby Kids." Office of Social Research, CBS, 1974.

MURRAY, J. P. Television and violence. *American Psychologist*, 1973, **28**, 472–478.

SINGER, J. L. & SINGER, D. G. Fostering imaginative play in pre-schoolers: Television and Live Adult Effects. Paper read at American Psychological Association Convention, New Orleans, 1974.

SINGER, J. L. The influence of violence portrayed in television or movies on overt aggression. In J. L. Singer (Ed.), *The Control of Aggression and Violence*. New York: Academic Press, 1971.

SINGER, J. L. *The Child's World of Make-Believe: Experimental Studies of Imaginative Play*. New York: Academic Press, 1973.

SPRUELL, N. Visual attention, modelling behaviors and other verbal and non-verbal meta-communication of pre-kindergarten children viewing Sesame Street. *American Educational Research Journal*, 1973, **10**, 101–114.

STEIN, L. & FRIEDRICH, L. K. Television content and young children's behavior. In J. P. Murray, E. P. Rubenstein, & G. Comstock (Eds.), *Television and social behavior*. Vol. 2. *Television and Social learning*. Washington, D.C.: U.S. Government Printing Office, 1972.

APPENDIX

THE COMPONENTS OF RESEARCH ON TELEVISION AND CHILDREN

I. Which processes related to TV can we measure
   A. Attention of child to content
      1. Looking behavior
      2. Ongoing behavior
      3. Restlessness or diversion from screen
   B. Affect of the child while watching and after
      1. Ratings of emotion of expressiveness (TV monitor of face—e.g., Ekman)
         Motor tendencies—thumbsucking, gestures, masturbating, sleepiness or boredom, anger
         e.g., evidence of fear as well as aggression or enjoyment
         Mixed emotion—approach-avoidance or puzzlement
      2. Affect after watching
         e.g., liveliness, restlessness, attitude toward following program
      3. Interaction with other children and with set (Misterogers on screen) vs. child alone and with adults [their role]
      4. Predispositional variables—High vs. Low anxiety children, High Fantasy vs. Low Fantasy children, Aggressive vs. Nonaggressive, boys vs. girls, age and stage levels and affective reaction
      5. Imitation as a function of positive or negative affect vs. neutral
      6. Does liveliness hold interest in itself or must there be conflict, danger, aggression, cognitive disconfirmation or novelty, suspense
   C. Cognitive elements
      1. Level of language usage
      2. Complexity of stimuli
      3. Children's comprehension of content [modeling cues—acquisition—imitation/disinhibition/counter imitation
      4. Measures of concept formation and cognitive levels at outset—age levels—predispositional variables (Boehm test)
      5. Changes in convergent and divergent processes [Piagetian notions—animism, conservation] cognitive aspects of humor
II. Outcome measures
   A. Cooperative
      1. Retention of material
      2. Generalization and conceptual level
      3. Insights into conflicts; self-awareness and body image and reality vs. fantasy
      4. Symbolic transformation (e.g., emergence in dreams or spontaneous play)
      5. Vocabulary and language changes and communication (verbal and nonverbal) [Meichenbaum studies on reflective and impulsive children] [Smilansky—critical and injunctive vs. descriptive] Self-references and alternations of role
      6. Imagery evidences—Reyher's semantic elaboration

       7. Competence and mastery level; task persistence

       8. Organization—structuring capacity

  B. Affective

       1. Joy and interest—positive affects, humor and playfulness

       2. Modifications of anger and alternatives to aggression—modeling of coping mechanisms in conflict situations

       3. Fear reduction—dentist, doctor, animals, hair cuts, dark, sleep, separation, strangers

       4. Tenderness, loving-warmth and love for animals, open affection

       5. Empathy, identification of own and others' emotions

  C. Socialization

       1. Cooperative behavior

       2. Sharing [Liebert's modeling and cooperation]

       3. Change in "ethical" level

       4. Self-control and delay

       5. Competence and mastery level

       6. Sociodramatic play—role playing and role reversal

       7. Tolerance for self and others—racial, handicapped

III. Parent and teacher training

  A. Delineation of major training areas

       1. Awareness of cognitive level differences, e.g., vocabulary, grasp of situations

       2. Awareness of stage in social development

       3. Identification of conflicts and negative affects

       4. Communication of positive affects

       5. Awareness of environmental reinforcement contingencies (careful observation)—monitoring behavior

  B. Specific training

       1. Role playing of techniques for conflict resolution or reinforcement

       2. Imaginative games

       3. Expression of own positive affect and awareness of own styles—touching and physical contact

       4. Developing specific dependency or independence

       5. Preparation for specific life situations

          a. Separation and attachment

          b. Sibling rivalries

          c. Need satisfaction and delay of gratification

          d. Doctors, dentists, operations

          e. Refusal to eat, toilet training, sleep resistance, regressive behavior, temper tantrums, social withdrawal, shyness, timidity, sadness

          g. General and specific aggression situations

          h. Natural phenomena—storms, dark

          i. Phobias and compulsions

          j. Development of competencies and failures (e.g., athletics)

Chapter 5
An Overview of Human Life and Growth

All of existence is continuous and related. A search for beginnings and causes of life reveals psychological, physiological, biological, biochemical, and physical structures built upon and of each other.

Every organism and its environment have dynamic, reciprocal relationships. Affecting each other and being affected by each other, neither can be understood without the other, nor can either be what it *is* without the other. The cool air under the tree does not exist without the tree, nor would the tree exist without air. An interesting interaction between plants and landscape can be seen in coastal areas where conservation projects are carried out. A beach that was washed away by a hurricane now stretches smoothly into the Atlantic Ocean, backed by sand dunes built by plants. The plants were dead Christmas trees stuck into the sand and then reinforced by living plants which, finding nutrients and moisture enough in the sand, sent down a network of tough roots, which held the sand in the dunes.

More remarkable even than the building of beaches is the interaction of the human baby with his environment, his family. A human baby grows into a human child as he lives in a human family, calling forth maternal and paternal responses from two adults whose behavior could not be parental if he were not there.

Varieties of Interaction Between the Individual and His World

The story of child development begins with the interactions of a small package of DNA and ends with an adult human being living in a complex social network. Everyone has some beliefs and hypotheses as to how these many changes take place. Nobody has explained it all in a comprehensive theory, but many theorists have described and explained parts of it. A theory depends first of all on the point of view from which the observer looks at the human scene and consequently on the phenomena that he observes. Theories of growth and development usually have a biological flavor. Learning experiments may suggest the influence of physics. Research in social relationships often involves sociology and perhaps anthropology. This chapter deals with six types of interactions that represent different ways of looking at human phenomena. They are equilibration, growth and development, learning, maturation, evolutionary adaptation, and heredity.

Equilibration

The organism constantly regulates its life processes so as to maintain physical and mental states within certain limits.

HOMEOSTASIS

Homeostasis is a balance that the organism maintains within itself during the processes of living and as environmental influences affect its internal conditions. Since the balance is continually upset and re-created, through a complex of interactions, it can be called a *dynamic equilibrium*. Through activities that are mostly unconscious, the individual keeps his blood sugar at a definite level, his water content within a given range, his oxygen content just so. Breathing and heartbeat speed up or slow down from their average rates to restore disturbed balances. The mechanisms of homeostasis regulate sleeping and waking states, activity and rest. Pressures and depleted tissues may register consciously as felt needs, leading to such purposeful interactions with the environment as eating, drinking, and eliminating.

Looming large in the life of a newborn infant, the problems of homeostasis dwindle throughout infancy and childhood. By about 3 months of age, basic physiological processes are well controlled. At any time throughout the life span, however, when the balance is seriously threatened, when biological demands become crucial or urgent, the individual drops his higher-order activities, such as giving a lecture or playing tennis, in order to restore the balance within his body.

PSYCHOLOGICAL EQUILIBRIUM

The search for balance occurs in the mental realm as well as in the physical. Equilibration is the process of achieving a state of balance. Sooner or later, the state of equilibrium is upset and a new one must be created. Equilibration includes selecting stimuli from the world, seeking this or that kind, more or less, paying attention to some of them and using some in more complex mental operations. When you consider all the sounds, sights, tastes, and other perceptions available, it follows that a person could not possibly attend to all of them at once. The mother or principal caretaker protects the infant and young child from excessive stimulation, helping the child gradually to take over the functions of selecting and ignoring stimuli [65].

Equilibration is one of Piaget's principles of mental development [50, pp. 5–8]. Action can be provoked when equilibrium is upset by finding a new object, being asked a question, identifying a problem; in fact, by any new experience. Equilibrium is re-established by reaching a goal, answering a question, solving a problem, imitating, establishing an effective tie or any other resolution of the difference between the new factor or situation and the mental organization already existing. Equilibration results in the successive stages of intelligence that Piaget describes.

Equilibration, in Piaget's theory, includes two complementary processes through which the person proceeds to more complex levels of organization—*assimilation,* which is the taking in from the environment what the organism can deal with and *accommodation,* the changing of the organism to fit external circumstances. Just as the body can assimilate foods and not other substances, so the mind can take in certain aspects and events in the external world and not others. Existing structures or *schemas* incorporate experiences that fit them or that almost fit them.

A schema is a pattern of action and/or thought. A baby develops some schemas before he is born and has them for starting life as a newborn. With simple schemas, he interacts with his environment, working toward equilibration. He achieves equilibrium over and over again, by using the schemas available to him at the moment. For example, a baby has a furry toy kitten that he knows as *kitty.* When given a small furry puppy he calls it *kitty,* strokes it and pats it, assimilating the puppy to an existing schema. A new little horse on wheels requires accommodation, since it is too different to be assimilated into the schema for dealing with *kitty.* It looks different; it feels different; it is not good for stroking and patting, but something can be done with the wheels that cannot be done with *kitty.* A new pattern of action is required. The child accommodates by changing and organizing existing schemas to form a schema for dealing with *horsey.* Thus the child grows in his understanding of the world and his ability to deal with his experiences in meaningful ways. Assimilation conserves the structural systems that he has while accommodation effects changes through which he copes more adequately with his environment and behaves in increasingly complex ways.

When homeostasis presents no problems, such as hunger, thirst, or fatigue, a person looks for something to do, something interesting, a new experience. If equilibrium were completely satisfying in itself, then surely he would sit or lie quietly doing nothing. In looking for action, the child seems to be trying to upset his state of equilibrium, as though equilibration were fun! And so it is. Activity is intrinsic in living tissue, brain cells included. The nervous system demands input, just as the digestive system does. Curiosity, exploration, competence, and achievement motivation are all outgrowths of the human propensity for enjoying the process of equilibration. The first stage of the process, perception of a problem, an incongruity or discrepancy, involves tension and a feeling of incompleteness. Something is missing or something is wrong.

The baby pushes himself forward to grasp a toy that is out of reach. The 4-year-old makes a mailbox that is necessary for his game of postman. The first grader sounds out a new word. Each child reduces a feeling of tension as he creates a new equilibrium. The equilibration (achievement of new balance) makes him into a slightly different person from what he has been, a person who can move forward a bit, a person who has made his own mailbox and can therefore make other things, a person who can read another word. Thus, equilibration is a way of describing behavior development. New and more complex behavior occurs as it is demanded by the person's relationship with his surroundings.

When a person's schemas are adequate to deal with the situation in which he finds himself, he reacts automatically. For example, the response of a hungry breast-fed baby of 3 months would be quite automatic when offered his mother's breast. A 10-year-old would automatically answer the question "What is two times two?" When the schemas are not quite adequate to the situation, the child uses what he has, changing them slightly into actions which do solve the problem. For instance, the baby would change his behavior sufficiently to cope with a bottle and the 10-year-old with "$2x = 4$. What does x equal?" The change that takes place at the same time within the child is the development of a new behavior pattern or schema. A pleasant feeling of curiosity and satisfaction accompanies successful adjustments to demands for new behavior.

A person feels uneasy when he encounters a situation in which his resources are very inadequate. In order to provoke uneasiness, the problem must be somewhat similar to those that a person can solve, but not similar enough for him to succeed with. Such a problem for the baby mentioned might be a cup of milk. For the 10-year-old it might be an equation such as $5x - 49/x = 20x/5$. If the situation is so far removed from a person's past experience that his schemas for dealing with it are extremely inadequate, then he will have no reaction to it. He will not notice it. He will not select from the environment the stimuli that would pose the problem. The baby will not try to drink out of a carton full of cans of milk. The child won't attempt to solve:

$$5x + 6y = 145$$
$$12x - 3y = 21$$

Familiar objects in unfamiliar guise produce unpleasantness, uneasiness, or even fear. (Chimpanzees are afraid of the keeper in strange clothes, an anesthetized chimp, or a plaster cast of a chimp's head. Human babies are afraid of strangers.) In order to be frightened or to get the unpleasant feeling, the subject must first have residues of past experience with which to contrast the present experience. Thus does incongruity arise, with its accompanying unpleasant feeling tone. If the individual can cope with the situation successfully, he achieves equilibration and its accompanying pleasant feeling tone. Stimuli preferred and chosen are those that are slightly more complex than the state of equilibrium that the individual has already reached. Thus he moves on to a new state of equilibrium [51].

Growth and Development

The child's body becomes larger and more complex while his behavior increases in scope and complexity. If any distinction is made between the two terms, growth refers to size, and development to complexity. However, the two terms are often used interchangeably, and this is what we have done. The terms *growth* and *development* were borrowed from the physical field, but they are commonly understood in connection with mental and personality characteristics. One can say, "He has grown mentally," or "He has developed mentally." The statement means "He is now functioning on a more complex intellectual level." Or one can speak of growth of personality and development of attitudes. Listening in on second-grade and fifth-grade classrooms in the same school building will reveal differences in subject matter interests and in mode of thinking.

Growth or development can be shown to have taken place either by comparing younger and older individuals at the same moment of time or by comparing the same individuals at two different points of time. When the measures of some characteristic of a number of individuals are averaged by age groups, the averages of the successive age groups show what growth has taken place. If each individual is measured only once, that is, if there are different people at each age, the study is *cross-sectional*. If the same individuals are measured at each successive age, the study is *longitudinal*. If some individuals do not remain available for continued study and new ones are added, the study is called *mixed longitudinal*. In a cross-sectional study, growth status at each age is investigated, and inferences regarding growth are drawn from *differences* between any groups. *Change* in status from age to age can be inferred only if the individuals at the two ages can be assumed to be comparable in all relevant ways. In a longitudinal study both growth status at each age and change in status from age to age can be investigated more precisely, because the same individuals are involved and actual growth patterns are established for individuals.

PRINCIPLES OF GROWTH

There are a number of generalizations about growth that are more apparent with respect to physical growth but that, as far as research can show, are also true for psychological growth. We elaborate on nine such statements about growth at this point, some of them with subheadings.

Variation of Rates. Rates of growth vary from one individual to another, and they vary within one individual. An organism grows at varying rates, from one time to another. The organs and systems grow at varying rates and at different times. There is a sex difference in rates and terminals. Various group differences can be shown. It is no wonder that comparisons of growth require facts obtained by highly controlled methods.

An organism and its parts grow at rates that are different at different times. The body as a whole, as measured by height and weight, shows a pattern of velocity that is fast in infancy, moderate in the preschool period, slow during the school years, and fast in the beginning of adolescence. Figure 5-1 illustrates growth

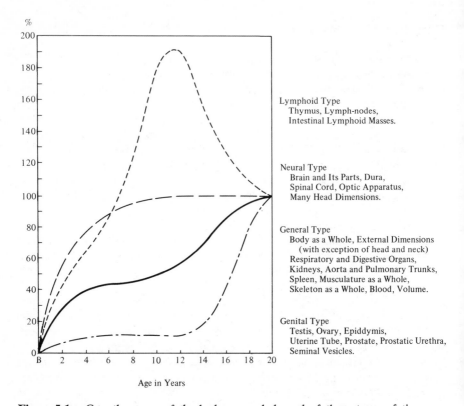

Figure 5-1. Growth curves of the body as a whole and of three types of tissue. Values at each age are computed as percentages of values for total growth.

Source: Reproduced by permission from J. A. Harris, C. M. Jackson, D. G. Paterson, and R. E. Scammon. *The measurement of man*. Minneapolis: University of Minnesota Press, 1930.

of four types of tissue, expressed at each age as percentages of the values for total growth. The general type of growth, which represents not only height and weight but muscles, skeleton, and most of the internal organs, is illustrated by a sigmoid curve, an elongated S. The brain and related tissues grow in a different pattern of velocity, very fast during the first 2 years, moderately until about 6, and very little after that. The growth curve for genital tissue is almost the reverse of that of neural tissue. The genital system grows very little during infancy and childhood and very fast in adolescence. The fourth curve in Figure 5-1 represents the lymph system which grows rapidly throughout infancy and childhood, reaches a peak just before puberty, and then decreases in size throughout adolescence.

Rates of growth vary from one individual to another. Some children are fast growers, some moderate, and some slow in regard to the number of years taken to reach maturity. Periods of fast and slow growth vary as to when they occur and for how long. One child begins the pubescent growth spurt earlier or later than another, grows faster or slower during the spurt, and finishes sooner or later.

There are sex differences in rates. Early in fetal life, girls show evidence of maturing faster than boys, especially in skeletal development. At birth, girls are four weeks ahead of boys skeletally. Boys' skeletal development is about 80 per cent of that of girls' from birth to maturity [59, p. 43]. Girls are ahead of boys in dentition, as measured by eruption of permanent teeth. Although sex differences in height and weight before the preadolescent growth spurt are very slight, favoring boys, sexual maturity and its antecedent growth spurt occur in girls about two years before they do in boys. Therefore, there is a period of about two years when girls are taller and heavier than boys. At all ages, girls are more mature physiologically than boys.

Individual Differences in Terminals. It is obvious, yet it is essential in understanding growth, to recognize that for different people maturity comes at different points. You have only to walk down the street to observe that some people grow until they are over six feet tall, others stop at five feet, and most people stop in between. Measurable mental growth stops at different times for different individuals too. The average girl reaches height and weight terminals before the average boy. Little is known about mental growth terminals.

Dynamic Interrelations in Growth. It would be surprising if different measures of growth were not related to each other. A tremendous number of studies have probed into the question of interrelationships of growth-controlling and regulating mechanisms.

Correlations between measures of growth can be between measures in the same field (physical–physical, mental–mental, and so on), or in different fields (physical–mental, mental–emotional). Skeletal development, assessed by X rays of the wrist, is at present the best indicator of physiological maturity, although if body proportions could be quantified and scaled in some manageable way, this might prove even more useful. Fat thickness in childhood is also a measure of general physiological maturity [24]. Sexual maturity and eventual height can be predicted with good accuracy from measurements of skeletal maturity. A general factor of bodily maturity operating throughout the growth period influences the child's growth as a whole, including his skeleton, size, physiological reactions, and possibly intelligence. Influencing factors of more limited scope operate independently of the general factor and of each other. One of these limited factors controls baby teeth, another permanent teeth, another the ossification centers in the skeleton, and probably several others regulate brain growth. This is why various measures of physical growth have low positive correlations with each other. If there were only one controlling factor, then the different measures would presumably all correlate highly or even perfectly with one another [59].

Studies of the relation between physical and mental growth show a small but consistent positive correlation, bearing out the hypothesis of a general factor that influences all growth processes. This relationship has been documented by a variety of studies [1, 9, 11, 33, 56, 57]. A study of children at the extremes of distributions of mental traits showed gifted boys to be significantly ahead of retarded boys in measures of physical growth [33]. A small positive correlation between mental ability and size is also found in adults [60]. As an example of the relationships between growth and personality, there is evidence that early maturers feel more adequate and more comfortable about themselves than do late maturers [32, 45].

Optimal Tendency. An organism behaves as though it were seeking to reach its maximum potential for development in both structure and function. Even though growth is interrupted, such as in periods of inadequate food supply, the child (or organism) makes up for the lean period as soon as more and better food is available, returning to his characteristic pattern of growth. Only if the deprivation is severe, or if it occurs throughout a critical period, will he show permanent effects from it. During the deprivation period, the organism adapts by slowing growth and cutting down on the use of energy.

All sorts of adaptive arrangements are worked out when there are interferences with the normal course of development, as though the child is determined to reach his best potential by another route when one is blocked. The child with poor eyesight seeks extra information from his other senses. Babies with a tendency toward rickets drink cod liver oil freely if permitted to, selecting their own diets from a wide variety of simple foods [14]. For white children in the northern United States, the characteristics of the home were found to be most important in determining how well the child did at school, but for southern black children the characteristics of the school were more important than those of the home. "It is as if the child drew sustenance from wherever it was available. When the home had more intellectual stimulation to offer, it became more determining; but when the school could provide more stimulation than the home, then the school became the more influential factor." [10, p. 106].

Gesell has stated the principle of optimal tendency as follows. "Every breach in the normal complex of growth is filled through regenerative, substantive, or compensatory growth of some kind. . . . Insurance reserves are drawn upon whenever the organism is threatened. . . . Herein lies the urgency, the almost irrepressible quality of growth" [26, p. 165]. This principle has been recognized as working in physical realms as well as organic, where there seems to be a self-stabilizing or target-seeking property of certain systems [62].

Differentiation and Integration. From large global patterns of behavior, smaller, more specific patterns emerge. Later the small, specific patterns can be combined into new, complicated, larger patterns. For example, a photographic study of human beginnings shows an 11½ weeks' fetus reacting to being stroked on the right cheek [26, p. 25]. The fetus contracted the muscles of its neck, trunk, and shoulder, causing its whole body to bend away from the stimulus and the arms and hands to move backward. When a newborn infant is stroked on the cheek he turns toward the stimulus, pursing his lips and opening his mouth when his lips touch something. Thus, he shows a new, specialized response pattern that involves a small part of his body instead of the whole. As he grows older, the rooting response changes and becomes integrated with other behavior patterns. Instead of turning toward food when he is touched near the mouth, he turns toward the breast or bottle when he sees it. His hands come into play in guiding food toward his mouth. Later he uses a knife and fork. He is integrating behavior patterns of eyes and hands with the rooting pattern, forming a smoothly functioning whole.

Bower analyzes the process of reaching and grasping in terms of differentiation and integration. The newborn baby will reach for a seen object, opening the hand before contact and closing it on contact, but too quickly for hand closure to have been released by the contact. The reaching and grasping is a unitary act. Reaching rarely occurs after 4 weeks, but reappears at around 20 weeks, in a different form. The infant can now reach without grasping and can also combine them. Reaching and grasping are differentiated. Either reaching or grasping can be corrected during the act instead of having to be corrected by starting again. Reaching and grasping are integrated. They are separate but combinable [7, pp. 150–166].

Examples can also be taken from purely intellectual fields, such as mathematics. There is a stage of maturity at the end of infancy when a child knows *one, two* and *a-lot-of*. At 5, he has differentiated *three* and *four* out of *a-lot-of*. By 6, numbers up to ten have true meaning. Using these differentiated concepts, the child next combines them in addition and subtraction to form new and more complicated concepts. Conceptual differentiation and integration are at work as the student moves up through algebra and geometry into higher mathematics. There remains an undifferentiated sphere where each person stops in his progress in mathematics.

Developmental Direction. Certain sequences of development take place in certain directions, in reference to the body. The motor sequence takes two such directions, *cephalocaudal* (head to tail) and *proximodistal* (midline to outer extremities). Like all animals, the child grows a relatively large, complex head region early in life, whereas the tail region or posterior is small and simple. As he becomes older, the region next to the head grows more, and finally, the end region grows. Coordination follows the same direction, the muscles of the eyes coming under control first, then the neck muscles, then arms, chest, and back, and finally the legs. The motor sequence illustrates the proximodistal direction by the fact that the earliest controlled arm movements, as in reaching, are large movements, controlled mostly by shoulder muscles. Later the elbow is brought into play in reaching, then the wrist, and then the fingers.

Normative Sequence. The sequence of motor development has long been noticed and understood as one of the ways of nature. "A child must creepe ere he walke."

As the structures of the body mature in their various sequences, they function in characteristic ways, provided that the environment permits appropriate interaction. The resulting behavior patterns appear in an orderly sequence. Sequences have been described for locomotion, use of hands, language, problem solving, social behavior, and other kinds of behavior [12, 27, 28]. During the decade of the 1930s, the bulk of research in child development was normative, delineating sequences of development and designating average ages for the patterns observed. The classic studies, exemplified by Gesell's work, viewed normative sequences as an unfolding. Although the role of the environment was implicit in these early writings, the focus was on regulation from innate forces. Today interaction between organism and environment is emphasized as basic to development. The change in viewpoint has come about to some extent because of the broadening of areas of child study to include a variety of cultures, at home and abroad. Although child development continues to take place in orderly sequences, exceptions can be found [16]. Hence normative sequences cannot be considered as universal, but must be understood as occurring in particular kinds of environments.

Epigenesis. Growth takes place upon the foundation that is already there. New parts arise out of and upon the old. Although the organism becomes something new as it grows, it still has continuity with the past and hence shows certain consistencies over time. Through interactions with the environment, the organism continues to restructure itself throughout life, being at each moment the product of the interaction that took place in the previous moment between organism and environment. A toddler's body results from interactions of a baby's body with food, water, and air. The motor pattern of walking is derived and elaborated from creeping and standing. Writing is built from scribbling.

Critical Periods. There are certain limited times during the growth period of any organism when it will interact with a particular environment in a specific way. The result of interactions during critical periods can be especially beneficial or harmful. The prenatal period includes specific critical periods for physical growth. The first three months are critical for the development of eyes, ears, and brain, as shown by defects in children whose mothers had rubella during the first three months of pregnancy. Apparently those organs are most vulnerable to the virus of rubella when they are in their periods of rapid growth.

Experiments on vision with human and animal infants reveal critical ages for the development of visual responses, times when the infant will either show the response without experience or will learn it readily [21]. If the visual stimulus is not given at the critical age (as when baby monkeys are reared in darkness), the animal later learns the response with difficulty, or not at all.

Psychological development also shows critical periods in the sense that certain behavior patterns are acquired most readily at certain times of life. Critical periods in personality development include the period of primary socialization, when the infant makes his first social attachments [55] and develops basic trust [18]. A warm relationship with a mother figure is thought to be essential among the experiences that contribute to a sense of trust [8]. This type of critical period is probably not so final and irreversible as is a critical period for the development of an organ in the embryo. If the term *critical period* is applied to the learning of skills such as swimming and reading, then it should be understood that it signifies the most *opportune* time for learning and not the only one [43].

STAGE THEORIES OF DEVELOPMENT

The last three principles of growth are incorporated in theories of child development that present growth occurring in stages. Each stage is created through *epigenesis,* behavior patterns being organized and reorganized or transformed in an orderly sequence. Thus, past, present, and future development are related and can be understood as an ongoing process. Small pieces of behavior can be interpreted in terms of the stage when they occur instead of being invested with one meaning. For example, crying at 1 month of age was seen to be an active attempt to overcome interference with sucking, whereas crying at 1 year of age was found to be a passive mode of response to environmental frustration [36]. Stage theories encourage research that establishes ways of predicting future development [31].

This book is organized in stages of development, leaning heavily on two stage theories: Erikson's theory of personality growth, and Piaget's theory of the growth of intelligence. The ages corresponding with the various stages are only approximations or rough landmarks. Although it is useful to be able to anchor stage concepts to some sort of chronology, it is important to realize that stages are only age-related and not age-determined. The growth principle, *variation of rates,* applies here.

Erikson's Stages. Erikson's theory might be called epigenetic in a double sense. Not only does it portray epigenetic stages but it was built upon Freud's theory and yet is a new organization and a unique creation. Freud proposed psychosexual stages of development, each of which used a certain zone of the body for gratification of the *id* (the unconscious source of motives, strivings, desires, and energy). The *ego,* which mediates between the demands of the id, the outside world, and the superego, "represents what may be called reason and common sense, in contrast to the id, which contains the passions" [23, p. 15]. The *superego* or ego ideal corresponds roughly to *conscience.* Freud's psychosexual stages are *oral,* when the mouth is the main zone of satisfaction, about the first year; *anal,* when pleasure comes from anal and urethral sensations, the second and third years; *phallic,* the third and fourth years, a time of pleasure from genital stimulation; *oedipal,* also genital but now, at 4 and 5 years, the child regards the parent of the opposite sex as a love object and the same-sex parent as a rival; *latency,* from 6 to around 11, when sexual cravings are repressed (made unconscious) and the child identifies with the parent and peers of his own sex; *puberal* when mature genital sexuality begins.

Erikson uses Freud's concepts in his theory of psychosocial development, adding to the complexity of each stage and also adding three stages above the puberal, thus dealing with adulthood as a time for growth. Progress through the stages takes place in an orderly sequence. In making his stages psychosocial as well as psychosexual, Erikson recognizes the interaction between individual and culture as contributing to personal growth. Although Freud's theory has a great deal to say about pathology, Erikson's offers a guide to both illness and health of personality. For each stage, there are problems to be solved within the cultural context. Thus, each stage is a critical period for the development of certain attitudes, convictions, and abilities. After the satisfactory solution of each crisis, the person emerges with an increased sense of unity, good judgment, and capacity to "do well" [19, p. 92]. The conflicts are never completely resolved nor are the problems disposed of forever. Each stage is described with a positive and negative outcome of the crisis involved. The stages are [18, pp. 247–274]:

1. *Basic trust versus basic mistrust.* Similar to Freud's oral stage, the development of a sense of trust dominates the first year. Success means coming to

trust the world, other people, and oneself. Since the mouth is the main zone of pleasure, trust grows on being fed when hungry, pleasant sensations when nursing, and the growing conviction that his own actions have something to do with pleasant events. Consistent, loving care is trust-promoting. Mistrust develops when trust-promoting experiences are inadequate, when the baby has to wait too long for comfort, when he is handled harshly or capriciously. Since life is never perfect, shreds of mistrust are woven into the fabric of personality. Problems of mistrust recur and have to be solved later, but when trust is dominant, healthy personality growth takes place.

2. *Autonomy versus shame and doubt.* The second stage, corresponding to Freud's anal period, predominates during the second and third year. Holding on and letting go with the sphincter muscles symbolizes the whole problem of autonomy. The child wants to do for himself with all of his powers: his new motor skills of walking, climbing, manipulating; his mental powers of choosing and deciding. If his parents give him plenty of suitable choices, times to decide when his judgment is adequate for successful outcomes, then he grows in autonomy. He gets the feeling that he can control his body, himself, and his environment. The negative feelings of doubt and shame arise when his choices are disastrous, when other people shame him or force him in areas where he could be in charge.

3. *Initiative versus guilt.* The Oedipal part of the genital stage of Freudian theory, at 4 and 5 years, is to Erikson the stage of development of a sense of initiative. Now the child explores the physical world with his senses and the social and physical worlds with his questions, reasoning, imaginative, and creative powers. Love relationships with parents are very important. Conscience develops. Guilt is the opposite pole of initiative.

4. *Industry versus inferiority.* Solutions of problems of initiative and guilt bring about entrance to the stage of developing a sense of industry, the latency period of Freud. The child is now ready to be a worker and producer. He wants to do jobs well instead of merely starting them and exploring them. He practices and learns the rules. Feelings of inferiority and inadequacy result when he feels he cannot measure up to the standards held for him by his family or society.

5. *Identity versus role diffusion.* The Freudian puberal stage, beginning at the start of adolescence, involves resurgence of sexual feelings. Erikson adds to this concept his deep insights into the adolescent's struggles to integrate all the roles he has played and hopes to play, his childish body concept with his present physical development, his concepts of his own society, and the value of what he thinks he can contribute to it. Problems remaining from earlier stages are reworked.

6. *Intimacy versus isolation.* A sense of identity is the condition for the ability to establish true intimacy, "the capacity to commit himself to concrete affiliations and partnerships and to develop the ethical strength to abide by such commitments" [18, p. 263]. Intimacy involves understanding and allowing oneself to be understood. It may be, but need not be, sexual. Without intimacy, a person feels isolated and alone.

7. *Generativity versus self-absorption.* Involvement in the well-being and development of the next generation is the essence of generativity. While it includes being a good parent, it is more. Concern with creativity is also part of it. Adults need to be needed by the young, and unless the adults can be concerned and contributing, they suffer from stagnation.

8. *Ego integrity versus despair.* The sense of integrity comes from satisfaction with one's own life cycle and its place in space and time. The individual feels that his actions, relationships, and values are all meaningful and acceptable. Despair arises from remorseful remembrance of mistakes and wrong decisions plus the conviction that it is too late to try again.

Figure 5-2 shows the normal timing of Erikson's stages of psychosocial development. The critical period for each stage is represented by a swelling of the rope that stretches throughout life. The ropes indicate that no crisis is ever solved completely and finally, but that strands of it are carried along, to be dealt with at different levels. As one rope swells at its critical period, the other ropes are affected and interact. Solutions to identity problems involve problems in all the other stages. The metaphor of the rope can also be extended by thinking of the personalities of a family's members as being intertwined ropes. When the parents' Generativity strands are becoming dominant, the infant's Trust strand is dominant. The two ropes fit smoothly together, indicating a complementary relationship between the personalities of infant and parents.

Piaget's Stages. Figure 5-2 shows Piaget's stages in the development of intelligence. Piaget is concerned with the nature of knowledge and how it is acquired. His studies of infants and children have revealed organizations of structures by which the child comes to know the world. The structural units are *schemas,* patterns of action and/or thought. As the child matures, he uses his existing schemas to interact, transforming them through the process of equilibration. Each stage of development is an advance from the last one, built upon it by reorganizing it and adapting more closely to reality. Reorganization and adaptation go on continuously, but from one time to another the results differ from each other. Piaget has broken this series of organizations of structures into units called *periods* and stages. There are three periods, each of which extends the previous one, reconstructs it, and surpasses it [51, pp. 152–159]. Periods are divided into stages that have a constant sequence, no matter whether the child achieves them at a slow or fast pace. Progress through the periods and stages is affected by organic growth, exercise and experience, social interaction or equilibration. The periods are

1. *Sensorimotor.* Lasting from birth until about 2, sensorimotor intelligence exists without language and symbols. Practical and aimed at getting results, it works through action-schemas [51, p. 4]. Beginning with the reflex patterns present at birth, the baby builds more and more complex schemas through a succession of six stages. Figure 5-2 lists the names of the stages. During this period the baby constructs a schema of the permanence of objects. He comes to know that things and people continue to exist even when he cannot see them and he realizes that they move when he is not looking. He learns con-

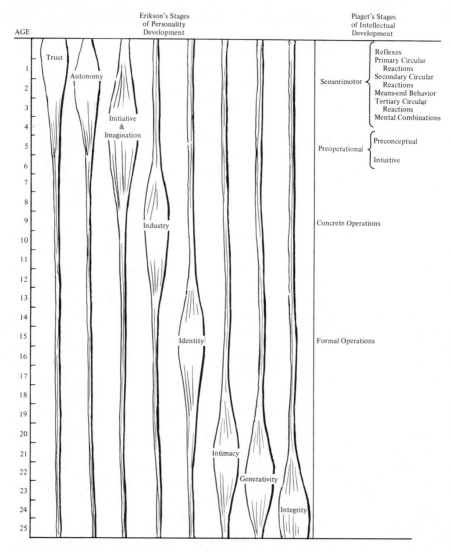

Figure 5-2. Schematic representation of Erikson's stages of psychosocial development, with names of Piaget's stages of the development of intelligence.

trol of his body in space. He begins to use language to imitate and to make internal representations of reality.

2. *Preoperational.* Sometimes this period, from about 2 to 7, is considered a subperiod of the whole time from 2 to 11. It is distinctly different, however, from the sensorimotor period and the period that comes around 7, the period of concrete operations. Two stages, preconceptual and intuitive thought, are

included. The preoperational period is marked by the *semiotic* function and imitation. The semiotic function, often called *symbolizing,* is the use of an indicator or sign as distinct from the object or event to which it refers [51, pp. 52–91]. For example, the bell that announces dinner is perceived as distinct from the food but as indicating food. Achievements show much use of his new representational abilities, in deferred imitation (imitation starting after the model has disappeared), symbolic play, drawing, mental images, and verbal representation. The child thinks that names are essential parts of the objects to which they refer. When he gives a reason, it is in terms of how he wants things to be. He sees no need to come to the same conclusions as anyone else because he does not realize the existence of viewpoints other than his own. Throughout this stage the child becomes more flexible in his thinking, more able to use past experience, and to consider more than one aspect of an event at a time.

3. *Concrete operations.* The period from about 7 to 11 years of age is essentially the time when the child can think about real, concrete things in systematic ways, although he has great difficulty in thinking about abstractions. He orders, counts, classifies, and thinks in terms of cause and effect. He develops a new concept of permanence, called *conservation,* through which he realizes that amount, weight, volume, and number stay the same when outward appearances of objects or groups are changed. Although he finds it difficult to change his hypotheses, he learns to take other people's points of view and comes to feel that his reasoning and his solutions to problems should check with other people's. His thinking has become socialized.

4. *Formal operations.* The period of formal operations or logical thought begins at about 11 and continues to develop until about 15, when the individual has the mental operations for adult thinking. Instead of having to think about concrete objects, he can think and reason in purely abstract terms. He can think systematically, combining all factors in a situation so as to exhaust all possibilities. He makes hypotheses and tests them. This type of thinking is basic to logic and to the scientific method. The limitation of this stage is a confusion of what could and should be with what is practically possible. The adolescent resists the imperfections in the world when he can construct ideal arrangements in his mind.

Memory

Both remembering and learning refer to changes in the organism that result from interactions with the environment. In remembering, as in all interactions, the child brings his own resources to bear on the particular environment in which he lives. Some cultures stress memorizing more than others do. Children may be encouraged and assisted in remembering what is considered important to remember. Until recently, it was important for a Maori to be able to recite the names of his ancestors, right back to the one who came to New Zealand in a particular one of the canoes that brought the first Maoris. Because textbooks are scarce in India, college students memorize extensively. In North America, organizing and understanding are often preferred to memorizing.

Memory means the storing of experience within the person, in all likelihood in his brain, in such ways that he can hold it and retrieve it. *Learning* occurs when behavior changes as a result of experience. Therefore, many learning experiments involve memory and many memory experiments involve learning. For many years, psychologists have been exploring the conditions under which children learn everything from swimming to moral behavior. More recently, scientists from different disciplines have been trying to discover the processes by which human beings take in information from their senses, process it, store it, and take it out for use when they need it.

THE STRUCTURES AND PROCESSES OF MEMORY

The *hippocampus,* a deep part of the brain, is a place where memories are made, or, more exactly, the hippocampus is essential for the process of long-term storing of new experience in retrievable form [44]. Biochemical changes occur in the brain as the processes of memory are carried on. One of the mysteries of the process is the form in which the brain stores experience and the method by which it converts perceptual input into items that can be stored and found for later use. Pribram suggests that memory works on the principle of the *hologram* (a construct from physics), a mechanism that codes 10 billion bits of information in the space of about a cubic centimeter [52].

The various sense organs react to stimuli. The processes of attention select certain features. *Perception* involves analyzing stimuli, first in terms of physical or sensory features and later matching them with stored memories and extracting meaning. If processing continues to a deeper level, the material is enriched by associating it with additional stored material. Thus, more meaning is added. A theory of memory holds that the more deeply a stimulus is processed, the longer and more fully it is remembered [13]. Some researchers think that there are different storage structures for long-term and short-term memory, but others think that the same processes are at work and that the level of processing determines how long and how well an experience will be remembered.

The term *control processes* refers to the ways in which an individual uses his perceptual processes, puts material into his memory store (or stores), and finds (retrieves) the stored material when he wants it. The methods of analyzing and coding material and extracting meaning from it will depend, of course, on the type of mental operations used. As Piaget has shown, mental operations are stage-related, depending upon the maturity and experience of the child. Some control processes can be modified by the individual as he adapts to new conditions and learns new techniques [53]. "Learning to learn" includes adopting new patterns of control that improve remembering.

Developmental research deals with age-related changes in the various aspects of memory. Topics include long-term and short-term memory and their connections with each other and with input, response, and control systems. Experimenters vary input, such as visual or verbal, color or form. They require different responses, such as recall or recognition, after different time lags. They consider the effects of intelligence and nutrition, and even of sibling position [13, 53].

Learning

Learning occurs when behavior changes as a result of experience. Behavior includes inner processes as well as actions. Different approaches to the study of learning give different emphases. Some of the terms of behaviorism focus on something being done to the learner. Thus, the learner may be seen as passive. *Behavior shaping,* for example, sounds very much like a "psychosculptor" hewing out a neat set of behavior patterns from a rough bundle of mass activity. (Such is not really the case, as is seen later.) Presently, however, the self is seen as an active shaper of personal destiny, as evaluator, decision-maker, and active learner. The view of self as active is illustrated in the following section on academic learning and in the discussion of social learning. The self can also be seen as active in reinforcement and conditioning.

ACADEMIC LEARNING

A new way of measuring and understanding school learning is offered by Bloom's use of *time* as a yardstick [6]. A child takes a measurable length of time to reach criteria of achievement in reading, mathematics, science, literature, a foreign language, and so on. Bloom reviews studies of the length of time required by children in different countries to reach the same criteria. The average student in the highest-scoring of the developed nations achieved 12 years of learning in 12 years. For children in low-scoring developed nations, the achievement was 8 years in 12 years. The average child in an underdeveloped country achieved 6 years in 12 years. United States research has shown that if the highest 20 per cent of students reach the criterion level one year, 50 per cent will reach it the next year and 80 per cent in 2 years. When mastery teaching is used and students spend extra time during the first year in learning, 80 per cent can reach the same criterion as the upper 20 per cent in one year. (Mastery teaching includes identifying gaps in learning and then using corrective procedures designed especially for the child's particular needs.)

When mastery learning procedures are first offered to students who are not learning fast, the slowest 5 per cent of learners take about five times as long to reach criterion as do the fastest 5 per cent of learners. After achieving several learning units through mastery procedures, the slowest learners reach criterion in three times or less what was required by the fastest. Thus, it pays off to help the slow learners in the early stages. Most likely they will increase in self-esteem and self-confidence as they achieve more and as they learn more effective ways of learning.

Further studies reviewed by Bloom show that the fastest learners spend more time *on task,* or actually learning. From both observation and interviews, the fast learners were found to spend large amounts of time in school actively engaged with the subject matter. Slower learners were likely to spend the first 20 minutes talking, arranging their materials, and fixing their hair and clothing. Then they worked for about 20 minutes. The next 15 or 20 minutes were spent getting ready to leave. *Time on task* explains many of the differences between fast learners and slow learners. In ghetto schools, apathy and hostility depress the amount of time spent on task. Here and in poor countries, hunger and malnutrition contribute to apathy.

Although human beings vary in their initial learning ability, all need to learn basic academic subjects in order to get along in the modern world. Nearly all can learn them if enough time is allowed, but nearly all can learn them much faster and with greater satisfaction if teaching procedures enlist all of their learning potential.

Social Learning

One of the most remarkable features of human beings is that they learn so much and so easily from one another. People learn from the experience of those who lived in the past as well as from face-to-face encounters, learning from others' errors and successes instead of having to try out all kinds of actions. Very often, a person can acquire a new piece of behavior by simply watching another person perform it or by listening to the other person telling how to do it. However, a learner does not imitate everything she sees or hears. She chooses to do what is rewarding, or what she thinks will have positive reinforcement value.

SOCIALIZATION

Children learn by observing their parents and listening to them. Parents teach children through a variety of techniques, as they *socialize* the children. *Socialization* is the teaching done by members of a group or institution in order that the individual will learn to think, feel, and behave as a member of that group. Socialization occurs in people of all ages, but much of it takes place during childhood, as the developing person acquires appropriate values, attitudes, and behavior patterns. Parents are the primary socializers. Siblings and other family members also teach. Teachers and peers are important socializing agents as are, to a lesser extent, other members of the community.

Socialization refers to both the present and the future. The child learns to behave appropriately as the child he now is, but he also learns attitudes, values, and skills that he will use in the future. From interacting with his father, he learns the father role as well as the son role. Similarly, he observes his various socializers as worker, manager, host, citizen, and teacher, and in all the many roles that they play in his society. The child learns some specific information and skills, as well as values and attitudes. Thus, he is gradually socialized into his family, community, and nation through a process that maintains the values and behavior patterns of that group.

MODELING

Infants begin to imitate toward the end of the sensorimotor period. Piaget observes that imitation is always active, never automatic or nonintentional [49]. Imitation is accommodation, a way of modifying present schemas. Imitation is the child's first mode of representing an action. Throughout life, imitation continues to serve as an important mode of learning.

Bandura, who has conducted basic experiments on observational learning, concludes that "virtually all learning phenomena resulting from direct experience can occur on a vicarious basis by observing other people's behavior and its consequences for them" [4]. An action can be learned from one observation. It can be stored for a long time, to be used if and when an appropriate time comes.

Influences on Modeling. Although children will imitate spontaneously, various factors and circumstances have been shown to affect whether they do imitate. Age and developmental level are related to whether children will imitate the ways in which toys are manipulated [22]. The child's past experience with peers affects his tendency to imitate peers [29]. Children who had often been reinforced by peers were more likely to imitate a rewarding peer; children who had seldom been reinforced by peers were more likely to imitate a nonrewarding peer. What happens to the model also has an effect on the child. In one of Bandura's famous experiments, children saw a film of an aggressive model either being punished, rewarded, or having no consequences [3]. Then they were left in a room with the aggressed-against clown and the instruments of aggression, as well as other toys. Those who saw the model being punished did less imitating of his aggressive behavior than did those who saw the model being rewarded or having no consequences. When the children were offered reinforcers for imitating the aggression, the difference between the groups disappeared. Boys imitated more aggressive acts than girls after seeing the model punished, but when rewards were given, the sex difference disappeared. Thus, it seems that children inhibit aggressive imitation when they see the model punished, but they learn the behavior just as readily. Girls are more inhibited than boys by punishment for aggression, but they learn the behavior just as well. Bandura says that one of the most interesting questions in regard to modeling is whether one can keep people from learning what they have seen [4]. Presumably the answer is *no*.

These experiments, and many additional ones, give insight into modeling, but they cannot predict what a given individual will imitate. The situation is analogous to language. One can test a child's level of language development, but one cannot tell just what the child will say. Modeling involves abstracting from what is observed, storing it in memory in some symbolic form, making generalizations and rules about behavior, mentally putting together and trying out different kinds of behavior, and choosing which forms to act out at what times. Thus, other people's behavior is used creatively by the individual in an extraordinarily efficient way of developing new ways of acting that are suited to the particular occasion. Bandura has summarized the component processes of observational learning [4].

Component Processes. First, *attention* regulates the perception of modeled actions. Second, what is observed is transformed into representations that are preserved in *memory*. Coding and symbolic rehearsal make these transformations. Memory keeps the symbolically represented actions available as guides to performance. Third, new response patterns are integrated from *motor* acts. Fourth, *incentive* or *motivational* processes govern the choice of action patterns to be used.

Thus, it is the *person* who actively observes, remembers, judges, decides, and creates a response. The person's own values are the context in which the processes of modeling occur.

CONDITIONING

Conditioning, or learning by association, is the establishing of a connection between a stimulus and a response. In *classical conditioning,* the kind made famous by Pavlov, a neutral stimulus is presented with another stimulus that elicits an innate response. After several such presentations, the neutral stimulus is given without the other stimulus and the response occurs. Pavlov sounded a buzzer when he gave food to his dog. Eventually the dog salivated at the sound of the buzzer.

Operant, or *instrumental,* conditioning is done by rewarding the desired response whenever it occurs. Operant conditioning techniques have been developed for use in a wide variety of situations, with animal and human subjects. By rewarding small pieces of behavior, complex patterns can be built up, thus "shaping" or modifying the behavior of the subject. This technique has proven to be very useful in treating behavior disorders in infants, children, retardates, and the mentally ill.

Conditioning has been used to explore the abilities of infants and to show that newborn babies do learn [37]. Papoušek taught newborn babies to turn their heads to the sound of a buzzer by using a combination of classical and operant conditioning methods [47]. A bell was sounded and if the infant turned to the left, he was given milk. If he did not turn, head turning was elicited by touching the corner of his mouth with a nipple. Then he was given milk. Newborns were slow to condition, taking an average of 18 days, whereas at 3 months, only 4 days were required and by 5 months, 3 days were required. Two-month-old infants learned to operate a mobile by means of pressing their heads on their pillows [63].

REINFORCEMENT

Reinforcements are consequences of events, or so they are seen by the subject. A *positive* reinforcement makes the reoccurrence of the event more likely, a *negative* reinforcement, less likely. Positive reinforcement functions not only through being pleasant or rewarding but because it gives information, such as, "That was right," "You succeeded." Likewise, negative reinforcement is not only unpleasant; it informs the person, "You did wrong." Reinforcement is, therefore, not just a mechanical procedure by which one person manipulates another, but a means by which people can regulate their own behavior [4].

Reinforcement comes from both external and internal sources. People reward themselves when they think they have done well and punish themselves when they fail or do wrong. Or they may try to cheer themselves up after failure, by a reward. The reinforcement may be just a comment to oneself, such as "That was a great job!" Or a person may buy a present for herself or indulge in a fancy dessert. Children's self-rewarding behavior has been studied under various conditions. Although preschool children tend to reward themselves liberally [35], school-age children make complex judgments about giving themselves appropriate reinforcements. School-age children rewarded themselves differently for different types of altruistic behavior [40]. They also apparently considered the length of task and quality of performance in dispensing self-rewards [39]. Thus do children evaluate and direct their own behavior. When children receive inappropriate reinforcement at school, their learning behavior is likely to be depressed [30].

Modern behavior modification programs take account of the individual's capacity for self-regulation rather than simply administering external reinforcements [4]. The person who wants to change his behavior is helped to plan inducements for the desired behavior, to evaluate his own performance, and to dispense the reinforcers.

Successful socialization of children also makes use of children's growing powers of self-regulation. Even if behavior could be controlled by extrinsic rewards and punishments, the result would be a child who could not control herself. And, of course, external rewards and punishments will not give predictable results because the child herself is also active in the process. Experiments with adults have shown that external rewards and punishments sometimes decrease self-motivation [46]. The reason may be that the person sees himself as less self-controlled and with less freedom of choice when someone else is dispensing reinforcements.

Punishment especially is a risky technique of influence. Although punishment is often effective in suppressing behavior, it does not teach new, positive behavior. Parke has summarized the effects of punishment on children as shown by research [48]. Punishment suppressed behavior more effectively when it occurred close in time to the deviation. High-intensity punishment was more effective than low, but when it occurred promptly, high- and low-intensity punishment were equally effective. When the adult withdrew affection or was inconsistent with affection, children were likely to suppress undesired behavior in order to win back the affection. When reasoning and explanation accompanied punishment, light punishment was as effective as severe. Reviewing the deviance had the same effect. Inconsistency delayed the effect. Indiscriminate and harsh punishment may make the child avoid the punisher or may lead to passivity and withdrawal.

Maturation

As the child's bodily structures grow, they change in size and complexity, becoming more and more the way they will be in the mature state. Bodily functions likewise change as the structures do. The whole process is called *maturation*. Although maturation is controlled by hereditary factors, the environment must be adequate to support it. The growth principle of normative sequence is reflected in maturation, since structures and functions mature in an orderly, irreversible sequence. Since maturation is little affected by experience, its effects are the same throughout a species. An impoverished environment slows the process of maturation more than it changes quality or sequence.

Certain behavior patterns are the result of maturation more than of learning because they are relatively independent of experience. Many developmental processes involve both maturation and learning. Examples of processes that are largely maturational are the motor sequence and the emergence of language. In all but the most abnormal environments, infants go through regular sequences of raising the head, raising the chest, sitting, creeping, standing with support, and so on.

Another explanation of maturation is that certain experiences are encountered by everyone and are, therefore, not recognized as experience. Behavior patterns attributed to maturation are really the results of interactions with the universal environment. For instance, everyone makes postural adjustments to gravity, but nobody notices gravity. Another example is that everyone learns to chew food because everyone receives food. The emergence of language is a response to an almost universal experience, the hearing of spoken language.

Some theories of development, such as Gesell's, emphasize the role of maturation in determining behavior. Gesell's descriptions of behavior stages led some parents to think that they could do little to influence their children's behavior and that they must enjoy his good stages and wait patiently while he grew out of unattractive, annoying, or disturbing stages. In contrast, although Piaget recognizes that the body matures, he stresses the necessity for the child to interact, explore, and discover for himself in order to build his mental structures. Mental growth cannot be forced or hurried, however, since its counterpart is physical maturation. "Mental growth is inseparable from physical growth: the maturation of the nervous and endocrine systems, in particular, continues until the age of 16" [51, p. vii].

Evolutionary Adaptation

Evolutionary changes can be considered in terms of behavior patterns or behavior systems.

ETHOLOGY

The behavior patterns that develop through maturation can be traced back in the history of the species or the phylum. These fixed action patterns evolved as the animal adapted to a certain environment. *Ethology,* the study of the relation between animal behavior and environment, has influenced the study of human development, offering insight into certain kinds of behavior that cannot be explained as learning or fully understood as maturation. Lorenz pointed out the implications of ethology for understanding certain forms of human behavior [38]. Bowlby has integrated psychoanalytic theory with ethology [8]. Ainsworth [2] has done extensive research on attachment behavior, a main focus of the ethological approach to human development.

The adaptive behavior pattern becomes fixed in form, appearing as an innate skill in every member of a species, even though he has not had opportunities to learn [17]. A specific stimulus from the environment activates the particular behavior pattern, as though it were a key, unlocking the mechanism. Thus, the behavior is sometimes called an *innate response mechanism,* or IRM. For example, a toad's catching response is released by a small, moving object, a nine-week-old gosling gives an intense fear reaction to his first sight of a hawk, and a stickleback fish will attack a red spot that resembles the red underbelly of another stickleback.

Bowlby points out that the environment to which a species is adapted is the environment in which it evolved into its present form [8, p. 59]. Most likely, when man first emerged as a distinct species, he lived by hunting and gathering in a savannah environment, much like today's most primitive societies and not unlike the ground-dwelling primates [2]. Mother–infant reciprocal behavior was adapted to protecting the infant so as to ensure his survival. The baby's unlearned, spontaneous patterns of crying, clinging, and sucking brought him (and still bring him) into contact with the mother. Other aspects of attachment behavior, maturing a little later, serve to maintain and strengthen the contacts with the mother, who was (and still is) adapted or genetically programmed to respond with specific action patterns. In the urban environment of today, close physical contact of mother and baby is not necessary for protecting the baby from predators, but babies still behave as though it were and mothers still respond to their infants' behavior with innate action patterns. Closeness of mother and baby has other advantages, however, in terms of normal development.

BEHAVIOR SYSTEMS

Ascending the evolutionary scale, the nervous system and brain become more complex. Their first function is to control and integrate the other bodily systems and organs. In the higher animals and most notably in man, the cognitive system has its own needs and demands, in addition to its function as controller and co-ordinator. Curiosity, information seeking, and exploration are modes of obtaining what the cognitive system must have in order to function optimally. Dember maintains that the brain is not like a computer that acts only on demand, but rather it is "an instrument with needs of its own" [15]. Cognitive actions may even result in states that oppose the demands of other systems. Ideas or ideologies can be so strong that the person harms his own body or even kills himself. Such is the case with martyrs, political prisoners resisting torture, and people who accept dares.

Disharmony between behavioral systems is also discussed by Wolff [64]. He points out that different behavioral systems have evolved at different times and with considerable independence between them. Autonomic reactivity appears first followed by organized reflex action and diffuse nonreflex activity. Next, the voluntary behavior system develops and then language. Although all systems influence each other to some extent, there are times when a person's actions do not coincide with her feelings, or words with actions. Many therapies and techniques are presently trying to bring these systems into closer relationships. Such methods include Gestalt techniques, yoga, meditation, brain-wave conditioning, and control of the autonomic system. Wolff suggests that success in these efforts will have survival value for the species and may bring happiness to the individual.

Heredity

Although most students of child development will study the mechanisms of heredity in a biology course, we include a brief account here. After all, the mechanisms of heredity are what start the child developing and guide the course of development.

BIOLOGICAL INHERITANCE

The human being is composed of two main types of cells. By far the larger number of cells are the *body* cells. These are the cells that compose the skeleton, skin, kidneys, heart, and so on. A minority of cells are the *germ* cells. In the male, germ cells are called *spermatazoa* (the singular is *spermatazoon*), usually shortened to *sperm:* in the female, the germ cells are *ova* (the singular is *ovum*).

Each body cell is composed of several different parts, the most important of which for our present discussion are the *chromosomes,* of which there are 46, arranged in 23 pairs. The sizes and shapes of the chromosomes can be determined by viewing a prepared cell through an electron microscope. Twenty-two of the pairs of chromosomes are composed of two highly similar chromosomes, though each pair differs in certain respects from every other pair. These 22 pairs are similar in males and females. In males, the twenty-third pair is composed of two chromosomes that are unequal in size. The larger one is an *X chromosome;* the smaller is a *Y chromosome.* In females, the twenty-third pair is composed of two X chromosomes. When, in the course of growth, a body cell divides to form two

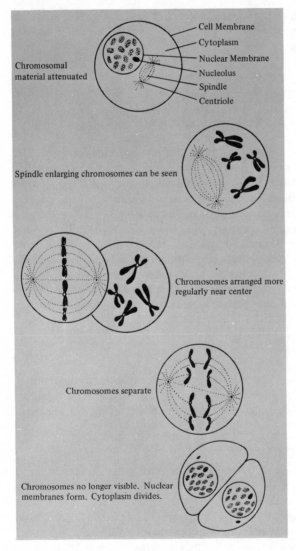

Figure 5-3. Stages in the process of mitosis.

SOURCE: Adapted from P. A. Moody. *Genetics of man.* New York: W. W. Norton & Company, Inc., 1967. Figure 3–2, p. 28.

Cell Membrane
Cytoplasm
Nuclear Membrane
Nucleolus
Spindle
Centriole

Chromosomal material attenuated

Spindle enlarging chromosomes can be seen

Chromosomes arranged more regularly near center

Chromosomes separate

Chromosomes no longer visible. Nuclear membranes form. Cytoplasm divides.

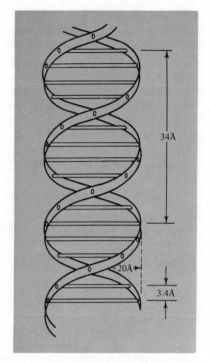

Figure 5-4. DNA takes the form of a double helix.

SOURCE: Adapted from G. W. Burns. *The science of genetics*. New York: Macmillan Publishing Co., Inc. 1969. Figure 14–9, p. 258.

new cells, it goes through the process of *mitosis*. The result of mitosis is that each of the new cells has exactly the same kind and number of chromosomes as the first cell had before it divided. Figure 5-3 shows the process of mitosis.

DNA, a substance in the chromosomes, is the carrier of the genetic code that transmits characteristics from one generation to the next. Figure 5-4 shows a model of the DNA molecule, in the shape of a double helix or spiral ladder. The *genes,* carriers of specific instructions for growth, are arranged in linear order on the spirals. The two spirals can come apart like a zipper. Then each half produces another half.

Dominant and Recessive Genes. A story [58] that might be called *science prediction* rather than *science fiction* went like this: a young couple had been quietly holding hands in a secluded corner of the campus. Then one of them said, "Let's match cards." Each pulled out a printed card containing a few holes. They put one on top of the other. None of the holes matched. They embraced happily. Like most human beings, each carried a few dangerous recessive genes out of the thousand or more that can cause birth defects. Since it takes a recessive gene from each parent to produce a characteristic that does not show in either parent, the young couple could safely plan to have children. Or if not with complete assurance, at least they would know that they were not endangering their future children as far as their own dangerous recessives were concerned. Suppose two of the holes had matched such that each of the couple was carrying a recessive gene for cystic fibrosis. For each conception, chances would be one in four for a child with two recessives and hence having cystic fibrosis, two in four for a child carrying one recessive, like the parents, and not showing the defect, and one in four for a normal child with two normal genes. And suppose they conceived a defective embryo. It could be diagnosed early in pregnancy and aborted, if they so chose.

Although at the moment when this is being written, the story is only prediction, the technology on which it is based is of the present. Many physical characteristics, including a large number of defects, are inherited according to simple Mendelian law, as illustrated in our story. Some other defects, such as color blindness, are sex linked, which means that they are dominant in the male and recessive in the female. A male shows the defect when he carries only one gene for it, but the female does not suffer unless she has two such genes.

Heredity works in more complicated ways, also. Genes work in concert with one another and with the environment. The mechanisms of *crossing over* and *independent assortment* add enormously to the variety of genetic combinations that are possible. Genes "turn on" and off at various times during the life cycle. For example, the control of sexual maturation is considerably influenced by heredity.

Gene Blends. Many characteristics are the results of more than one pair of genes. Skin color in human beings is such a characteristic. It is not determined in all-or-none way, as is seed color in peas. Rather, in spite of popular belief to the contrary, a child's skin color is almost never darker than the skin of the darker parent, nor lighter than the skin of the lighter parent. If the child's skin is darker than either parent's, it is only a shade darker. At least two pairs of genes are considered to be active in determining skin color; there may be three or more.

Standing height is another human characteristic that is the result of many different genes working at least in part in a literally additive way, although blending of the kind that determines skin color may also be operating. A human being's height is the sum of the lengths of many different bones and many pieces of cartilage. Each bone's length is probably determined by one or more genes, and varies somewhat independently of the length of every other bone. Height is, therefore, a *polygenic* trait. (In addition, of course, the variation in heights of a group of individuals is affected by environmental factors such as diet and disease.)

Meiosis. Although each individual receives the chromosomes from germ cells of the parents, the offspring of the same parents do not receive identical chromosomes. The explanation of this difference between brothers and sisters lies in the process of *meiosis,* the formation of germ cells, sperm and ova.

Figure 5-5 shows the development of sperm that contain only two single chromosomes, since to show 23 chromosomes would unnecessarily complicate the diagram. In the diagram the primordial germ cell, the *spermatogonium,* is shown as containing two pairs of chromosomes. In the process of meiosis, the spermatogonium divides into two cells called *secondary spermatocytes,* each of which has one of the members of each pair of chromosomes. Each chromosome is composed of two *chromatids.* Each spermatocyte divides into two *spermatids,* each of which has one of the chromatids from the eight chromatids that are shown to have been in the original spermatogonium. From each spermatid develops a sperm. Therefore,

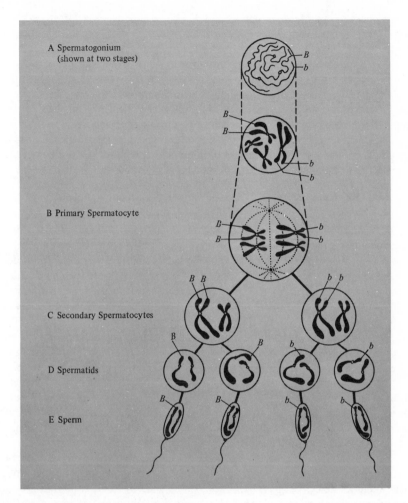

A Spermatogonium
(shown at two stages)

B Primary Spermatocyte

C Secondary Spermatocytes

D Spermatids

E Sperm

Figure 5-5. Meiosis provides the mechanism by which a heterozygous male produces sperm of two kinds: half of them containing the dominant gene, *B,* half of them containing its recessive allele, *b.*

SOURCE: Adapted from P. A. Moody. *Genetics of man.* New York: W. W. Norton & Company, 1967. Figure 3–7, p. 34.

from each male primordial germ cell result four sperm, each containing 23 single chromosomes.

The development of each ovum is similar to the development of each sperm, except that from each female primordial germ cell (called an *obgonium*) there result not four ova, but one. But it, like each sperm, contains 23 chromatids from among the 92 chromatids present in the obgonium. Since the obgonium begins meiosis with two X chromosomes, every ovum contains an X chromosome. The spermatogonium, which begins meiosis with one X and one Y chromosome, results in four sperms, two of which contain an X apiece and two a Y. If an X-bearing sperm fertilizes an ovum, the new individual will have two X chromosomes, and will be female. If a Y-bearing sperm fertilizes an ovum, the new individual will have one Y chromosome and one X chromosome, and will be a male.

In the same way, if one parent has two genes for any trait, each offspring will receive from that parent the same kind of genetic material as any other offspring. But if a parent has unlike genes for a trait, half of the offspring (other things being equal, which they often are not) will receive one kind of gene (for example, the dominant gene) and half will receive the other. The process of meiosis explains part of the genetic difference between brothers and sisters, including the fact that a given father and mother are likely to have both sons and daughters.

BEHAVIOR GENETICS

Not only are body form and coloration inherited from generation to generation but different kinds of functioning are, also. The ability to roll the tongue is one of these functions. One of the authors of this book (MSS) can roll her tongue; RCS cannot. All three of their daughters can. Since this ability is known to be a dominant characteristic, we know that RCS is homozygous recessive. Some of our grandchildren may turn out to be like Grandpa. Our daughters are heterozygous for this characteristic. If their husbands are also heterozygous, we could predict that our grandchildren will be tongue-rollers in the ratio of 3:1.

(Incidentally, the genetic ratios hold only for large populations, not for small samples. Since we expect that the total number of our grandchildren will be no more than six, they might all be tongue-rollers.)

The inheritance of certain defects in mental functioning can be described in terms of chromosomes [42]. Down's syndrome (Mongolism), a type of mental retardation accompanied by distinctive physical anomalies, occurs when an extra chromosome is attached to the chromosome numbered 21, making a total of 47 instead of the normal 46 chromosomes. Klinefelter's syndrome, incomplete sexual development along with lowered intelligence in males, involves two X chromosomes in addition to a Y. Turner's syndrome, in which females have only one X chromosome, includes defective spatial abilities. Males with an XXY condition are more likely than normals to be tall, aggressive, and mentally defective.

The transmission of all-or-none traits, such as tongue-rolling and Down's syndrome, can be explained by basic rules of genetics. When many genes are involved and when the characteristic is highly complex, such as intelligence or emotional stability, *heritability* is studied by *quantitative genetics*. Heritability of a characteristic can be estimated by comparing correlations between groups of known genetic similarity. Since the heredity of animals can be controlled, they can be used for experimental work in heredity. In working with humans, investigators have to use groups that vary in known degrees, from identical twins to unrelated persons. Results of many studies on inheritance of intelligence and personality indicate that there are indeed significant hereditary components in both [61].

Intelligence. Figure 5-6 shows median (average) sizes of correlations between measured intelligence of persons of different degrees of genetic similarity [20]. Unrelated persons living apart show no correlation (−.01). Identical twins

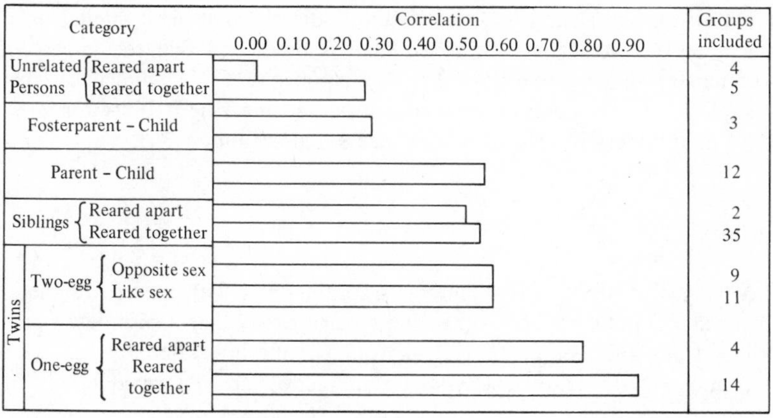

Category	Correlation 0.00 0.10 0.20 0.30 0.40 0.50 0.60 0.70 0.80 0.90	Groups included
Unrelated Persons { Reared apart		4
{ Reared together		5
Fosterparent – Child		3
Parent – Child		12
Siblings { Reared apart		2
{ Reared together		35
Two-egg { Opposite sex		9
{ Like sex		11
One-egg { Reared apart		4
{ Reared together		14

(Twins label spans the Two-egg and One-egg rows)

Figure 5-6. Median correlation coefficients for intelligence test scores showing degree of similarity between performances of people of varying degrees of relatedness under different and similar environmental conditions.

SOURCE: Data from L. Erlenmeyer-Kimling and L. F. Jervik. *Science,* 1964, **142,** 1477–79.

reared together are very similar (.87). Identical twins reared apart are more closely correlated than those in any other relationship group (.75). Intelligence of parents and children correlates significantly (.50). Heredity components have been found in the following intellectual abilities, listed in order of weight of influence by heredity: word fluency, verbal ability (including spelling and grammar), spatial ability, clerical speed and accuracy, reasoning, number ability, and memory [61]. Sensorimotor intelligence scores were found to be more highly correlated in identical twins than in fraternals [41].

Personality. There is evidence for heritability of several dimensions of personality, the main ones of which are usual activity level; expression of emotions frankly in interpersonal relationships; degree of planning ahead rather than behaving impulsively [61]; extraversion–introversion [54].

Age Trends. Correlations between intelligence of children and parents are low negative in early infancy, zero at around a year, low positive at the end of the second year, and moderate (.5) in early childhood and thereafter [17a]. This pattern is true of children and parents living apart, as well as of those living together. Correlations between stature of parents and children also increase throughout the early preschool years [25].

Sex Differences in Heritability. There is evidence that girls are controlled by heredity more than boys are, most likely because the X chromosome, of which girls have two and boys one, carries more hereditary material than does the Y chromosome. After age 13, measurements of stature correlate more highly for father–daughter than for father–son and for mother–daughter than for mother–son

[25]. Data from the Berkeley Growth Study indicated that girls' intellectual functioning is more genetically determined than is boys, and that the impact of the environment is greater upon boys than it is upon girls [5]. High school boys and girls, studied by a twin control method, showed stronger heritability for girls than for boys on a battery of tests of achievements and aptitudes [34].

Summary

A baby, like all organisms, interacts continuously with the environment. She and her parents influence each other and change each other. Child development is described from different theoretical viewpoints, offering different ways of interpreting and understanding. Six types of interaction are described briefly in this chapter.

Equilibration is a process of regulation that the organism carries on in physical and intellectual modes. Homeostasis is the maintaining of the organism within certain physical limits such as those of chemical content and temperature. Psychological equilibrium involves regulating stimulation to an optimal level and also progressing toward more complex levels of mental organization. Piaget's notion of equilibration includes two complementary processes, accommodation and assimilation. Assimilation is the taking in and using of material from the environment; accommodation is changing the schemas to adjust to reality as it is experienced. Equilibration is enjoyable, as shown by children's curiosity and exploration, looking for problems and incongruities to be solved.

Growth and development, terms that can be used interchangeably, refer to increasing size and complexity of structure and function. The following principles or generalizations hold for many kinds of growth and development: variation in rates between individuals, between sexes, within the organism and of the organism in time; individuals differ in time of reaching maturity; measures of growth are interrelated; organisms behave as though they were seeking to achieve maximum potential, searching for substitute sources of nurture when the usual ones are not available; specific patterns of behavior are differentiated out of larger, global patterns, and then specific patterns are integrated into larger, complex patterns; certain sequences of physical and motor development take place in directions (cephalo-caudal and proximo-distal) in relation to the body; certain behavior patterns mature in orderly sequences; growth is based on a foundation, the organism interacting with the environment to transform itself; critical periods are specific times when the organism will interact with the environment in specific ways that may be harmful or beneficial.

Stage theories, including Erikson's and Piaget's, explain development as proceeding epigenetically, being transformed or reorganized on more and more complex levels that occur in an orderly sequence. Erikson's psychosocial theory uses Freud's psychosexual stages as a base and develops a theory of the healthy personality. The eight stages of man's development involve the development of basic trust versus basic mistrust; autonomy versus doubt and shame; initiative versus guilt; industry versus inferiority; identity versus role diffusion; intimacy versus isolation; generativity versus self-absorption; ego integrity versus despair. Piaget shows how children develop intelligence in the process of dealing with the world and coming to know it. His sensorimotor period, spanning infancy, is subdivided into six stages. The preoperational period, from around 2 to 7, includes the stages of preconceptual and intuitive thought. The period of concrete operations comprises the school years, and the period of formal operations (logical thought) comprises the years of adolescence.

Memory means the storing of experience in such ways that it can be retrieved and used. The process includes perception, attention, coding, and enriching with meaning. Memory performance varies with age, input, and various environmental aspects. Learning is an active process, not something that is done to a person. When academic learning is measured in terms of time, focused aid can help slow learners to achieve more and to increase their self-esteem and motivation. Human beings learn easily from observing one another and hearing or reading of the experiences of others. Through socialization, children and, to some extent, others learn to think, feel, and behave as members of social groups. Selecting among what she sees, hears, and reads, an individual imitates behavior that she expects will be rewarding to her. The components of modeling are attention, symbolic representations in memory, new integrations of motor acts, and control of selection through incentive or motivational processes. Classical conditioning involves linking a new response with an old one, operant conditioning involves strengthening a response when it occurs. Positive reinforcements increase the likelihood of recurrence of an event, negative reinforcements decrease it. Individuals can use reinforcement systematically to change their own behavior. Manipulation of reinforcements is complicated and often does not bring the desired results because not all variables are understood.

Maturation is the growth toward maturity of the body, its structures, and functions—growth that is relatively independent of experience. Most developmental processes involve both maturation and learning.

Evolutionary adaptation accounts for certain behavior patterns that mature quickly into a complex and relatively fixed form. The environment to which a species is adapted is the one in which it emerged in its present form. Attachment behavior in the human infant is most easily understood in terms of evolutionary adaptation. Behavioral systems have also evolved. They are not always in harmony with each other.

Hereditary characteristics in human beings are sometimes the result of single pairs of genes, but often of numbers of genes working together. Most human beings carry several dangerous recessive genes, which will do no harm unless they are matched with the same dangerous genes from the partner in reproduction. Birth defects can be predicted on a chance basis, and some can be predicted with certainty. An ovum contains an X chromosome, a sperm either an X or a Y chromosome. The source of sex differences is in the X and Y chromosomes, including differences in heritability, females being more influenced by heredity. These functions include intelligence and many of its components and also certain personality dimensions. Correlations between physical and mental measurements of parents and children increase during the preschool period.

References

1. Abernathy, E. M. Relationships between physical and mental growth. *Monographs of the Society for Research in Child Development,* 1936, **1**:7.
2. Ainsworth, M. D. S. The development of infant-mother attachment. In B. M. Caldwell and H. N. Ricciuti (eds.). *Review of child development research,* vol. 3. Chicago: University of Chicago Press, 1973.
3. Bandura, A. Influence of models' reinforcement contingencies on the acquisition of imitative responses. *Journal of Personality & Social Psychology,* 1965, **1**, 589–595.
4. Bandura, A. Behavior theory and the models of man. *American Psychologist,* 1974, **29**, 859–869.
5. Bayley, N., and E. S. Schaefer. Correlations of maternal and child behaviors with the development of mental abilities: Data from the Berkeley growth study. *Monographs of the Society for Research in Child Development,* 1964, **29**:6.
6. Bloom, B. S. Time and learning. *American Psychologist,* 1974, **29**, 682–688.
7. Bower, T. G. R. *Development in infancy.* San Francisco: W. H. Freeman & Co., Publishers, 1974.
8. Bowlby, J. *Attachment and loss.* vol. I: *Attachment.* London: Hogarth, 1969.
9. Brenner, A. and L. H. Stott. *School readiness factor analyzed.* Detroit: Merrill-Palmer Institute (undated).
10. Bronfenbrenner, U. *Two worlds of childhood.* New York: Russell Sage Foundation, 1970.
11. Brucefors, A., I. Johannesson, P. Karlberg, I. Klackenberg-Larsson, H. Lichtenstein, and I. Svenberg. Trends in development of abilities related to somatic growth. *Human Development,* 1974, **17**, 152–159.
12. Bühler, C. *The first year of life.* New York: Day, 1930.
13. Craik, F. I. M., and R. S. Lockhart. Levels of processing: A framework for memory research. *Journal of Verbal Learning and Behavior,* 1972, **11**, 671–684.
14. Davis, C. M. Self-selection of diet by newly weaned infants. *American Journal of Diseases of Children,* 1928, **36**, 651–679.
15. Dember, W. N. Motivation and the cognitive revolution. *American Psychologist,* 1974, **29**, 161–168.
16. Dennis, W. *Children of the crèche.* New York: Meredith Corporation, 1973.
17. Eibl-Eibesfeldt, I. Concepts of ethology and their significance in the study of human behavior. In H. W. Stevenson, E. H. Hess, and H. L. Rheingold (eds.). *Early behavior.* New York: John Wiley & Sons, Inc., 1967, pp. 127–146.
17a. Eichorn, D. H. Developmental parallels in the growth of parents and their children. *Newsletter of the Division on Developmental Psychology of the American Psychological Association,* Spring, 1970.
18. Erikson, E. H. *Childhood and society.* New York: W. W. Norton & Company, 1963.
19. Erikson, E. H. *Identity, youth and crisis.* New York: W. W. Norton & Company, 1968.
20. Erlenmeyer-Kimling, L. K., and L. F. Jarvik. Genetics and intelligence: A review. *Science,* 1964, **142**, 1477–1479.
21. Fantz, R. L. The origin of form perception. *Scientific American,* 1961, **204**, 66–72.
22. Fouts, G., and P. Liikanen. The effects of age and developmental level on imitation in children. *Child Development,* 1975, **46**, 555–558.
23. Freud, S. *The ego and the id,* New York: W. W. Norton & Company, 1962.
24. Garn, S. M. Fat thickness and developmental status in childhood and adolescence. *Journal of the American Medical Association,* 1960, **99**, 746–751.

25. Garn, S. M. Body size and its implications. In L. W. Hoffman and M. L. Hoffman (eds.). *Review of child development research.* vol. 2, New York: Russell Sage Foundation, 1966, pp. 529–561.

26. Gesell, A. *The embryology of behavior.* New York: Harper, 1945.

27. Gesell, A. and H. Thompson. *The psychology of early growth.* New York: Macmillan Publishing Co., Inc., 1938.

28. Halverson, H. M. An experimental study of prehension in infants by means of systematic cinema records. *Genetic Psychology Monographs,* 1931, **10,** 107–286.

29. Hartup, W. W., and B. Coates. Imitation of a peer as a function of reinforcement from the peer group and rewardingness of the model. *Child Development,* 1967, **38,** 1003–1016.

30. Havighurst, R. J. Minority subcultures and the law of effect. *American Psychologist,* 1970, **25,** 313–322.

31. Hunt, J. V., and N. Bayley. Explorations into patterns of mental development and prediction from the Bayley scales of infant development. *Minnesota Symposium on Child Psychology,* 1971, **5,** 52–71.

32. Jones, M. C., and P. H. Mussen. Self-conception, motivations, and interpersonal attitudes of early- and late-maturing girls. *Child Development,* 1958, **29,** 492–501.

33. Ketcham, W. A. Relationship of physical and mental traits in intellectually gifted and mentally retarded boys. *Merrill-Palmer Quarterly,* 1960, **6,** 171–177.

34. Klinger, R. Sex differences in heritability assessed by the Washington precollege test battery of achievement/aptitude measures. Paper presented at the meeting of the Society for Research in Child Development, Santa Monica, 1969.

35. Lane, I. M., and R. C. Coon. Reward allocation in preschool children. *Child Development,* 1972, **43,** 1382–1389.

36. Lewis, M. The meaning of a response, or why researchers in infant behavior should be Oriental metaphysicians. *Merrill-Palmer Quarterly,* 1967, **13,** 7–18.

37. Lipsitt, L. P. Learning in the human infant. In H. W. Stevenson, E. H. Hess, and H. L. Rheingold (eds.). *Early behavior,* New York: John Wiley & Sons, Inc., 1967, pp. 225–247.

38. Lorenz, K. *King Solomon's ring.* New York: Thomas Y. Crowell Company, 1952.

39. Masters, J. C., and M. D. Christy. Achievement standards for contingent self-reinforcement: Effects of task length and task difficulty. *Child Development,* 1974, **45,** 6–13.

40. Masters, J. C., and P. A. Pisarowicz. Self-reinforcement and generosity following two types of altruistic behavior. *Child Development,* 1975, **46,** 313–318.

41. Matheny, A. P. Twins: Concordance for Piagetian-equivalent items derived from the Bayley Mental Test. *Developmental Psychology,* 1975, **11,** 224–227.

42. McClearn, G. E. Behavioral genetics: An overview. *Merrill-Palmer Quarterly,* 1968, **14,** 9–24.

43. McGraw, M. B. Major challenges for students of infancy and early childhood. *American Psychologist,* 1970, **25,** 754–756.

44. Milner, B. Memory and the medial regions of the brain. In K. H. Pribram and D. E. Broadbent. *Biology of memory.* New York: Academic Press, Inc., 1970, pp. 29–50.

45. Mussen, P. H., and M. C. Jones. The behavior-inferred motivations of late- and early-maturing boys. *Child Development,* 1958, **29,** 61–67.

46. Notz, W. W. Work motivation and the negative effects of intrinsic rewards: A review with implications for theory and practice. *American Psychologist,* 1975, **30,** 884–891.

47. Papoušek, H. Experimental studies of appetitional behavior in human newborns

and infants. In H. W. Stevenson, E. H. Hess, and H. L. Rheingold (eds.). *Early behavior*. New York: John Wiley & Sons, Inc., 1967, pp. 249–277.

48. Parke, R. D. Some effects of punishment on children's behavior. *Young Children,* 1969, **24,** 225–240.

49. Piaget, J. *Play, dreams and imitation in childhood*. New York: W. W. Norton & Company, 1962.

50. Piaget, J. *Six psychological studies*. New York: Random House, Inc., 1967.

51. Piaget, J., and B. Inhelder. *The psychology of the child*. New York: Basic Books, Inc., 1969.

52. Pines, M. *The brain changers*. New York: Harcourt Brace Jovanovich, Inc., 1973.

53. Reese, H. W. Models of memory and models of development. *Human Development,* 1973, **16,** 397–416.

54. Scarr, S. Social introversion-extraversion as a heritable response. *Child Development,* 1969, **40,** 823–832.

55. Scott, J. P. *Early experience and the organization of behavior*. Belmont, Calif.: Brooks/Cole Publishing Co., 1968.

56. Shuttleworth, F. K. The physical and mental growth of girls and boys age six to 19 in relation to age at maximum growth. *Monographs of the Society for Research in Child Development,* 1939, **4**:3.

57. Stone, C. P., and R. G. Barker. Aspects of personality and intelligence in post-menarcheal and premenarcheal girls of the same chronological age. *Journal of Comparative Psychology,* 1937, **23,** 439–455.

58. Sullivan, W. If we master the gene. *New York Times,* June 14, 1970.

59. Tanner, J. M. *Education and physical growth*. London: University of London Press, 1961.

60. Tanner, J. M. Relation of body size, intelligence test scores and social circumstances. In P. Mussen, J. Langer, and M. Covington (eds.). *Trends and issues in developmental psychology*. New York: Holt, Rinehart and Winston, Inc., 1969.

61. Vandenberg, S. G. Human behavior genetics: Present status and suggestions for future research. *Merrill-Palmer Quarterly,* 1969, **15,** 121–154.

62. Walter, G. Comments. In J. M. Tanner and B. Inhelder (eds.). *Discussions on child development*. vol. I. New York: International Universities Press, 1953.

63. Watson, J. S., and C. T. Ramey. Reactions to response-contingent stimulation in early infancy. *Merrill-Palmer Quarterly,* 1972, **18,** 219–227.

64. Wolff, P. Autonomous systems in human behavior and development. *Human Development,* 1974, **17,** 281–291.

65. Zern, D. S. An interpretation of the effects of stimulation on development: Its role as a resolvable disequilibrator. *Genetic Psychology Monographs,* 1974, **90,** 532–547.

Readings in
An Overview of Human Life and Growth

In an earlier, and possibly in some ways happier, time, man was considered the final and triumphant item of creation, the master and user of other living things. Even the early evolutionary biologists considered that man stood at the apex of evolution; they did not seem aware of the possibility that the process of evolution might continue, resulting in the appearance of new species. They seemed even less aware of the possibility that the evolutionary process of man resulted in a creature who had within him the seeds of his own destruction, like the sabre-toothed tiger, whose overdeveloped canine teeth prevented him from ingesting his prey.

Ecology is the branch of biology that studies the relationship of living things to their environment, including other living things. Recently ecologists have included man as the subject of their study. In general, the results of their investigations have been frightening. Especially in North America man is seen as a fouler of his environment—air, water, and soil—to such an extent that ecologists say that if present trends go unchecked, man may make his continued existence impossible.

In the first article in this chapter, William W. Ballard, a biologist, describes some of the facts about man's evolutionary development and speculates about the future. He makes the important distinction between man as a species and men as individuals who together make up the species. Each individual has characteristics of the species that have arisen during the course of evolution, but each individual has his own personal history, during which he has learned some ways of behaving that may be, in the long run, maladaptive for the species. Ballard's article has been very useful to us in teaching child development courses. We found ourselves referring frequently to his notion of the two computers when we discussed opposing processes or ideas in all sorts of contexts.

Lawrence K. Frank, the author of the second article, gave form, direction, and impetus to the field of child development. Frank's genius provided a flow of ideas for research, education, and theory. He was responsible for establishing child development centers, the parent education movement, and interdisciplinary research. In the article presented here, Frank demonstrates his characteristic warmth and wonder while analyzing the growth processes at work in infants. He describes how the child elaborates his individuality through interaction. In the terms used by Ballard in the first article, Frank shows how the "second computer" begins, based on the beginnings of the "first computer."

Erikson and Piaget, the authors of the third and fourth selections, are also primarily concerned with the development of the "second computer." But both are explicit in their statement that their theories are based on biology. Although both are dealing with psychological material, they start from biological characteristics of man.

The epigenetic theory of Erik H. Erikson is represented by the next essay, taken from his book Identity, Youth and Crisis. An artist, teacher, and philosopher thoroughly trained in Freudian psychoanalysis, Erikson has made enormous contributions to the field of child development. His theory is built upon Freudian theory, which he extends and develops into a way of understanding and describing the healthy personality throughout life. Erikson describes stages of personality growth, showing for each one a relation of personality to bodily development and to interaction with the culture. Each stage is derived from and built upon the one preceding it. The organization of this book is shaped by Erikson's stages in childhood and adolescence. The content is influenced by his thinking.

Jean Piaget, the world-famous Swiss psychologist, is the author of the fourth piece in this section. Piaget is primarily a genetic epistemologist, a scientist-philosopher who investigates the production of knowledge. He has developed a comprehensive theory of the mental structures through which human beings build their concept of reality and deal with it. Piaget has stimulated psychological research all over the world. Americans have produced hundreds of studies in response to his theories and findings. Like Erikson's theory of personality development, Piaget's account of the growth of intelligence is epigenetic and interactional. Piaget's theory is very compatible with a child development point of view, because the child's mind is seen as resulting from biologically given beginnings actively engaged with the environment.

The Rise and Fall of Humanity

William W. Ballard

The reading that follows is the last part of a lecture titled " The Rise and Fall of Humanity." In the first part Ballard summarizes the development of living things during the course of four billion years of earth history, the accelerating growth of knowledge in the last few thousand years, and the serious threats to man's continued existence that have stemmed from this knowledge. Basically, Ballard says, the present crisis has arisen because there are too many people on the earth and they are demanding more than the earth can provide. These events have occurred because man as a species of animal is composed of men and women as individuals.

To maximize the amount of life that can be supported in a given ecosystem, a large number of species of plants, animals, and decomposers are brought into balance, each occupying its own niche and following its own instructions to make the best of the things available to it while contributing to the flow of energy and the recycling of materials. If one species in the ecosystem gets out of balance the whole community develops an instability that may either result in an irreversible change in its character, or in the control or rejection of the destabilizing element.

From Dartmouth Alumni Magazine, 1970, **62** (6), 60–64. Reprinted by permission of the author, the Dartmouth Alumni College, and the Dartmouth Alumni Magazine.

The human species has been manipulating its environment since the invention of agriculture, favoring the plants and animals that serve it for food, repressing or even exterminating others. Where this was overdone—e.g., Mesopotamia, the Near East, Yucatan—ghost cities and records of dead cultures remain to show how powerfully nature can strike back. Quite recently we have begun to use the treasure trove of fossil fuels to grow the food to satisfy the multiplying demands of our own population, and we congratulate ourselves on having temporarily freed ourselves from the normal restrictions of the natural world. It is a dangerous game we are playing.

No good asking why the human *species* takes these risks. A species is an invention of the mind, a generalization. Only human *individuals* actually walk and breathe and make decisions and it is the collection of individuals who have been doing what I say the species has been doing. What went wrong with human individuals, that they have gotten their species and their environment into such a mess? The other face of this question is, what is an indvidual supposed to be doing, and within what limits is he supposed to be held?

THE PRIMARY COMPUTER   To simplify, I shall restrict the latter question to animals rather than plants or decomposers. I shall pick animals that are not on a rampage, animals that have (so far as we can tell) no conscious reasoning ability, no thoughts, loyalties, hopes, or faiths. Some kind of earthworm or some frog will do. I assume that whatever one of these animals does, any choice that it makes, is determined by its inherited computer system. It receives from its ancestors a scanning mechanism which reports what all the circumstances around and inside it are at the moment. This information is checked against an inherited memory encoded in its central nervous system. The computer then not only orders up the strategy and tactics that had met that sort of situation successfully before, but directs what every cell, what every organ, what the whole earthworm or frog must be doing to contribute to that response. (Directions for unsuccessful responses are not encoded in this primary computer, because they simply are not inherited.)

To see what this genetic computer requires the individual worm or frog to do, let us follow his life history, watching him obey and reconstructing from what he does the nature of the commands.

1. As a member of a bisexual species he (or she) starts as a fertilized egg, a single diploid individual with unique heterozygous genic individuality. First, *he develops*. Since the fertilized egg is insulated to a degree from the outside world, his computer works at first mostly on internal information. It refers to the inherited memory in the chromosomes and brings out instructions of various intricate sorts to the ultrastructures of the cell, programmed so that the cell divides into two, then four, then eight cells . . . until the word gets back to the multiplied computers in the multiplied cells that it is time to activate their inherited instructions for differentiation. Tissues and organs are formed, in such sorts and such patterns as have enabled the species to survive so far. The new individual acquires the sensory and neural apparatus for bringing in more and more information from the outside, and this is referred to the more and more specialized computer developing out of the inherited instructions, in a central nervous system (in the case of a frog, a brain and spinal cord). He begins

to move about, respire, feed, excrete, defend himself, in directions and at rates calculated to be appropriate to the sensed state of affairs from moment to moment. This is quite a trick for a self-built computer to bring off, and as an embryologist I wish I understood more of how it is done.

2. The young earthworm or pollywog, having broken loose from its protective envelopes and used up its dowry of yolk, is next under orders to *reach adulthood*. He recognizes dangers and opportunities by continually referring the information flowing in from his sensory apparatus to his inherited memory. He certainly has not learned his behavioral responses from his parents, never having met them. It is the inherited computer which tells him what to do from one millisecond to the next. He survives or not, partly by luck but also partly according to whether his own inherited variant of the species-specific computer will deliver the right answers to the problems of his own day and place. (The *species* survives by offering up enough varieties so that some individuals will have what the new situations demand, the wastage of the other individuals being a necessary part of the cost. No other way has yet been discovered for meeting the demands of an unpredictable future, i.e. winning a game the rules for which have not yet been written.)

3. Our earthworm or frog, if lucky, finds himself a sexually mature individual, with his instructions to reproduce now turned on. These instructions, activated by seasonal or other environmental signals, operate upon particular genes, particular cells, particular organs, and particular behavioral mechanisms set off through the nervous system. Without knowing it, much less knowing why, the animals seeks out a mate, copulates, and shares in the production of fertilized eggs that bring us again to phase 1 of the cycle.

4. Having blindly and without thought followed his instructions to (1) develop, (2) make do, survive, gain strength, and (3) reproduce, our earthworm or frog subsequently (4) *dies*. It is the ancient law. So far as the interests of the individual are concerned, it is absurd.

But now how about man? How unique is he? Does he not learn by experience and education, manage his own life, consciously determine what jobs he shall tackle, what ends he shall serve? My argument that he too is run by an inherited computer program rests partly on the observed fact that (1) he develops, (2) he makes every effort to reach maturity, (3) if lucky enough he sets the cycle going again, and (4) he dies. There is nothing unique about that. Experience, learning, individual preferences serve only for minor embellishments.

I select one case to illustrate that an animal's program is mostly inherited. Four to six weeks after fertilization (depending on temperature) a salamander embryo will have used up its yolk and must by then have acquired an elaborate repertoire of locomotor, hunting-sensory, food-grabbing, and swallowing behavior to keep itself fed and growing. Does the individual learn this behavior by trial and error? No. Starting a day before any of his muscles were mature enough to contract, you can rear him in a dilute anesthetic solution until he has reached the feeding stage. Put him back into pond water, and in twenty minutes the anesthetic will have worn off and he is swimming, hunting, grabbing, and swallowing like a normal tadpole. One is seeing here the computer-controlled maturation of a computer-controlled behavior. No practice, no learning.

The individual within which this remarkable apparatus matures is an expendable pawn, and the apparatus is not for his enjoyment of life, it is to keep the species going.

THE SECONDARY COMPUTER   There is such an inherited program in the human individual, but there is much more. The baby does not so much learn to walk as to develop the inherited capacity to walk; but then he can learn a dance that no man has ever danced before, he can paint a picture with a brush clasped between his toes. During late fetal life and his first six or eight years he gradually matures a second computer system superimposed on, controlling and almost completely masking the ancient frog-type computer. The evolutionary history of this new device is traceable back to, and in some respects beyond, the time of origin of the modern mammals 70 million or more years ago. It has progressed farthest in particular mammalian orders—the carnivores, hoofed animals, bats, whales and primates, and least in the egg-laying mammals and marsupials.

The new trend has worked certain real advantages, and has been kept under reasonable control, in the higher mammals, but it is my strong suspicion that its over-development in man is the root of our trouble. Like the dinosaurs, we contain in our own structure the reason why we will have to go. Robinson Jeffers [1] said it: "We have minds like the fangs of those forgotten tigers, hypertropied and terrible."

Up to a point, the development of brain and spinal cord follows the same course in frog and man. Sense organs, cranial and spinal nerves, principal subdivisions of the brain, basic fiber tract systems, all form in strictly comparable fashion in both. But the adult human brain is a far different thing from the adult frog brain. It continues the multiplication and interconnection of neurons during a far longer growth period, and adds to the elementary or frog-type apparatus two principal complicating tissues that far overshadow the earlier developments. One is often called reticular substance, the other is the cerebral cortex.

The reticular substance is so called because it is an interweaving of small centers of gray substance with short bundles and interspersed mats of axons (the white substance), quite different from the simple contrast between gray and white substance seen in primitive animals and in early embryos. The frog brain is not without this sort of tissue, but in the brains of advanced vertebrates like the teleost fishes, the reptiles, and the birds, it becomes indescribably complex. The modern mammals push this development to still higher orders of magnitude.

Although neurological science is not yet ready with answers to most specific questions about what happens where in the central nervous system, the new techniques of exploration within the brain suggest that in and through the reticular substance the connections for integrating sensory information with the devices for evaluation and for making decisions and coordinated responses are multiplied exponentially.

Thus, an electrode planted within a single neuron in the reticular substance of the hindbrain can give startling evidence that this one cell is receiving and

[1] R. Jeffers, "Passenger Pigeons," in *The Beginning and the End.*

reacting to sensations reported from widely scattered parts of the body, and sending out coded pulses as a calculated response. Your own brain contains hundreds of millions, probably billions of such cells, every one individually a computer.

The neurologists can now stimulate chosen localized areas through implanted electrodes, either hooked up to wires dangling from the cage ceiling or activated through miniaturized transmitters healed in under the scalp and controlled by radio transmission. In such experiments, stimuli delivered to many parts of the reticular substance cause the animal to react as though he were flooded with agreeable sensation. If the cat or rat or monkey learns how to deliver the stimulus to himself by pressing a pedal, he will do so repeatedly and rapidly, until he falls asleep exhausted. As soon as he wakes up, he goes to pounding the pedal again.

There are other reticular areas which have the reverse effect. If the stimulus comes at rhythmical intervals and the animal discovers that he can forestall it by pressing the pedal, he quickly learns to regulate his life so as to be there and step on it just in time. What kind of sensation such a stimulus produces in him can only be guessed by the experimenter. One might suppose that these areas of reticular substance which have such opposite effects are there to add into the computer's analysis of the situation at the moment a go signal or a stop signal for particular alternative choices, or a sense of goodness or badness, satisfaction or distress, urgency or caution, danger or relaxation. A value judgment, in other words.

It is not difficult to see the survival value of such a device. No doubt the basic mechanism exists in the brains of fishes and frogs, though I am not aware that experiments have been done to locate it. In the reticular substance of mammals, however, we see it hugely developed. The result of overdoing this might produce an awareness of the good and bad features of so very many facets of a situation as to delay and perplex the individual in calculating his single coordinated response.

Mammals are also conspicuously good at remembering experiences from their own lives as individuals, and these memories are loaded with value judgments. There is still no clear answer as to where or in what coded form these new personal memories are stored. But an animal with all this added to the ancestral memory, enhanced with perhaps casually acquired and unwisely generalized connotations of goodness and badness, might predictably be endowed with excessive individuality, prone to unnecessarily variable behavior, chosen more often for self-satisfaction than in the interest of species survival.

The other evolutionary development, the formation of the cerebral cortex, is almost unknown in vertebrates other than mammals, and is feeble in some of these. Cerebral cortex is a tissue of awesome complexity, and our techniques for analyzing what happens in it are still highly inadequate. Stimulation of willing human subjects, in chosen spots exposed surgically, or radio stimulation of these areas through permanently installed electrodes operated by healed-in transistor devices, evoke feelings referred to a particular part of the body, or cause normal-appearing localized movements, e.g. the flexion of an arm or a finger, time and again, upon repetition of the signal. Other areas produce more generalized sensory or motor or emotional or physiologic effects. The patient, his brain exposed under local anesthesia, does not know when the stimulus is applied. When the electrode touches a particular spot of his cortex he may report that he is suddenly remembering a scene identifiable as to time and place, but the memory blacks out when the current is cut off. Stimulation of other areas may elicit emotions of sexual attraction or anxiety or rage graded according to the intensity of the signal.

More wide-ranging experiments with cats, monkeys, or barnyard stock, singly or in groups, free to move in large caged areas, show the possibility of turning on and off a great range of complex emotions, behavior, and even personality traits, by local stimulation.[2] The effect produced through a permanently planted electrode is area specific. Though not predictable before the first stimulus is given, the response is repeated with each stimulus, many times a day or over periods of months or years.

In subjective comparison of mammals with greater or less personal individuality one gets the impression that the degrees of freedom of choice, of imaginative recognition of possible ways to react to situations, of storage capacity and retentiveness of memory, and the richness of association, are correlated with the intricacy and amount of the cerebral cortex and reticular substance. Animals highest on both scales include porpoises, elephants, cats and dogs, apes, and people.

One cannot underestimate the effects on the human species of other evolutionary trends that came to a climax in us, for instance the development of upright posture that frees the hands, the reshaping of the fingers for grasping and manipulating, the perfection of binocular vision that can bring into focus either the hands or the far distance at will. Far more significant than these was the development of speech, made possible by and controlled in a particular small area of the new cerebral cortex. This expanded the powers of the human secondary computer by orders of magnitude, even in comparison with that of close relatives like apes.

We no longer communicate with each other by baring teeth, raising hackles and flaunting rumps, but in symbolic language. We can make abstractions and generalizations, and artificial associations. Through speech we can feed into the recording apparatus of each others' secondary computers not only the vast and rather accidental store of individually acquired and long-lasting memories of our own experience, but also the loads of approval or disapproval which we deliberately or unwittingly put upon them. We increasingly remove ourselves into created worlds of our own, calculating our choices by reference to a memory bank of second-hand ghosts of other people's experiences and feelings, prettied up or uglified with value judgments picked up who knows where, by whom, for what reason.

Language gave a fourth dimension to the powers of the secondary computer, and writing a fifth dimension. We can now convince each other that things are good or bad, acceptable or intolerable, merely by agreeing with each other, or by reciting catechisms. With writing we can color the judgments of people unborn, just as our judgments are tailored to the whim of influential teachers in the past.

[2] J. M. R. Delgado, 1969, *Physical Control of the Mind.*

Symbols have given us the means to attach a value judgment to some abstract noun, some shibboleth, and transfer this by association to any person or situation at will. We invent, we practice, we delight in tricks for saying things indirectly by poetry and figures of speech, that might sound false or trite or slanderous or nonsensical if we said them directly. A more normally constructed animal, a porpoise or an elephant, mercifully spared such subtleties, might well look at human beings and see that each one of us has become to some degree insane, out of touch with the actual world, pursuing a mad course of options in the imagined interest of self rather than of species.

The primary computer is still there, programmed in the interest of species survival. With his new powers, man should do better than any other animal at understanding the present crisis and generating an appropriate strategy and tactics. Instead, the effort is drowned out in the noise, the flicker-bicker, the chattering flood of directives from the personalized secondary computer. In pursuit of his own comfort and his own pleasure, man wars against his fellows and against the good earth.

The frame of each person is like a racing shell with two oarsmen in it, back to back, rowing in opposite directions. The one represents the ancient computer system, comparing the personal situation of the moment with an inherited value system and driving the person to perform in such a way that the species will survive, irrespective of how absurd his own expendable life may be. The other represents the secondary computer system, probably located in reticular substance and cerebral cortex, surveying chiefly the memories of childhood and adult life, and deciding how to act according to the value-loaded store of personal experience.

It is this runaway evolutionary development of our superimposed second computer that has produced our inventors, our artists, our saints and heroes, our poets, our thinkers. Our love and hate, ecstasy and despair. The infinite variety of human personalities. It has also atomized the species into a cloud of ungovernable individuals. We split our elections 48 to 52, make laws to break them, and either ignore community priorities or establish them by political blind-man's-buff in frivolous disregard of real emergencies. Six experts will come violently to six different decisions on how to meet a crisis because their personal histories lead them to weigh the same data differently. Each of us can see bad logic and conflicts of interest affecting the judgment of most of our associates; it is more difficult to detect them in ourselves. Our individually acquired prejudices have been built into our secondary computers.

Yet it is a glorious thing to feel the uniqueness, the power of decision, the freedom of being human. Who would prefer to be even so wonderful a creature as a dog, an elephant, a horse, a porpoise? I believe nevertheless that just this ungovernable power of the human individual, the essence of our humanity, is the root of the trouble.

The California biologist Garrett Hardin, in a famous essay called "The Tragedy of the Commons," showed that this accounts for practically all the facets of our apocalyptic crisis, from the population explosion to runaway technology.[3] He is referring to the community pasture where anyone may feed

[3] G. Hardin, 1968, *Science* 162: 1243. "The Tragedy of the Commons."

his animals. Overgrazing will bring erosion and irreversible deterioration in it. Each herdsman, calculating the advantage and disadvantage to himself of putting out one more animal to graze, balancing his small share of the possible damage against his sole ownership of the extra income, adds another animal in his own interest, and another, and another. All do, and all lose together. The tragedy is the inescapable disaster when each herdsman pursues his own advantage without limit, in a limited commons. This is the tragedy that leaves us with too many human mouths to feed, soil impoverished and washed or blown away, forests skinned off, lakes ruined, plastic bottles and aluminium cans scattered over the countryside, rivers clogged with dead fish, bilge oil spreading on public waters, streets and highways made obscene with advertisements. It is what gives us choking smog, the stink and corruption below paper mills and slaughter houses, the draining of one well by another in a falling water table, the sneaking of radioactive wastes into the air and the oceans.

All these, Hardin makes clear, are problems with *no technological solution*. To be sure, the technology stands ready, but the trouble starts with some individual, you, me, whose response to a situation is to give highest priority to his personal chance of profit, or his family's, or his country's. He has a vivid sense of the value to himself of his own freedom, but the total effects of all such freedoms on the species and on the natural world which supports it is invisible or far out of focus. The technology might just as well not exist.

Some of these problems that will not be solved by technology alone can indeed be brought under control by compacts, treaties, and other agreements between willing groups, or by laws imposed by the majority upon a minority in the common interest. Hardin, however, puts the finger on the population problem as the worst example of the worst class of problems, in which all of us must restrict the freedom of all of us, when none of us want to. He is properly skeptical of conscience or altruism as forces for uniting the community when nearly all of us are still daring to gamble on the continued capacity of the commons to withstand collapse. What is needed, he says, is a fundamental extension of morality.

My way of agreeing with him is to say that human nature is our chief enemy because the species-preserving function of our primary computer has not yet been built into the secondary computer which generates our human nature. It is by now clear that our nature as individuals is not so much inherited as learned by babies as they grow into people, in and from their individual, accidental, and culture-bound experiences. We need to incorporate into the decision-making apparatus that will really control them a new survival morality, a system of values the principal axiom of which is that anything which threatens the welfare of the species is bad, anything that serves to bring the species into harmony with its environment is good. We must, each of us, because of this inner drive, regulate our numbers and our selfish wants as rigorously as the forces of natural selection would have done had we not learned how to set them aside.

Do we know how to create a human nature that can keep the species going without undue sacrifice of the privilege and joy of being human? How much freedom must we give up? Do we want to? Is there time?

Basic Processes in Organisms

Lawrence K. Frank

If we are to understand the infant as a persistent, but ever changing, organism, we need to think in terms that are dynamic, which calls for a recognition of the ongoing processes by which the infant grows, develops, matures, and ages while continually functioning and behaving. As a young mammalian organism, the human infant lives by much the same basic physiological processes as other mammals.

The recognition of process has come with the acceptance of such recently formulated conceptions as that of self-organization, self-stabilization, self-repair, and self-direction which are characteristic not only of organisms but of various man-made machines such as computers and systems designed to operate a planned sequence of activities with the use of positive and negative feedbacks (Wiener 1961; Von Foerster and Zopf 1962). The organism may be said to be "programmed" by its heredity but capable of flexible functioning through the life cycle.

Moreover, it must be re-emphasized that each infant differs to a greater or lesser extent from all other infants, exhibiting not only individual variation but also displaying a considerable range of intra-individual variability, or continually changing functioning and physiological states, especially during the early months of life when the infant is not yet fully organized or capable of adequate self-stabilization.

Since most of our knowledge of infancy and childhood is derived from observations and measurements of selected variables, responses to stimuli, at a given time or a succession of times, we do not gain an adequate conception of the continuous, dynamic processes of living organisms, especially since we tend to focus upon the outcomes, without recognizing the processes which produce them. Accordingly, some account of these basic processes and how they operate may provide a conceptual model for understanding the multidimensional development of infants during the first year of life. Whatever is done to and for the infant, what privations, frustrations and deprivations he may suffer, what demands and coercions he must accept, what spontaneous activity and learning he displays, may be viewed as expressions of his basic functioning processes.

Every experience in the life of an infant evokes some alteration in these organic processes whereby he manages not only to survive but to grow and develop, to learn while carrying on his incessant intercourse with the surrounding world. Thus, by focusing on the organic processes we may discover what is taking place when we speak of adjustment, learning, adaptation, and the transitions encountered at critical stages in his development.

The concept of mechanism indicates or implies a deterministic relationship between antecedent and consequent, usually as a *linear* relationship in which the consequent is proportional to the antecedent. The concept of *process* involves a dynamic, *non-linear* operation, whereby the same process, depending upon where, what, how, and in what quantities or intensities it operates, may produce different products which may be all out of proportion to that which initiates or touches off the process. For example the process of fertilization and gestation operates in all mammals to produce the immense variety of mammalian young. But different processes may produce similar or equivalent products, an operation which has been called "equifinality" by Bertalanffy (1950).

A brief discussion of the six basic processes operating in organisms will indicate how the infant organism is able to persist and survive by continually changing and is thereby able to cope with the particular version of infant care and rearing to which he is subjected.

These six processes are: The Growth Process, The Organizing Process, The Communicating Process, The Stabilizing Process, The Directive or Purposive Process, and The Creative Process. (Frank, 1963).

THE GROWTH PROCESS   The infant who has been growing since conception continues, with a brief interruption and often some loss of weight, to grow incrementally, adding gradually to his size and weight. His growth may be slowed down by inadequate or inappropriate feeding, by some difficulties in digesting and assimilating whatever foodstuff he be given, or by a variety of disturbances and dysfunctions. A continuing upward trend in weight is expected as an expression of normal development, although recent cautions have been expressed on the undesirability of too rapid increase in weight and the vulnerability of a fat, waterlogged infant.

This incremental growth in size and weight indicates that the infant is maintaining an excess of growth over the daily losses through elimination of urine and feces, through skin and lungs, and also in the replacement of many cells that are discarded. Thus, millions of blood corpuscles are destroyed and replaced each day, the iron of those destroyed being salvaged and reused. Likewise, cells of the skin and lining of the gastrointestinal tract, of the lungs, kidneys, liver, indeed of almost all organ systems, except the central nervous system and brain, are continually being replaced at different rates.

Probably more vitally significant but less clearly recognized is the continual replacement of the chemical constituents of cells, tissues, and bony structures, like the skeleton and the teeth in which different chemicals are discarded and new materials are selected out of the blood stream to replace them. Here we see a dramatic illustration of the statement that an organism is a configuration which must continually change in order to survive, a conception which is wholly congruous with the recently formulated assumption of the world as an aggregate of highly organized complexes of energy transformations.

Growth, incremental and replacement, is a major functioning process, gradually producing an enlarging infant as the growing cells differentiate, specialize and organize to give rise to the varied tissues and organ systems in the developing embryo and fetus. In this prenatal development the creative process is also operating to produce the unique, unduplicated human infant along with the operation of the organizing process.

THE ORGANIZING PROCESS   Only recently has the process of self-organization been recognized in scientific thinking as basic to all organisms which start with some kind of genetic inheritance and undergo multiplication and duplication of cells with differentation and specialization of components that become organized into a living organism. (Von Foerster and Zopf, 1962). Thus the initial development of an infant takes place through the operation of the growth and the organizing processes which continue to operate throughout its life, maintaining the organism as it undergoes various transitions and transformations and copes with the many discontinuities encountered in its life cycle.

Since the normal infant arrives fully equipped with all the essential bodily components and organ systems, the growth process and the organizing process operate to incorporate the intakes of food, water, and air into its ever changing structure-functioning. Most of the highly organized foodstuffs, proteins, fats, and carbohydrates, are progressively broken down, disorganized, and random-ized, and the products of these digestive operations are then circulated through the blood stream from which the constituent cells, tissues, and fluids select out what they need for metabolism and organize these into their specialized structure-functioning components. The recent dramatic findings in molecular biology show how this organizing process operates within the cell as the DNA (the carrier of the genetic information) of the genes directs the production of the various proteins and the utilization of the minerals and vitamins for the growth and multiplication of cells and the maintenance of their functioning.

Also of large significance for the understanding of organic processes are the sequential steps in the utilization of food stuffs for metabolism involving many steps and numerous specialized enzymes and catalysts. Unfortunately some infants suffer from so-called metabolic errors when one or more of these steps in the metabolic sequence is missing or inadequate and therefore his growth and development and healthy functioning are jeopardized.

In the self-organizing organism we encounter circular and reciprocal operations in which every component of the organism by its specialized function-ing, gives rise to, and maintains, the total organism of which it is a participant; concurrently, the total organism reciprocally governs when, what, and how each of these components must function and operate to maintain the organized whole. This capacity for self-organizing arises from the autonomy of each component of an organism which over millions of years of evolution has developed its own highly individualized and specialized functioning within the total organic complex but functions according to the requirements of the organ-ism in which it operates.

COMMUNICATION PROCESS   Obviously, these autonomous components which give rise to growth and organization must continually communicate, internally and with the external "surround." The infant has an inherited communication network in his nervous system, his circulatory system, and his lymphatic system. Through these several channels every constituent of an organism continually communicates with all others, directly or indirectly, and with different degrees of speed in communication. Each component continually sends and receives messages whereby its functioning operations are regulated, synchronized, articulated, and related to all others, with greater or less immediacy. The infant is born with most of these internal communications already functioning, having been in operation for varying periods of its prenatal development but with the central nervous system still immature. The infant also has the sensory apparatus for various inputs, of light, of sound, touch, taste and smell, also for pain, heat and cold, and for gravity and for atmospheric pressure changes. But the infant is also initially prepared for dealing with the varying intensities and durations of these intakes and impacts, gradually increasing his capacity for filtering, buffering, mingling, and transducing these inputs whereby he may monitor these sensory communications according to his ever changing internal, physiological states and the kinesthetic and proprioceptive messages by which he continually orients himself and gradually achieves an equilibrium in space.

The infant must carry on this incessant intercourse with the world more or less protected by adults from too severe or hazardous impacts and provided with the food and care required by his helpless dependency. But the infant often must try to defend himself from what his caretakers try to impose on him or compel him to accept, as in feeding, toilet training, etc. Under this treatment much of the infant's energies may be expended in these efforts to maintain his stability and integrity against unwelcomed and uncongenial treatment which may interfere with his normal functioning and compromise his growth and development and learning as a unique organism. Thus we may say that the growth and organizing processes contribute to and are dependent upon the communication process, which operates through the inherited receptors of the infant which may become progressively altered, refined, and increasingly sensitized through learning. Quite early the infant may become receptive to nonverbal communications such as tones of voice, smiling, tactile comforting, or painful treatment.

STABILIZING PROCESS   Since the world presents so many different and continually varying messages and impacts, organisms must be able to cope with the ever changing flux of experience and maintain their integrity and functional capacities by monitoring all their organic functions. While all other organisms have evolved with their species-specific range of sensory awareness and capacity for perception and for living in their ancestral life zones, the human infant, and a few other mammals are able to live in a wide variety of climates and habitations and maintain their internal world within fairly close limitations upon intraorganic variability. This becomes possible through the operation of the stabilizing process.

The stabilizing process operates through a network of physiological feedbacks, both negative and positive, to maintain a dynamic equilibrium and is not limited to the concept of homeostasis which Cannon used to describe the maintenance of the fluid internal environment. The stabilizing process maintains continually changing physiological states. At birth it is not fully developed or operationally effective and hence the infant needs continual care, protection, and appropriate nutrition. But as he grows and develops he increasingly regulates his internal functioning by responding appropriately to the various inputs and outputs, intakes, and outlets. Obviously an infant who must grow, both incrementally and by replacement, cannot tolerate too stable an internal environment which might prevent or limit such growth and adaptive functioning. With his increasing exposure to the world the infant learns to calibrate all his sensory inputs and increasingly to "equalize his thresholds," as Kurt Goldstein (1939) has pointed out.

Not the least significant and often stressful experience under which an infant must maintain his internal stability are the varying practices of child care and feeding, the efforts of parents to regularize his functioning and compel him to conform to whatever regimen of living they wish to establish. Clearly the stabilizing process is essential to the infant's survival and to his continuing growth and development and the variety of learning which he must master. Happily, most infants achieve a progressive enlargement of their capacity for living and for self-regulation and self-stabilization to assume an autonomy expressing their integrity in the face of often uncongenial treatment and surroundings.

THE DIRECTIVE OR PURPOSIVE PROCESS   With the achievement of motor coordination and locomotion, by creeping and crawling, and then assuming an erect posture and learning to walk, the infant enlarges the purposive or goal seeking process which involves continual scanning, probing, and exploring the world and developing his selective awareness and patterned perception, and especially the ability to ignore or to reject what may interfere or distract him in his endeavour to attain remote or deferred goals. Obviously, the purposive process cannot operate effectively until the infant has achieved a considerable degree of internal stabilization and of neuro-muscular coordination, and the ability to cope with a three dimensional, spatial world.

Since the child initially is attracted or impelled by whatever he may become aware of or has an impulse to seek, to handle, to put into his mouth, or otherwise to manipulate, the purposive process is frequently blocked and the child may be severely punished in his attempts to develop his autonomous mastery of his small world. Thus the purposive process operates differentially in each infant who is likely to be attracted by and responsive to different dimensions of his environment at different times; these early explorations provide an endless sequence of learning experiences which involve, not only the actual world of nature, but the wide range of artifacts and of highly individuated personalities with whom he is in contact. With language the infant learns to deal with people and verbal symbols of language for goal seeking.

THE CREATIVE PROCESS   As noted earlier, the creative process begins to operate early in gestation to produce a unique infant as a human organism with the same basic organic functions and similar or equivalent components which, however, are different in each infant. From birth on, therefore, each infant is engaged in creating a highly selective environment or a "life space" that is as congenial and appropriate for his individualized organism, with its peculiar needs and capacities, as is possible under the constraints and coercions imposed by others upon his growth, development, functioning, and learning. In infancy and childhood the individual is more creative than in any other period in his life cycle, but this creativity may be either ignored or discouraged by those who are intent upon making the child conform as nearly as possible to their image or ideal of attainment.

Within recent years the purposive and creative processes have become major foci in the studies of early child growth, development, and education, but it must be remembered that the purposive and creative processes cannot operate independently because they are inextricably related to and dependent upon the other four basic processes which reciprocally contribute to the operation of these two processes.

Most of the training and education of the infant and young child involves curbing, regulating, focusing, and patterning, and also evoking the communicating and stabilizing and directive processes which are more amenable to intervention and control by others. Through supervision and regulation of these processes the child is largely molded, patterned, and oriented into the kind of organism-personality favored by his parents and appropriately prepared for living in his cultural and social order. As he grows older the infant is expected to learn the required conduct for group living and to master the various symbol systems by which he can relate cognitively to the world and negotiate with other people. It appears that learning as an expression of the purposive and the creative processes may be compromised and sometimes severely distorted or blocked when the child is expected or compelled to alter the organizing, communicating, and stabilizing processes, as required by his parents and other more experienced persons.

In the discussion of humanization we will see how the young mammalian organism is transformed into a personality for living in a symbolic cultural world and for participating in a social order, through the various practices of infant care and rearing that are focused upon, and directly intervene in, the operation of these six basic organic processes. But each infant is a highly individualized organism who develops his own idiosyncratic personality through the development and utilization of his basic organic processes.

References

BERTALANFFY, L. VON, "Theory of Open Systems in Physics and Biology," *Science*, CXI, 1950, pp. 27–29. See also Yearbooks of Society for General Systems Research.

FRANK, L. K., "Human Development—An Emerging Discipline," in *Modern Perspectives in Child Development*, In honor of Milton J. E. Senn, Eds. Albert J. Solnit and Sally Provence, New York: International Universities Press, 1963.

———. "Potentiality: Its Definition and Development," in *Insights and the Curriculum*, Yearbook, Association for Supervision and Curriculum Development, Washington, D.C.: National Education Association, 1963.

GOLDSTEIN, KURT, *The Organism*, New York: American Book Company, 1939.

VON FOERSTER, HEINZ, and ZOPF, JR., GEORGE W., Eds., *Principles of Self Organizing Systems*, London: Pergamon Press, 1962.

WIENER, NORBERT, *Cybernetics*, Cambridge and New York: M.I.T. Press and John Wiley and Sons, Inc., 1961.

The Life Cycle : Epigenesis of Identity

Erik H. Erikson

HARVARD UNIVERSITY

Whenever we try to understand growth, it is well to remember the *epigenetic principle* which is derived from the growth of organisms *in utero*. Somewhat generalized, this principle states that anything that grows has a ground plan, and that out of this ground plan, the parts arise, each part having its time of special ascendancy, until all parts have arisen to form a functioning whole. This, obviously, is true for fetal development where each part of the organism has its critical time of ascendance or danger of defect. At birth the baby leaves the chemical exchange of the womb for the social exchange system of his society, where his gradually increasing capacities meet the opportunities and limitations of his culture. How the maturing organism continues to unfold, not by developing new organs but by means of a prescribed sequence of locomotor, sensory, and social capacities, is described in the child-development literature. As pointed out, psychoanalysis has given us an understanding of the more idiosyncratic experiences, and especially the inner conflicts, which constitute the manner in which an individual becomes a distinct personality. But here, too, it is important to realize that in the sequence of his most personal experiences the healthy child, given a reasonable amount of proper guidance, can be trusted to obey inner laws of development, laws which create a succession of potentialities for significant interaction with those persons who tend and respond to him and those institutions which are ready for him. While such interaction varies from culture to culture, it must remain within "the proper rate and the proper sequence" which governs all epigenesis. Personality, therefore, can be said to develop according to steps predetermined in the human organism's readiness to be driven toward, to be aware of, and to interact with a widening radius of significant individuals and institutions.

It is for this reason that, in the presentation of stages in the development of the personality, we employ an epigenetic diagram analogous to the one employed in *Childhood and Society* for an analysis of Freud's psychosexual stages.[1] It is, in fact, an implicit purpose of this presentation to bridge the theory of infantile sexuality (without repeating it here in detail) and our knowledge of the child's physical and social growth.

In Diagram 1 the double-lined squares signify both a sequence of stages and a gradual development of component parts. In other words, the diagram formalizes a progression through time of a differentiation of parts. This indicates (1) that each item of the vital personality to be discussed is systematically related to all others, and that they all depend on the proper development in

[1] See Erik H. Erikson, *Childhood and Society*, 2nd ed., New York: W. W. Norton & Company, Inc., 1963, Part I.

DIAGRAM 1

	1	2	3	4	5	6	7	8
VIII	Temporal Perspective vs. Time Confusion							INTEGRITY vs. DESPAIR
VII							GENERATIVITY vs. STAGNATION	
VI						INTIMACY vs. ISOLATION		
V		Self-Certainty vs. Self-Consciousness	Role Experimentation vs. Role Fixation	Apprentice-ship vs. Work Paralysis	IDENTITY vs. IDENTITY CONFUSION	Sexual Polarization vs. Bisexual Confusion	Leader- and Followership vs. Authority Confusion	Ideological Commitment vs. Confusion of Values
IV				INDUSTRY vs. INFERIORITY	Task Identification vs. Sense of Futility			
III			INITIATIVE vs. GUILT		Anticipation of Roles vs. Role Inhibition			
II		AUTONOMY vs. SHAME, DOUBT			Will to Be Oneself vs. Self-Doubt			
I	TRUST vs. MISTRUST				Mutual Recognition vs. Autistic Isolation			

339

the proper sequence of each item; and (2) that each item exists in some form before "its" decisive and critical time normally arrives.

If I say, for example, that a sense of basic trust is the first component of mental vitality to develop in life, a sense of autonomous will the second, and a sense of initiative the third, the diagram expresses a number of fundamental relations that exist among the three components, as well as a few fundamental facts for each.

Each comes to ascendance, meets its crisis, and finds its lasting solution in ways to be described here, toward the end of the stages mentioned. All of them exist in the beginning in some form, although we do not make a point of this fact, and we shall not confuse things by calling these components different names at earlier or later stages. A baby may show something like "autonomy" from the beginning, for example, in the particular way in which he angrily tries to wriggle his hand free when tightly held. However, under normal conditions, it is not until the second year that he begins to experience the whole critical alternative between being an autonomous creature and being a dependent one, and it is not until then that he is ready for a specifically new encounter with his environment. The environment, in turn, now feels called upon to convey to him its particular ideas and concepts of autonomy in ways decisively contributing to his personal character, his relative efficiency, and the strength of his vitality.

It is this encounter, together with the resulting crisis, which is to be described for each stage. Each stage becomes a crisis because incipient growth and awareness in a new part function go together with a shift in instinctual energy and yet also cause a specific vulnerability in that part. One of the most difficult questions to decide, therefore, is whether or not a child at a given stage is weak or strong. Perhaps it would be best to say that he is always vulnerable in some respects and completely oblivious and insensitive in others, but that at the same time he is unbelievably persistent in the same respects in which he is vulnerable. It must be added that the baby's weakness gives him power; out of his very dependence and weakness he makes signs to which his environment, if it is guided well by a responsiveness combining "instinctive" and traditional patterns, is peculiarly sensitive. A baby's presence exerts a consistent and persistent domination over the outer and inner lives of every member of a household. Because these members must reorient themselves to accommodate his presence, they must also grow as individuals and as a group. It is as true to say that babies control and bring up their families as it is to say the converse. A family can bring up a baby only by being brought up by him. His growth consists of a series of challenges to them to serve his newly developing potentialities for social interaction.

Each successive step, then, is a potential crisis because of a radical change in perspective. Crisis is used here in a developmental sense to connote not a threat of catastrophe, but a turning point, a crucial period of increased vulnerability and heightened potential, and therefore, the ontogenetic source of generational strength and maladjustment. The most radical change of all, from intrauterine to extrauterine life, comes at the very beginning of life. But in postnatal existence, too, such radical adjustments of perspective as lying relaxed, sitting firmly, and running fast must all be accomplished in their own good time.

With them, the interpersonal perspective also changes rapidly and often radically, as is testified by the proximity in time of such opposites as "not letting mother out of sight" and "wanting to be independent." Thus, different capacities use different opportunities to become full-grown components of the ever-new configuration that is the growing personality.

Equilibrium

Jean Piaget
UNIVERSITY OF GENEVA

The psychological development that starts at birth and terminates in adulthood is comparable to organic growth. Like the latter, it consists essentially of activity directed toward equilibrium. Just as the body evolves toward a relatively stable level characterized by the completion of the growth process and by organ maturity, so mental life can be conceived as evolving toward a final form of equilibrium represented by the adult mind. In a sense, development is a progressive equilibration from a lesser to a higher state of equilibrium. From the point of view of intelligence, it is easy to contrast the relative instability and incoherence of childhood ideas with the systematization of adult reason. With respect to the affective life, it has frequently been noted how extensively emotional equilibrium increases with age. Social relations also obey the same law of gradual stabilization.

An essential difference between the life of the body and that of the mind must nonetheless be stressed if the dynamism inherent in the reality of the mind is to be respected. The final form of equilibrium reached through organic growth is more static and, above all, more unstable than the equilibrium toward which mental development strives, so that no sooner has ascending evolution terminated than a regressive evolution automatically starts, leading to old age. Certain psychological functions that depend closely on the physical condition of the body follow an analogous curve. Visual acuity, for example, is at a maximum toward the end of childhood, only to diminish subsequently; and many other perceptual processes are regulated by the same law. By contrast, the higher functions of intelligence and affectivity tend toward a "mobile equilibrium." The more mobile it is, the more stable it is, so that the termination of growth, in healthy minds, by no means marks the beginning of decline but rather permits progress that in no sense contradicts inner equilibrium.

It is thus in terms of equilibrium that we shall try to describe the evolution of the child and the adolescent. From this point of view, mental development is a continuous construction comparable to the erection of a vast building that becomes more solid with each addition. Alternatively, and perhaps more appropriately, it may be likened to the assembly of a subtle mechanism that goes through gradual phases of adjustment in which the individual pieces become more supple and mobile as the equilibrium of the mechanism as a whole becomes more stable. We must, however, introduce an important distinction between two complementary aspects of the process of equilibration. This is the distinction between the variable structures that define the successive states of equilibrium and a certain constant functioning that assures the transition from any one state to the following one.

There is sometimes a striking similarity between the reactions of the child and the adult, as, for example, when the child is sure of what he wants and acts as adults do with respect to their own special interests. At other times there is a world of difference—in games, for example, or in the manner of reasoning. From a functional point of view, i.e., if we take into consideration the general motives of behavior and thought, there are constant functions common to all ages. At all levels of development, action presupposes a precipitating factor: a physiological, affective, or intellectual need. (In the latter case, the need appears in the guise of a question or a problem.) At all levels, intelligence seeks to understand or explain, etc. However, while the functions of interest, explanation, etc., are common to all developmental stages, that is to say, are "invariable" as far as the functions themselves are concerned, it is nonetheless true that "interests" (as opposed to "interest") vary considerably from one mental level to another, and that the particular explanations (as opposed to the function of explaining) are of a very different nature, depending on the degree of intellectual development. In addition to the constant functions, there are the variable structures. An analysis of these progressive forms of successive equilibrium highlights the differences from one behavioral level to another, all the way from the elementary behavior of the neonate through adolescence.

The variable structures—motor or intellectual on the one hand and affective on the other—are the organizational forms of mental activity. They are organized along two dimensions—intrapersonal and social (interpersonal). For greater clarity we shall distinguish six stages or periods of development which mark the appearance of these successively constructed structures:

1. The reflex or hereditary stage, at which the first instinctual nutritional drives and the first emotions appear.

2. The stage of the first motor habits and of the first organized percepts, as well as of the first differentiated emotions.

3. The stage of sensorimotor or practical intelligence (prior to language), of elementary affective organization, and of the first external affective fixations. These first three stages constitute the infancy period—from birth till the age of one and a half to two years—i.e., the period prior to the development of language and thought as such.

4. The stage of intuitive intelligence, of spontaneous interpersonal feelings, and of social relationships in which the child is subordinate to the adult (ages two to seven years, or "early childhood").

5. The stage of concrete intellectual operations (the beginning of logic) and of moral and social feelings of cooperation (ages seven to eleven or twelve, or "middle childhood").

6. The stage of abstract intellectual operations, of the formation of the personality, and of affective and intellectual entry into the society of adults (adolescence).

Each of these stages is characterized by the appearance of original structures whose construction distinguishes it from previous stages. The essentials of these successive constructions exist at subsequent stages in the form of substructures onto which new characteristics have been built. It follows that in the adult each stage through which he has passed corresponds to a given level in the total hierarchy of behavior. But at each stage there are also temporary and secondary characteristics that are modified by subsequent development as a function of the need for better organization. Each stage thus constitutes a particular form of equilibrium as a function of its characteristic structures, and mental evolution is effectuated in the direction of an ever-increasing equilibrium.

We know which functional mechanisms are common to all stages. In an absolutely general way (not only in comparing one stage with the following but also in comparing each item of behavior that is part of that stage with ensuing behavior), one can say that all action—that is to say, all movement, all thought, or all emotion—responds to a need. Neither the child nor the adult executes any external or even entirely internal act unless impelled by a motive; this motive can always be translated into a need (an elementary need, an interest, a question, etc.).

As Claparède (1951) has shown, a need is always a manifestation of disequilibrium: there is need when something either outside ourselves or within us (physically or mentally) is changed and behavior has to be adjusted as a function of this change. For example, hunger or fatigue will provoke a search for nourishment or rest; encountering an external object will lead to a need to play, which in turn has practical ends, or it leads to a question or a theoretical problem. A casual word will excite the need to imitate, to sympathize, or will engender reserve or opposition if it conflicts with some interest of our own. Conversely, action terminates when a need is satisfied, that is to say, when equilibrium is re-established between the new factor that has provoked the need and the mental organization that existed prior to the introduction of this factor. Eating or sleeping, playing or reaching a goal, replying to a question or resolving a problem, imitating successfully, establishing an affective tie, or maintaining one's point of view are all satisfactions that, in the preceding examples, will put an end to the particular behavior aroused by the need. At any given moment, one can thus say, action is disequilibrated by the transformations that arise in the external or internal world, and each new behavior consists not only in re-establishing equilibrium but also in moving toward a more stable equilibrium than that which preceded the disturbance.

Human action consists of a continuous and perpetual mechanism of re-adjustment or equilibration. For this reason, in these initial phases of construction, the successive mental structures that engender development can be considered as so many progressive forms of equilibrium, each of which is an advance upon its predecessor. It must be understood, however, that this functional mechanism, general though it may be, does not explain the content or the structure of the various needs, since each of them is related to the organization of the particular stage that is being considered. For example, the sight of the same object will occasion very different questions in the small child who is still incapable of classification from those of the older child whose ideas are more extensive and systematic. The interests of a child at any given moment depend on the system of ideas he has acquired plus his affective inclinations, and he tends to fulfill his interests in the direction of greater equilibrium.

Before examining the details of development we must try to find that which is common to the needs and interests present at all ages. One can say, in regard to this, that all needs tend first of all to incorporate things and people into the subject's own activity, i.e., to "assimilate" the external world into the structures that have already been constructed, and secondly to readjust these structures as a function of subtle transformations, i.e., to "accommodate" them to external objects. From this point of view, all mental life, as indeed all organic life, tends progressively to assimilate the surrounding environment. This incorporation is effected thanks to the structures of psychic organs whose scope of action becomes more and more extended. Initially, perception and elementary movement (prehension, etc.) are concerned with objects that are close and viewed statically; then later, memory and practical intelligence permit the representation of earlier states of the object as well as the anticipation of their future states resulting from as yet unrealized transformations. Still later intuitive thought reinforces these two abilities. Logical intelligence in the guise of concrete operations and ultimately of abstract deduction terminates this evolution by making the subject master of events that are far distant in space and time. At each of these levels the mind fulfills the same function, which is to incorporate the universe to itself, but the nature of assimilation varies, i.e., the successive modes of incorporation evolve from those of perception and movement to those of the higher mental operations.

In assimilating objects, action and thought must accommodate to these objects; they must adjust to external variation. The balancing of the processes of assimilation and accommodation may be called "adaptation." Such is the general form of psychological equilibrium, and the progressive organization of mental development appears to be simply an ever more precise adaptation to reality.

Reference

CLAPARÈDE, E. *Le développement mental.* Neuchâtel: Delachaux et Niestlé, 1951.

Appendix A
Recommended Daily Nutrients

1. For Canadians

Age (years)	Sex	Weight (kg)	Height (cm)	Energy[a] (kcal)	Protein (g)	Water-Soluble Vitamins						
						Thiamin (mg)	Niacin[e] (mg)	Riboflavin (mg)	Vitamin B₆[f] (mg)	Folate[a] (µg)	Vitamin B₁₂ (µg)	Ascorbic Acid (mg)
0–6 mos.	Both	6	—	kg × 117	kg × 2.2 (2.0)[d]	0.3	5	0.4	0.3	40	0.3	20[h]
7–11 mos.	Both	9	—	kg × 108	kg × 1.4	0.5	6	0.6	0.4	60	0.3	20
1–3	Both	13	90	1400	22	0.7	9	0.8	0.8	100	0.9	20
4–6	Both	19	110	1800	27	0.9	12	1.1	1.3	100	1.5	20
7–9	M	27	129	2200	33	1.1	14	1.3	1.6	100	1.5	30
	F	27	128	2000	33	1.0	13	1.2	1.4	100	1.5	30
10–12	M	36	144	2500	41	1.2	17	1.5	1.8	100	3.0	30
	F	38	145	2300	40	1.1	15	1.4	1.5	100	3.0	30
13–15	M	51	162	2800	52	1.4	19	1.7	2.0	200	3.0	30
	F	49	159	2200	43	1.1	15	1.4	1.5	200	3.0	30
16–18	M	64	172	3200	54	1.6	21	2.0	2.0	200	3.0	30
	F	54	161	2100	43	1.1	14	1.3	1.5	200	3.0	30
19–35	M	70	176	3000	56	1.5	20	1.8	2.0	200	3.0	30
	F	56	161	2100	41	1.1	14	1.3	1.5	200	3.0	30
36–50	M	70	176	2700	56	1.4	18	1.7	2.0	200	3.0	30
	F	56	161	1900	41	1.0	13	1.2	1.5	200	3.0	30
51	M	70	176	2300[b]	56	1.4	18	1.7	2.0	200	3.0	30
	F	56	161	1800[b]	41	1.0	13	1.2	1.5	200	3.0	30
Pregnant				+300[c]	+20	+0.2	+2	+0.3	+0.5	+50	+1.0	+20
Lactating				+500	+24	+0.4	+7	+0.6	+0.6	+50	+0.5	+30

Recommendations assume characteristic activity pattern for each age group.

[a] Recommended energy allowance for age 66½ years reduced to 2,000 for men and 1,500 for women.

[b] Recommended energy allowance recommended during second and third trimesters. An increase of 100 kcal per day is recommended during the first trimester.

[c] Increased energy allowance recommended during second and third trimesters. An increase of 100 kcal per day is recommended during the first trimester.

[d] Recommended protein allowance of 2.2 g per kg body weight for infants age 0–2 mos. and 2.0 g per kg body weight for those age 3–5 mos. Protein recommendation for infants, 0–11 mos., assumes consumption of breast milk or protein of equivalent quality.

[e] Approximately 1 mg of niacin is derived from each 60 mg of dietary tryptophan.

[f] Recommendations are based on the estimated average daily protein intake of Canadians.

[g] Recommendation given in terms of free folate.

346

Age (years)	Sex	Fat-Soluble Vitamins			Minerals					
		Vitamin A (μg RE)[i]	Vitamin D (μg cholecalciferol)[j]	Vitamin E (mg α-tocopherol)	Calcium (mg)	Phosphorus (mg)	Magnesium (mg)	Iodine (μg)	Iron (mg)	Zinc (mg)
0-6 mos.	Both	400	10	3	500[l]	250[l]	50[l]	35[l]	7[l]	4[l]
7-11 mos.	Both	400	10	3	500	400	50	50	7	5
1-3	Both	400	10	4	500	500	75	70	8	5
4-6	Both	500	5	5	500	500	100	90	9	6
7-9	M	700	2.5[k]	6	700	700	150	110	10	7
	F	700	2.5[k]	6	700	700	150	100	10	7
10-12	M	800	2.5[k]	7	900	900	175	130	11	8
	F	800	2.5[k]	7	1000	1000	200	120	11	9
13-15	M	1000	2.5[k]	9	1200	1200	250	140	13	10
	F	800	2.5[k]	7	800	800	250	110	14	10
16-18	M	1000	2.5[k]	10	1000	1000	300	160	14	12
	F	800	2.5[k]	6	700	700	250	110	14	11
19-35	M	1000	2.5[k]	9	800	800	300	150	10	10
	F	800	2.5[k]	6	700	700	250	110	14	9
36-50	M	1000	2.5[k]	8	800	800	300	140	10	10
	F	800	2.5[k]	6	700	700	250	100	14	9
51	M	1000	2.5[k]	8	800	800	300	140	10	10
	F	800	2.5[k]	6	700	700	250	100	14	9
Pregnant		+100	+2.5[k]	+1	+500	+500	+25	+15	+1[m]	+3
Lactating		+400	+2.5[k]	+2	+500	+500	+75	+25	+1[m]	+7

[h] Considerably higher levels may be prudent for infants during the first week of life to guard against neonatal tyrosinemia.

[i] One μg retinol equivalent (1 μg RE) corresponds to a biological activity in humans equal to 1 μg retinol (3.33 IU) and 6 μg β-carotene (10 IU).

[j] One μg cholecalciferol is equivalent to 40 IU vitamin D activity.

[k] Most older children and adults receive enough vitamin D from irradiation but 2.5 μg daily is recommended. This recommended allowance increases to 5.0 μg daily for pregnant and lactating women and for those who are confined indoors or otherwise deprived of sunlight for extended periods.

[l] The intake of breast-fed infants may be less than the recommendation but is considered to be adequate.

[m] A recommended total intake of 15 mg daily during pregnancy and lactation assumes the presence of adequate stores of iron. If stores are suspected of being inadequate, additional iron as a supplement is recommended.

SOURCE: Committee for Revision of the Canadian Dietary Standard. Recommended daily nutrients. Bureau of Nutritional Sciences, Health and Welfare, Canada, 1974.

2. For Americans[a]

	Age (years)	Weight (kg)	(lbs)	Height (cm)	(in)	Energy (kcal)[b]	Protein (g)	Vitamin A Activity (RE)[c]	(IU)	Vitamin D (IU)	Vitamin E Activity (IU)
								Fat-Soluble Vitamins			
Infants	0.0–0.5	6	14	60	24	kg × 117	kg × 2.2	420[d]	1,400	400	4
	0.5–1.0	9	20	71	28	kg × 108	kg × 2.0	400	2,000	400	5
Children	1–3	13	28	86	34	1,300	23	400	2,000	400	7
	4–6	20	44	110	44	1,800	30	500	2,500	400	9
	7–10	30	66	135	54	2,400	36	700	3,300	400	10
Males	11–14	44	97	158	63	2,800	44	1,000	5,000	400	12
	15–18	61	134	172	69	3,000	54	1,000	5,000	400	15
	19–22	67	147	172	69	3,000	54	1,000	5,000	400	15
	23–50	70	154	172	69	2,700	56	1,000	5,000		15
	51+	70	154	172	69	2,400	56	1,000	5,000		15
Females	11–14	44	97	155	62	2,400	44	800	4,000	400	12
	15–18	54	119	162	65	2,100	48	800	4,000	400	12
	19–22	58	128	162	65	2,100	46	800	4,000	400	12
	23–50	58	128	162	65	2,000	46	800	4,000		12
	51+	58	128	162	65	1,800	46	800	4,000		12
Pregnant						+300	+30	1,000	5,000	400	15
Lactating						+500	+20	1,200	6,000	400	15

[a] The allowances are intended to provide for individual variations among most normal persons as they live in the United States under usual environmental stresses. Diets should be based on a variety of common foods in order to provide other nutrients for which human requirements have been less well defined.

[b] Kilojoules (kJ) = 4.2 × kcal.

[c] Retinol equivalents.

[d] Assumed to be all as retinol in milk during the first six months of life. All subsequent intakes are assumed to be half as retinol and half as β-carotene when calculated from international units. As retinol equivalents, three fourths are as retinol and one fourth as β-carotene.

	Age (years)	Ascorbic Acid (mg)	Folacin[f] (μg)	Niacin[g] (mg)	Riboflavin (mg)	Thiamin (mg)	Vitamin B_6 (mg)	Vitamin B_{12} (μg)	Calcium (mg)	Phosphorus (mg)	Iodine (μg)	Iron (mg)	Magnesium (mg)	Zinc (mg)
		Water-Soluble Vitamins							Minerals					
Infants	0.0–0.5	35	50	5	0.4	0.3	0.3	0.3	360	240	35	10	60	3
	0.5–1.0	35	50	8	0.6	0.5	0.4	0.3	540	400	45	15	70	5
Children	1–3	40	100	9	0.8	0.7	0.6	1.0	800	800	60	15	150	10
	4–6	40	200	12	1.1	0.9	0.9	1.5	800	800	80	10	200	10
	7–10	40	300	16	1.2	1.2	1.2	2.0	800	800	110	10	250	10
Males	11–14	45	400	18	1.5	1.4	1.6	3.0	1,200	1,200	130	18	350	15
	15–18	45	400	20	1.8	1.5	2.0	3.0	1,200	1,200	150	18	400	15
	19–22	45	400	20	1.8	1.5	2.0	3.0	800	800	140	10	350	15
	23–50	45	400	18	1.6	1.4	2.0	3.0	800	800	130	10	350	15
	51+	45	400	16	1.5	1.2	2.0	3.0	800	800	110	10	350	15
Females	11–14	45	400	16	1.3	1.2	1.6	3.0	1,200	1,200	115	18	300	15
	15–18	45	400	14	1.4	1.1	2.0	3.0	1,200	1,200	115	18	300	15
	19–22	45	400	14	1.4	1.1	2.0	3.0	800	800	100	18	300	15
	23–50	45	400	13	1.2	1.0	2.0	3.0	800	800	100	18	300	15
	51+	45	400	12	1.1	1.0	2.0	3.0	800	800	80	10	300	15
Pregnant		60	800	+2	+0.3	+0.3	2.5	4.0	1,200	1,200	125	18+[h]	450	20
Lactating		80	600	+4	+0.5	+0.3	2.5	4.0	1,200	1,200	150	18	450	25

[e] Total vitamin E activity, estimated to be 80 per cent as α-tocopherol and 20 per cent other tocopherols. See text for variation in allowances.

[f] The folacin allowances refer to dietary sources as determined by Lactobacillus casei assay. Pure forms of folacin may be effective in doses less than one fourth of the recommended dietary allowance.

[g] Although allowances are expressed as niacin, it is recognized that on the average 1 mg of niacin is derived from each 60 mg of dietary tryptophan.

[h] This increased requirement cannot be met by ordinary diets; therefore, the use of supplemental iron is recommended.

SOURCE: Food and Nutrition Board, National Research Council. Recommended dietary allowances. Eighth rev. ed., 1974. Washington, D.C.: National Academy of Sciences, 1974.

Appendix B
Height and Weight Interpretation Charts

These charts make it possible to show graphically a child's *status* as to height and weight for any one measurement of size. If two or more measurements are made, separated by a time interval, the child's *progress* will also be shown graphically.

How to Measure Weight and Height Accurately

Use a beam-type platform scale. Weigh the child without shoes, barefoot, or in stockings, wearing minimal clothing, underwear or gym clothes. For children under 24 months, recumbent length is measured between the crown of the head and the bottom of the heel, with the back flat, the knees extended, and the soles of the feet at right angles with the ankles. For children above two, stature is measured as standing height. Without shoes, the feet should be together. Have the child stand normally erect, chin tucked in, eyes looking straight ahead. Stature is the distance between the floor and a horizontal board or bar firmly touching the crown of the head. Up to 36 months, record weight to the nearest quarter kilo (250 grams) and height to the nearest centimeter. At older ages, the nearest kilogram and the nearest centimeter are close enough.

GRAPHING HEIGHT AND WEIGHT STATUS

On the day he was measured, Carl was 7 years and 4 months old. His stature was 122 centimeters and his weight 22 kilograms. To plot his growth status, first find on the age scale of the weight graph a point one third of the way between 7 and 8 years. Imagine a line drawn vertically upward to the point where it intersects with another imaginary horizontal line drawn through a point on the weight scale at 22. Put a dot on the graph at this point. Similarly, find the imaginary vertical line at the bottom of the height scale. Put a dot at the point where that line intersects with an imaginary horizontal line through 122 centimeters. Each of these dots falls just below the 50th percentile line on the graph. These show that Carl is slightly below the average child of 7 years and 4 months, slightly lighter and slightly shorter; he is neither heavy nor light for his height.

GRAPHING HEIGHT AND WEIGHT PROGRESS

On his eighth birthday Carl weighs 25 kilograms and is 126 centimeters tall. As in the earlier measurement, put a pencil dot on the eight-year vertical line where it intersects with the imaginary line through 25 kilograms on the weight graph, and the imaginary line through 126 centimeters on the height graph. Lines connecting the two pairs of dots are roughly parallel with the printed 50th percentile lines. In the eight months between measurements Carl grew proportionately in height and weight.

EVALUATION OF WEIGHT AND HEIGHT MEASUREMENTS

If the points representing a child's height and weight are not about the same distance above or below the same percentile curve, the difference may indicate that the child is normally slender or normally stocky. If the difference between the stature and weight percentile is more than 25 percentiles, a further check on his or her health should be made.

Normal progress in height and weight gives lines for such a child that stay roughly the same distance from adjacent printed lines on the graph. When the lines go steeply up, or if one goes up and the other is nearly horizontal, a medical investigation of the child's health or nutritional condition is called for. Around the age of 11, a child's lines may cross the printed percentile lines, because there are individual differences in the timing and strength of the puberal growth spurt. A child's lines may go up more steeply for a period of time, or be more horizontal than the printed lines.

Girls'   Stature and Weight by Age Percentiles: Ages 2 to 18 Years

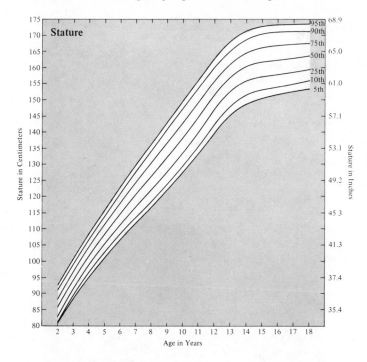

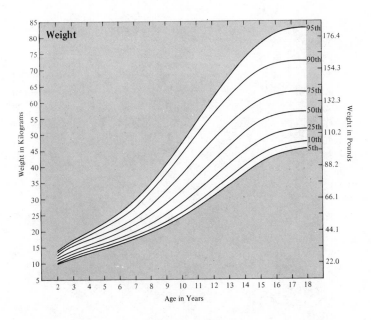

Boys' Stature and Weight by Age Percentiles: Ages 2 to 18 Years

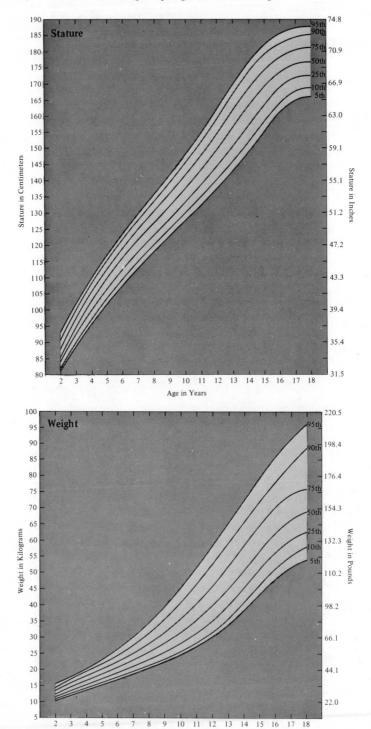

Appendix C
Communicable Diseases of Childhood

	Chickenpox	Diphtheria	Measles	Mumps	Polio
Cause	A virus: Present in secretions from nose, throat and mouth of infected people.	Diphtheria bacillus: Present in secretions from nose and throat of infected people and carriers.	A virus: Present in secretions from nose and throat of infected people.	A virus: Present in saliva of infected people.	3 strains of polio virus have been identified: Present in discharges from nose, throat, bowels of infected people.
How spread	Contact with infected people or articles used by them. Very contagious.	Contact with infected people and carriers or articles used by them.	Contact with infected people or articles used by them. Very contagious.	Contact with infected people or articles used by them.	Primarily, contact with infected people.
Incubation period (from date of exposure to first signs)	13 to 17 days. Sometimes 3 weeks.	2 to 5 days. Sometimes longer.	About 10 to 12 days.	12 to 26 (commonly 18) days.	Usually 7 to 12 days.
Period of communicability (time when disease is contagious)	From 5 days before, to 6 days after appearance of skin blisters.	From about 2 to 4 weeks after onset of disease.	From 4 days before until about 5 days after rash appears.	From about 6 days before symptoms to 9 days after. Principally at about time swelling starts.	Apparently greatest in late incubation and first few days of illness.
Most susceptible ages	Under 15 years.	Under 15 years.	Common at any age during childhood.	Children and young people.	Most common in children 1 to 16 years.
Seasons of prevalence	Winter.	Fall, winter and spring.	Mainly spring. Also fall and winter.	Winter and spring.	June through September.
Prevention	No prevention.	Vaccination with diphtheria toxoid (in triple vaccine for babies).	Measles vaccine.	Mumps vaccine.	Polio vaccine.
Control	Exclusion from school for 1 week after eruption appears. Avoid contact with susceptibles. Immune globulin may lessen severity. (Cut child's fingernails.) Immunity usual after one attack.	Booster doses (see Appendix D). Antitoxin and antibiotics used in treatment and for protection after exposure. One attack does not necessarily give immunity.	Isolation until 7 days after appearance of rash. Immune globulin between 3 and 6 days after exposure can lighten attack. Antibiotics for complications. Immunity usual after one attack.	Isolation for 9 days from onset of swelling. Immunity usual after one attack but second attacks can occur.	Booster doses (see Appendix D). Isolation for about one week from onset. Immunity to infecting strain of virus usual after one attack.

	Rheumatic Fever	Rubella	Smallpox	Strep Infections	Tetanus	Whooping Cough
Cause	Direct cause unknown. Precipitated by a strep infection.	A virus: Present in secretions from nose and mouth of infected people.	A virus: Present in skin pocks and discharges from mouth, nose and throat of infected people. Rare in U.S.	Streptococci of several strains cause scarlet fever and strep sore throats: Present in secretions from mouth, nose and ears of infected people.	Tetanus bacillus: Present in a wound so infected.	Pertussis bacillus: Present in secretions from mouth and nose of infected people.
How spread	Unknown. But the preceding strep infection is contagious.	Contact with infected people or articles used by them. Very contagious.	Contact with infected people or articles used by them.	Contact with infected people; rarely from contaminated articles.	Through soil, contact with horses, street dust, or articles contaminated with the bacillus.	Contact with infected people and articles used by them.
Incubation period (from date of exposure to first signs)	Symptoms appear about 2 to 3 weeks after a strep infection.	14 to 21 (usually 18) days.	From 8 to 17 (usually 12) days.	1 to 3 days.	4 days to 3 weeks. Sometimes longer. Average about 10 days.	From 7 to 10 days.
Period of communicability (time when disease is contagious)	Not communicable. Preceding strep infection is communicable.	From 7 days before to 5 days after onset of rash.	From 2 to 3 days before rash, until disappearance of all pock crusts.	Greatest during acute illness (about 10 days).	Not communicable from person to person.	From onset of first symptoms to about 3rd week of the disease.
Most susceptible ages	All ages; most common from 6 to 12 years.	Young children, but also common in young adults.	All ages.	All ages.	All ages.	Under 7 years.
Seasons of prevalence	Mainly winter and spring.	Winter and spring.	Usually winter, but anytime.	Late winter and spring.	All seasons, but more common in warm weather.	Late winter and early spring.
Prevention	No prevention, except proper treatment of strep infections. (See Strep Infections.)	Rubella (German measles) vaccine.	Vaccination (no longer given routinely in U.S.).	No prevention. Antibiotic treatment for those who have had rheumatic fever.	Immunization with tetanus toxoid (in triple vaccine for babies).	Immunization with whooping cough vaccine (in triple vaccine for babies).

	Rheumatic Fever	Rubella	Smallpox	Strep Infections	Tetanus	Whooping Cough
Control	Use of antibiotics. One attack does not give immunity.	Isolation when necessary, for 5 days after onset. Immunity usual after one attack.	Vaccinia immune globulin may prevent or modify smallpox if given within 24 hours after exposure. Isolation until all pock crusts are gone. Immunity usual after one attack.	Isolation for about 1 day after start of treatment with antibiotics—used for about 10 days. One attack does not necessarily give immunity.	Booster dose of tetanus toxoid for protection given on day of injury. Antitoxin used in treatment and for temporary protection for child not immunized. One attack does not give immunity.	Booster doses (see Appendix D). Special antibiotics may help to lighten attack for child not immunized. Isolation from susceptible infants for about 3 weeks from onset or until cough stops. Immunity usual after one attack.

SOURCE: *The Control of Communicable Diseases*, American Public Health Association, 1975, and *Report of Committee on Control of Infectious Diseases*, American Academy of Pediatrics, 1974. Courtesy of Metropolitan Life.

Appendix D
Vaccination Schedule

This schedule for first vaccinations is based on recommendations of the American Medical Association and the American Academy of Pediatrics. A first test for TB (tuberculosis) may be recommended at one year. Your physician may suggest a slightly different schedule suitable for your individual child. And recommendations change from time to time as science gains new knowledge.

Disease	No. of Doses	Age for First Series	Booster
Diphtheria	4 doses	2 months	At 4 to 6 years—
Tetanus		4 months	before entering
Whooping		6 months	school. As recom-
Cough		18 months	mended by physician.
Polio	4 doses	2 months	At 4 to 6 years—
(Oral		4 months	before entering
vaccine)		6 months	school. As recom-
		18 months	mended by physician.
Rubella	1 vaccination	After 1 year	None
(German			
measles)			
Measles	1 vaccination	1 to 12 years	None
Mumps	1 vaccination	1 to 12 years	None

Courtesy of Metropolitan Life.

Author Index

Entries in *italics* refer to pages on which bibliographic references are given. Entries in **boldface** refer to selections by the authors cited.

361

Subject Index